Game Physics Pearls

Game Physics Pearls

Edited by
Gino van den Bergen
and
Dirk Gregorius

A K Peters, Ltd.
Natick, Massachusetts

Editorial, Sales, and Customer Service Office

A K Peters, Ltd.
5 Commonwealth Road, Suite 2C
Natick, MA 01760
www.akpeters.com

Cover image taken from DiRT2, courtesy of Codemasters Software Co., Ltd.
Background cover image © YKh, 2010. Used under license from Shutterstock.com.

Library of Congress Cataloging-in-Publication Data

Game physics pearls / edited by Gino van den Bergen and Dirk Gregorius.
  p. cm.
ISBN 978-1-56881-474-2 (alk. paper)
  1. Computer games–Programming. 2. Physics–Programming. I. Bergen,
Gino van den. II. Gregorius, Dirk.

QA76.76.C672G359 2010
794.8'1526–dc22

2010021721

Printed in the United States of America
14 13 12 11 10   10 9 8 7 6 5 4 3 2 1

Contents

Foreword

I am not a fan of gems-style books. Typically, they are assembled and glued together as a collection of loosely related articles, and no attempt is made to unify them by emphasizing common themes and ideas. When I was asked to write the foreword for this book, my initial reaction was to decline politely, thinking this was yet another such book. However, knowing the editors and their reputations in the physics engine industry, I agreed to read the book in hopes that there might be a few articles that make the book a worthwhile purchase.

I am delighted to say that this book is much more than I imagined. Those few articles I hoped to find interesting turned out to be all the articles! I congratulate the editors and the authors for producing the finest collection of game physics articles I have seen to date. The common theme is experience. Each author describes not only a topic of interest, but provides an in-the-trenches discussion of the practical problems and solutions when implementing the algorithms, whether for a physics engine or game application. Moreover, I found it comforting that the authors were consistent in their findings, giving me hope that writing a fast and robust physics engine actually can be a scientific process rather than an endeavor that combines art, hacks, and voodoo. Also of importance is that several of the topics are about nonsequential programming, whether multicore or for game consoles, which is important given the evolution of modern computing hardware towards multiprocessing and multithreading.

This book is a must-have if you plan on exploring the world of physics programming. And I hope the editors and authors have plans on producing more books of the same great quality.

—Dave Eberly

Preface

It took some time before I considered myself a physics programmer. Like most game programmers, I started out toying with physics in hobby game projects. These early attempts at getting physical behavior out of an 8-bit home computer did involve concepts such as velocity, mass, and force, but in my head they were far from "real" physics. In the following years at the university I learned how to program properly and got proficient in linear algebra, geometric algorithms, and computer graphics. I took courses in theoretical mechanics and numerical analysis, expecting that after overcoming these hurdles, developing a physics engine would be easy.

It never did get easy. In the coming years I was struggling to get even the simplest of rigid body simulations stable on computers that were a thousand times more powerful than the 8-bit home computer from my junior years. It would take a considerable number of hacks to stop my "resting" contacts from oscillating and from bouncing all over the place. And even then, the hacks would work only for objects within certain ranges of masses and sizes. In the end, most of the hacks that seemed to work would make Sir Isaac Newton turn in his grave. My inner physicist was nagging at me, telling me that what I was doing was not "real" physics. I was failing to truly capture classical mechanics as it was taught to me in the code of a real-time physics engine. Surely, anyone who needs to resort to the use of cheap hacks to get things working could never be considered a genuine physics programmer.

After spending a couple of years in the game industry I learned that an understanding of classical mechanics and the ability to apply it in code are not the prime skills of a physics programmer. Of course, any physics programmer should feel comfortable with the science and mathematics behind physics, but being too concerned about the science can become a burden as well. Games that involve physics should primarily be targeted at playability and robustness rather than showcase a maximum realism level. I had to overcome some hesitation before I willingly started breaking the laws of physics and came up with hacks that created "unnatural" behavior that fixed some game design issues. For example, in an arcade racing game, cars should drift nicely, should rarely tip over, and if they do, should always land back on their wheels—but most of all, they should never get stuck in parts of the scenery. A game physics programmer can start with a realistic driving behavior and then add helper forces and impulses to govern down force, balance, turn rate, and what not, in order to get just the right behavior. It takes creativity and a lot of experience to make a game that relies heavily on physics and is fun.

This book is written by and targeted at game physics programmers. We seek to provide experience and proven techniques from experts in the field and focus on what is actually used in games rather than on how to achieve maximum realism. You will find a lot of hacks here, but they should not be regarded as "cheap." They are the result of many years of hard work balancing playability, robustness, and visual appeal. Such information was previously found only on internet forums and at game developers conferences. This is the first gems-type book that collects articles on tricks of the trade in game physics written by people in the trade, and as such, seeks to fill a gap in game technology literature.

Source code and demos that accompany this book will be made available at http://www.gamephysicspearls.com.

It was not easy to set this book in motion. There were two main forces working against us during production. Firstly, in the game industry developers usually do not have nine-to-five jobs. Dedicating the little spare time that one has to a book article is not a light decision for many people. Secondly, physics programmers tend to be quite modest about their work and need some encouragement to make them share their ideas. Perhaps many of us are plagued by the same inner physicist who nags about our disregard for the laws of physics. Nevertheless, once the project gained momentum, great stuff came out of the gang of contributors we managed to lure in.

I very much enjoyed editing for this book; it's great to see a coherent book taking form when each of the authors is adding a piece to the puzzle. I would like to thank everyone who contributed to this book. My gratitude goes to the authors, the staff at A K Peters, all external reviewers, copy editors, the cover designer, and last but not least to Dirk, my fellow co-editor and physics buddy.

—Gino van den Bergen
June 16, 2010

My initial contact with game physic programming was totally accidental. I had just finished my studies of civil engineering and I was sitting in a cafe talking to an old girlfriend I hadn't seen for a while. As she asked me what I would do next I replied that I would be maybe interested in game development. As it turned out her husband (who just returned from GDC) was a veteran in the game industry, and he invited me for an interview. In this interview I learned that his company was working on a release title for the PS3 and was currently looking for a physics programmer. I had no idea what this meant, but I happily accepted.

When I started my work, I was overwhelmed by the huge amount of books, papers, and especially rumors that were around. People on public forums had many ideas and were gladly sharing them, but sadly these ideas often worked reliably only in very specific situations. I quickly learned that it was very hard to get accurate information that was actually useable in a game. At this point I wished for a collection of proven algorithms that actually were used in a shipped title, but sadly no such source existed at that time.

As Gino mentioned his idea of such a book, I was immediately excited and felt flattered to support him as editor. It is my very strong belief that game physics programming is about choosing the right algorithms rather then inventing everything yourself. Having a collection of proven techniques is a great help in architecturing a solution for the specific needs of any game.

It was a great experience editing this book, and I enjoyed every minute working with every author. They all showed a great enthusiasm for contributing to this book. I would like to thank all the authors, the staff at A K Peters, all the external reviewers, the copy editors, the cover designer, and especially Gino for getting me on board of this project.

—Dirk Gregorius
June 18, 2010

– I –

Game Physics 101

– 1 –

Mathematical Background

James M. Van Verth

1.1 Introduction

It has been said that, at its core, all physics is mathematics. While that statement
may be debatable, it is certainly true that a background in mathematics is indis-
pensable in studying physics, and game physics is no exception. As such, a single
chapter cannot possibly cover all that is useful in such a broad and interesting
field. However, the following should provide an essential review of the mathematics needed for the remainder of this book. Further references are provided at
the end of the chapter for those who wish to study further.

1.2 Vectors and Points

1.2.1 Definitions and Relations

The core elements of any three-dimensional system are points and vectors. Points
represent positions in space and are represented graphically as dots. Vectors represent direction or rate of change—the amount of change indicated by the length,
or *magnitude*, of the vector—and are presented graphically as arrows. Figure 1.1

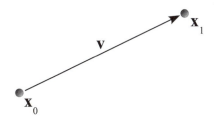

Figure 1.1. Relationship between points and vectors.

3

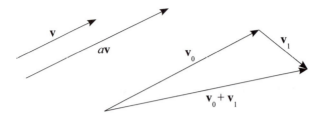

Figure 1.2. Vector scaling and addition.

shows the relationship between points and vectors—in this case, the vector is acting as the difference between two points. Algebraically, this is

$$\mathbf{v} = \mathbf{x}_1 - \mathbf{x}_0$$

or

$$\mathbf{x}_1 = \mathbf{x}_0 + \mathbf{v}.$$

In general, vectors can be scaled and added. Scaling (multiplying by a single factor, or scalar) changes the length of a vector. If the scalar is negative, it can also change the direction of the vector. Adding two vectors together creates a new vector that points from the tail of one to the head of another (see Figure 1.2).

Scaling and adding together an arbitrary number of vectors is called a *linear combination*:

$$\mathbf{v} = \sum_i a_i \mathbf{v}_i.$$

A set of vectors $\mathbf{v}$ is *linearly dependent* if one of the vectors in S can be represented as the linear combination of other members in S. Otherwise, it is a *linearly independent* set.

Points cannot be generally scaled or added. They can only be subtracted to create a vector or combined in a linear combination, where

$$\sum_i a_i = 1.$$

This is known as an *affine combination*. We can express an affine combination as follows:

$$\mathbf{x} = \left(1 - \sum_i^{n-1} a_i\right)\mathbf{x}_n + \sum_i^{n-1} a_i \mathbf{x}_i$$

$$\begin{aligned}
&= \mathbf{x}_n - \sum_{i}^{n-1} a_i \mathbf{x}_n + \sum_{i}^{n-1} a_i \mathbf{x}_i \\
&= \mathbf{x}_n + \sum_{i}^{n-1} a_i (\mathbf{x}_i - \mathbf{x}_n) \\
&= \mathbf{x}_n + \sum_{i}^{n-1} a_i \mathbf{v}_i.
\end{aligned}$$

So an affine combination can be thought of as a point plus a linear combination of vectors.

We represent points and vectors relative to a given coordinate frame. In three dimensions, or $\mathbb{R}^3$, this consists of three linearly independent vectors $\mathbf{e}_1$, $\mathbf{e}_2$, and $\mathbf{e}_3$ (known as a basis) and a point $\mathbf{o}$ (known as an origin). Any vector in this space can be constructed using a linear combination of the basis vectors:

$$\mathbf{v} = x\mathbf{e}_1 + y\mathbf{e}_2 + z\mathbf{e}_3.$$

In practice, we represent a vector in the computer by using the scale factors (x, y, z) in an ordered list.

Similarly, we can represent a point as an affine combination of the basis vectors and the origin:

$$\mathbf{x} = \mathbf{o} + x\mathbf{e}_1 + y\mathbf{e}_2 + z\mathbf{e}_3.$$

Another way to think of this is that we construct a vector and add it to the origin. This provides a one-to-one mapping between points and vectors.

1.2.2   Magnitude and Distance

As mentioned, one of the quantities of a vector $\mathbf{v}$ is its magnitude, represented by $\|\mathbf{v}\|$. In $\mathbb{R}^3$, this is

$$\|\mathbf{v}\| = \sqrt{x^2 + y^2 + z^2}.$$

We can use this to calculate the distance between two points $\mathbf{p}_1$ and $\mathbf{p}_2$ by taking $\|\mathbf{p}_1 - \mathbf{p}_2\|$, or

$$\text{dist}(\mathbf{p}_1, \mathbf{p}_2) = \sqrt{(x_1 - x_2)^2 + (y_1 - y_2)^2 + (z_1 - z_2)^2}.$$

If we scale a vector $\mathbf{v}$ by $1/\|\mathbf{v}\|$, we end up with a vector of magnitude 1, or a *unit vector*. This is often represented by $\hat{\mathbf{v}}$.

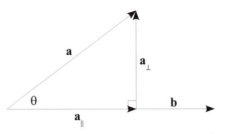

Figure 1.3. Projection of one vector onto another.

1.2.3   Dot Product

The dot product of two vectors **a** and **b** is defined as

$$\mathbf{a} \cdot \mathbf{b} = \|\mathbf{a}\| \|\mathbf{b}\| \cos \theta, \tag{1.1}$$

where θ is the angle between **a** and **b**.

For two vectors using a standard Euclidean basis, this can be represented as

$$\mathbf{a} \cdot \mathbf{b} = a_x b_x + a_y b_y + a_z b_z.$$

There are two uses of this that are of particular interest to game physics developers. First of all, it can be used to do simple tests of the angle between two vectors. If $\mathbf{a} \cdot \mathbf{b} > 0$, then $\theta < \pi/2$; if $\mathbf{a} \cdot \mathbf{b} < 0$, then $\theta > \pi/2$; and if $\mathbf{a} \cdot \mathbf{b} = 0$, then $\theta = \pi/2$. In the latter case, we also say that the two vectors are *orthogonal*.

The other main use of the dot product is for projecting one vector onto another. If we have two vectors **a** and **b**, we can break **a** into two pieces $\mathbf{a}_{||}$ and $\mathbf{a}_{\perp}$ such that $\mathbf{a}_{||} + \mathbf{a}_{\perp} = \mathbf{a}$ and $\mathbf{a}_{||}$ points along the same direction as, or is *parallel* to, **b** (see Figure 1.3). The vector $\mathbf{a}_{||}$ is also known as the scalar projection of **a** onto **b**.

From Equation (1.1), if $\|\mathbf{b}\| = 1$, then $\mathbf{a} \cdot \mathbf{b}$ is simply $\|\mathbf{a}\| \cos \theta$, which we can see from Figure 1.3 is the length of the projection of **a** onto **b**. The projected vector itself can be computed as

$$\mathbf{a}_{||} = (\mathbf{a} \cdot \mathbf{b})\mathbf{b}.$$

The remaining, or orthogonal portion of **a** can be computed as

$$\mathbf{a}_{\perp} = \mathbf{a} - \mathbf{a}_{||}.$$

1.2.4   Cross Product

The cross product of two vectors **a** and **b** is defined as

$$\mathbf{a} \times \mathbf{b} = (a_y b_z - a_z b_y, a_z b_x - a_x b_z, a_x b_y - a_y b_x).$$

This produces a vector orthogonal to both **a** and **b**. The magnitude of the cross product is

$$\|\mathbf{a} \times \mathbf{b}\| = \|\mathbf{a}\|\|\mathbf{b}\| \sin\theta,$$

where θ is the angle between **a** and **b**. The direction of the cross product is determined by the right-hand rule: taking your right hand, point the first finger in the direction of **a** and the middle finger along **b**. Your extended thumb will point along the cross product.

Two useful identities to be aware of are the anticommutativity and bilinearity of the cross product:

$$\mathbf{a} \times \mathbf{b} = -\mathbf{b} \times \mathbf{a},$$
$$\mathbf{a} \times (s\mathbf{b} + t\mathbf{c}) = s(\mathbf{a} \times \mathbf{b}) + t(\mathbf{a} \times \mathbf{c}).$$

1.2.5 Triple Product

There are two possible triple products for vectors. The first uses both the dot product and the cross product and produces a scalar result. Hence it is known as the *scalar triple product*:

$$s = \mathbf{a} \cdot (\mathbf{b} \times \mathbf{c}).$$

The scalar triple product measures the signed volume of the parallelepiped bounded by the three vectors **a**, **b**, and **c**. Thus, the following identity holds:

$$\mathbf{a} \cdot (\mathbf{b} \times \mathbf{c}) = \mathbf{b} \cdot (\mathbf{c} \times \mathbf{a}) = \mathbf{c} \cdot (\mathbf{a} \times \mathbf{b}).$$

The second triple product uses only the cross product and produces a vector result. It is known as the *vector triple product*:

$$\mathbf{v} = \mathbf{a} \times (\mathbf{b} \times \mathbf{c}).$$

The vector triple product is useful for creating an orthogonal basis from linearly independent vectors. One example basis is **b**, **b** × **c**, and **b** × (**b** × **c**).

The following relationship between the vector triple product and dot product is also helpful in derivations for rigid-body dynamics and geometric algorithms:

$$\mathbf{a} \times (\mathbf{b} \times \mathbf{c}) = (\mathbf{a} \cdot \mathbf{c})\mathbf{b} - (\mathbf{a} \cdot \mathbf{b})\mathbf{c}.$$

1.2.6 Derivatives

We mentioned that vectors can act to represent rate of change. In particular, a vector-valued function is the derivative of a point-valued function. If we take the standard equation for a derivative of a function as in

$$\mathbf{x}'(t) = \lim_{h \to 0} \frac{\mathbf{x}(t + h) - \mathbf{x}(t)}{h},$$

we can see that the result $\mathbf{x}'(t)$ will be a vector-valued function, as we are sub-tracting two points and then scaling by $1/h$. It can be similarly shown that the derivative of a vector-valued function is a vector-valued function. Note that we often write such a time derivative as simply $\dot{\mathbf{x}}$.

1.3   Lines and Planes

1.3.1   Definitions

If we parameterize an affine combination, we can create new entities: lines and planes. A line can be represented as a point plus a parameterized vector:

$$\mathbf{l}(t) = \mathbf{x} + t\mathbf{v}.$$

Similarly, a plane in $\mathbb{R}^3$ can be represented as a point plus two parameterized vectors:

$$\mathbf{p}(s, t) = \mathbf{x} + s\mathbf{u} + t\mathbf{v}.$$

An alternative definition of a plane is to take a vector $\mathbf{n}$ and a point $\mathbf{p_0}$ and state that for any given point $\mathbf{p}$ on the plane,

$$0 = \mathbf{n} \cdot (\mathbf{p} - \mathbf{p_0}).$$

If we set $(a, b, c) = \mathbf{n}$, $(x, y, z) = \mathbf{p}$, and $d = -\mathbf{n} \cdot (\mathbf{p_0} - \mathbf{o})$, we can rewrite this as

$$0 = ax + by + cz + d, \tag{1.2}$$

which should be a familiar formula for a plane.

For an arbitrary point $\mathbf{p}$, we can substitute $\mathbf{p}$ into Equation (1.2) to test whether it is on one side or another of the plane. If the result is greater than zero, we know the point is on one side, if less than zero, it is on the other. And if the result is close to zero, we know that the point is close to the plane.

We can further restrict our affine combinations to create half-infinite or fully finite entities. For example, in our line equation, if we constrain $t \geq 0$, we get a ray. If we restrict t to lie between 0 and 1, then we have a line segment. We can rewrite the line equation in an alternate form to make it clearer:

$$\mathbf{S}(t) = (1 - t)\mathbf{x_0} + t\mathbf{x_1}.$$

In this case, $\mathbf{x_0}$ and $\mathbf{x_1}$ are the two endpoints of the line segment.

We can perform a similar operation with three points to create a triangle:

$$\mathbf{T}(s, t) = (1 - s - t)\mathbf{x_0} + s\mathbf{x_1} + t\mathbf{x_2},$$

where, again, s and t are constrained to lie between 0 and 1.

1.4 Matrices and Transformations

1.4.1 Definition

A *matrix* is an $m \times n$ array of components with m rows and n columns. These components could be complex numbers, vectors, or even other matrices, but most of the time when we refer to a matrix, its components are real numbers. An example of a 2×3 matrix is

$$\begin{bmatrix} 5 & -1 & 0 \\ 12 & 0 & -10 \end{bmatrix}.$$

We refer to a single element in the ith row and jth column of the matrix $\mathbf{A}$ as a_{ij}. Those elements where $i = j$ are the *diagonal* of the matrix.

A matrix whose elements below and to the left of the diagonal (i.e., those where $i > j$) are 0 is called an *upper triangular* matrix. Similarly, a matrix whose elements above and to the right of the diagonal (i.e., those where $i < j$) are 0 is called a *lower triangular* matrix. And those where all the non-diagonal elements are 0 are called *diagonal* matrices.

A matrix is called *symmetric* if, for all i and j, the elements $a_{ij} = a_{ji}$, i.e., it is mirrored across the diagonal. A matrix is *skew symmetric* if for all i and j the elements $a_{ij} = -a_{ji}$. Clearly, the diagonal elements must be 0 in this case.

1.4.2 Basic Operations

Matrices can be added and scaled like vectors:

$$\begin{aligned} \mathbf{C} &= \mathbf{A} + \mathbf{B}, \\ \mathbf{D} &= k\mathbf{A}. \end{aligned}$$

In the first case, each element $c_{ij} = a_{ij} + b_{ij}$, and in the second, $d_{ij} = ka_{ij}$.

Matrices can be transposed by swapping elements across the diagonal, i.e., a matrix $\mathbf{G}$ is the transpose of matrix $\mathbf{A}$ if for all i and j, $g_{ij} = a_{ji}$. This is represented as

$$\mathbf{G} = \mathbf{A}^{\mathrm{T}}.$$

Finally, matrices can be multiplied:

$$\mathbf{H} = \mathbf{AB}.$$

Here, for a given element h_{ij}, we take the corresponding row i from $\mathbf{A}$ and corresponding column j from $\mathbf{B}$, multiply them component-wise, and take the sum, or

$$h_{ij} = \sum_k a_{ik}b_{kj}.$$

Note also that matrix multiplication is noncommutative. That is, we cannot say in general that $\mathbf{AB} = \mathbf{BA}$.

1.4.3   Vector Representation and Transformation

We can represent a vector as a matrix with one column, e.g.,

$$\mathbf{x} = \begin{bmatrix} x_1 \\ x_2 \\ \vdots \\ x_n \end{bmatrix},$$

or with one row, e.g.,

$$\mathbf{b}^{\mathrm{T}} = \begin{bmatrix} b_1 & b_2 & \cdots & b_m \end{bmatrix}.$$

In this book, we will be using column matrices to represent vectors. Should we want to represent a row matrix, we shall use the transpose, as above. Using this notation, we can also represent a matrix as its component columns:

$$\mathbf{A} = \begin{bmatrix} \mathbf{a}_1 & \mathbf{a}_2 & \cdots & \mathbf{a}_n \end{bmatrix}.$$

A *linear transformation* $\mathcal{T}$ is a mapping that preserves the linear properties of scale and addition; that is, for two vectors $\mathbf{x}$ and $\mathbf{y}$,

$$a\mathcal{T}(\mathbf{x}) + \mathcal{T}(\mathbf{y}) = \mathcal{T}(a\mathbf{x} + \mathbf{y}).$$

We can use matrices to represent linear transformations. Multiplying a vector $\mathbf{x}$ by an appropriately sized matrix $\mathbf{A}$, and expanding the terms, we get

$$\begin{bmatrix} b_1 \\ b_2 \\ \vdots \\ b_m \end{bmatrix} = \begin{bmatrix} a_{11} & a_{12} & \cdots & a_{1n} \\ a_{21} & a_{22} & \cdots & a_{2n} \\ \vdots & \vdots & \ddots & \vdots \\ a_{m1} & a_{m2} & \cdots & a_{mn} \end{bmatrix} \begin{bmatrix} x_1 \\ x_2 \\ \vdots \\ x_n \end{bmatrix}.$$

This represents a linear transformation $\mathcal{T}$ from an n-dimensional space to an m-dimensional space. If we assume that both spaces use the standard Euclidean bases $\mathbf{e}_1, \mathbf{e}_2, \ldots, \mathbf{e}_n$ and $\mathbf{e}_1, \mathbf{e}_2, \ldots, \mathbf{e}_m$, respectively, then the column vectors in matrix $\mathbf{A}$ are the transformed basis vectors $\mathcal{T}(\mathbf{e}_1), \mathcal{T}(\mathbf{e}_2), \ldots, \mathcal{T}(\mathbf{e}_n)$.

Multiplying transformation matrices together creates a single matrix that represents the composition of the matrices' respective transformations. In this way, we can represent a composition of linear transformations in a single matrix.

1.4.4 Inverse and Identity

Just as we can multiply a scalar by 1 to no effect, there is an identity transformation that produces the original vector. This is represented by the matrix $\mathbf{E}$, which is a square diagonal matrix, sized appropriately to perform the multiplication on the vector and with all 1s on the diagonal. For example, the following will work for vectors in $\mathbb{R}^3$:

$$\mathbf{E} = \begin{bmatrix} 1 & 0 & 0 \\ 0 & 1 & 0 \\ 0 & 0 & 1 \end{bmatrix}.$$

Intuitively, this makes sense. If we examine the columns, we will see they are just $\mathbf{e}_1$, $\mathbf{e}_2$, and $\mathbf{e}_3$, thereby transforming the basis vectors to themselves.

Note that the identity matrix is often represented in other texts as $\mathbf{I}$. We are using $\mathbf{E}$ to distinguish it from the inertial tensor, as discussed below.

The equivalent to standard division is the inverse. The inverse reverses the effect of a given transformation, as represented by the following:

$$\mathbf{x} = \mathbf{A}^{-1}\mathbf{A}\mathbf{x}.$$

However, just as we can't divide by 0, we can't always find an inverse for a transformation. First, only transformations from an n-dimensional space to an n-dimensional space have inverses. And of those, not all of them can be inverted. For example, the transformation $\mathcal{T}(\mathbf{x}) = \mathbf{0}$ has no inverse.

Discussing how to invert matrices in a general manner is out of the scope of this chapter; it is recommended that the reader see [Anton and Rorres 94], [Golub and Van Loan 93], or [Press et al. 93] for more information.

1.4.5 Affine Transformations

An affine transformation on a point $\mathbf{x}$ performs the basic operation

$$\mathbf{z} = \mathbf{A}\mathbf{x} + \mathbf{y},$$

where $\mathbf{A}$ and $\mathbf{y}$ are a matrix and vector, respectively, of the appropriate sizes to perform the operation. We can also represent this as a matrix calculation:

$$\begin{bmatrix} \mathbf{z} \\ 1 \end{bmatrix} = \begin{bmatrix} \mathbf{A} & \mathbf{y} \\ \mathbf{0}^T & 1 \end{bmatrix} \begin{bmatrix} \mathbf{x} \\ 1 \end{bmatrix}.$$

In general, in physical simulations, we are concerned with two affine transformations: translation (changing position) and rotation (changing orientation). (See Figure 1.4.)

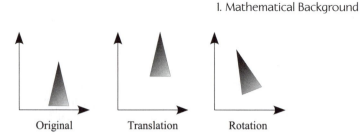

Figure 1.4. Translation and rotation.

The affine transformation will end up adding the vector $\mathbf{y}$ to any point we apply it to, so $\mathbf{y}$ achieves translation for us. Rotation is stored in the matrix $\mathbf{A}$. Because it is for us convenient to keep them separate, we will use the first form more often. So in three dimensions, translation will be stored as a 3-vector $\mathbf{t}$ and rotation as a 3×3 matrix, which we will call $\mathbf{R}$.

The following equation, also known as the Rodrigues formula, performs a general rotation of a point $\mathbf{p}$ by θ radians around a rotation axis $\hat{\mathbf{r}}$:

$$\cos\theta\,\mathbf{p} + [1 - \cos\theta](\hat{\mathbf{r}} \cdot \mathbf{p})\hat{\mathbf{r}} + \sin\theta(\hat{\mathbf{r}} \times \mathbf{p}). \tag{1.3}$$

This can be represented as a matrix by

$$\mathbf{R}_{\hat{\mathbf{r}}\theta} = \begin{bmatrix} tx^2 + c & txy - sz & txz + sy \\ txy + sz & ty^2 + c & tyz - sx \\ txz - sy & tyz + sx & tz^2 + c \end{bmatrix},$$

where

$$\begin{aligned} \hat{\mathbf{r}} &= (x, y, z), \\ c &= \cos\theta, \\ s &= \sin\theta, \\ t &= 1 - \cos\theta. \end{aligned}$$

Both translation and rotation are invertible transformations. To invert a translation, simply add $-\mathbf{y}$. To invert a rotation, take the transpose of the matrix.

One useful property of rotation is its interaction with the cross product:

$$\mathbf{R}(\mathbf{a} \times \mathbf{b}) = \mathbf{R}\mathbf{a} \times \mathbf{R}\mathbf{b}.$$

Note that this does not hold true for all linear transformations.

1.5   Quaternions

1.5.1   Definition

Another useful rotation representation is the quaternion. In their most general form, quaternions are an extension of complex numbers. Recall that a complex number can be represented as

$$c = a + bi,$$

where $i^2 = -1$.

We can extend this to a quaternion by creating two more imaginary terms, or

$$\mathbf{q} = w + xi + yj + zk,$$

where $i^2 = j^2 = k^2 = ijk = -1$. All of a quaternion's properties follow from this definition. Since i, j, and k are constant, we can also write this as an ordered 4-tuple, much as we do vectors:

$$\mathbf{q} = (w, x, y, z).$$

Due to the properties of $xi + yj + zk$, the imaginary part of a quaternion is often referred to as a vector in the following notation:

$$\mathbf{q} = (w, \mathbf{v}).$$

Using the vector form makes manipulating quaternions easier for those who are familiar with vector operations.

Note that most software packages store a quaternion as (x, y, z, w), which matches the standard layout for vertex positions in graphics.

1.5.2   Basic Operations

Like vectors, quaternions can be scaled and added, as follows:

$$\begin{aligned} a\mathbf{q} &= (aw, a\mathbf{v}), \\ \mathbf{q}_0 + \mathbf{q}_1 &= (w_0 + w_1, \mathbf{q}_0 + \mathbf{q}_1). \end{aligned}$$

There is only one quaternion multiplication operation. In vector form, this is represented as

$$\mathbf{q}_0 \mathbf{q}_1 = (w_0 w_1 - \mathbf{v}_0 \cdot \mathbf{v}_1, w_0 \mathbf{v}_1 + w_1 \mathbf{v}_0 + \mathbf{v}_0 \times \mathbf{v}_1).$$

Note that due to the cross product, quaternion multiplication is noncommutative.

Quaternions, like vectors, have a magnitude:

$$\|\mathbf{q}\| = \sqrt{w^2 + \mathbf{v} \cdot \mathbf{v}} = \sqrt{w^2 + x^2 + y^2 + z^2}.$$

Quaternions of magnitude 1, or unit quaternions, have properties that make them useful for representing rotations.

Like matrices, quaternions have a multiplicative identity, which is $(1, \mathbf{0})$. There is also the notion of a multiplicative inverse. For a unit quaternion $(w, \mathbf{v})$, the inverse is equal to $(w, -\mathbf{v})$. We can think of this as rotating around the opposing axis to produce the opposite rotation. In general, the quaternion inverse is

$$\mathbf{q}^{-1} = \frac{1}{w^2 + x^2 + y^2 + z^2}(w, -\mathbf{v}).$$

1.5.3 Vector Rotation

If we consider a rotation of angle θ around an axis $\mathbf{r}$, we can write this as a quaternion:

$$\mathbf{q} = (\cos(\theta/2), \sin(\theta/2)\hat{\mathbf{r}}).$$

It can be shown that this is, in fact, a unit quaternion.

We can use a quaternion of this form to rotate a vector $\mathbf{p}$ around $\hat{\mathbf{r}}$ by θ by using the formulation

$$\mathbf{p}_{\text{rot}} = \mathbf{q}\mathbf{p}\mathbf{q}^{-1}.$$

Note that in order to perform this multiplication, we need to rewrite $\mathbf{p}$ as a quaternion with a zero-valued w term, or $(0, \mathbf{p})$.

This multiplication can be expanded out and simplified as

$$\mathbf{p}_{\text{rot}} = \cos\theta\mathbf{p} + [1 - \cos\theta](\hat{\mathbf{r}} \cdot \mathbf{p})\hat{\mathbf{r}} + \sin\theta(\hat{\mathbf{r}} \times \mathbf{p}),$$

which as we see is the same as Equation (1.3) and demonstrates that quaternions can be used for rotation.

1.5.4 Matrix Conversion

It is often useful to convert a quaternion to a rotation matrix, e.g., so it can be used with the graphics pipeline. Again, assuming a unit rotation quaternion, the following is the corresponding matrix:

$$\mathbf{R_q} = \begin{bmatrix} 1 - 2y^2 - 2z^2 & 2xy - 2wz & 2xz + 2wy \\ 2xy + 2wz & 1 - 2x^2 - 2z^2 & 2yz - 2wx \\ 2xz - 2wy & 2yz + 2wx & 1 - 2x^2 - 2y^2 \end{bmatrix}.$$

Figure 1.5. Space curve with position and velocity at time t.

1.6 Rigid-Body Dynamics

1.6.1 Constant Forces

Suppose we have an object in motion in space. For the moment, we will consider only a particle with position $\mathbf{x}$, or linear motion. If we track this position over time, we end up with a function $\mathbf{x}(t)$. In addition, we can consider at a particular time how fast the object is moving and in what direction. This is the velocity $\mathbf{v}(t)$. As the velocity describes how $\mathbf{x}$ changes in time, it is also the derivative of its position, or $\dot{\mathbf{x}}$. (See Figure 1.5.)

Assuming that the velocity $\mathbf{v}$ is constant, we can create a formula for computing the future position of an object from its current position $\mathbf{x}_0$ and the time traveled t:

$$\mathbf{x}(t) = \mathbf{x}_0 + \mathbf{v}t.$$

However, most of the time, velocity is not constant, and we need to consider its derivative, or acceleration $\mathbf{a}$. Assuming $\mathbf{a}$ is constant, we can create a similar formula for $\mathbf{v}(t)$:

$$\mathbf{v}(t) = \mathbf{v}_0 + \mathbf{a}t.$$

Since velocity is changing at a linear rate, we can substitute the average of the velocities across our time steps for $\mathbf{v}$ in our original equation:

$$\begin{aligned}
\mathbf{x}(t) &= \mathbf{x}_0 + t\left[\frac{1}{2}(\mathbf{v}_0 + \mathbf{v}(t))\right] \\
&= \mathbf{x}_0 + t\left[\frac{1}{2}(\mathbf{v}_0 + \mathbf{v}_0 + \mathbf{a}t)\right] \\
&= \mathbf{x}_0 + \mathbf{v}_0 t + \frac{1}{2}\mathbf{a}t^2.
\end{aligned} \tag{1.4}$$

Acceleration in turn is derived from a vector quantity known as a force $\mathbf{F}$. Forces act to push and pull an object around in space. We determine the acceleration from force by using Newton's second law of motion,

$$\mathbf{F} = m\mathbf{a},$$

where m is the mass of the object and is constant.

The standard example of a force is gravity, $\mathbf{F}_{grav} = m\mathbf{g}$, which draws us to the Earth. There is also the normal force that counteracts gravity and keeps us from sinking through the ground. The thrust of a rocket, an engine moving a car along—these are all forces.

There can be multiple forces acting on an object. To manage these, we take the sum of all forces on an object and treat the result as a single force in our equations:

$$\mathbf{F} = \sum_{j} \mathbf{F}_j.$$

1.6.2   Nonconstant Forces

Equation (1.4) is suitable when our forces are constant across the time interval we are considering. However, in many cases, our forces are dependent on position or velocity. For example, we can represent a spring force based on position,

$$\mathbf{F}_{spring} = -k\mathbf{x},$$

or a drag force based on velocity,

$$\mathbf{F}_{drag} = -m\rho\mathbf{v}.$$

And as position and velocity will be changing across our time interval, our forces will as well.

One solution is to try and find a closed analytical solution, but (a) such a solution may not be possible to find and (b) the solution may be so complex that it is impractical to compute every frame. In addition, this constrains us to a single set of forces for that solution, and we would like the flexibility to apply and remove forces at will.

Instead, we will use a numerical solution. The problem we are trying to solve is this: we have a physical simulation with a total force dependent generally on time, position, and velocity, which we will represent as $\mathbf{F}(t, \mathbf{x}, \mathbf{v})$. We have a position $\mathbf{x}(t) = \mathbf{x}_0$ and a starting velocity $\mathbf{v}(t) = \mathbf{v}_0$. The question is, what is $\mathbf{x}(t + h)$?

One solution to this problem is to look at the definition of a derivative. Recall that

$$\mathbf{x}'(t) = \lim_{h \to 0} \frac{\mathbf{x}(t + h) - \mathbf{x}(t)}{h}.$$

For the moment, we will assume that h is sufficiently small and obtain an approximation by treating h as our time step.

Rearranging terms, we get

$$\mathbf{x}(t + h) \doteq \mathbf{x}(t) + h\mathbf{x}'(t),$$

or
$$\mathbf{x}(t+h) \doteq \mathbf{x}(t) + h\mathbf{v}(t).$$

This is known as the explicit Euler's method. Another way of thinking of this is that the derivative is tangent to the curve of $\mathbf{x}(t)$ at time t. By taking a small enough step in the tangent direction, we should end up close to the actual solution.

Note that since we are taking a new time step each frame, the frame positions are often represented in terms of a sequence of approximations $\mathbf{x}_0, \mathbf{x}_1, \mathbf{x}_2, \ldots$ So an alternative form for Euler's method is

$$\mathbf{x}_{i+1} = \mathbf{x}_i + h\mathbf{x}_i'.$$

Including the update for velocity, our full set of simulation equations is

$$\begin{aligned}
\mathbf{v}_{i+1} &= \mathbf{v}_i + h\mathbf{F}(t_i, \mathbf{x}_i, \mathbf{v}_i)/m, \\
\mathbf{x}_{i+1} &= \mathbf{x}_i + h\mathbf{v}_{i+1}.
\end{aligned}$$

Note that we use the result of the velocity step in our position equation. This is a variant of the standard Euler known as symplectic Euler, which provides more stability for position-based forces. We will discuss symplectic Euler and other integration methods below in more detail.

1.6.3 Updating Orientation

Updating orientation for a rigid-body simulation is similar to, yet different from, updating position. In addition to the linear quantities, we now have an object with the last frame's orientation $\mathbf{R}_i$ or $\mathbf{q}_i$, the last frame's angular velocity vector ω_i, an inertial tensor $\mathbf{I}$, and a sum of torques τ. From that, we wish to calculate the current frame's orientation $\mathbf{R}_{i+1}$ or $\mathbf{q}_{i+1}$ and the current frame's angular velocity ω_{i+1}.

The orientation itself we represent with either a rotation matrix $\mathbf{R}$ or a quaternion $\mathbf{q}$, both encapsulating rotation from a reference orientation (much as we can use a vector from the origin to represent a point). Which form we use depends on our needs. For example, rotation matrices can be convenient because they are easily converted into a form efficient for rendering. However, quaternions take up less space and need fewer operations to update and, thus, can be more efficient in the simulation engine itself.

Angular velocity is the rotational correspondence to linear velocity. As linear velocity represents a change in position, angular velocity represents a change in orientation. Its form is a three-element vector pointing along the axis of rotation and scaled so that its magnitude is the angle of rotation, in radians. We

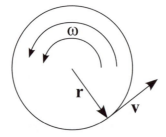

Figure 1.6. Converting between angular and linear velocities.

can determine the linear velocity at a displacement **r** from the center of rotation (Figure 1.6) using the following equation:

$$\mathbf{v} = \omega \times \mathbf{r}. \qquad (1.5)$$

If the object is also moving with a linear velocity $\mathbf{v}_l$, this becomes

$$\mathbf{v} = \mathbf{v}_l + \omega \times \mathbf{r}.$$

The inertial tensor **I** is the rotational equivalent to mass. Rather than the single scalar value of mass, the inertial tensor is a 3×3 matrix. This is because the shape and density of an object affects how it rotates. For example, consider a skater doing a spin. If she draws her arms in, her angular velocity increases. So by changing her shape, she is changing her rotational dynamics.

Computing the inertial tensor for an object is not always easy. Often, we can approximate it by using the inertial tensor for a simpler shape. For example, we could use a box to approximate a car or a cylinder to approximate a statue. If we want a more accurate representation, we can assume a constant density object and compute it based on the tessellated geometry. One way to think of this is as the sum of tetrahedra, where each tetrahedron shares a common vertex with the others, and the other vertices are one face of the original geometry. As the inertial tensor for a tetrahedron is a known quantity, this is a relatively straightforward calculation [Kallay 06]. A quantity that has no linear complement is the center of mass. This is a point, relative to the object, where applying a force invokes no rotation. We can think of this as the perfect balance point. The placement of the center of mass varies with the density or shape of an object. So a uniformly dense and symmetric steel bar will have its center of mass at its geometric center, whereas a hammer, for example, has its center of mass closer to its head. Placement of the center of mass can be done in a data-driven way by artists or designers, but more often, it comes out of the same calculation that computes the inertial tensor.

The final quantity is torque, which is the rotational equivalent to force. Applying force to an object at any place other than its center of mass will generate torque. To compute the torque, we take a vector $\mathbf{r}$ from the center of mass to the point where the force is applied and perform a cross product as follows:

$$\tau = \mathbf{r} \times \mathbf{F}.$$

This will apply the torque counterclockwise around the vector direction, as per the right-hand rule. We can sum all torques to determine the total torque on an object:

$$\tau_{\text{tot}} = \sum_j \mathbf{r}_j \times \mathbf{F}_j.$$

As with force, we can use Newton's second law to find the relationship between torque and angular acceleration α:

$$\tau = \mathbf{I}\alpha.$$

1.6.4 Numerical Integration for Orientation Using Matrices

To update our orientation, we ideally would want to do something like this:

$$\mathbf{R}_{i+1} = \mathbf{R}_i + h\omega_i.$$

However, as $\mathbf{R}_i$ is a matrix and ω_i is a vector, this is not possible. Instead, we do the following:

$$\mathbf{R}_{i+1} = \mathbf{R}_i + h[\omega]_{\times i}\mathbf{R}_i,$$

where

$$[\omega]_\times = \begin{bmatrix} 0 & -\omega_3 & \omega_2 \\ \omega_3 & 0 & -\omega_1 \\ -\omega_2 & \omega_1 & 0 \end{bmatrix}.$$

To understand why, let us consider the basis vectors of the rotation matrix $\mathbf{R}$ and how they change when an infinitesimal angular velocity is applied. For simplicity's sake, let us assume that the angular velocity is applied along one of the basis vectors; Figure 1.7 shows the other two. Recall that the derivative is a linear quantity, whereas angular velocity is a rotational quantity. What we need to do is change the rotational change of each axis to a linear change. We can do this by computing the infinitesimal linear velocity at the tip of a given basic vector and then adding this to get the new basis vector.

Recall that Equation (1.5) gives the linear velocity at a displacement $\mathbf{r}$ for angular velocity ω. So for each basis vector $\mathbf{r}_j$, we could compute $\omega \times \mathbf{r}_j$ and,

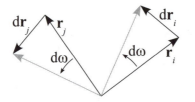

Figure 1.7. Change in basis vectors due to angular velocity.

from that, create a differential rotation matrix. However, there is another way to do a cross product and that is to use a skew symmetric matrix of the appropriate form, which is just what $[\omega]_\times$ is. Multiplying $\mathbf{r}_j$ by the skew symmetric matrix $[\omega]_\times$ will perform the cross product $\omega \times \mathbf{r}_j$, and multiplying $\mathbf{R}$ by $[\omega]_\times$ will perform the cross product on all the basis vectors as a single operation, giving us our desired result of $d\mathbf{R}/dt$.

1.6.5 Numerical Integration for Orientation Using Quaternions

Performing the Euler step for quaternions is similar to matrices. Again, we use an equation that can turn our angular velocity vector into a form suitable for adding to a quaternion:

$$\mathbf{q}_{i+1} = \mathbf{q} + \frac{h}{2}\mathbf{w}\mathbf{q},$$

where $\mathbf{w}$ is a quaternion of the form

$$\mathbf{w} = (0, \omega).$$

There are a number of proofs for this, though none are as intuitive as the one for rotation matrices. The most straightforward is from [Hanson 06]. If we take a quaternion $\mathbf{q}$ to the t power, we find that

$$\mathbf{q}^t = \exp(t \log \mathbf{q}).$$

For a rotation quaternion,

$$\log \mathbf{q} = \left(0, \frac{\theta}{2}\hat{\mathbf{r}}\right),$$

and hence,

$$\exp(t \log \mathbf{q}) = \exp\left(0, t\frac{\theta}{2}\hat{\mathbf{r}}\right)$$

$$= \left(\cos\frac{t\theta}{2}, \sin\frac{t\theta}{2}\hat{\mathbf{r}}\right).$$

Taking the derivative of $\mathbf{q}^t$ with respect to t gives us

$$
\begin{aligned}
\frac{d\mathbf{q}^t}{dt} &= \frac{d\exp(t\log\mathbf{q})}{dt} \\
&= \log\mathbf{q}\exp(t\log\mathbf{q}) \\
&= (\log\mathbf{q})\mathbf{q}^t.
\end{aligned}
$$

At $t = 0$, this is just

$$
\begin{aligned}
\frac{d\mathbf{q}}{dt} &= \log\mathbf{q} \\
&= \left(0, \frac{\theta}{2}\hat{\mathbf{r}}\right).
\end{aligned}
$$

Pulling out the $\frac{1}{2}$ term, we get

$$
\frac{1}{2}(0, \theta\hat{\mathbf{r}}) = \frac{1}{2}\mathbf{w}.
$$

Multiplying this quantity by the quaternion $\mathbf{q}$ gives the change relative to $\mathbf{q}$, just as it did for matrices.

1.6.6   Numerical Integration for Angular Velocity

As angular velocity and torque/angular acceleration are both vectors, we might think we could perform the followoing:

$$
\omega_{i+1} = \omega_i + h\mathbf{I}^{-1}\tau.
$$

However, as

$$
\tau = \mathbf{I}\dot{\omega} + \omega \times \mathbf{I}\omega,
$$

we cannot simply multiply τ by the inverse of $\mathbf{I}$ and do the Euler step.

One solution is to ignore the $\omega \times \mathbf{I}\omega$ term and perform the Euler step as written anyway. This term represents the precession of the system—for example, a tipped, spinning top will spin about its local axis but will also slowly precess around its vertical axis as well. Removing this term will not be strictly accurate but can add some stability.

The alternative is to do the integration in a different way. Consider the angular momentum $\mathbf{L}$ instead, which is $\mathbf{I}\omega$. The derivative $\dot{\mathbf{L}} = \mathbf{I}\dot{\omega} = \mathbf{I}\alpha = \tau$. Hence we can do the following:

$$
\begin{aligned}
\mathbf{L}_{i+1} &= \mathbf{L}_i + h\tau, \\
\omega_{i+1} &= \mathbf{I}_i^{-1}\mathbf{L}_{i+1}.
\end{aligned}
$$

The final piece is the calculation of $\mathbf{I}_i^{-1}$. The problem is that $\mathbf{I}$ is calculated relative to the object, but the remaining quantities are computed relative to the world. The solution is to update $\mathbf{I}$ each time step based on its current orientation thusly:

$$\mathbf{I}_i^{-1}\mathbf{L}_{i+1} = \mathbf{R}_i\mathbf{I}_0^{-1}\mathbf{R}_i^{-1}\mathbf{L}_{i+1}.$$

We can think of this as rotating the angular momentum vector into the object's local orientation, applying the inverse inertial tensor, and then rotating back into world coordinates.

This gives us our final formulas:

$$\tau = \sum_k \mathbf{r}_k \times \mathbf{F}_k,$$

$$\mathbf{L}_{i+1} = \mathbf{L}_i + h\tau,$$

$$\mathbf{I}_i^{-1} = \mathbf{R}_i\mathbf{I}_0^{-1}\mathbf{R}_i^{-1},$$

$$\omega_{i+1} = \mathbf{I}_i^{-1}\mathbf{L}_{i+1},$$

$$\mathbf{R}_{i+1} = \mathbf{R}_i + h\omega_{i+1}.$$

1.7 Numerical Integration

1.7.1 Issues with Euler's Method

Euler's method has the advantage of simplicity, however, it has its problems. First of all, it assumes that the derivative at the current point is a good estimate of the derivative across the entire interval. Secondly, the approximation that Euler's method produces adds energy to the system. And this approximation error is propagated with each Euler step. This leads to problems with stability if our system oscillates, such as with springs, orbits, and pendulums, or if our time step is large. In either case, the end result is that our approximation becomes less and less accurate.

We can see an example of this by looking at Euler's method used to simulate an orbiting object (Figure 1.8). The first time step clearly takes us off the desired path, and each successive step only makes things worse. We see similar problems with so-called "stiff" equations, e.g., those used to simulate stiff springs (hence the name).

Recall that the definition of the derivative assumes that h is infinitesimally small. So one solution might be to decrease our time step: e.g., divide our time in half and take two steps. While this can help in some situations (and some physics

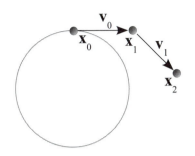

Figure 1.8. Using Euler's method to approximate an orbit.

engines do just that for that reason), because of the nature of Euler's method the error will still accumulate.

1.7.2   Higher-Order Explicit Methods

One solution to this problem is to realize that we are trying to approximate a non-linear function with a linear function. If we take a weighted average of samples of the derivative across our interval, perhaps we can construct a better approximation. The higher-order Runge-Kutta methods do just this. The most notable example is Runge-Kutta Order 4, or just RK4, which takes four samples of the derivative.

In general, RK4 will provide a better approximation of the function. However, it does come with the cost of more invocations of the derivative function, which may be expensive. In addition, it still does not solve our problem with stiff equations. For particularly stiff equations, RK4 will still add enough energy into the system to cause it to spiral out of control. Fortunately, there are other possibilities.

1.7.3   Implicit Methods

One method uses an alternative definition of the derivative:

$$\mathbf{x}'(t) = \lim_{h \to 0} \frac{\mathbf{x}(t) - \mathbf{x}(t - h)}{h}.$$

If we assume small h and again rearrange terms, we get

$$\mathbf{x}(t) \doteq \mathbf{x}(t - h) + h\mathbf{x}'(t).$$

Substituting $t + h$ for t, we end up with

$$\mathbf{x}(t + h) \doteq \mathbf{x}(t) + h\mathbf{x}'(t + h).$$

This is known as the *implicit Euler method*. The distinction between the implicit and explicit methods is that with the implicit methods, the right side includes terms that are not yet known. Implicit Euler is a first-order implicit method—it is possible to create higher-order methods just as we did for explicit methods.

Whereas explicit methods add energy to the system as they drift away from the actual function, implicit methods remove energy from the system. So while implicit methods still do not handle oscillating or stiff equations perfectly, they do not end up oscillating out of control. Instead, the system will damp down much faster than expected. The solution converges, which is not ideal, but does maintain stability.

We do have the problem that $x'(t + h)$ is unknown. There are three possible ways to solve this. One is to try to solve for an analytic solution. However, as before, this is not always possible, and often we do not have an equation for $x'(t)$—it is a function we call in our simulator that returns a numeric result. That result could be computed from any number of combinations of other equations. So, for both reasons, it is usually not practical to compute an explicit solution. In this case, we have two choices.

The first is to compute $x(t + h)$ using an explicit method and then use the result to compute our implicit function. This is known as a predictor-corrector method, as we predict a solution using the explicit equation and then correct for errors using the implicit solution. An example of this is using the result of an explicit Euler step in a modified implicit Euler solution:

$$\tilde{x}_{i+1} = x_i + hv_i,$$
$$\tilde{v}_{i+1} = v_i + hF(t_i, x_i, v_i)/m,$$

$$x_{i+1} = x_i + \frac{h}{2}(\tilde{v}_{i+1} + v_i),$$
$$v_{i+1} = v_i + \frac{h}{2}(F(\tilde{t}_{i+1}, \tilde{x}_{i+1}, \tilde{v}_{i+1}) + F(t_i, x_i, v_i))/m.$$

An alternative method for implicit Euler is to treat it as a linear equation and solve for it. We can do this for a force dependent on position as follows:

$$x_{x+1} = x_i + h_i x'_{i+1},$$
$$x_i + \Delta x_i = x_i + h_i F(x_i + \Delta x_i),$$
$$\Delta x_i = h_i F(x_i + \Delta x_i),$$
$$\Delta x_i \approx h_i (F(x_i) + J(x_i)\Delta x_i),$$
$$\Delta x_i \approx \left[\frac{1}{h_i}E - J(x_i)\right]^{-1} F(x_i),$$

where $\mathbf{J}$ is a matrix of partial derivatives known as the Jacobian. The resulting matrix is sparse and easy to invert, which makes it useful for large systems, such as collections of particles.

1.7.4 Verlet Methods

A popular game physics method, mainly due to [Jakobsen 01], is Verlet integration. In its most basic form, it is a velocity-less scheme, instead using the position from the previous frame. As we often don't care about the velocity of particles, this makes it very useful for particle systems.

The general formula for the Verlet method is as follows:

$$\mathbf{x}_{i+1} = 2\mathbf{x}_i - \mathbf{x}_{i-1} + h^2 \mathbf{a}_i.$$

While standard Verlet is quite stable, it has the disadvantage that it doesn't incorporate velocity. This makes it difficult to use with velocity-dependent forces.

One possible solution is to use Leapfrog Verlet:

$$
\begin{aligned}
\mathbf{v}_{i+1/2} &= \mathbf{v}_{i-1/2} + h\mathbf{a}_i, \\
\mathbf{x}_{i+1} &= \mathbf{x}_i + h\mathbf{v}_{i+1/2}.
\end{aligned}
$$

However, this does not compute the velocity at the current time step, but instead at the half-time step (this is initialized by using a half-interval Euler step). While we can take an average of these over two time steps for our force calculation, we still have problems with impulse-based collision systems, which instantaneously modify velocity to simulate contact forces. One solution to this is use the full velocity Verlet:

$$
\begin{aligned}
\mathbf{v}_{i+1/2} &= \mathbf{v}_i + h/2\mathbf{a}_i, \\
\mathbf{x}_{i+1} &= \mathbf{x}_i + h\mathbf{v}_{i+1/2}, \\
\mathbf{v}_{i+1} &= \mathbf{v}_{i+1/2} + h/2\mathbf{a}_{i+1}.
\end{aligned}
$$

However, unlike Euler's method, this does require two force calculations, and we can get similar stability with the last method we'll consider.

More information on Verlet methods can be found in Chapter 11.

1.7.5 Symplectic Euler Method

We've already seen the symplectic Euler method previously—in fact, it's the method we were using for the simulation equations in Section 1.6. It is a semi-implicit method, in that it uses the explicit Euler method to update velocity but

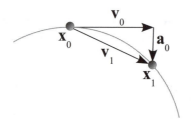

Figure 1.9. Using the symplectic Euler method to approximate an orbit.

uses an implicit value of velocity to update position:

$$\mathbf{v}_{i+1} = \mathbf{v}_i + h\mathbf{F}(t_i, \mathbf{x}_i, \mathbf{v}_i)/m,$$
$$\mathbf{x}_{i+1} = \mathbf{x}_i + h\mathbf{v}_{i+1}.$$

This takes advantage of the fact that velocity is the derivative of position, and the end result is that we get a very stable method that only requires one force calculation. It does have the disadvantage that it is not as accurate with constant forces, but in those cases, we should consider using Equation (1.4) anyway.

In Figure 1.9, we see the result of using symplectic Euler with one step of our orbit example. Admittedly this is a bit contrived, but we see that, in principle, it is extremely stable—neither spiraling outward as explicit Euler would do nor spiraling inward as implicit Euler would do.

1.8   Further Reading

This chapter is mainly intended as an overview, and the interested reader can find more details in a wide variety of sources. Good references for linear algebra with widely varying but useful approaches are [Anton and Rorres 94] and [Axler 97]. Kenneth Joy also has a good series on vectors, points, and affine transformations, found in [Joy 00c], [Joy 00b], and [Joy 00a].

The standard quaternion reference for graphics is [Shoemake 85], which has been expanded to excellent detail in [Hanson 06]. An early series of articles about game physics is [Hecker 97], and [Witkin and Baraff 01] provides thorough coverage of the early Pixar physics engine. It is also worth mentioning [Catto 06], which first introduced me to the symplectic Euler method, for which I am eternally grateful.

Finally, without modesty, a good general source for all of these topics is my own work, cowritten with Lars Bishop [Van Verth and Bishop 08].

Bibliography

[Anton and Rorres 94] Howard Anton and Chris Rorres. *Elementary Linear Algebra: Applications Version*, Seventh edition. New York: John Wiley and Sons, 1994.

[Axler 97] Sheldon Axler. *Linear Algebra Done Right*, Second edition. New York: Springer, 1997.

[Catto 06] Erin Catto. "Fast and Simple Physics using Sequential Impulses." Paper presented at GDC 2006 Tutorial "Physics for Game Programmers," San Jose, CA, March, 2006.

[Golub and Van Loan 93] Gene H. Golub and Charles F. Van Loan. *Matrix Computations*. Baltimore, MD: Johns Hopkins University Press, 1993.

[Hanson 06] Andrew Hanson. *Visualizing Quaternions*. San Francisco: Morgan Kaufmann, 2006.

[Hecker 97] Chris Hecker. "Behind the Screen: Physics." Series published in *Game Developer Magazine*, 1996–1997.

[Jakobsen 01] Thomas Jakobsen. "Advanced Character Physics." Paper presented at Game Developers Conference 2001, San Jose, CA, March, 2001.

[Joy 00a] Kenneth Joy. "On-Line Geometric Modeling Notes: Affine Combinations, Barycentric Coordinates and Convex Combinations." Technical report, University of California, Davis, 2000.

[Joy 00b] Kenneth Joy. "On-Line Geometric Modeling Notes: Points and Vectors." Technical report, University of California, Davis, 2000.

[Joy 00c] Kenneth Joy. "On-Line Geometric Modeling Notes: Vector Spaces." Technical report, University of California, Davis, 2000.

[Kallay 06] Michael Kallay. "Computing the Moment of Inertia of a Solid Defined by a Triangle Mesh." *journal of graphics tools* 11:2 (2006), 51–57.

[Press et al. 93] William H. Press, Brian P. Flannery, Saul A. Teukolsky, and William T. Vetterling. *Numerical Recipes in C: The Art of Scientific Computing*, Second edition. New York: Cambridge University Press, 1993.

[Shoemake 85] Ken Shoemake. "Animating Rotation with Quaternion Curves." *Computer Graphics (SIGGRAPH '85 Proceedings)* 19 (1985), 245–254.

[Van Verth and Bishop 08] James M. Van Verth and Lars M. Bishop. *Essential Mathematics for Games and Interactive Applications*, Second edition. San Francisco: Morgan Kaufmann, 2008.

[Witkin and Baraff 01] Andrew Witkin and David Baraff. "Physically Based Modelling: Principles and Practice." ACM SIGGRAPH 2001 Course Notes. Available at http://www.pixar.com/companyinfo/research/pbm2001/, 2001.

- 2 -

Understanding
Game Physics Artifacts

Dennis Gustafsson

2.1 Introduction

Physics engines are known for being notoriously hard to debug. For most people, physics artifacts are just a seemingly random stream of weird behavior that makes no sense. Few components of a game engine cause much frustration and hair loss. We have all seen ragdolls doing the funky monkey dance and stacks of "rigid" bodies acting more like a tower of greasy mushrooms, eventually falling over or taking off into the stratosphere. This chapter will help you understand the underlying causes of this behavior and common mistakes that lead to it. Some of them can be fixed, some of them can be worked around, and some of them we will just have to live with for now. This is mostly written for people writing a physics engine of their own, but understanding the underlying mechanisms is helpful even if you are using an off-the-shelf product.

2.2 Discretization and Linearization

Physics engines advance time in discrete steps, typically about 17 ms for a 60 Hz update frequency. It is not uncommon to split up the time step into smaller steps, say two or three updates per frame (often called substepping) or even more, but no matter how small of a time step you use, it will still be a discretization of a continuous problem. Real-world physics do not move in steps, not even small steps, but in a continuous motion. This is by far the number one source for physics artifacts, and any properly implemented physics engine should behave better with more substeps. If a physics artifact does not go away with more substeps, there is most likely something wrong with your code. The bullet-through-paper problem illustrated in Figure 2.1 is a typical example of a problem that is caused by discretization.

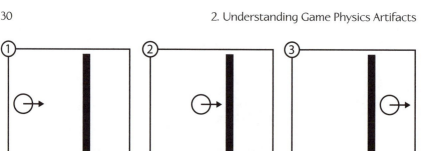

Figure 2.1. Discretization can cause fast-moving objects to travel through walls.

Another big source of artifacts is the linearization that most physics engines employ—the assumption that during the time step everything travels in a linear motion. For particle physics, this is a pretty good approximation, but as soon as you introduce rigid bodies and rotation, it falls flat to the ground. Consider the ball joint illustrated in Figure 2.2. The two bodies are rotating in opposite directions. At this particular point in time, the two bodies are lined up as shown. Even if the solver manages to entirely solve the relative velocity at the joint-attachment point to zero, as soon as time is advanced, no matter how small the amount, the two attachment points will drift apart. This is the fundamental of linearization, which makes it impossible to create an accurate physics engine by solving just for relative linear velocities at discrete points in time.

Even though linearization and discretization are two different approximations, they are somewhat interconnected. Lowering the step size (increasing the number of substeps) will always make linearization less problematic, since any nonlinear motion will appear more and more linear the shorter the time span. The ambitious reader can make a parallel here to the Heisenberg principle of uncertainty!

The major takeaway here is that as long as a physics engine employs discretization and linearization, which all modern physics engines and all algorithms

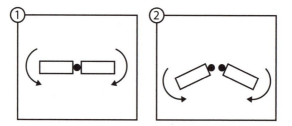

Figure 2.2. Even if relative linear velocity at the joint attachment is zero, objects can separate during integration due to rotation.

and examples in this book do, there will always be artifacts. These artifacts are not results of a problem with the physics engine itself, but the assumptions and approximations the engine is built upon. This is important to realize, because once you accept the artifacts and understand their underlying causes, it makes them easier to deal with and work around.

2.3   Time Stepping and the Well of Despair

Since the physics engine is advanced in discrete steps, what happens if the game drops a frame? This is a common source of confusion when integrating a physics engine, since you probably want the motion in your game to be independent of frame rate. On a slow machine, or in the occasion of your modern operating system going off to index the quicksearch database in the middle of a mission, the graphical update might not keep up with the desired frequency. There are several different strategies for how to handle such a scenario from a physics perspective. You can ignore the fact that a frame was dropped and keep stepping the normal step length, which will create a slow-motion effect that is usually highly undesirable. Another option is to take a larger time step, which will create a more realistic path of motion but may introduce jerkiness due to the variation in discretization. The third option is to take several, equally sized physics steps. This option is more desirable, as it avoids the slowdown while still doing fixed-size time steps.

2.3.1   The Well of Despair

Making several physics updates per frame usually works fine, unless the physics is what is causing the slowdown to begin with. If physics is the bottleneck, the update frequency will go into the well of despair, meaning every subsequent frame needs more physics updates, causing a slower update frequency, resulting in even more physics updates the next frame, and so on. There is unfortunately no way to solve this problem other than to optimize the physics engine or simplify the problem, so what most people do is put a cap on the number of physics updates per frame, above which the simulation will simply run in slow motion. Actually, it will not only run in slow motion but it will run in slow motion at a lower-than-necessary frame rate, since most of what the physics engine computes is never even shown! A more sophisticated solution is to measure the time of the physics update, compare it to the overall frame time, and only make subsequent steps if we can avoid the well of despair. This problem is not trivial, and there is no ultimate solution that works for all scenarios, but it is well worth experimenting with since it can have a very significant impact on the overall update frequency.

2.4   The Curse of Rotations

Since rotation is the mother of most linearization problems, it deserves some special attention. One fun experiment we can try is to make the inertia tensor for all objects infinite and see how that affects our simulation. The inertia tensor can roughly be described as an object's willingness to rotate and is often specified as its inverse, so setting all values to zero typically means rotations will be completely disabled. You will be surprised how stable those stacks become and how nicely most scenarios just work. Unfortunately, asking the producer if it is okay to skip rotations will most likely not be a good idea, but what we can learn is that the more inertia we add, the less rotation will occur, problems with linearization will decrease, and the simulation will get more stable.

The problem is especially relevant on long, thin rods. So if you experience instability with such objects, try increasing the inertia, especially on the axis along the rod (compute inertia as if the rod was thicker). Increasing inertia will make objects look heavy and add a perceived slow-motion effect, so you might want to take it easy, but it can be a lifesaver and is surprisingly hard to spot.

2.5   Solver

Just to freshen up our memory without getting into technical detail, the solver is responsible for computing the next valid state of a dynamic system, taking into account various constraints. Now, since games need to be responsive, this computation has to be fast, and the most popular way of doing that is using an iterative method called *sequential impulse*. The concept is really simple: given a handful of constraints, satisfy each one of them, one at a time, and when the last one is done, start over again from the beginning and do another round until it is "good enough," where good enough often means, "Sorry man, we are out of time, let's just leave it here."

What is really interesting, from a debugging perspective, is how this early termination of a sequential impulse solver can affect the energy of the system. Stopping before we are done will not add energy to the system, it will drain energy. This means it is really hard to blame the solver itself for energy being added to the system.

When you implement a sequential impulse solver with early termination, stacked, resting objects tend to sink into each other. Let's investigate why this is happening: at each frame, gravity causes an acceleration that increases an object's downward velocity. Contact generation creates a set of points and at each contact, the solver tries to maintain a zero-relative velocity. However, since greedy game programmers want CPU cycles for other things, the solver is terminated before it is completely done, leaving the objects with a slight downward velocity instead of zero, which is desired for resting contact. This slight downward velocity causes objects to sink in, and the process is repeated.

To compensate for this behavior, most physics engines use a geometric measure for each contact point: either penetration depth or separation distance. As the penetration depth increases, the desired resulting velocity is biased, so that it is not zero but is actually negative, causing the objects to separate. This translates to objects being soft instead of rigid, where the softness is defined by how well the solver managed to solve the problem. This is why most solvers act springy or squishy when using fewer iterations. Hence, the best way to get rid of the mushroom is to increase the number of iterations in the solver!

2.5.1   Keeping the Configuration Unchanged

A solver that uses this kind of geometric compensation running at the same step size and same number of iterations every frame will eventually find an equilibrium after a certain number of frames. Understanding that this equilibrium is not a relaxed state but a very complex ongoing struggle between gravity, penetrating contacts, and penalty forces is key to stability. Removing or adding even a single constraint, or changing the number of iterations, will cause the solver to redistribute the weight and find a new equilibrium, which is a process that usually takes several frames and causes objects to wiggle. The set of constraints for a specific scenario is sometimes called its configuration; hence keeping the configuration unchanged from one frame to the next is very important, and we will revisit this goal throughout the chapter.

2.5.2   Warm Starting

Assuming that the configuration does not change and objects are at rest, the impulses at each contact point will be essentially the same every frame. It seems kind of unnecessary to recompute the same problem over and over again. This is where warm starting comes into the picture. Instead of recomputing the impulses from scratch every time, we can start off with the impulses from the previous frame and use our solver iterations to refine them instead. Using warm starting is almost always a good idea. The downside is that we have to remember the impulses from the last frame, which requires some extra bookkeeping. However, since most physics engines keep track of pairs anyway, this can usually be added relatively easily.

I mentioned before that a sequential impulse solver does not add energy but rather drains energy from a system. This unfortunately no longer holds true if

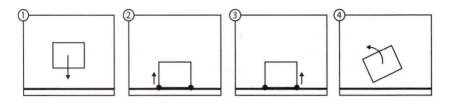

Figure 2.3. A sequential impulse solver can cause an aligned box falling flat to the ground to bounce off with rotation.

warm starting is being used. Full warm starting can give a springy, oscillating behavior and prevents stacks from ever falling asleep. Because of this, the current frame's impulses are usually initialized with only a fraction of the previous frame's impulses. As we increase this fraction, the solver becomes more springy, but it can also handle stacking better. It could be worth experimenting with this to find the sweet spot.

2.5.3   Who Is Tilting My Box

A sequential impulse solver, as described above, is called in mathematical terms Gauss-Seidel iteration. Another method is Jacobi iteration, in which all contact points are solved independently, and then the resulting impulses are applied all at once, hence removing the *sequential* in sequential impulse. Jacobi solvers have some nice properties, especially when it comes to parallelization, but they generally take way more iterations to converge. One effect of sequential contact solving is that symmetric problems often have seemingly unpredictable solutions. Consider a perfectly aligned box dropped on a horizontal plane. All four corners hit the plane at the same time, even forming four identical contact points. A sequential impulse solver will start solving one contact point without considering the other three, apply the resulting impulse and then consider the next one. While solving the second contact, the problem is no longer symmetric, since the box is rotating after applying the first impulse. The resulting motion will behave as if one corner of the box hit the ground slightly before the others (see Figure 2.3). Hence, whenever we see this type of behavior, it is most likely not an error, just brother Gauss-Seidel pulling a prank.

2.5.4   Friction

Friction is usually a little trickier than nonpenetration constraints since the maximum applied force depends on the normal force. The more pressure there is on an object, the better it sticks. This interdependence results in a nonlinear problem that is very tricky to solve accurately.

Coupled or decoupled. There are two main approaches to solving friction—coupled and decoupled. In the coupled approach, the maximum friction force changes while iterating, basically trying to solve a nonlinear problem with a toolbox that is designed for linear problems (Gauss-Seidel), which may sound inappropriate but actually works fairly well in practice. The decoupled involves using a fixed maximum friction force that is determined before iterating. In the case of decoupled friction, there are two popular methods: either using the normal force from the last time step, which requires some bookkeeping, or using a fixed value, regardless of normal force. Such a fixed value is often based on the normal force to keep the body at rest when affected by gravity. This may sound like a very crude approximation, but it works surprisingly well, requires no bookkeeping, and is perfectly linear. The main drawback is, of course, that friction is unaffected by how much pressure is on the object. An object at the bottom of a stack slides out just as easily as the ones on top!

Friction in stacks. It is worth mentioning the importance of proper friction for handling stable stacking. Even in a scenario that seems largely unaffected by friction, like a pyramid of boxes, friction plays a very important role. Remember that the solver causes objects to rotate as an artifact of Gauss-Seidel iteration. This rotation introduces a tangential motion that causes a stack to tip over if no friction is used.

Friction drift. Remember the description above, about early solver termination causing stacked objects to sink into each other? The exact same thing happens to friction constraints, so if not compensated for, stacked objects might slide around slowly on top of each other, eventually causing the whole thing to fall over. Tracking friction drift is cumbersome because it involves tracking pairs of objects over several frames. For penetration depth it is rather straightforward since the desired configuration is determined by the shape of the objects. For static friction, it is not quite that easy. Static friction can be seen as a temporary joint holding two objects together in the contact plane. If the maximum joint force is exceeded, the objects should actually slide, but as long as the force is within the maximum friction force, the relative net motion should ideally be zero. Hence, any motion that actually occurs is due to early solver termination, linearization, or any other of our artifact friends. Measuring this drift and compensating for it over time can therefore help maintain stable stacking and natural friction behavior.

2.5.5   Shock Propagation

As a way to counteract the squishiness of iterative solvers, a shock-propagation scheme can be used. The idea is to analyze the configuration and set up the problem in such a way so that the solver can find a solution more quickly. Some engines maintain an explicit graph of how the objects connect, whereas other engines temporarily tweak mass ratios, inertia, or gravity. There is a lot of creativity in shock propagation, but the artifacts are usually similar.

Large stacks require many iterations because the impulses at the bottom of the stack are many times bigger than they would be for any pair of objects solved in isolation. It takes many iterations to build up these large impulses. With shock propagation, objects at the bottom of a stack will not feel the entire weight of the objects on top. This can show up as the unnatural behavior of stacks tipping over and can also be very obvious when observing friction—an object at the bottom of a stack can be as easily pulled out as one on top.

2.6   Collision Detection

The collision-detection problem is often broken down into two or three phases. First a broad phase, detecting objects in close proximity, and then sometimes a mid phase, breaking down structures into smaller parts, before the near phase, computing the actual contact points.

2.6.1   Phases

Broad phase. Let us start with the broad phase, which has a relatively well-defined task: report overlaps of bounding volumes, most often axis-aligned bounding boxes. If the bounding box is too small, we might experience weird shootouts as the broad phase reports nonoverlap until the objects are already in penetration. Having the bounding boxes too big, on the other hand, has a performance implication, so we have to be sure to make them *just right*. Remember that if we use continuous collision detection or intentional separation distance, these must be included in the bounding-box computation, so that the bounding box is no longer tight-fitting around the object. These errors can be hard to spot since it looks right most of the time.

Mid phase. The mid phase often consists of a bounding-volume hierarchy to find convex objects in close proximity. Again, incorrect bounding-box computation can lead to shootouts. Another common problem is that objects can get stuck in between two convex parts of a compound geometry. Consider the object consisting of two spheres in Figure 2.4. Convex geometries are usually treated in isolation, causing two conflicting contact points with opposite normals and penetration depths. Feeding this problem to the solver is a dead end—there is no valid solution! The objects will start shaking violently and act very unstable. There

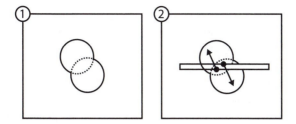

Figure 2.4. Compound geometries can cause artifacts when objects get stuck in between parts.

is no good solution to this, but avoid using many small objects to make up compound bodies. In the case above, a capsule or cylinder would have avoided the problem.

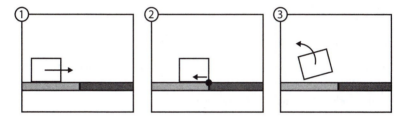

Figure 2.5. An object sliding over a compound geometry can catch on invisible hooks due to penetration.

Sliding. A similar problem can occur when an object is sliding over a flat surface that is made up of multiple parts. Imagine the scene in Figure 2.5. The box should ideally slide over the seam without any glitches, but they way the object is constructed, the seam can create invisible "hooks" causing the sliding object to

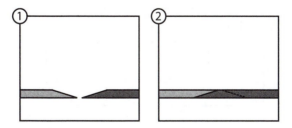

Figure 2.6. Making a ramp on each side and letting them overlap is a simple work-around to avoid objects getting stuck in compound objects.

stop. This is a typical frustrating artifact in certain car racing games where the car can get trapped on invisible hooks while sliding along the fence. A simple workaround is to construct the geometry as suggested in Figure 2.6.

Near phase. The near phase is by far the most complex part, where the actual contact generation occurs. The poor solver is often blamed for unstable and jittering simulations, but surprisingly often, shaking objects, general instability, and jerkiness can be attributed to inadequate contact generation. A sequential-impulse solver can be blamed for squishy stacks, improper friction, and many other things, but it is actually quite hard to make a solver that causes objects to rattle and shake. Near-phase contact generation often has many special cases and can be prone to numerical floating-point precision issues. Some engines use contact pruning to remove excess contact points. Special care should then be taken to make sure the same contacts are pruned every frame. Remember that keeping the configuration unchanged is key to stability.

2.6.2   Continuous Collision Detection

Ah, continuous collision detection, a technique that prevents objects from slipping through walls—how about that! Just enable it, sit back, and enjoy how everything magically works? Not quite, unfortunately.

Let us start by splitting the problem domain into two categories. First, there are artifacts caused by discretization, typically, a small object passing through a wall, called the bullet-through-paper problem already mentioned in the beginning of this chapter. The other category is when contact is detected and generated, but the solver fails to find a proper solution, usually because of early termination. This artifact can be very significant when a light object is getting squished in between two heavy objects and is sometimes referred to as the sandwich case (see Figure 2.7).

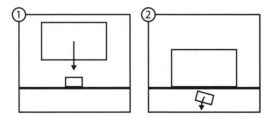

Figure 2.7. Fast-moving objects are not the only ones taking shortcuts through walls. Early solver termination can cause objects to get squished even if contacts are detected and generated.

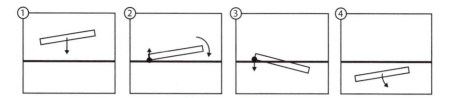

Figure 2.8. Fast-moving objects could potentially get rotated through the floor even if a contact is generated.

There is also a fairly common case that is a combination of the two. Imagine a thin rod, slightly inclined, falling onto a flat surface, as illustrated in Figure 2.8. The initial impact on the left side can cause a rotation so severe that by the next time step, more than half of the rod has already passed through the floor, and contact generation pushes it out on the other side. This example is a good illustration of the sometimes complex interaction between linearization and discretization that can bring a seemingly simple case like this to epic failure, even with continuous collision detection switched on. Note that some physics engine actually do have a really sophisticated nonlinear continuous collision detection that does consider rotation as well, in which case the example mentioned above would have actually worked.

Sandwich case. The sandwich case can be somewhat worked around by prioritizing contacts. It is always the last constraints in a sequential impulse solver that will be the most powerful and less prone to be violated upon early termination. Therefore, it is best to rearrange the stream of contacts so that the ones that touch important game-play mechanics, such as walls, are solved at the very last. A good common practice to avoid having objects get pushed through walls or the floor is to solve all contacts involving a static object after any other contact or do an extra iteration or two after termination to satisfy only static contacts.

Bullet-through-paper. An engine that aims to solve only the bullet-through-paper case typically uses a raycast or linear sweep operation to find a time of impact, then either splits up the time step—simulates the first half until the object is touching and then does the rest—or employs an early-engage method that inserts a contact point before the object has actually reached the surface. The early-engage method can sometimes be noticed as an invisible wall in front of obstacles, especially when using zero restitution, in which case a falling object could come to a full stop some distance above the floor before finally falling the last bit.

2.7   Joints

Joints are at the most fundamental level simpler than contacts. It is an equality constraint, keeping the relative velocity between two bodies to zero. No inequalities, no interdependent friction, etc. However, the way we combine constraints, and add limits, breakable constraints, joint friction, and damping typically make them fairly complex.

2.7.1   Drift

The most common artifact with joints is drifting, i.e., an unintended separation between the two jointed objects. It is the joint counterpart to stacked objects sinking into each other. The solver simply fails to find a valid solution within the limited number of iterations. However, as described in the introduction to this chapter, even with an unlimited number of iterations, joints can still drift due to the linearization of velocities. Most engines cope with drifting in the same way they cope with penetration or friction drift: simply add a geometric term, acting as a spring to compensate for the drift.

2.7.2   Solving Direct

A good way to reduce joint drift is to solve as many constraints as possible at the same time. Since joints are made up of equality constraints, they can be solved as a system of linear equations, sometimes referred to as a direct solver. Solving a system of linear equations is more complicated than applying sequential impulses, but it does pay off in stability. On the upside, these two methods can be easily combined. Some engines solve systems of three orthogonal constraints (this particular assembly is found in many joint types) as a special case with a three-by-three matrix inversion and then interweave the rest of the constraints using sequential impulses.

The way the constraints are placed also matters when it comes to stability. Consider a ball joint. It might be tempting to use a single constraint in the direction of maximum separation or in the direction of relative velocity. But remember that whatever constraints go into the solver are the only constraints avoiding motion, so a single constraint will naturally transfer motion from the constraint axis to the other two. A proper ball joint needs three constraints to be stable, and even the way the three constraints are aligned matters. Keeping the constraints aligned roughly the same way every frame helps stability. World axes are a good starting point, but using the axes of one of the objects can be even better, since they will then be stationary to at least one of the objects, keeping the configuration as similar as possible.

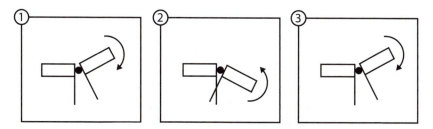

Figure 2.9. Hard joint limits might start oscillating due to discretization.

2.7.3 Joint Limits

Some joints support limits that block either linear or angular motion. This is very similar to a contact constraint. A common artifact with jointed structures with limits is that they tend to shake and never come to rest. Even if a joint limit is supposed to be a hard limit, it is usually a good idea to soften it up a tiny bit. A hard limit that fully engages when limit is exceeded and fully disengaged otherwise is very hard to get stable. Consider the limited hinge joint in Figure 2.9. Before it hits the limit, the joint can move freely. Now, since the simulation is carried out in discrete steps, this means that the joint limit will not kick in until the limit is already exceeded. Once it is exceeded, the geometric term that is supposed to correct the joint will kick the joint back, causing the limit to disengage and fall back down again. This is a good example of how rapidly changing the configuration causes instability.

Using soft limits, so that the hinge is allowed to rest on a spring for a certain distance, will give the solver a chance to find equilibrium without changing the configuration every frame.

2.7.4 Dealing with the Dead Guy

Ragdolls might qualify as the number one physics frustration worldwide, and numerous games are still shipped with ragdolls doing the monkey dance while "dead." In my experience, ragdoll instability is due to two main factors—hard joint limits and excess inter-bone collisions. Applying soft limits as described above will get you halfway there. A ragdoll is a pretty complex structure, especially since it can end up on the ground in any pose, including one that engages multiple joint limits.

Shaking usually appears either when the configuration changes or when there are conflicting constraints. The more constraints there are to solve, the higher chance there is for conflicting ones. Therefore, it is usually a good idea to disable as many collisions as possible. Start with a ragdoll with all bone–bone collisions turned off. You will be surprised how good it still looks. You might want to enable certain collisions, such as hips–lower arms, and calf-calf collisions, but in general, it is fine to leave most of the other ones, assuming you have a decent setup of joint limits.

Finally, add a certain amount of damping or friction to all joints. The flesh in the human body naturally dampens any motion, so some amount of friction will look more natural, at the same time helping our ragdoll get some sleep.

2.7.5 Geometric Joint Recovery

Since joint drifting cannot be completely avoided, it is tempting to do a final geometric translation to pull joints back together. This can work well in some situations, but for the most part, it will add instability and energy to the overall system. Consider the scene illustrated in Figure 2.10. Translating the joint back into position introduces a penetration that will at the next frame push the body up and add energy to the system, possibly causing a new joint displacement. If we really want to get our hands dirty and implement geometric recovery, we should consider the whole system, also doing it for collisions to resolve penetrations, and modify both position and rotation.

A better way to do this correction is to do joint translation as a pure visual effect. In the ragdoll case, many games use only rotation from the physics representation, while keeping a fixed displacement, efficiently hiding joint drifting. However, if the joint displacement is large, it can cause visual penetration, especially at the outermost limbs of the ragdoll.

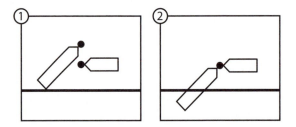

Figure 2.10. Compensating for joint drift by moving the objects is usually a really bad idea.

2.8 Direct Animation

Sometimes we might want to simply animate physical objects, having them affect other objects but not be affected themselves. There are several ways to do this, including using joint motors, to physically drive the object. However, sometimes we simply want to move an object along an animated path, totally unaffected by collisions. Animating an object by simply setting its position is never a good idea. It might still affect objects in its environment, but collisions will be soft and squishy. This is partly because the velocity of the object is not updated correctly, so for all the solver knows, there is a collision with penetration, but it is not aware that any of the objects are moving. To avoid this, make sure to update the velocity to match the actual motion. Some engines have convenience functions for this.

Even when the velocity is correct, if the animated object is not considerably heavier than the objects it is colliding with, the collisions will be soft and squishy. For an animated object to fully affect the environment, its mass and inertia tensor should be infinite. Only then will other objects fully obey and move out of the way. Hence, if we animate objects by setting their position, make sure to give them correct velocity, both linear and angular, and make the mass and inertiatensor temporarily infinite.

2.9   Artifact Reference

Following is a list of artifacts and their causes.

- *Frame rate gradually slows down to grinding halt.* You might have hit the well of despair, where the physics engine tries to compensate for its own slow down. Put a cap on the number of physics steps per frame or implement a more sophisticated time-stepping algorithm.

- *Simulation runs in slow motion.* Check that the physics step size corresponds to actual time. Keep an eye on simulation scale. A larger scale will result in slow-motion effects.

- *Stacked objects are shaking or rattling.* Check the contact-generation code and make sure the configuration is not rapidly changing.

- *An aligned object dropped on a flat surface bounces off in a weird way.* This is natural behavior of Gauss-Seidel iteration.

- *Objects at the bottom of a stack do not feel the weight of the ones on top.* This is caused by a shock-propagation scheme or decoupled friction with fixed maximum force.

- *Highly asymmetric objects act unstable.* The low inertia around one of the axes causes a lot of rotation. Increase inertia tensors, as if the objects were more symmetric.

- *Stacked objects act springy and objects get squashed.* The solver iteration count might be too low. We can also try adding warm starting or a shock-propagation scheme.

- *Stacks are oscillating and tend to never come to rest.* Too much warm starting is being used.

- *Stacked objects slide around on each other, eventually falling over.* There is a lack of friction-drift compensation.

- *An object penetrate freely and then suddenly shoots out.* This can be an incorrect bounding box or a contact-generation problem.

- *Objects are getting pushed through walls by other objects.* The contact stream might not favor static contacts. Rearrange the contact stream so that static contacts are at the end of the stream.

- *Small, fast objects pass through walls.* Enable continuous collision detection or early engage. If the problem still does not go away, it can be due to rotation. Make the object thicker or increase inertia tensor.

- *Falling object stop before hitting the floor and then fall down the last bit.* This is cased by early-engage contact generation. You can add some restitution to hide the problem or implement more sophisticated continuous collision detection.

- *Jointed structures drift apart, causing visual separation.* This cannot entirely be avoided due to the nature of iterative solvers and linearization. Use a direct solver to minimize the problem. You can also try a visual joint displacement, if applicable.

- *Ragdolls are shaking and never come to rest.* There can be conflicting joint limits, too many inter-bone collisions, or joint limits that are too hard.

- *An animated object does not affect the environment properly.* The animated object might have incorrect velocity, or the mass or inertia is not infinite.

– II –

Collision Detection

– 3 –

Broad Phase and Constraint Optimization for PlayStation®3

Hiroshi Matsuike

3.1 Introduction

The Cell Broadband Engine™(Cell/BE) is a heterogeneous multi-core processor installed in PlayStation®3 as its CPU. Because of this structure, Cell/BE demands that programmers take advantage of parallel computation to draw on its vast computational power. However, many existing codes that have been used by game developers are made for serial computation. So it is difficult to get better performance if we simply port existing codes to Cell/BE.

Rigid-body simulation has several stages, such as broad phase, collision detection, constraint solver, and integration. In these stages, it is easy to parallelize collision detection and integration because there aren't any dependencies between the data. On the other hand, it is difficult to parallelize broad phase and constraint solver. First, we describe the basic approach of how to optimize for Cell/BE and then focus on optimization of broad phase and constraint solver. Some optimization techniques showed in this chapter will also be useful for other general programs, such as ray casting or particle simulation. In this chapter, we describe how to draw on the power of the Cell/BE processor through optimizing the rigid body simulation.

3.2 Overview of Cell/BE

The Cell/BE is a multi-core processor composed of one power processing unit (PPU) and eight synergistic processor units (SPUs) in one chip (for PlayStation®3, available SPUs are seven out of eight because of improving chip yields). The PPU is designed to handle general-purpose operation such as system control or handling SPUs. On the other hand, an SPU is designed to perform a single-instruction multiple-data (SIMD) program effectively, such as image processing

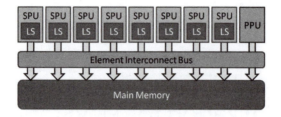

Figure 3.1. Cell/BE architecture.

or three-dimentional calculations. However, there is a big difference between an SPU and other general coprocessors. Each SPU has its own memory space and can run a full C/C++ program. And 90% of the computational power of Cell/BE lies in SPUs. So optimizing for Cell/BE is equivalent to optimizing for SPUs. (See Figure 3.1.)

Each SPU has its own local memory called the local storage. Before running a program on an SPU, transferring the program and data into the local storage is crucial. Because SPUs and the PPU don't share memory space, SPUs can't directly access the main memory. Whenever they have to access the main memory, they use the direct memory access unit (DMA) to transfer data to and from the main memory. SPUs can access the local storage faster than they can the main memory, but the size of the local storage is limited to 256 KB in each SPU. Moreover, the program, data, and stack also consume local storage. That is, the amount of available memory is very limited. Whenever we write an SPU program, we have to take into account the size of the available memory. To achieve the highest performance from an SPU, we must always use the local storage effectively. Fortunately, SPUs can run DMA transfer and computation simultaneously, so we can hide the latency of DMA transfer by using the method of double buffering.

3.2.1 Basic Approach for Cell/BE Optimization

A typical rigid-body simulation pipeline has four stages, and rigid-body data are processed through these stages in order. Because there are dependencies between stages, they can't be processed simultaneously. In order to parallelize the whole pipeline, we take the approach of parallelizing each stage using multiple SPUs (see Figure 3.2).

Each stage is divided into various tasks. A task is a basic element of the computation processed in parallel on an SPU. If a task becomes too small, the cost of starting tasks or data transferring may exceed calculation cost. In the worst case, the parallelized version becomes slower than the original. It is therefore important to carefully balance the tasks.

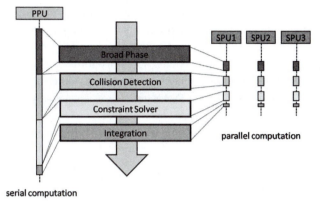

Figure 3.2. Parallel computation of rigid-body simulation.

If stages are divided into independent tasks properly, we can execute tasks run on multiple SPUs. The PPU performs preprocessing to assign data to each task and postprocessing to summarize the results, and tasks are executed on SPUs in parallel. It is important that each SPU take responsibility for only its given work, and not care about work processed by other SPUs. By doing this, it is not necessary to implement complicated mechanisms to synchronize between tasks. In general, such a complicated synchronization mechanisms can easily cause bugs or performance problems.

It would be optimal if we could move all stages into parallelized tasks. But usually, there is a task that can't be parallelized, or at least there is no effect if it is parallelized. In such a case, it is still useful to move as much PPU work as possible to the SPU because the PPU will become overloaded with work that can't be processed by the SPU.

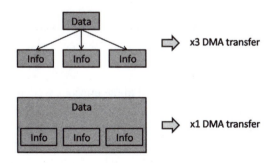

Figure 3.3. Suitable structure for DMA.

Data structure suitable for the SPU. Due to the limitation of the memory capacity of SPUs, the available space for data is very limited; using local storage limits the amount of data. Therefore, it is best to store all data in main memory and have the SPU transfer only the data necessary for a calculation to the local storage using DMA at runtime. When processing is completed, the SPU returns data to the main memory. To use DMA transfer, it is necessary to align data at a 16-byte boundary; nonaligned data cause DMA alignment-error interrupts. For optimal performance, transfer efficiency rises if data are aligned at a 128-byte boundary.

In addition, because accessing the main memory is slower than accessing the local storage, it is important to reduce the number of DMA transfers. The effective way to reduce the transfer number is to store all the information necessary for a single process in a single data structure. Many DMA transfers are needed to process a structure where all the necessary information is linked with many pointers, in which case performance would be slower (see Figure 3.3).

Hiding the latency of DMA transfer. SPUs can hide the latency of DMA transfer by executing computation and DMA transfer simultaneously. Using the mechanism of double buffering, SPUs can process the computation using one buffer while at the same time the other buffer is used for DMA transfer. A structure connected with pointers, such as a tree or a linked list, is not recommended because, to use double buffering effectively, we need to know an address of data in main memory before it is used. If we use a tree or a linked-list structure, we can only know the next data linked with the current data. If possible, use a simple array as a substitute for a linked structure.

Figure 3.4 shows the mechanism of double buffering. The data in an array in main memory are transferred into the local storage (`Get`). After the data are calculated (`Calc`), they returned to main memory (`Put`) in order. Two buffers in the local storage are used in turn to store the data—one is used for transfer, while the other is used simultaneously for calculation. In this way, accessing the main memory and performing calculations are executed in parallel in each step.

Execute tasks in parallel. As described in the previous section, we can largely improve computation performance by assigning tasks to multiple SPUs and processing them in parallel. If there are dependencies between data, SPUs must control the order of processing tasks with various synchronization mechanisms. But the cost of synchronization is not zero. So before starting tasks, it is better to gather the data without dependencies.

3.3   Optimization of the Broad Phase

A role of the broad phase in rigid-body simulation is to find a pair of bodies that could possibly collide. Because a fast algorithm is required rather than an accurate one in the broad phase, a bounding volume (AABB) that surrounds a real shape of a rigid body along each x-, y-, and z-axis is used. Then, if the AABBs of two rigid bodies cross one another, broad phase outputs this as a pair with a possibility of colliding. The collision-detection sequel to the broad phase can be done only for these colliding pairs, using real shapes of rigid bodies that belong to a pair. Therefore, useless operations will be largely avoided.

3.3.1   "Sweep and Prune" Algorithm

The mechanism of the "sweep and prune" (SAP) algorithm is very simple yet effective [Ericson 05]. In this algorithm, minimum and maximum values of AABB are stored in a node of the list along the x-, y-, and z-axes. All nodes in the lists are maintained as sorted along each axis. Then, select one axis and find nodes crossing one another. When the intersection is found, also check the intersection of nodes along the other axis. If nodes of two AABBs are crossing all axes, two AABBs are output as an overlapped pair. If the state of a rigid body is changed (moved, added, or removed), the algorithm's operation is to just change the pointer to the nodes, so the update of nodes is completed fast when there are not so many moving objects in the world.

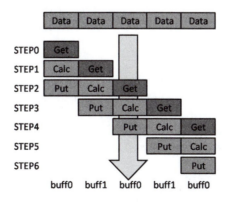

Figure 3.4. The mechanism of double buffering.

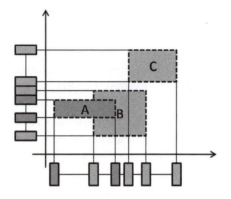

Figure 3.5. Sweep and prune.

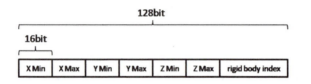

Figure 3.6. Structure of AABB node.

3.3.2   An Optimized SAP Algorithm

First, remove the data structure connected with many pointers because that structure is hard for SPUs to deal with. As in Figure 3.5, linked lists are created along the x-, y-, and z-axes, and each node in these lists is linked with a previous node. When traversing all lists, such a structure causes calling too many DMA operations and ends up with a low performance. Therefore, to reduce traversing pointers, it is better to use a structure that holds all necessary information without pointers.

An Optimized Structure of AABB. Figure 3.6 shows the structure of the node that holds all AABB values in one structure. For efficient use of the local storage, we take a value of AABB as a 16-bit integer instead of using a 32-bit float, and this structure is represented as a 128-bit length so that SPUs can handle it at a peak performance.

Using a sorted array as a list. To parallelize computation and DMA transfer in double-buffering mode, a sorted array is better than a linked list. As for a linked list in which all nodes are connected by pointers, the current node is always needed to access the next node. We can't use the method of double buffering due to this dependency.

However, with a sorted array we can calculate the address of each node by adding an offset address and an index of a node. Thus, we can calculate an address of a node used in the future. We prepare two buffers and assign one for DMA transfer of data and the other for computation and then execute computation and DMA transfer in parallel to hide the latency of DMA transfer.

The following two operations are needed to replace the operations of a linked list (see Figures 3.7 and 3.8).

- *Insert.* Add new nodes to the last of an array, then sort the whole array.

- *Remove.* Set sort keys of removed nodes to the maximum number as a sentinel value, then sort the whole array.

Parallelize the sort algorithm. For faster operation, a sort algorithm is also needed to run in parallel when using multiple SPUs (see Figure 3.9). First, we need to load as much data from main memory as we can store into the local storage and then sort the data on each SPU. The straightforward implementation of this sort is not complicated because sorting is executed on a single SPU, and all the necessary data is in its local storage. Actually, we use the combination of the bitonic and the merge sort for sorting on a single SPU.

The next step is to merge two sorted data sets using two SPUs, just putting data from both sides while comparing the value of data. Then repeat these procedures a few times and all the data will be sorted correctly, as shown in Figure 3.10.

How to find overlapped pairs using sorted AABB arrays. First, prepare AABB arrays that are sorted along the x-, y-, and z-axes, taking the minimum value as a sort key. Then, find the axis along which all rigid bodies are most widely

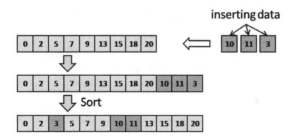

Figure 3.7. Insert operation.

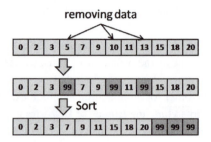

Figure 3.8. Remove operation.

positioned. We can calculate variance of rigid bodies by checking how far away each rigid body's position is from the average position (see Listing 3.1). The axis with the largest distance can be selected. Then, an AABB array along only the selected axis is used to find overlapping pairs.

```
// Calculate average
Vector average(0.0f,0.0f,0.0f);
for(int i=0;i<numRigidBodies;i++) {
    average.x += position[i].x;
    average.y += position[i].y;
    average.z += position[i].z;
}
    average.x /= (float)numRigidBodies;
    average.y /= (float)numRigidBodies;
    average.z /= (float)numRigidBodies;

// Calculate variance
Vector total_distance(0.0f,0.0f,0.0f);
```

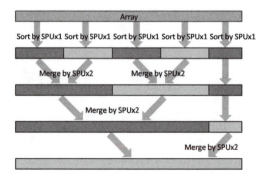

Figure 3.9. Parallel sort algorithm.

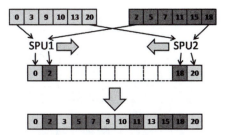

Figure 3.10. Merging data sets from two SPUs.

```
for(int i=0;i<numRigidBodies;i++) {
    Vector direction;
    distance.x = position[i].x − average.x;
    distance.y = position[i].y − average.y;
    distance.z = position[i].z − average.z;
    total_distance.x += distance.x * distance.x;
    total_distance.y += distance.y * distance.y;
    total_distance.z += distance.z * distance.z;
}


// Select the axis along which all rigid bodies are
// spread most widely.
if(total_distance.x > total_distance.y) {
    if(total_distance.x > total_distance.z) {
        // Select X axis
    }
    else {
        // Select Z axis
    }
}
else {
    if(total_distance.y > total_distance.z) {
        // Select Y axis
    }
    else {
        // Select Z axis
    }
}
```

Listing 3.1. Calculate variance of rigid bodies to find the axis.

For example, Figure 3.11 shows a scene with seven rigid bodies. The x-axis is selected as all rigid bodies are positioned mostly along this axis. When checking the overlapping of A with other AABBs (B, F, C, E, D, and G), we note that the AABBs are sorted in the order A, B, F, C, E, D, G . We can see AABBs of both A and F are separated along the axis, so we don't need to check later AABBs.

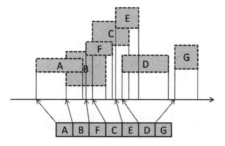

Figure 3.11. AABB array on the selected axis.

Parallelize finding overlapped pairs algorithm. To find the intersection of AABBs, continue to traverse the AABB array until a maximum value of the current AABB becomes smaller than a minimum value of the next AABB. This process is implemented as a simple double loop, shown in Listing 3.2. Figure 3.12 illustrates this algorithm using an extreme case. Actually, pairs with a dotted line aren't processed because any unnecessary processing is removed by checking the end condition.

```
for(int i=0;i<total;i++) {
    for(int j=i+1;j<total;j++) {
        // axis : 0,1,2 = X,Y,Z
        if(AABBs[i].max[axis] < AABBs[j].min[axis]) {
            break;
        }
        if(checkOverlap(AABBs[i],AABBs[j])) {
            submitOverlappedPair(i,j);
        }
    }
}
```

Listing 3.2. The example code of finding overlapped pairs.

The next step is to parallelize this process. Because there is more efficient parallelization if we can divide by a large processing element, we divide by the outside loop instead of the inner loop. Since there are no data dependencies between AABBs, we can divide the total number of AABBs by the number of the possible parallel batches as in Figure 3.12. As soon as each SPU finds a batch that hasn't been processed, it starts finding overlapping pairs within this batch. We can't know the execution time of each batch beforehand, as the amount of data included in each batch isn't uniform. It is necessary to choose the number of batches carefully so that an SPU does not become free.

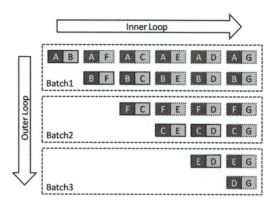

Figure 3.12. Double loop of finding overlapped pairs.

Each SPU executes the process of finding the overlapping of AABBs and DMA transfer in parallel with the double-buffering method because the AABB array is just a simple array structure. When the number of necessary AABBs becomes too small to use double buffering at a later stage of the process, we load the rest of the AABBs to the local storage and execute processes one at a time. For example, Batch 3 in Figure 3.12, includes only three AABBs.

The PPU has to allocate buffers where output pairs are stored before starting tasks because SPUs can't allocate buffers in the main memory. Each SPU finds overlapping pairs and then puts them back to the main memory when enough pairs are stored in the local storage. After all overlapping pairs are found by SPUs, the PPU gathers these pairs and merges them into one array.

3.4   Optimization of the Constraint Solver

Constraint is a condition that limits the behavior of a rigid body; it is used for collision response or ragdoll joints in many real games. Often, impulses that directly change the velocity of a rigid body are used to also control the behavior of a rigid body. To solve the constraint condition for many related rigid bodies, the general solution is to construct a huge matrix of linear equations and solve these with an iterative method known as projected Gauss-Seidel (PGS) or sequential impulse (SI) [Catto 05]. In this section, we don't describe the details of this method but rather focus on how to optimize the solver computation for Cell/BE. If needed, please refer to Chapter 2 for details.

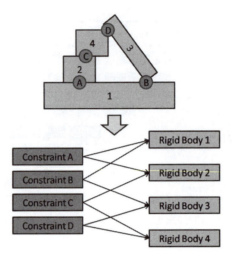

Figure 3.13. Constraints for collision response.

3.4.1　Overview of Solver Calculation

In the iterative method, one row of linear equations represents one constraint. A row of equations is solved and its output is used immediately by other rows. Then, by repeating the calculation for all rows, a result will be close to the suitable solution. Calculation continues until the calculation times reach the specified iteration limit, and a result will be a solution.

```
for(int i=0;i<iterationLimit;i++) {
    for(int n=0;n<numConstraints;n++) {
        Constraint &constraint = constraintArray[n];
        RigidBody &rigidbodyA = constraint.getRigidBodyA();
        RigidBody &rigidbodyB = constraint.getRigidBodyB();

        solveConstraintRow(constraint,rigidbodyA,rigidbodyB);
    }
}
```

Listing 3.3. Example code for the solver iteration.

Information about two related rigid bodies is necessary to calculate one constraint (see Figure 3.13). An output is applied to two related rigid bodies immediately in calculation, but there are dependencies between rigid bodies when some constraints share rigid bodies. We can't parallelize this solver calculation simply to assign divided constraints into each SPU.

3.4.2   Optimize Solver Calculation

The easiest way to convert the solver calculation for parallel computation is to break constraints into small independent batches without sharing rigid bodies between batches. It is too complicated to divide all constraints at the same time. However, it is easy to create small independent batches. Then we gather these batches into a group. Independent batches in a group can be processed by SPUs in parallel. We continue to create groups in the same way until all constraints are assigned.

Figure 3.14 shows some groups containing batches that can be executed in parallel. After the calculation of batches in a group is completed, we synchronize all SPUs and continue to calculate batches for the next group until all groups are completed. However, the cost of synchronization is not free. As the number of groups increases, the cost of synchronization will also increase. However, Cell/BE has a mechanism by which it can operate synchronization between SPUs without PPU operation. The cost of the SPU synchronization is low enough when the number of synchronizations is not too large.

Double buffering with two phases.   In using the constraint solver, we need to be careful about DMA transfer when double buffering. As described in the previous section, each SPU calculates an assigned batch. But each constraint in a batch has data dependencies if the constraints share rigid bodies. In a worst case, the Put and Get DMA operations for the same data occur at the same time; then double buffering causes an irregular result.

Moreover, we need a constraint and two related rigid bodies to calculate one constraint. The structure of a constraint has links to related rigid bodies. So we have to get a constraint first, then we can get two related rigid bodies before calculation. But such a dependency causes a disabling of double buffering.

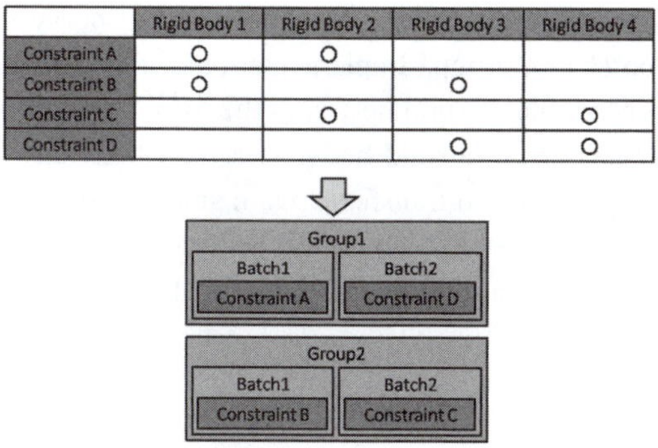

	Rigid Body 1	Rigid Body 2	Rigid Body 3	Rigid Body 4
Constraint A	O	O		
Constraint B	O		O	
Constraint C		O		O
Constraint D			O	O

⬇

Group1	
Batch1	Batch2
Constraint A	Constraint D

Group2	
Batch1	Batch2
Constraint B	Constraint C

Figure 3.14. Constraints assigned to batches.

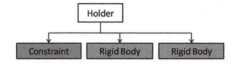

Figure 3.15. A data-holder structure.

To enable double buffering, we need to transfer all the data used for one calculation. As shown in Figure 3.15, we prepare the array of a structure that holds
related indices (or pointers) of necessary data. Figure 3.16 then shows double
buffering with two phases. In the first phase, we transfer the data-holder array
with double buffering. Then, in the second phase, we calculate real addresses of
necessary data and call the Get DMA command to transfer data used in the future to the local storage. We then continue to process in the same way as normal
double buffering.

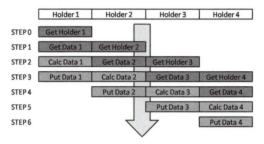

Figure 3.16. Double buffering with two phases.

To solve dependencies between rigid bodies in double-buffering mode in one
batch, once the rigid body is stored in the local storage, we keep it and don't load
the same rigid body again. Updated rigid bodies are returned to main memory at
the last step of the processing of a batch. It works well because no SPU shares
the same rigid bodies in a group. Implementation of this algorithm is easy. We
prepare the reference table of rigid bodies in the local storage and always check
this table before transferring a rigid body. If a rigid body already exists in the
local storage, we don't need to transfer it again since we can just use the one in
the local storage. We can specify the number of rigid bodies in a batch so that all
rigid bodies in this batch can be stored in the local storage.

3.5   Conclusion

Finally, we check how much speed-up we were able to achieve through our implementation. In the test scene, 3,000 boxes are dropped on the ground. The

number of solver iterations is specified as 10. All rigid bodies are always moving, and the maximum number of constraints is about 20,000. We can easily imagine how difficult this scene would be for both broad phase and constraint solver. See Figure 3.17 for the result. The vertical bars show the time of computation in a simulation frame. The optimized version with five SPUs is about 12 times faster than the original PPU version. It shows that we can achieve a large performance improvement with the effective combination of parallel computation and double buffering on multiple SPUs.

Note that computation on a single SPU is three and one-half times faster than on a PPU; that is, it shows that even a single SPU without parallelism is faster than a PPU.

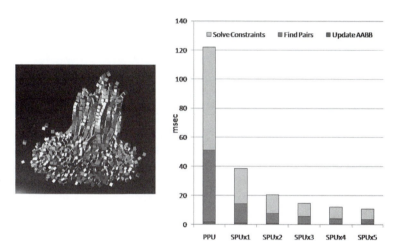

Figure 3.17. The result of the performance.

Bibliography

[Catto 05] Erin Catto. "Iterative Dynamics with Temporal Coherence." Technical Report, Crystal Dynamics, Menlo Park, CA, 2005.

[Ericson 05] Christer Ericson. *Real-Time Collision Detection*. San Francisco: Morgan Kaufmann, 2005.

– 4 –

SAT in Narrow Phase and Contact-Manifold Generation

Sergiy Migdalskiy

4.1 Introduction

Collision detection is a large part of physics simulations (Figure 4.2), responsible for objects colliding rather than sinking into each other. This chapter discusses approaches to generation and optimization of contacts between polygonal meshes.

Collision detection often occurs in two phases. A first *broad phase* determines whether two objects may potentially collide, then a subsequent *narrow phase* determines exact separation or penetration and generates a contact manifold. The *solver* stage follows and updates the simulated object states. The narrow phase may consume a considerable share of processing time, and the stability of the simulation and the speed of the subsequent solver stage depend directly on the quality of the generated manifold. However, the narrow phase is well suited to parallel computation, which can greatly improve execution time.

We present both approximate and exact algorithms for finding full contact manifolds. Furthermore, we present a linear-time heuristic approach to finding a dynamically stable subset of contact points. Next we present a linear complexity SIMD algorithm for finding an approximate contact manifold using a direction perturbation method, as well as a heuristic to reduce contacts (see Section 4.6).

Please refer to Tables 4.1, 4.4, and 4.5 for some notation used throughout this chapter.

4.2 Contact Manifold

When two rigid bodies are in contact, the force (or impact) direction is along the surfaces' normals, or within the cone coaxial with the normal—the Coulomb friction cone. Other friction models exist, but we don't consider them in this chapter. The point of contact is where the forces or impulses are applied and

```
struct ContactPoint
{
        Vector point; // world−space contact point
        Vector normal; // from object B to object A
        float penetration; // negative for separated objects
}
```

Listing 4.1. A contact point.

affect the torques or angular impulses acting on the contacting bodies. Physical simulation is discrete and must accommodate small errors. The rigid bodies may penetrate (or not exactly touch, but be very close) at the point of contact.

Coordinates of the point of contact, the normal, and the penetration are the main components of a contact point.

Collision response (the reaction, or how the objects bounce off of each other) depends on relative velocities or accelerations at the point of contact (the action, or how the objects push each other). This response is computed in the solver (see Section 4.3), where it's better not to access the geometric shape data (vertices, edges, faces) for performance reasons. Computing penetration at a point is non-trivial and requires the knowledge of the geometric shape [Ganjugunte 07]. This is why penetration is part of the ContactPoint structure in Listing 4.1.

Relative velocity and acceleration aren't in the ContactPoint structure, although they could be. They are easy to compute in the solver, thus trading CPU for memory bandwidth. And a discrete collision-detection routine doesn't need access to velocity or accelerations.

A contact manifold is a set of contact points between a pair of objects. It's not necessary to generate all contact points, only the corners of the contact shape is enough. More specifically, for any set of contact points with the same friction cone, it's enough to only generate the points forming a convex hull enclosing all the other points; for example, all of the shapes in Figure 4.1 should ideally have just four contact points generated, which are shown by their normal vectors. The shape in Figure 4.1(d) is very irregular, and the contact area's convex hull is a slightly rounded rectangle, but for a game simulation, it's still best approximated by a rectangle. Some useless contacts from the interior of the convex hull are marked with the ∅ symbol. They don't contribute to the contact area/volume convex hull (the wavy shapes), assuming their friction cones are the same. They eat up time during the dynamic solver stage, and although an iterative solver may be more stable with them, they generally need to be culled.

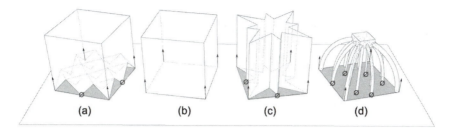

Figure 4.1. Equivalency of contact volumes: (a), (c), and (d) show irregular shapes with contact manifolds that are best approximated by a rectangle; (b) shows a regular rectangle contact manifold.

Culling contacts is only possible for contacts with (almost) the same normals and friction. One simple solution to deal with concave objects (and thus varying normals across contact points) is to put contacts into buckets depending on their normal. Simple $3 \times 3 \times 3$ or $4 \times 4 \times 4$ cubemaps worked fine in practice for me. If we assign a contact to a bucket in the cubemap, sometimes very similar contacts will be in different buckets, but we can have the solver deal with it.

4.3   Physics Engine Pipeline

Very roughly, we can dissect a typical physics simulation loop into pipelined stages. The same object or simulation island, if not asleep, usually has to "flow" its data through different stages sequentially. Not all the data about the object(s) are required at each stage. For example, the constraint solver cares about the object's inertia, contact, or constraint points, but not about its geometry. Discrete collision detection (DCD), and often continuous collision detection (CCD), too, only care about the object's trajectory and geometry, but not its mass properties.

In this chapter, we're mainly concerned with the DCD stage, dealing with just two shapes in close contact. This stage is also called the *narrow phase* of collision detection, as opposed to the *broad phase*, where all possible contacting pairs of objects are detected. Understanding up- and downstream connections is crucial for making the right choices in implementing this important part of the physics engine.

4.3.1   Narrow Phase

In the narrow phase, we take two objects in close vicinity (sometimes penetrating) and find contact points. We then optimize the contacts and form a contact manifold for the solver (see Figure 4.1). In this chapter, we'll describe one algorithm

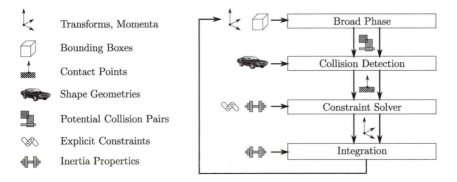

Figure 4.2. Simplified physics engine pipeline stages and data flow. (Car image from www.public-domain-photos.com.)

for finding penetration depth, direction, and location, all of which combined form one contact point. We can stop there and accumulate contact points over multiple frames. Or we can find the whole contact manifold, which is more CPU intensive, but we don't have to keep it in memory if we regenerate it every frame. We'll describe an algorithm based on the separating axis theorem (SAT).[1] We'll describe a simple algorithm to find an approximate contact manifold by perturbing penetration direction, finding outlines of the contact surfaces from two convex bodies, and intersecting them.

The shape in Figure 4.1(d) is a complex rigid object, and our algorithm will generate many contact manifolds—one for each leg. But the additional pass of these contacts may eliminate many of them, leaving only four essential corner points. As far as the solver is concerned, these four points are even better because the object stays stable, and it is faster to solve. Also notice that the solver uses the object's inertia tensor and mass, but does not care what geometrical shape it has. It may as well be a box on a plane (in this particular case); the solver will work just the same. This has a practical consequence: we need to design and optimize in-memory representations of collision shapes primarily for the narrow phase, and only the narrow phase needs to precache collision shapes for performance or direct memory access them to the local store on a PlayStation®3 or other nonunified memory architectures. Generally, only the narrow phase needs access to the precise definition of the shape of colliding objects. Just an axis-aligned bounding box usually suffices for the broad phase, where the solver doesn't care about the shapes at all, just the contact points.

---

[1]The acronym SAT is also commonly used to refer to a class of algorithms due to the theorem.

Our SAT-based method can only work with a pair of convex objects. Concave objects would need to be subdivided into convex pieces. The approximate contact-manifold method is also good only for convex pairs of objects. Concave shapes will generate a manifold for each convex subshape pair. That may amount to a lot of contacts. An additional contact-optimizing pass may eliminate a lot of them.

The narrow phase of collision detection is concerned with finding the contact point or points between a pair of objects. Narrow phase follows broad phase and is computationally much more intensive than broad phase. On the flip side, narrow phase is very easily parallelizable. It arguably scales better than both the preceding broad phase and the following dynamic solver. The output of the narrow phase goes to the dynamics solver and consists of one or more contacts between the pair of objects. It is the last stage where the shapes of colliding objects matter: the dynamics solver will only look at the contact points, without giving any thought to the object's shape.

Narrow phase collision detection deals with two objects in close vicinity, sometimes penetrating. Depending on our approach, we may allow penetration universally (i.e., require all objects to penetrate by a small margin) or disallow it (e.g., require all objects to have a small distance between them). Effectively, our strategy will change the shape of the objects, either "imploding" them or extruding and beveling them.

If we require all objects to penetrate, we don't need to compute the exact distance between them if they don't penetrate. We may still want to generate contacts with "negative penetration" speculatively for the velocity solver to be more stable in subsequent iterations or for the positional solver to prevent them from penetrating. If the velocity solver knows objects are about to collide, it can reduce the relative speed in anticipation of impact, speculatively. It's a hack, and friction should not be applied in such a case. The penetration solver may use a contact with negative penetration as a safeguard against making objects penetrate each other to prevent penetration with other objects.

4.3.2   Constraint Solver

Sometimes, after a contact manifold is completely generated, it consists of more points than necessary for stable simulation. The sampling algorithm from Section 4.6.7 partly takes care of that, but if we sample many directions or use the direct method of support-shape computation as in Section 4.6.3, we still may end up with more points than necessary. It may be desirable to remove some points from the manifold.

We care about spending time to reduce the contact points because extra contact points that don't add much to the simulation quality may add to the simulation

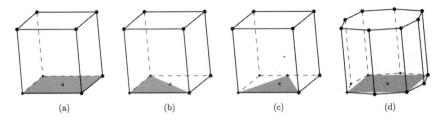

Figure 4.3. Contact reduction and stability. For stability, the center-of-mass projection (the ×) should be within the contact manifold. (a) Stable full-contact manifold. (b) Unstable reduced-contact manifold. (c) and (d) Stable reduced-contact manifold.

$\mathcal{F}$	Feature (vertex, edge, or face)
$\mathcal{P}$	Plane

Table 4.1. Notation guide.

time. However, more contact points will often mean more-precise simulations, so it's a trade-off between quality and speed. If speed is of higher priority, then reducing the contact manifold is probably a win. The solver will generally go through the contact points multiple times and execute more complex code than contact reduction. So it's rather safe to assume that the time spent reducing contact points will be a net win.

In case of concave contact areas, we only need to keep the convex hull of contact points as the contact manifold, as in Figure 4.1. But even then, we may reduce the contact points further, as in Figure 4.3(d).

Three or more contact points are necessary to keep an object statically stable. As a rule of thumb, the center of mass should project along the gravity vector (*not* along the contact normal) well inside the contact manifold formed by them, as in Figure 4.3(a), (c), and (d) (obviously, only when it's possible). It's convenient to choose those points among the unreduced contact manifold corners, as shown in Figure 4.3(c), but it's not always stable. Instead we may opt to leave four or more points, like in Figure 4.3(a) and (d), of the originally computed manifold, potentially using some heuristic to reduce other points, like in Figure 4.3(d).

One heuristic is to sort manifold vertices by their angle and reduce those with the highest angle (updating the neighboring vertex angles). We need to always keep the contact point with the most penetration, or otherwise compensate for the penetration by assigning high penetration to other points to resolve it.

Resampling the contact manifold is another possible heuristic. If we choose to resample every $90°$, we are guaranteed not to miss manifold vertices with $90°$ or sharper angle. See Figure 4.14.

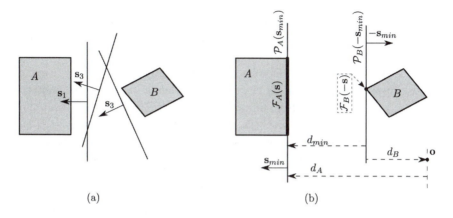

Figure 4.4. Separating directions s, support features $\mathcal{F}$, and support planes $\mathcal{P}$: (a) continuum of separating planes and (b) support planes.

4.4 SAT Basics

SAT states that two convex shapes A and B are disjoint if and only if there is a plane that separates them:

$$\begin{cases} \mathbf{s} \cdot \mathbf{x} - d_S = 0, \|\mathbf{s}\| = 1 & \text{Separating plane (SP)}, \\ \mathbf{s} \cdot \mathbf{x}_A - d_S \geq 0, \mathbf{x}_A \in A & A \text{ in front of SP}, \\ \mathbf{s} \cdot \mathbf{x}_B - d_S \leq 0, \mathbf{x}_B \in B & B \text{ behind SP}. \end{cases}$$

Let's call $\mathbf{s}$ the separating direction.[2] Note that for strictly disjoint shapes, there is a continuum of separating planes: there are many possible values for both $\mathbf{s}$ and d_S (see Figure 4.4(a)).

Let's call the plane $\mathbf{s} \cdot \mathbf{x} - d_A = 0$ touching A the *support plane* of A in direction $\mathbf{s}$, or $\mathcal{P}_A(\mathbf{s})$:

$$\begin{cases} \mathbf{s} \cdot \mathbf{x}_A - d_A \geq 0, \forall \mathbf{x}_A \in A & A \text{ in front of } \mathcal{P}_A(\mathbf{s}), \\ \exists \mathbf{x}_A : \mathbf{s} \cdot \mathbf{x}_A - d_A = 0 & \mathcal{P}_A(\mathbf{s}) \text{ must touch } A. \end{cases} \tag{4.1}$$

And let's consider $\mathcal{P}_B(-\mathbf{s})$ to be

$$\begin{cases} \mathbf{s} \cdot \mathbf{x}_B - (-d_B) \leq 0, \forall \mathbf{x}_B \in B & B \text{ in front of } \mathcal{P}_B(-\mathbf{s}), \\ \exists \mathbf{x}_B : \mathbf{s} \cdot \mathbf{x}_B - (-d_B) = 0 & \mathcal{P}_B(-\mathbf{s}) \text{ must touch } B. \end{cases} \tag{4.2}$$

Denote the minimal translation distance (MTD) and direction as

$$(d_{\min}, \mathbf{s}_{\min}) = \sup_d \{(d, \mathbf{s}) : \mathbf{s} \in \mathbb{S}^2\}. \tag{4.3}$$

---

[2] Without loss of generality, we assume that $\|\mathbf{s}\| = 1$.

The signed distance $d_{min} = d_A - (-d_B) = d_A + d_B$ is between the planes $\mathcal{P}_A(\mathbf{s}_{min})$ and $\mathcal{P}_B(-\mathbf{s}_{min})$. Equation (4.3) maximizes d over all unit directions $\mathbf{s} \in \mathbb{S}^2$. (See Figure 4.4(b).)

It's easy to see that d_{min} is the same as the standard Euclidean distance in the case of disjoint shapes A and B. In the case of colliding shapes, it's the minimal distance and direction we have to translate one of the shapes to get them into a nonpenetrating but contacting state. Just translate A by $-d_{min}\mathbf{s}_{min}$ or B by $d_{min}\mathbf{s}_{min}$. Empirically, that's one of the least intrusive and most robust ways to resolve penetration error between two rigid bodies in physics simulation, which is why we're after it.

Let's call all points from shape S lying in plane $\mathcal{P}_S(\mathbf{s})$ the support feature $\mathcal{F}_S(\mathbf{s}) \equiv A \cap \mathcal{P}_S(\mathbf{s})$. For a convex shape S, $\mathcal{F}_S$ is either a point, a straight line segment, or a flat convex area on the surface of S. Obviously, in polytopes $\mathcal{F}$ can only be a vertex, edge, or face. In Figure 4.4(b), $\mathcal{F}_A(\mathbf{s})$ is the bold edge on A and $\mathcal{F}_B(-\mathbf{s})$ is a vertex of B.

It may not be trivially apparent, but $\mathcal{F}_A(\mathbf{s})$ and $\mathcal{F}_B(-\mathbf{s})$ projected onto any plane $\mathcal{P}_A(\mathbf{s})$ or $\mathcal{P}_B(-\mathbf{s})$ always intersect. If the projections don't intersect and we translate B by $d_{min}\mathbf{s}_{min}$, the shapes would not touch, which contradicts the definition of d_{min}. This observation will help us limit the set of possible MTDs given the pair of support features.

The important point is that $\mathbf{s}_{min}$ defines d_{min}, $\mathcal{F}_A(\mathbf{s}_{min})$, and $\mathcal{F}_B(-\mathbf{s}_{min})$ unambiguously.

4.4.1 Polytopes

Even though most of this chapter may be generalized to any convex shape, all subsequent conclusions and algorithms are described in the domain of polytopes. For practical reasons, it is assumed that the vertices, edges, and faces, as well as their connectivity, are easily available during most computations.

It is easy to directly apply the described algorithms to a sphere, capsule, and wedge. Note that those shapes are Minkowski differences between shape A (point, segment, and polygon, correspondingly) and sphere B of radius r_B located at $\mathbf{o}$. Just compute the separating axis (SA)[3] and distance for the corresponding shape A and subtract the r_B from the distance.

It is less obvious and more complex, but still possible, to generalize the algorithms to curved (not polytope) shapes. The resulting algorithms may be constructed to be iterative or direct computation, but to be efficient and concise, they must be restricted to relatively limited subclasses of convex shapes, at least from my experience. These algorithms are not the main topic of this chapter.

---

[3]SA is normally the contact normal.

4.4.2   SAT Algorithm

While s_{min} defines support features, the opposite also happens to be true. For various reasons, a feature pair may only correspond to one possible (s_{min}, d_{min}) (see Table 4.3) if it is in fact the support-feature pair in MTD. The basic SAT algorithm enumerates every feature pair and checks whether that feature pair realizes MTD by finding the one with the highest d_{min}. Many (most, actually) feature pairs cannot possibly be the supporting-feature pairs in MTD. Finding and eliminating these pairs is a major source of SAT optimizations.

There are just nine possible combinations of $\mathcal{F}_A(s)$ and $\mathcal{F}_B(-s)$ to consider, since a feature can only be a vertex (V), edge (E), or face (F). Three of them are completely redundant: face-face (FF), edge-face (EF), and face-edge (FE) are special cases of the face-vertex (FV) and vertex-face (VF) variety and yield the same (s_{min}, d_{min}). Edge-edge (EE) is a degenerate case if the edges are parallel. Degenerate EE is the special case of either the edge-vertex (EV) or vertex-edge (VE) variety, which in turn may be a vertex-vertex (VV) case. (See Table 4.2.) We can just skip and ignore all special cases for the purposes of finding (s_{min}, d_{min}).

Case	Degeneracy Condition	General Cases
FF, FE, EF	always a special case	FV, VF
EE	parallel edges, $e_A \parallel e_B$	EV, VE, VV
VE, EV	vertex is inside the other shape's edge	VF, FV
VE, EV	vertex is on the edge line outside the edge	VV
VV	coinciding vertices, $v_A = v_B$	FV, VF, EE

Table 4.2. Special and degenerate case classes.

Each nondegenerate feature pair corresponds to just one possible support direction s. This limits the set of potential MTD directions.

Ignoring special cases restricts all possible directions for s_{min} to the classes enumerated in Table 4.3. The basic SAT algorithm is to evaluate (s, d) for every feature pair and find the best (maximum) one. Basic optimizations aim at reducing the number of feature pairs and at reducing the cost of evaluating d, since it involves computing support planes.

There are generally just three classes of support-feature pairs possible for a colliding pair of polytopes: FV, EE, and VF[4] (See Figure 4.5(a) and (b)). This means we only need to consider directions along face normals and edge-pair cross products to find s_{min} in the colliding case. This restricts Equation (4.3) to

---

[4]Proof is out of the scope of this article.

Case	Candidate MTD Direction $\mathbf{s}_{\min}$
FV^5	$\mathbf{s} = -\mathbf{n}(f_A)$
VF	$\mathbf{s} = \mathbf{n}(f_B)$
EE	$\mathbf{s} = \pm\mathbf{norm}_{\|\cdot\|}(\mathbf{e}_A \times \mathbf{e}_B)$
VE^6	$\mathbf{s} = \mathbf{norm}_{\|\cdot\|}(\mathbf{v}_A - \mathbf{proj}_\perp(\mathbf{v}_A, e_B))$
EV	$\mathbf{s} = \mathbf{norm}_{\|\cdot\|}(\mathbf{proj}_\perp(\mathbf{v}_B, e_A) - \mathbf{v}_B)$
VV^7	$\mathbf{s} = \mathbf{norm}_{\|\cdot\|}(\mathbf{v}_A - \mathbf{v}_B)$

Table 4.3. Candidate support directions in nondegenerate feature pair cases. Every undefined case is degenerate (see Table 4.2).

Equation (4.4):

$$(\mathbf{s}_{\min}, d_{\min}) = \max_d \{(\mathbf{s}, d) : \mathbf{s} \in FV \cup VF \cup EE\}. \qquad (4.4)$$

For each potential direction $\mathbf{s}_i$, we can find support planes $\mathcal{P}_{A,i}(\mathbf{s}_i)$ and $\mathcal{P}_{B,i}(-\mathbf{s}_i)$ and signed distance $d_i = d_{A,i} + d_{B,i}$. Computing every d_i, we compute the

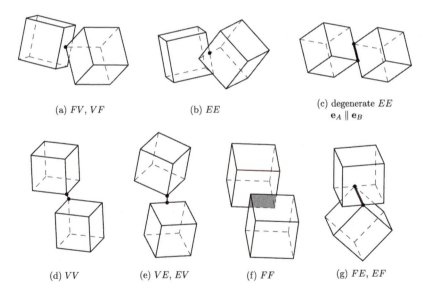

(a) FV, VF (b) EE (c) degenerate EE
                                                    $\mathbf{e}_A \parallel \mathbf{e}_B$

(d) VV (e) VE, EV (f) FF (g) FE, EF

Figure 4.5. SAT cases.

---

[5]The face must lie in the support plane $\mathcal{P}$, $\mathbf{n} \perp f \parallel \mathcal{P} \perp \mathbf{s}_{\min} \Rightarrow \mathbf{s}_{\min} \parallel \mathbf{n}$.

[6]If the vertex and the edge are the supporting features, the vertex will always project into the interior of the edge, so no bound checking is necessary.

[7]Vertices must project into each other along $\mathbf{s}$: $\mathbf{v}_A - \mathbf{v}_B \parallel \mathbf{s}$.

new lower bound on d_{min}. Note that it is neither simple nor practical to literally search through all vertices for a given face in FV and VF cases. Obviously, since we know the potential $\mathbf{s}_{min}$ direction for the face, we can just directly find the opposing-shape support vertex, which is faster and easier. The support-plane search can be accelerated using the Dobkin-Kirkpatrick (DK) hierarchy [Dobkin and Kirkpatrick 90] or gradient walk. Most of the signed distance values will usually be deeply negative, if we enumerate all of the possibilities.

If $d_{min} \leq 0$, it means the polytopes intersect and we found the correct $(\mathbf{s}_{min}, d_{min})$. Otherwise, we have the following choices:

1. Stop and detect no collision.

2. Stop and return d_{min} as the lower bound of distance.

3. Continue to find the exact Euclidean distance (Equation (4.5)).

In the latter case, we need to incrementally compute $(\mathbf{s}, d)$ for the remaining sets VE, EV, and VV (see Figure 4.5(d) and (e)):

$$(\mathbf{s}_{min}, d_{min}) = \max_{d}\{(\mathbf{s}, d) : \mathbf{s} \in FV \cup VF \cup EE \cup VE \cup EV \cup VV\}. \quad (4.5)$$

The algorithm from Equation (4.5) is in Listing 4.2. Please refer to Table 4.4 for the notation used.

$\mathbf{v}_0(e), \mathbf{v}_1(e)$	The two vertices of edge e; $\mathbf{v}_0(e) \neq \mathbf{v}_1(e)$
$\mathbf{norm}_{\|\cdot\|}(\mathbf{x})$	Normalization operator : $\mathbf{x}/\|\mathbf{x}\|$
$\mathbf{n}_0(e), \mathbf{n}_1(e)$	Normals of faces adjacent to edge e; $\mathbf{n}_0 \neq \mathbf{n}_1$
$\mathbf{e}(e)$	Edge e direction $\pm\mathbf{norm}_{\|\cdot\|}(\mathbf{v}_1(e) - \mathbf{v}_0(e))$
	$\mathbf{e}(e) = \mathbf{norm}_{\|\cdot\|}(\mathbf{n}_0(e) \times \mathbf{n}_1(e))$ if $\mathbf{n}_0 \neq \mathbf{n}_1$
$\mathbf{proj}_\perp(\mathbf{v}, e)$	Projection of $\mathbf{v}$ onto edge e: $\mathbf{v}_0(e) + \mathbf{e}(e)((\mathbf{v} - \mathbf{v}_0(e)) \cdot \mathbf{e}(e))$
$\mathbf{n}(f)$	Normal of face f
$\mathbf{V}(S), \mathbf{E}(S), \mathbf{F}(S)$	Sets of vertices $\{\mathbf{v}_i\}$, edges $\{e_i\}$, faces $\{f_i\}$ of shape S

Table 4.4. Notation guide.

$(\mathbf{s}_{\min}, d_{\min}) \leftarrow (\mathbf{o}, -\infty)$

for each $face_A \in \mathbf{F}(A)$ **do**   // check $FV \supset FE \cup FF$

      checkDirection($-\mathbf{n}(face_A)$)

for each $face_B \in \mathbf{F}(B)$ **do**   // check $VF \supset EF \cup FF$

      checkDirection($\mathbf{n}(face_B)$)

for each $edge_A \in \mathbf{E}(A)$ **and** $edge_B \in \mathbf{E}(B)$ **do** // check cases EE

      $\mathbf{s} \leftarrow \mathbf{e}(edge_A) \times \mathbf{e}(edge_B)$

      checkDirection(s) // to choose one of $\pm\mathbf{s}$,

      checkDirection($-\mathbf{s}$) // ...see Equation 4.9

if $d_{\min} \leq 0$ **then**   // penetrating case

      return $(\mathbf{s}_{\min}, d_{\min})$ // skip VV, VE, EV

for each $\mathbf{v}_A \in \mathbf{V}(A)$ **and** $\mathbf{v}_B \in \mathbf{V}(B)$ **do**   // check cases VV

      checkDirection($\mathbf{v}_A - \mathbf{v}_B$)

for each $\mathbf{v}_A \in \mathbf{V}(A)$ **and** $edge_B \in \mathbf{E}(B)$ **do**   // check cases VE

      if $\mathbf{proj}_\perp(\mathbf{v}_A, edge_B) \in edge_B$ **then**   // *optimization*

            checkDirection($\mathbf{v}_A - \mathbf{proj}_\perp(\mathbf{v}_A, edge_B)$)

for each $edge_A \in \mathbf{E}(A)$ **and** $\mathbf{v}_B \in \mathbf{V}(B)$ **do**   // check cases EV

      if $\mathbf{proj}_\perp(\mathbf{v}_B, edge_A) \in edge_A$ **then**   // optimization

            checkDirection($\mathbf{proj}_\perp(\mathbf{v}_B, edge_A) - \mathbf{v}_B$)

return $(\mathbf{s}_{\min}, d_{\min})$

procedure checkDirection(s)

      if $\|\mathbf{s}\| \neq 0$ **then**   // ignore degenerate cases

            $\mathbf{s} \leftarrow \mathbf{norm}_{\|\cdot\|}(\mathbf{s})$

            $d \leftarrow \text{support}(A, \mathbf{s}) + \text{support}(B, -\mathbf{s})$

            if $d > d_{\min}$ **then**

                  $(\mathbf{s}_{\min}, d_{\min}) \leftarrow (\mathbf{s}, d)$

function support($Shape$, s)

      return $min\{\mathbf{s} \cdot \mathbf{v} : \mathbf{v} \in \mathbf{V}(Shape)\}$

Listing 4.2. Basic SAT algorithm.

4.4.3   Negating Shape B Normals

We should never forget about asymmetry anytime we are dealing with shapes A and B. By this chapter's convention, direction s is used to find $\mathcal{P}_A$, but $-\mathbf{s}$ is used to find $\mathcal{P}_B$. See Figure 4.4(b)—the support features $\mathcal{F}_A$ and $\mathcal{F}_B$ always oppose each other. Equivalently, we can negate shape B's vertices and normals and B's position relative to A and use **s**. Another way to look at it is to remember that we implicitly operate on the Minkowski sum of $A \oplus -B$.

To adjust for this asymmetry, the Gauss map (see Section 4.5 for an introduction to Gauss maps) of B has to be negated (by negating normals of B) before superimposing it with the Gauss map A, as in Figure 4.17(a) and (b). All the formulae in this chapter take this negation into account, and both $\mathbf{n}_A$ and $\mathbf{n}_B$ denote nonnegated normals of shapes A and B, correspondingly.

4.5   Intuitive Gauss Map

At first encounter, the Gauss map may be a somewhat unintuitive and even intimidating concept. It is, however, a widely used tool [Fogel and Halperin 07]. This section is a short introduction to the Gauss maps of a polytope.

The Gauss map of the surface of a polytope is the surface of the unit sphere $\mathbb{S}^2$. Each point on the polytope surface maps simply to its normal. Hence the unit sphere: the normals are all unit length. Also, it means that all the points on a polytope face map to one single normal—also a point on a unit sphere—the face's normal. (See Figure 4.6(a).)

Edges don't have definite normals per se, but it's natural to assign them the range of normals between their adjacent faces. If you imagine the edge as a thin smooth bevel, it's a natural and intuitive extension. Thus, edges map to great arcs on $\mathbb{S}^2$. (See Figure 4.6(b).)

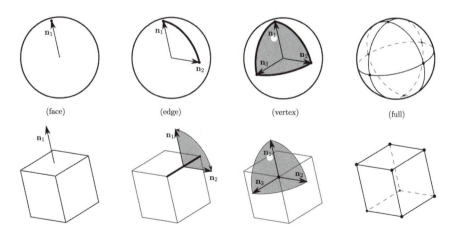

Figure 4.6. Gauss map components.

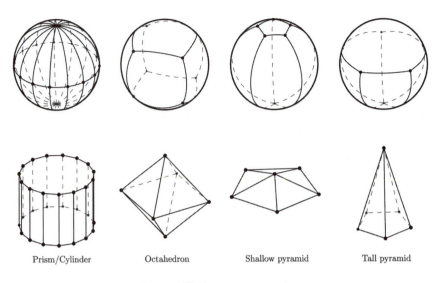

| Prism/Cylinder | Octahedron | Shallow pyramid | Tall pyramid |

Figure 4.7. Gauss map examples.

Vertices also, by extension, map to the hull enclosed by adjacent faces' normals, which is a spherical polygon on $\mathbb{S}^2$ (see Figure 4.6(c)). Figure 4.6(d) shows the full Gauss map of a cube.

The whole sphere is covered by a Gauss map and features overlap only at the borders of their corresponding images. Vertex areas are bounded by edge arcs, which have corresponding face points (normals) as their ends. See Figure 4.7 for examples.

A Gauss map is not reversible. Figure 4.8 shows two Gauss maps generated by six different polytopes.

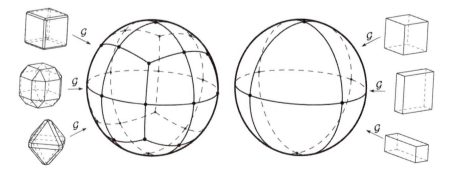

Figure 4.8. Gauss map nonreversibility.

Whatever feature vector $-\mathbf{s}$ hits on the Gauss map, that is the support feature in direction $\mathbf{s}$:

$$-\mathbf{s} \in \mathcal{G}(\mathcal{F}(\mathbf{s})), \quad \forall \mathbf{s} \in \mathbb{S}^2,$$

where $\mathcal{G}(\mathcal{F}(\mathbf{s}))$ is the Gauss map of feature $\mathcal{F}(\mathbf{s})$.

4.6 Computing Full Contact Manifolds

SAT is not particularly constructive. It doesn't tell us much about contact manifolds or explain how to compute collision response. We'll compute the collision response in the solver using the contact-manifold vertices, a.k.a. contact points, trying to reduce penetration distance, velocity, and/or acceleration in all of them at the same time. But for now, our algorithm of finding the contact manifold consists of the following three steps:

1. *Find the contact normal* **s**. It needs to be the MTD or something close to it for the contact-manifold generation to work because we need support polygons that actually intersect. SAT, the expanding polytope algorithm (EPA) [van den Bergen 01], and Gilbert-Johnson-Keerthi algorithm (GJK) [van den Bergen] all generate MTD. Approximate direction, like the one Xenocollide [Snethen 08] or Dual-CD [Choi et al. 05] produces, can be used, too. To warm start many algorithms, we may cache **s** found on the previous frame, exploiting coherence.

2. *Find the support shapes,* or the outlines of the shape surfaces "touching" (close enough to) the plane of contact and potentially the other shape.

3. *Intersect the contact areas* to get the final contact manifold. We need to choose a few representative points from the outline contour. It must be at least three points, but if we choose just the corners, it may be unstable (see Figure 4.3(b)): whatever three corners we choose at the base of a cube, the projection of the center of mass will not lie well inside their convex hull, a condition necessary for stability. Four points are practically enough in most cases (see below for a discussion on choosing the number of points).

4.6.1 Step 1: Find the Contact Normal

The $\mathbf{s}_{\min}$ as described in Section 4.4, or the approximation thereof, will be our contact normal. In convex shapes, the support features (along $\mathbf{s}_{\min}$) are also the closest features. Denote a plane in the middle of the support planes and the contact

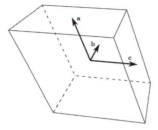

Figure 4.9. Parallelepiped.

planes, and assume the shapes are close enough or are penetrating, so that we have to generate a contact manifold and can't ignore their collision.

Of course, basic SAT (Listing 4.2) is a very nonscalable algorithm. But in case we have really simple shapes (for example, parallelepipeds (Figure 4.9)) with just a dozen features, brute force is the fastest algorithm ever. A parallelepiped has just three edge directions $\mathbf{a}$, $\mathbf{b}$, and $\mathbf{c}$ and three face directions $\mathbf{a} \times \mathbf{b}$, $\mathbf{b} \times \mathbf{c}$, and $\mathbf{c} \times \mathbf{a}$ to check. We need to normalize the directions and check both ends of each direction. If we aren't interested in nonpenetrating shapes, we don't have to check VV, VE, and EV pairs. Even if we are interested in nonpenetrating shapes, we can still skip checking vertex-vertex pairs. We will not have the correct MTD, but we'll have an approximation that's good enough for many purposes. As a side note, the support function for a parallelepiped is very simple due to its specific shape: $|\mathbf{s} \cdot \mathbf{a}| + |\mathbf{s} \cdot \mathbf{b}| + |\mathbf{s} \cdot \mathbf{c}| + \mathbf{s} \cdot \mathbf{o}$. If you have a general case polyhedron with 8–12 vertices, it's still very fast to compute dot products with all vertices on SIMD processors, four dot products at a time. In some cases, nothing beats brute force, but for other cases, we discuss some optimizations in Section 4.7.

4.6.2   Step 2a: Supporting Two-Dimensional Shapes— Low-Poly Case

There's no standard term for this, but it's a simple operation. We now found the support plane (and, equivalently, separating axis or contact normal), and we need to find the feature (point, line, or polygon) that lies in that plane.

When we have two shapes touching nontrivially, i.e., having an edge or a polygon in close contact, we need to find several contact points representative of that area of contact. For convex shapes, we can assume the same contact normal across the whole contact area.

Low-poly shapes are common in game physics, and they allow a specific luxury: they can rest on only one polygon and be stable (box versus high-poly curved surface). In the simplest case of low-poly shapes, e.g., stacked toy cubes, we just need to find at most one face aligned with the contact plane. Then intersect that face with the other shape's face—and we have our contact manifold. High-poly objects (like a curvy sports car) may need to have a lot of faces aligned with the contact plane, so this simple method needs to be adjusted. But let's examine the toy cubes.

Usually we can recover a shape feature (vertex, edge, or face) that is closest to the support contact plane from our collision algorithm. If we have a degenerate case like edge-face, face-face, or a pair of parallel edges, we'll usually have a vertex-face or edge-edge pair to start with, but we want to expand both features to larger features (edge-edge → face-face). From the smaller shape feature (vertex or edge), we can examine all adjacent edges and faces and choose the one (edge or face) that is most aligned with the support contact plane within some tolerance α. That is, we want to find a face that is tilted at most by angle α from s. If no face is aligned, we want an edge. And if no edge is aligned enough, we'll have to live with one vertex. Whatever feature we find, let's call it the contact feature (contact vertex, edge, or face).

To find a contact face, we just need to compute the alignment of the edges because for a face to be aligned with the contact plane, its edges need to be aligned. Another important reason is more subtle: to compute how aligned the edges are, we compute the dot product of the edge vector and the contact normal. When it's close to zero, the value of the dot product is approximately the length of the edge multiplied by the angle between the edge and the contact plane. That's a good number to compare to the threshold. Equivalently, we could compute the difference between the heights of the edge vertices above the contact plane—a value we may already have cached when we computed the support function, if we deal with really low-poly shapes like cubes.

If we compute a face's alignment with the contact plane using $\mathbf{n} \cdot \mathbf{s}$, we'll end up with the cosine of the face tilt angle relative to s. That value needs to be close to 1.0 for the face to be aligned, and it isn't very sensitive to the face tilt at small angles, but it is very sensitive to round-off errors. That is because unlike the dot product of the edge vector with the normal, this cosine is changing as $1 - o(x^2)$ instead of $o(x)$. The variable x is the very small angle between the face (or edge) and the contact plane, so x^2 isn't a good value to compare to a very

$\mathcal{G}(\mathcal{F})$	Gauss map of feature $\mathcal{F}$
$\mathbf{n}_0 \angle \mathbf{n}_1$	Angle between vectors $\mathbf{n}_0$ and $\mathbf{n}_1$
$\mathbb{S}^2$	Unit sphere: $\{\mathbf{n} \in \mathbb{R}^3 : \|\mathbf{n}\| = 1\}$
$\mathcal{C}(\alpha, \mathbf{s})$	Spherical cap on $\mathbb{S}^2$: $\{\mathbf{x} \in \mathbb{S}^2 : (\mathbf{s}\angle\mathbf{x}) \leq \alpha\}$
$\delta\mathcal{C}$	The border of $\mathcal{C}$, the circle: $\{\mathbf{x} \in \mathbb{S}^2 : (\mathbf{s}\angle\mathbf{x}) = \alpha\}$

Table 4.5. Notation guide.

small threshold. To find x in a stable way, we'd need to compute something like
the length of the cross product between the contact normal and the face's normal,
and that's awkward and expensive compared to just examining the edges.

4.6.3   Step 2b: Supporting Two-Dimensional Shapes— Exact Algorithms

In the case of mid- to high-polygon collision shapes, we may have to recover more
than just one feature $\mathcal{F}$ as the supporting shape. We may recover all features that
are aligned with s within the tolerance angle α. It's $\mathbf{s}_{min}$ for shape B and $-\mathbf{s}_{min}$
for shape A. If we look at the Gauss map $\mathcal{G}$ of the shape, we can view s as a
pole of $\mathbb{S}^2$. Let's draw a spherical cap $\mathcal{C}(\alpha, \mathbf{s})$ centered around s with the angular
radius α. We need to find all features with Gauss maps overlapping $\mathcal{C}$ at least
partially. For example, if a face f maps inside $\mathcal{C}$ like in Figure 4.10(c), it is tilted
no more than angle α from s, $f \angle \mathbf{s} \leq \alpha$. The area(s) on $\mathcal{G}$ intersecting $\delta \mathcal{C}$ are the
images of vertices on the boundary of the support shape (see Figure 4.10(a), for
example). And the arcs intersecting $\delta \mathcal{C}$ (if any) are the boundary of the support
shape (see Figure 4.10(b)). Figure 4.10(d) shows the same shape and its Gauss
map oriented differently for reference.

The support shape found this way is not completely flat (although it's not
steeper than α relative to the support plane) and is not always convex, so we need
to project it onto a support plane and find its convex hull. We really prefer to
deal with convex shapes. So, we'll need to walk the support shape once to find its

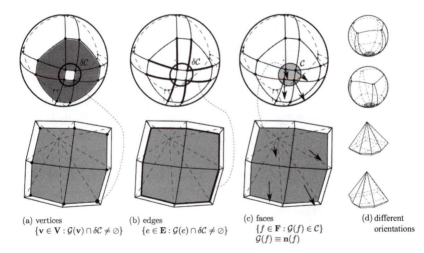

(a) vertices
$\{\mathbf{v} \in \mathbf{V} : \mathcal{G}(\mathbf{v}) \cap \delta \mathcal{C} \neq \varnothing\}$

(b) edges
$\{e \in \mathbf{E} : \mathcal{G}(e) \cap \delta \mathcal{C} \neq \varnothing\}$

(c) faces
$\{f \in \mathbf{F} : \mathcal{G}(f) \in \mathcal{C}\}$
$\mathcal{G}(f) \equiv \mathbf{n}(f)$

(d) different
orientations

Figure 4.10. Faces in $\mathcal{C}$ and edges and vertices intersecting $\delta \mathcal{C}$. Please refer to Figure 4.6
if this mapping is not clear enough.

convex hull. Although it may lead to generation of out-of-bounds contact points due to the projection, they will not be far outside.

One way to find the support shape (faces within $\mathcal{C}$), if we don't want to miss a single vertex (see Section 4.6.7 for an approximate algorithm), is to flood-fill all features inside $\mathcal{C}$ by following topological connectivity: from each feature inside $\mathcal{C}$, go to adjacent features and check if they are also inside. Repeat until all features inside $\mathcal{C}$ are found.

---

if $\mathcal{F}$ **is** vertex **then** $(V_{queue}, E_{queue}) \leftarrow (\mathcal{F}, \varnothing)$
if $\mathcal{F}$ **is** edge **then** $(V_{queue}, E_{queue}) \leftarrow (\varnothing, \mathcal{F})$
if $\mathcal{F}$ **is** face **then** $(V_{queue}, E_{queue}) \leftarrow (\mathbf{V}(\mathcal{F}), \mathbf{E}(\mathcal{F}))$

$(V, E) \leftarrow (\varnothing, \varnothing)$
while $(V_{queue}, E_{queue}) \neq (\varnothing, \varnothing)$
    for each $\mathbf{v}_{queue} \in V_{queue}$ **do**
        $V_{queue} \leftarrow V_{queue} \setminus \{\mathbf{v}_{queue}\}$ // move $\mathbf{v}_{queue}$ to V
        $V \leftarrow V \cup \{\mathbf{v}_{queue}\}$
        for each $e_{adj} \in \mathbf{E}(\mathbf{v}_{queue})$ **do**
            if $e_{adj} \notin E \cup E_{queue}$ **and** overlap$(e_{adj}, \mathcal{C}(\alpha, \mathbf{s}))$ **then**
                $E_{queue} \leftarrow E_{queue} \cup \{e_{adj}\}$
    for each $e_{queue} \in E_{queue}$ **do**
        $E_{queue} \leftarrow E_{queue} \setminus \{e_{queue}\}$ // move $\mathbf{e}_{queue}$ to E
        $E \leftarrow E \cup \{e_{queue}\}$
        $V_{queue} \leftarrow V_{queue} \cup \mathbf{V}(e_{queue}) \setminus V$
return V

function overlap$(e, \mathcal{C}(\alpha, \mathbf{s}))$
    if $\mathbf{s} \cdot \mathbf{n}_0(e) \leq \cos \alpha$ **or** $\mathbf{s} \cdot \mathbf{n}_1(e) \leq \cos \alpha$ **then return true**
    if $\mathbf{s} \cdot e > \sin \alpha$ **then return false**
    $\mathbf{n}^\perp \leftarrow \mathbf{s} \times \mathbf{e}$
    if $\text{sign}(\mathbf{n}^\perp \cdot \mathbf{n}_0(e)) = \text{sign}(\mathbf{n}^\perp \cdot \mathbf{n}_1(e))$ **then return false**
    return $(\mathbf{n}_0(e) + \mathbf{n}_1(e)) \cdot \mathbf{s} > 0$

Listing 4.3. Exact support shape flood-fill algorithm.

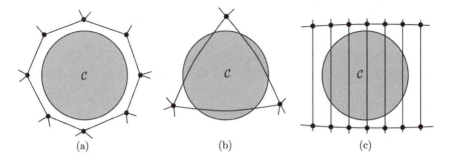

Figure 4.11. Flood-fill algorithm, no faces map onto $\mathcal{C}$: (a) $\mathcal{G}(\mathbf{v})$ covering full spherical cap $\mathcal{C}$; (b) vertex $\mathbf{v}$ and neighbors overlap $\mathcal{C}$, but faces of $\mathbf{v}$ map outside $\mathcal{C}$; (c) flood-fill goes from vertex to edge to vertex.

We can't use just faces for flood-fill because we won't always find adjacent vertices inside $\mathcal{C}$, like in Figure 4.11. We can use vertices, but we need to check if an area on $\mathcal{G}$ intersects $\mathcal{C}$ for each vertex then, which is possible but inconvenient.

Following edges is simple enough, and it guarantees that we find all edges, vertices, and faces mapping inside $\mathcal{C}$. Starting from the set of edges and vertices (perhaps just one edge or one vertex), we can find all vertices adjacent to the edges and edges intersecting $\mathcal{C}$ and adjacent to vertices. After a number of iterations, when the set of found edges and vertices doesn't grow, it will be the vertices comprising our supporting shape. Vertices that have all neighboring vertices inside $\mathcal{C}$ can be excluded. And we compute the two-dimensional convex hull for the rest of them. See Listing 4.3 for the pseudocode of this algorithm.

4.6.4   Edge (Arc)-Cap $\mathcal{C}$ Overlap Test

Let $\mathbf{n}_0$ and $\mathbf{n}_1$ be the normals of faces adjacent to edge e. The Gauss map $\mathcal{G}(e)$ obviously overlaps $\mathcal{C}$ if $\mathbf{n}_i \angle \mathbf{s} \le \alpha \Leftrightarrow \mathbf{n}_i \cdot \mathbf{s} \ge \cos\alpha$ (see Figure 4.12(a)).

Otherwise, let's consider the plane $\mathcal{P}(\mathcal{G}(e))$ passing through $\mathcal{G}(e)$ and $\mathbf{o}$. Let $\delta_{\mathcal{P}e}$ be the angle between the plane $\mathcal{P}(\mathcal{G}(e))$ and $\mathbf{s}$. The plane $\mathcal{P}(\mathcal{G}(e))$ normal is $\mathbf{e} \perp \mathbf{n}_0, \mathbf{n}_1$, hence Equation (4.6). If $\delta_{\mathcal{P}e} > \alpha$, like in Figure 4.12(b), obviously $\mathcal{G}(e)$ does not overlap $\mathcal{C}$:

$$\sin\delta_{\mathcal{P}e} = |\mathbf{e} \cdot \mathbf{s}|. \tag{4.6}$$

If $\delta_{\mathcal{P}e} \le \alpha \Leftrightarrow |\mathbf{e} \cdot \mathbf{s}| \le \sin\alpha$ and $\mathbf{n}_0, \mathbf{n}_1 \notin \mathcal{C}$ (see Figure 4.12(c), (d), and (e)), let's consider the plane $\mathcal{P}^{\perp}(\mathcal{G}(e))$ that is orthogonal to $\mathcal{P}(\mathcal{G}(e))$ and contains $\mathbf{o}$ and $\mathbf{s}$ (see Equation (4.7)). If points $\mathbf{n}_0, \mathbf{n}_1$ are on the same side of $\mathcal{P}^{\perp}(\mathcal{G}(e))$, then the edge does not intersect $\mathcal{C}$. If $\mathbf{n}_0, \mathbf{n}_1$ are on different sides, we just need to check against the situation depicted in Figure 4.12(e)—arc near the pole $-\mathbf{s}$.

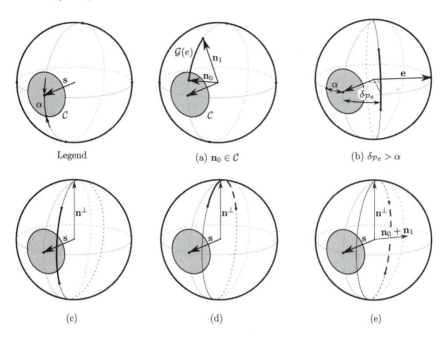

Figure 4.12. Edge(Arc)-Cap $\mathcal{C}$ overlap test: (a) $\mathbf{n}(e) \in \mathcal{C} \Rightarrow \mathcal{G}(e) \cap \mathcal{C} \not\equiv \varnothing$; (b) $\mathcal{G}(e) \cap \mathcal{C} \equiv \varnothing$, with $\delta_{\mathcal{P}e} > \alpha$; (c) $\mathbf{n}_0, \mathbf{n}_1 \notin \mathcal{C}$ but edge overlaps $\mathcal{C}$; (d) and(e) edge arc's great circle overlaps $\mathcal{C}$.

One test to do that is to check that the bisector $\mathbf{n}_0 + \mathbf{n}_1$ is in the hemisphere of $\mathbf{s}$ and not $-\mathbf{s}$. If $(\mathbf{n}_0 + \mathbf{n}_1) \cdot \mathbf{s} > 0$, the edge intersects $\mathcal{C}$ (see Listing 4.3, function `overlap`):

$$\mathcal{P}^\perp (\mathcal{G}(e)) = \{\mathbf{x} : \mathbf{n}^\perp \cdot \mathbf{x} = 0, \mathbf{n}^\perp = \mathbf{s} \times \mathbf{e}\}. \tag{4.7}$$

4.6.5 Supporting Shape Fallbacks

Sometimes the "almost aligned" contact features may be aligned with the contact plane but may not quite intersect when projected onto it. Even if there is a slight misalignment between them, we may still proceed to generate a single (approximate) contact point. This kind of misalignment is not statically stable and is rare enough to be usually corrected the next frame. If it's not, it means the objects in close contact do not have stable contact (edge firmly resting on face, or face on face). To generate an approximate contact point, we need to choose the point on one shape that's closest to the other shape. SAT always returns a vertex as one of the contact features, except in the case of the edge-edge feature pair. If we have a vertex, we can use it to generate the single contact point. If we have an edge-edge pair, we can find the closest points on the edges for that. We can treat the edges as infinite lines; the result will always be inside the edges, barring round-off errors.

This gives rise to another variant of contact-manifold generation: we can also only generate one single contact point per frame and have to cache the other points. We'll have to spend memory on persistent contacts and come up with an algorithm to cull the points, but that's a fast and viable alternative to generating the full contact manifold that is used in many of today's commercial physics engines. It is, unfortunately, out of the scope of this chapter. If for some reason we only have the separating axis direction (a.k.a. the contact normal), it's pretty easy to at least find the closest vertex: by scanning all vertices or by using the DK hierarchy. Although if we have to resort to the DK hierarchy to find the support vertex, we probably have a high-poly object and just one face won't be enough.

4.6.6   Contact Area Tolerance Angle $\delta_{\mathcal{P}e}$

To find the part of the shape surface close to the supporting contact plane, we could start from the feature we have from the collision algorithm, such as the GJK, EPA, and SAT, and expand to all neighboring features, stopping when we are getting too far from the supporting plane. We'll end up with a (hopefully convex) area on each. If a shape is high-poly, we'll have a lot of vertices to deal with, and if it's a curved or an implicit surface, we'll have a really complicated surface to deal with.

We really want to detect wide contact areas on both contact shapes for more stable support in the case of either very long time steps or static configurations (when the objects are stacked on top of each other and don't move or move very slowly). In static configuration cases, we expect the supporting shapes (contact

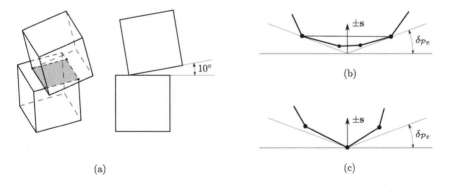

Figure 4.13. Contact area tolerance angle $\delta_{\mathcal{P}e}$: (a) misaligned support features, (b) vertices strictly inside support cone, and (c) "edge-on" contact.

area) to be aligned within a rather tight tolerance. But in the case of long time steps, the supporting features may be significantly misaligned, and yet it may be desirable to detect a large contact area, like the rectangular contact area in Figure 4.13(a).

We may start with the separating axis direction s_{min} and take a wide cone of directions around s_{min} within some tolerance angle $\delta_{\mathcal{P}e}$. Then we may find all vertices supporting that cone of direction. See Figure 4.13(b): we may have some vertices that do not support our cone. We often may ignore them and form a simplified contact area (unless the tolerance angle is too high). Sometimes, as in Figure 4.13(c), we have an "edge-on" contact, where stable stacking is not possible. The tolerance angle lets us make a clear distinction between these cases.

It may be better to illustrate this method with the Gauss map of the convex shape. To find the outline of the contact area, choose a $\delta_{\mathcal{P}e}$ ($5°$–$15°$ works fine) and cut out a cone with that angle around the contact-normal direction, like in Figure 4.10.

This gives rise to a sampling algorithm. If it's too slow to find the full contact area with all the vertices, we may only find a representative sample of those vertices. A vertex is mapped to an area on $\mathbb{S}^2$, so the cone will intersect a continuous circle of vertices around the base of the polytope (see Figure 4.10(a)). Those vertices will limit the area consisting of the faces with normals inside the tolerance angle from the contact normal (see Figure 4.10(c)). Sometimes there will be no such faces, but only one vertex (see Figure 4.11(a)) or several vertices with corresponding edges (see Figure 4.11(b) and (c)). This definition is completely independent from the linear scale of the shapes.

4.6.7 Contact Area Sampling

Of course, we could walk the circle on the Gauss map and find all vertices one by one. It is not particularly hard, but unless you want a very precise contact manifold, we can also just sample 8 (or 4, or 12) discrete directions from the cone. To decide how many samples we need, consider the two-dimensional Gauss map of the support shape (see Figure 4.14). If we sample every $45°$, we will never miss the contact area vertex with a $135°$ internal angle (see Figure 4.14 (right)). If we make n uniform samples, $\frac{360°}{n}$ each, we may only miss vertices on the contact polygon with internal angle of $180° - \frac{360°}{n}$. Eight samples worked well for me. If we miss a vertex on the contact polygon, and it's important, chances are the dynamic simulation will tilt the shape towards the missing vertex, and we'll find it the next time. Another good property of eight samples is that it's easily SIMD-izable: we can find support for all eight directions in parallel easily.

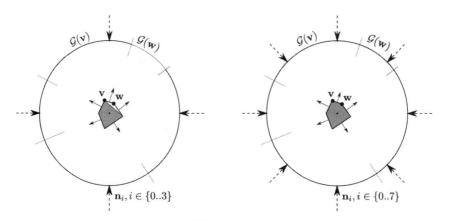

Figure 4.14. Two-dimensional Gauss map of the contact area. If we sample every 90° (left), we may randomly miss some vertices with a 90° internal angle or more, like vertex w. If we sample every 45° (right), we may only miss vertices with a 135° angle.

To find sampling directions, generate two directions $\mathbf{u}$ and $\mathbf{v}$ orthogonal to the normal and each other. The ith sampling direction is

$$\mathbf{n}_i = \mathbf{n} + \left(\mathbf{u} \cos \left(\frac{2\pi i}{n} \right) + \mathbf{v} \sin \left(\frac{2\pi i}{n} \right) \right) \tan (\text{threshold})$$

It's not normalized because, for finding the support vertex, it doesn't need to be. For fixed $\mathbf{n}$, it's very fast to compute these directions. The normal must be pointing away from the shape, so the sampling directions will have opposite-sign normals for the shapes.

After we sample the directions, we'll end up with n vertices, some of them the same. To weed out the duplicates, all we need to do is go through the array and check the vertices sequentially: for each vertex i, remove it from the array if the previous vertex $(i-1)$ is too close. We can only check one vertex because we kept the sequence of sampling directions.

4.6.8   Step 3: Intersect the Contact Areas

Once we have the contact areas, we need to find the actual contact manifold by intersecting the contact areas.

1. *Contact point.* The simplest case of the contact manifold (besides having no contact at all) is just one contact point. If we only have one point from either shape (see Figure 4.5(a), (d), and (e)), we conclude that the contact manifold consists of only one point, and we have that point's coordinates

already. Of course, we'll need to project that point onto the other shape to find out the penetration. We can just project it onto the aligned feature on the other shape—be it a face, an edge, or another point. We might also want to remember the midpoint (the point right in the middle between the two shapes) as the point of contact because it makes our computations independent on the order of the shapes. Since the distance is usually small, the difference is not significant, but it's good to be consistent for easier debugging. When projecting onto an edge or a face, we can project onto the corresponding infinite line or infinite plane. There's a chance that the resulting point will be slightly outside of the other shape (vertex-vertex converting to face-vertex), but the error will never be significant because we are using the closest features on both shapes.

2. *Edge-edge.* In the case of two contact edges, we need to intersect them approximately. We're actually intersecting their projections onto the contact plane because they don't generally intersect in $\mathbb{R}^3$. To produce stable contacts, we want to find two contact points when both edges are almost parallel (very parallel, not-so-parallel edges). A relatively simple heuristic is to find the extreme points at which both edges (or their projections onto the contact plane, whichever is simpler) are still closer than some threshold.

3. *Face-edge.* If we have a contact face on one side of the collision and a contact edge on the other, we just intersect the edge with the face either by projecting the edge onto the face (which is cleaner) or by intersecting their projections onto the contact plane (which may be simpler sometimes but may produce slightly inconsistent results). We've probably already spent linear time to generate the face, so linear-time, brute-force cutting of the edge by the face edges works fine to find the two contact-manifold vertices.

   The edge line will split the face vertices into two sides: left and right of the edge. We'll need to find the two polygon edges intersecting the edge's line and then intersect the edge with that segment. If the edge doesn't intersect the polygon, we probably want to fall back and generate one contact point.

4. *Face-face.* This is the most complicated of all because we need to intersect two polygons. If we sample with eight directions, we will never have more than eight vertices in each polygon. One thing to remember is that we don't really need the intersection polygon, we just need its vertices, so any order will do. So for small numbers of vertices in both polygons, we can use brute force and it will sometimes be fast. But in the more general case, we need to actually intersect two polygons in two dimensions and project them onto the contact plane. For each intersection, the contact point may

lie on the contact plane, and the contact penetration can be computed as the projection of the difference between the shapes' vertices onto the contact normal. We can also use the difference to compute the contact normal for each contact point separately. In any case, the contact points with the most penetration are the most important.

4.6.9 Contact Area Intersection

The brute-force algorithm is used to build bit-matrices $\mathbf{B}^a$ and $\mathbf{B}^b$ for polygons a and b, respectively: each element $\mathbf{B}^x_{i,j}$ will contain 0 if the vertex i of the polygon x is on the outside of edge j of the other polygon, and vice versa. For two quadrilaterals, it's just two 4×4 matrices, 32 two-dimensional tests total. Let's consider a vertex N in the N-gon the same as vertex 0. Vertices with all 1s in the row lie inside the other polygon and get admitted as contacts. We will also need to compute contact points for each pair of edges (one edge from each polygon) that intersects. Polygon a with edge i (E^a_i) with vertices $i, i+1$ intersects E^b_j if and only if $\mathbf{B}^a_{i,j} \oplus \mathbf{B}^a_{i+1,j}$ (that is, edge E^a_i is split in two by infinite line E^b_j) and, symmetrically, $\mathbf{B}^b_{j,i} \oplus \mathbf{B}^b_{j+1,i}$. See Figure 4.15 for an example. The symbol $\oplus$ denotes xor (exclusive or).

The brute-force algorithm is only good for triangles or quadrilaterals. If we don't care much about precision, we can always just cull extra vertices from the contact area and reduce it to a quadrilateral. For example, cull vertices with the highest angle until just four vertices are left in each shape's contact area. But if we want more precision, there are linear-time, convex polygon-polygon intersection algorithms [O'Rourke 98], and they deserve a lot more attention than we can give in this chapter. Next is a small illustration of one such algorithm.

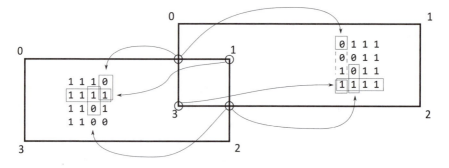

Figure 4.15. Bit-matrices for brute-force polygon intersection. Each polygon has its $\mathbf{B}$ matrix written inside. Each intersection vertex is linked to the bits in $\mathbf{B}$ that determine its status.

4.6.10   Shamos and Hoey Polygon Intersection Algorithm

This algorithm [Shamos and Hoey 76] is very easy to understand, hence easy to implement. First, split both polygons into two chains going top-to-bottom (from the vertex with max y to the vertex with min y). They will share the top and bottom vertices, and there will be left and right chains for each polygon. Then scan top-to-bottom and intersect trapezoids.

On every step, we need to check whether each side of the trapezoid intersects each other side. And every step means introduction of an additional vertex, so we'll need to check whether the other polygon's trapezoid contains the new vertex. If it does, we'll include it into our contact manifold.

4.7   SAT Optimizations

SAT is used to compute the contact normal and penetration or separation for two convex shapes. We describe the brute-force SAT in Sections 4.4 and 4.6.1. The notation $\mathbf{s}$ is used for the contact normal. To use SAT for concave shapes, we need to decompose them into convex pieces and generate a manifold for each pair of pieces from both rigid bodies. Ideally, we need to cull contacts then. If there are more than a few pieces, consider using some kind of bounding volume hierarchy (BVH), like sphere tree, or some other heuristic limiting many candidate features [Terdiman 08].

4.7.1   Limiting Candidate Features

One of the most obvious things to optimize is the number of candidate feature pairs to check, especially edge-edge pairs, as their count grows quadratically with the complexity of the polytopes and there's no obvious hill-climbing or DK-hierarchy-based algorithm to restrict that complexity, like in the FV, VF, and VV cases.

A Gauss map ($\mathcal{G}$) is a natural way to analyze support planes and features. A face maps to its normal, just one point on a unit sphere. An edge maps to an arc, and a vertex to a spherical polygon. Support features in direction $\mathbf{s}$ on a polytope have the Gauss map areas that include vector $-\mathbf{s}$. And $-\mathbf{s}$ is also a witness feature in the same direction on the Gauss map. For example, if vertex $\mathbf{v}$ supports polytope in direction $-\mathbf{s}$, then $\mathbf{s}$ is inside $\mathcal{G}(\mathbf{v})$, the solid angle or spherical polygon $\mathbf{v}$ maps to. When the supporting feature is an edge e (and its two vertices are $\mathbf{v}_0$ and $\mathbf{v}_1$), $-\mathbf{s}$ will happen to be on the arc $\mathcal{G}(e)$, which happens to be the shared border between areas $\mathcal{A}_0 = \mathcal{G}(\mathbf{v}_0)$ and $\mathcal{A}_1 = \mathcal{G}(\mathbf{v}_1)$. When the supporting feature is a face f with vertices $\mathbf{v}_i$, $i = 0, \ldots, n$, $-\mathbf{s} = \mathcal{G}(f)$ will be the face's normal and will be the point shared between areas $A_i = \mathcal{G}(\mathbf{v}_i)$, $i = 0, \ldots, n$.

In SAT, we seek supporting features for opposite directions in two colliding shapes A and B. Thus, to find the pair of supporting features for a direction $\mathbf{s}$, we can find where $-\mathbf{s}$ lies in $\mathcal{G}(A)$ for shape A support. For shape B, we'll find where $\mathbf{s}$ lies in $\mathcal{G}(B)$, or, equivalently, where $-\mathbf{s}$ lies in the negated Gauss map $-\mathcal{G}(B)$, with each $\mathbf{x} \in \mathcal{G}(B)$ mapped to $-\mathbf{x} \in -\mathcal{G}(B)$.

Let's superimpose $\mathcal{G}(A)$ and $-\mathcal{G}(B)$ and call the result $\mathcal{S}$. It lets us intuitively and quickly see the pair of features for any direction $\mathbf{s}$.[8] It also shows that if the Gauss maps $\mathcal{G}(f_A)$ and $-\mathcal{G}(f_B)$ with features f_A on A and f_B on B do not overlap, there is no separating direction where those features would be the pair of supporting features, and it doesn't make sense to check them. For example, if the Gauss maps of a pair of edges do not intersect, we don't have to check that pair of edges. This eliminates a lion's share of edge pairs to check. It also has another important consequence.

Whenever a pair of features overlap on $\mathcal{S}$, those two features *are* the supporting features in any direction that belongs to both of them on $\mathcal{S}$. There's no need to build a DK hierarchy or perform a supporting feature search: in that direction, we already have all the information to compute the translation distance. If edges are collinear on $\mathcal{S}$, we don't need to take them into account because there will be several face-vertex feature pairs attaining the same distance. Vertex-vertex intersections form an infinity of possible SA directions, but fortunately, we don't need to check them if our shapes penetrate. If they don't penetrate, we can easily establish a candidate SA as a line going through both vertices. If the vertices coincide (hence we can build no line), we can just assume the shapes penetrate.

If the normal $\mathbf{n}$ of a face in A is outside of $-\mathcal{G}(\mathbf{v}_B)$, we don't need to check that face-vertex pair. We probably still need to check direction $\mathbf{n}$ as a candidate SA, because $\mathbf{n}$ will surely be inside at least one spherical polygon $-\mathcal{A} = -\mathcal{G}(\mathbf{v}_B)$, unless we establish that the corresponding vertex cannot be a separating supporting feature. It is possible to establish, for example, whether the vertex is on the "far end" of the convex hull from the other shape (see http://www .codercorner.com/blog/?p=24 for details of the idea). But more importantly, it lets us reduce the support computation to a mere dot product. Wherever area $-\mathcal{A}$ is overlapped by $\mathbf{n}$, $-\mathcal{A}$ will correspond to the supporting vertex $\mathbf{v}_B$ on the shape B. The signed distance of $\mathbf{v}_B$ to f_A is the separating distance between shapes A and B in the direction $\mathbf{n}$.

---

[8]However, we are not interested in just any direction due to SAT. For penetrating objects, the only interesting directions are face normals and directions orthogonal to a pair of edges from both shapes. The latter are the points of intersection between edges on $\mathcal{S}$: remember that points on the Gauss map are also unit vectors, defining directions in $\mathbb{R}^3$.

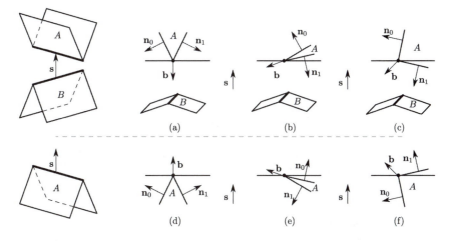

Figure 4.16. Filtering s in the case of EE: (a), (b), and (c) candidate support feature, requiring additional tests; (d), (e), and (f) noncandidate feature pair.

4.7.2 Limiting Edge-Edge Checks

Since we need to test only the edge pairs for which the respective Gauss maps overlap, we can quickly reject the majority of edge pairs. The Gauss map of an edge is an arc that connects the normals of the edge's adjoining faces. Figure 4.16 illustrates that, indeed, if the separating features are two edges the cross product of the edge directions corresponds to the point of intersection of the edges' Gauss maps.

In this section, we present a quick test that determines whether two arcs on a Gauss map intersect. The test boils down to a simple origin-in-tetrahedron test, which is many times faster than performing a supporting-feature search on the shapes. These tests work for polyhedra (i.e., polytopes that have volume). However, with a few simple measures, the test can be performed on arbitrary polytopes. See Section 4.7.3 for some additional considerations in the case of flat (non-three-dimensional) polytopes (such as single polygons, wedges, capsules, etc.).

The EE case deserves some special attention. The support direction is always $s = \pm\mathbf{norm}_{||\cdot||}(\mathbf{e}_A \times \mathbf{e}_B)$ in this case (see Table 4.3). However, most edge pairs $e_A \in \mathbf{E}(A)$, $e_B \in \mathbf{E}(B)$ fail to satisfy even the necessary conditions to be a support feature pair:

1. Shape A must be in front of $\mathcal{P}_A(s_{min})$ (Equation (4.1)).

2. Shape B must be in front of $\mathcal{P}_B(-s_{min})$ (Equation (4.2)).

Bisector $\mathbf{b} = \mathbf{n}_0(e) + \mathbf{n}_1(e)$ (Figure 4.16) shows the intuitive direction "outside" the edge. The inequalities in Equation (4.8) relate $\mathbf{b}$ and $\pm\mathbf{s}$. If neither direction $\mathbf{s}$ nor $-\mathbf{s}$ satisfy both conditions in Equation (4.8), then this EE case is clearly not the support feature pair.

$$\begin{cases} \mathbf{s} \cdot \mathbf{b}_A < 0, & \mathbf{b}_A = \mathbf{n}_0(e_A) + \mathbf{n}_1(e_A); \\ \mathbf{s} \cdot \mathbf{b}_B > 0, & \mathbf{b}_B = \mathbf{n}_0(e_B) + \mathbf{n}_1(e_B). \end{cases} \tag{4.8}$$

In Figure 4.16, cases (d), (e), and (f) are examples of noncandidate (filtered out) cases where $\mathbf{s} \cdot \mathbf{b}_A > 0$. Cases (a), (b), and (c) require the additional test of $\mathbf{b}_B$.

The inequalities in Equation (4.8) generate a lot of false positives and require computing $\mathbf{s}$, but they illustrate the EE case in $\mathbb{R}^3$. Let us consider the EE case on a Gauss map (see Figure 4.17). The arcs $\mathcal{G}(e_A)$ and $-\mathcal{G}(e_B)$ are the ones we need to test for intersection (note the negation). Their point of intersection is the candidate support direction $\mathbf{s}$. If the arcs don't intersect, then there are no parallel support planes $\mathcal{P}_A(\mathbf{s})$ and $\mathcal{P}_B(-\mathbf{s})$ for this edge pair, and we need not consider this edge pair.

The arcs $\mathcal{G}(e_A)$ and $-\mathcal{G}(e_B)$ intersect if and only if the tetrahedron $\mathbf{n}_{A,0}\mathbf{n}_{A,1}\mathbf{n}_{B,0}\mathbf{n}_{B,1}$ contains $\mathbf{o}$, like in Figure 4.17(c). The direction of the line from $\mathcal{G}(e_B)$ to $\mathcal{G}(e_A)$ through $\mathbf{o}$ is the candidate $\mathbf{s}$. Note that the $\mathbf{n}_{B,i}$ are not negated (see Figure 4.17(a) and (c)). If the arcs $\mathcal{G}(e_A)$ and $\mathcal{G}(e_B)$ intersect as in Figure 4.19(b), then $\mathcal{G}(e_A)$ and $-\mathcal{G}(e_B)$ do *not* intersect, and we skip the edge pair.

In Figure 4.17(c) it's easy to see that the tetrahedron contains the origin if and only if

1. the plane through $(\mathbf{o}, \mathbf{n}_{A,0}, \mathbf{n}_{A,1})$ splits chord $\mathbf{n}_{B,0}$ - $\mathbf{n}_{B,1}$,

2. the plane through $(\mathbf{o}, \mathbf{n}_{B,0}, \mathbf{n}_{B,1})$ splits chord $\mathbf{n}_{A,0}$ - $\mathbf{n}_{A,1}$, and

3. arcs $\mathcal{G}(e_A)$ and $\mathcal{G}(e_B)$ do not intersect.

See Figure 4.17(c): the plane through $(\mathbf{o}, \mathbf{n}_0, \mathbf{n}_1)$ has the equation $(\mathbf{n}_0 \times \mathbf{n}_1) \cdot \mathbf{x} = 0$, and $\mathbf{n}_0 \times \mathbf{n}_1 \parallel \mathbf{e}$ is the edge direction that we can (but don't have to) cache. Thus, the necessary condition for two edges to be supporting features in the direction $\mathbf{e}_A \times \mathbf{e}_B$ is

$$\begin{cases} \text{sign}(\mathbf{e}_A \cdot \mathbf{n}_{B,0}) \neq \text{sign}(\mathbf{e}_A \cdot \mathbf{n}_{B,1}), \\ \text{sign}(\mathbf{e}_B \cdot \mathbf{n}_{A,0}) \neq \text{sign}(\mathbf{e}_B \cdot \mathbf{n}_{A,1}). \end{cases}$$

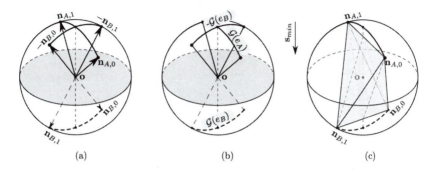

Figure 4.17. Testing if edge-edge is a candidate support pair: (a) edge face normals, (b) edge arcs, and (c) tetrahedron containing the origin.

The above do not detect arc intersections exactly. However, it is relatively easy to detect both the intersection and the direction of s at the same time. Next, we will present such a method.

For the shape S, we can compute the edge direction $e_S \parallel n_{S,0} \times n_{S,1}$ (the order is important). By projecting the arcs onto a plane orthogonal to $b = n_{A,0} + n_{A,1}$, as in Figure 4.18, it is easy to see that the candidate support direction s is as in Equation (4.9). The vector s is also the point of intersection of two arcs (see Figure 4.18(a) and (b)). If the arcs do not intersect, s is undefined, and the edge pair is not a candidate support feature pair. See Figure 4.18 for examples of the cases in Equation (4.9):

$$
s = \begin{cases}
-e_B \times e_A & \text{if } \begin{cases} e_A \cdot -n_{B,0} > 0 \\ e_A \cdot -n_{B,1} < 0 \\ -e_B \cdot n_{A,0} < 0 \\ -e_B \cdot n_{A,1} > 0 \end{cases} \\
e_A \times -e_B & \text{if } \begin{cases} e_A \cdot -n_{B,0} < 0 \\ e_A \cdot -n_{B,1} > 0 \\ -e_B \cdot n_{A,0} > 0 \\ -e_B \cdot n_{A,1} < 0 \end{cases} \\
\text{undefined otherwise}
\end{cases}
\tag{4.9}
$$

We only need to check nonparallel pairs of edges with intersecting arcs. Intersection and direction s can be detected according to Equation (4.9). See Figure 4.19 for examples of excluded cases. And for those pairs that we need to check, we just need to compute the distance between the edges along the direction s. If $e_A \times e_B$ is close to zero, we can skip that EE check as it is a degenerate case (shown in Figure 4.19(a)).

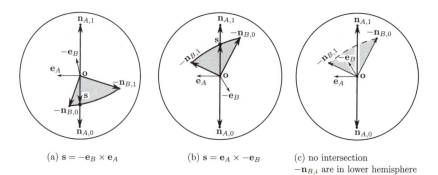

(a) $\mathbf{s} = -\mathbf{e}_B \times \mathbf{e}_A$ (b) $\mathbf{s} = \mathbf{e}_A \times -\mathbf{e}_B$ (c) no intersection

$-\mathbf{n}_{B,i}$ are in lower hemisphere

Figure 4.18. Detection of arc-arc intersection and the direction of $\mathbf{s}$.

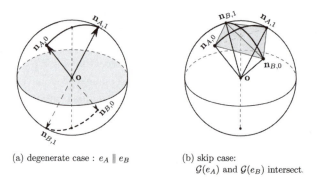

(a) degenerate case : $e_A \parallel e_B$ (b) skip case:

$\mathcal{G}(e_A)$ and $\mathcal{G}(e_B)$ intersect.

Figure 4.19. Edge-edge cases: not candidate support pairs.

4.7.3 Non-Three-Dimensional Polytopes

In order for the arc-arc intersection test in Equation (4.9) to work, direction $\mathbf{e}$ must be the right-screw direction for the rotation from $\mathbf{n}_0$ to $\mathbf{n}_1$ (see Figure 4.20(a)). It is easy to establish that $\mathbf{e} = \mathbf{norm}_{||\cdot||}(\mathbf{n}_0 \times \mathbf{n}_1)$ but that $\mathbf{n}_0 \times \mathbf{n}_1 = \mathbf{0}$ in the case where $\mathbf{n}_1 = -\mathbf{n}_0$, i.e., in the case of a wedge collision shape. Furthermore, the tetrahedron test also breaks down unless we replace $\mathbf{n}_0 \times \mathbf{n}_1$ with a valid nonzero direction.

Fortunately, this special case is easy to handle with a little bit of precomputation. The main requirements for $\mathbf{e}$ are that it is orthogonal to the arc plane and is the axis of right-hand-rule rotation from $\mathbf{n}_0$ to $\mathbf{n}_1$ (it also implies $\mathbf{e} \perp \mathbf{n}_0$ and $\mathbf{e} \perp \mathbf{n}_1$). This automatically holds in common cases ($\mathbf{e} = \mathbf{norm}_{||\cdot||}(\mathbf{n}_0 \times \mathbf{n}_1)$, see Figure 4.20(a)), and in the unfolded angle case (Figure 4.20(b)), we can

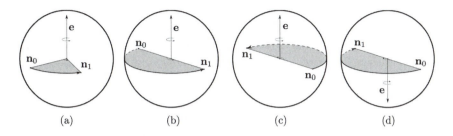

Figure 4.20. Computing $\mathbf{e}$ for a flat angle arc: (a) edge, normals, and arc orientation; (b) flat-angle arc direction; (c) flipped normal order; and (d) flipped edge direction, which is only free in the flat-angle case.

simply assume $\mathbf{e} = \pm\mathbf{norm}_{\|\cdot\|}(\mathbf{v}_1 - \mathbf{v}_0)$ and choose the sign $\pm$ according to the right-hand rule. See Figure 4.20(b) for an example. If we switch $\mathbf{n}_0$ and $\mathbf{n}_1$ and keep the direction of $\mathbf{e}$, we'll effectively flip the arc (see Figure 4.20(c)). If we flip the direction of $\mathbf{e}$, we'll also effectively flip the arc (see Figure 4.20(d)). Thus, it is always possible to choose the direction of $\mathbf{e}$ that works with our arc-arc test. Just keep in mind the direction of the arc from $\mathbf{n}_0$ to $\mathbf{n}_1$: it must be consistent with right-hand-rule rotation with regard to direction $\mathbf{e}$, and that is all that is needed for the arc-arc test to work.

Notice that the arc-arc test does not work with arcs of over $180°$. Neither does the origin-in-tetrahedron test work with such arcs. Fortunately, polytope SAT does not have to deal with such cases, as all normals of the collision shape must point "outwards" of the shape. In nonpolytope cases, special care must be taken. For example, the one edge in a capsule shape maps to a great circle on $\mathbb{S}^2$, so we must employ a different kind of edge-edge culling.

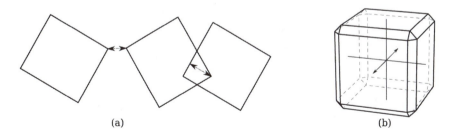

Figure 4.21. SAT traits: (a) SAT can skip vertex-vertex pairs for penetrating shapes; (b) SAT search space is inherently concave: the typical and simple Minkowski sum may have six (or more) local minima (corresponding penetrating distance vectors shown).

4.7.4   SAT versus GJK

A major advantage of SAT over GJK is that SAT works great for penetrating shapes. In fact, SAT works better in the penetrating case than in the separated shape case because there's no need to check vertex-vertex feature pairs if shapes penetrate (see, for example, Figure 4.21(a)).

A major disadvantage of SAT is its inherently slower asymptotic convergence rate. The GJK formulation is convex and implicit, so there is one and only one local minimum, which is a global minimum, too. And GJK needs only support mapping, it doesn't need features (edges, faces, connectivity), so implicit surfaces work just as well, and it's possible to stop when the solution is "close enough" (when the Minkowski sum support is within a small range of the simplex). SAT, on the other hand, solves potentially every concave problem with a lot of local optima. The Minkowski sum in Figure 4.21(b) has at least six local maxima, for example.

4.7.5   SAT versus EPA

EPA obtains the global minimum and is probably the best-known and widely used algorithm for finding a true MTD. It can also be warm-started with GJK. SAT doesn't require a priority queue data structure, so it may be more suitable for hardware with limited/slow conditional branching (like a GPU). It is also arguably much simpler to implement, especially without the optimizations, so it may run faster on very simple shapes (cube, octahedron).

4.7.6   SAT versus Xenocollide or Dual-CD

Both the Xenocollide [Snethen 08] and Dual-CD [Choi et al. 05] algorithms ultimately cast a ray from inside the Minkowski sum, find where the ray intersects the boundary, and thus detect the penetration distance in the given direction. It's possible to iterate the direction, but both algorithms perform a local search, whereas SAT finds the global minimal translation distance. Sometimes we may prefer one or the other, but when we prefer the MTD, SAT may be better.

4.8   Acknowledgments

I would like to extend a special thanks to my wife, Anna Bibikova, for her support and tremendous help with illustrations.

An algorithm similar to the one described here was used in the awesome PlayStation®3 title *Uncharted: Drake's Fortune* that sold one million copies in the first ten weeks.[9] Special thanks goes to the hardworking Naughty Dogs who let me realize the dream of writing the physics engine for *Uncharted*.

Bibliography

[Choi et al. 05] Yi-King Choi, Xueqing Li, Wenping Wang, and Stephen Cameron. "Collision Detection of Convex Polyhedra Based on Duality Transformation." Technical Report TR-2005-01, Hong Kong University Computer Science Department, 2005. Available at http://www.cs.hku.hk/research/techreps/document/TR-2005-01.pdf.

[Dobkin and Kirkpatrick 90] David P. Dobkin and David G. Kirkpatrick. "Determining the Separation of Preprocessed Polyhedra—A Unified Approach." In *ICALP '90: Proceedings of the 17th International Colloquium on Automata, Languages and Programming*, pp. 400–413. London, UK: Springer-Verlag, 1990.

[Fogel and Halperin 07] Efi Fogel and Dan Halperin. "Exact and Efficient Construction of Minkowski Sums of Convex Polyhedra with Applications." *Comput. Aided Des.* 39:11 (2007), 929–940.

[Ganjugunte 07] Shashidhara K. Ganjugunte. "A Survey on Techniques for Computing Penetration Depth.", 2007.

[O'Rourke 98] Joseph O'Rourke. "Comp.Graphics.Algorithms Frequently Asked Questions: Section 2. 2D Polygon Computations." Available online (http://www.faqs.org/faqs/graphics/algorithms-faq/), 1998.

[Shamos and Hoey 76] Michael Ian Shamos and Dan Hoey. "Geometric Intersection Problems." In *SFCS '76: Proceedings of the 17th Annual Symposium on Foundations of Computer Science*, pp. 208–215. Washington, DC: IEEE Computer Society, 1976.

[Snethen 08] Gary Snethen. "XenoCollide: Complex Collision Made Simple." In *Game Programming Gems 7*, edited by Scott Jacobs, pp. 165–178. Boston: Charles River Media, 2008.

[Terdiman 08] Pierre Terdiman. "Faster Convex-Convex SAT." *Coder Corner.* Available at http://www.codercorner.com/blog/?p=24, 2008.

---

[9]n4g.com. 2008-01-25.

[van den Bergen] Gino van den Bergen. "A Fast and Robust GJK Implementation for Collision Detection of Convex Objects." *journal of graphics tools* 4:2 (1999), 7–25.

[van den Bergen 01] Gino van den Bergen. "Proximity Queries and Penetration Depth Computation on 3D Game Objects.", 2001. Paper presented at Game Developers Conference, San Francisco, March 9–13, 2001.

– 5 –

Smooth Mesh Contacts with GJK

Gino van den Bergen

5.1 Introduction

Contacts are without doubt the toughest constraints that a game physics engine needs to deal with. Contacts constrain the relative motions of two bodies in one direction only, often act for a short period of time, and involve sliding and rolling. But most importantly, contacts require a detailed representation of a body's geometry, since a contact between two bodies can occur anywhere on their surfaces.

This chapter discusses how to obtain proper contact points and normals for convex shapes that collide with each other or with possibly concave shapes represented by polygon meshes. The case of a convex shape hitting a mesh is very common in games. Meshes are typically used for representing the static environment, such as buildings and terrain, whereas the moving objects, like player and nonplayer characters, (parts of) vehicles, projectiles, debris, and third-person cameras, are represented by convex shapes. The trouble with polygon meshes is that they, having zero thickness, actually only represent the surface but need to physically represent solid objects.

One immediate problem we see is that not only is the position on the surface important but also the time of impact. Physics engines compute body positions at discrete time steps. Collisions usually happen in between these time steps. Problems occur when performing collision detection for fast-moving bodies at these discrete time steps, since collisions may be detected too late or not at all. This effect, called *tunneling*, can be reduced by taking smaller time steps. If we had the computational budget to reduce the time step to a millisecond or less, then we would rid ourselves of the grossest tunneling mishaps for the average game scene. However, in game development we usually do not have that kind of budget.

This suggests that for fast-moving objects we need to detect collisions in continuous four-dimensional space-time in order to catch colliding bodies before they interpenetrate. This also seems to suggest that we need to take substeps in our physics integration, since velocities may radically change in between time steps.

However, the prospect of having to break the time step at each instant a collision occurs is not very rosy, since theoretically, a body could have an infinite number of collisions within a time interval. So, even though collision detection is performed in space-time, our physics scheme should change velocities and positions at a limited number of time steps only.

In any case, we will never be able to fully keep bodies from interpenetrating, and we shouldn't. We simply need to make sure that penetrations are shallow enough to allow for accurate contact data to be computed. We will present a definition of "shallow enough" further on, but for now, let us assume that we want to keep the depths at which bodies interpenetrate within a certain tolerance.

The body trajectories through space-time are not known, or at least, cannot be derived from the underlying physical simulation model. Using the trajectories prescribed by the physics model would take a little too much of our math skills. Even for something as simple as a tumbling brick in free fall, the equations for the trajectory are way too complex for continuous collision detection. Instead, we will assume simplified trajectories for moving bodies.

Solutions to the four-dimensional intersection detection problem have been presented for a restricted class of shapes and motions [Cameron 85, Cameron 90, Canny 86, Hubbard 93, Schömer and Thiel 95, Eckstein and Schömer 99, Redon et al. 02]. In the literature on continuous collision detection, the class of shapes is usually restricted to polytopes and the motions are restricted to rotations and translations. We use *polytope* as a generic term for all shapes that are formed by taking the convex hull of a finite point set. The set of polytopes includes points, line segments, triangles, tetrahedra, and convex polyhedra. In this chapter, we discuss solutions for convex objects in general. Besides polytopes, we also consider quadrics, such as spheres, cylinders, and cones, and shapes that are constructed from these primitive shapes through convex hulls and Minkowski sums.

The freedom of having any imaginable convex shape type as a collision primitive comes at the cost of restricting the set of continuous motions to translations. Bodies can still rotate but only at the given time steps. Often, we can get away with using piecewise linear trajectories for translations only. Angular velocities of moving bodies are usually not so high, and in cases where they are, the physical shape usually does not depend on the orientation, for example, wheels of a race car that are represented by cylinders are invariant under rotations along their axes.

Our solutions for continuous collision detection and contact data computation are all based on the use of support mappings and the Gilbert-Johnson-Keerthi algorithm (GJK). GJK is an iterative method for computing the distance between convex objects [Gilbert et al. 88]. GJK turns out to be extremely versatile and is applicable to all kinds of proximity queries on a large family of convex shape

Figure 5.1. Two convex objects (left) and their CSO (right).

types. An overview of GJK is presented in this chapter. But first let us get acquainted with the concept of translational configuration space.

5.2 Configuration Space

Proximity queries on pairs of objects are often expressed more conveniently in terms of the pair's configuration space. The *translational configuration space* of two objects is the space of relative translations between the two objects. For objects A and B being simultaneously translated over, respectively, vectors c_A and c_B, the relative translation between A and B is the vector $c_B - c_A$. From a collision detection point of view, we do not care too much about the absolute translations and only need to focus on the relative translation.

We regard relative translations of a pair of objects as points in the objects' configuration space. Some relative translations result in a configuration of intersecting objects. The set of such relative translations is called the *configuration space obstacle* (CSO) of the pair of objects. (See Figure 5.1.) For convex shapes, the CSO is convex as well. In formal terms, the CSO of objects A and B is the set of all vectors from a point of B to a point of A:

$$A - B = \{a - b : a \in A, b \in B\}.$$

The term "configuration space obstacle" originates from robot-motion planning, where it denotes the set of coordinates in configuration space that are not admissible. The CSO can be visualized as the object we get by "brushing" $-B$, the reflection of B in the origin, along each point of A. For example, the CSO of an arbitrary object and a sphere centered at the origin is the original object enlarged in all directions by the sphere's radius. Figure 5.1 shows the CSO of a box and a cone.

Expressing proximity queries in terms of configuration space results in a more convenient problem description and fewer special cases, since only one object needs to be considered in our computations. For instance, the point closest to the origin in $A - B$ is unique for convex objects, whereas multiple closest-point pairs may exist for a pair of convex objects. All closest-point pairs collapse to a single closest point in the CSO.

Let us take a closer look at a number of proximity queries and their equivalent in configuration space. Object A and B intersect if and only if the origin (zero vector) is contained in $A - B$:

$$A \cap B \neq \emptyset \equiv \mathbf{0} \in A - B.$$

This can be seen by the fact that if A and B intersect, they have a common point, and thus, the vector from this point to itself is contained in $A - B$. Phrased differently, the zero translation trivially results in a configuration of intersecting objects.

The distance between A and B is the distance from the origin to $A - B$, i.e., the length of the shortest vector in $A - B$:

$$d(A, B) = \min\{\|\mathbf{x}\| : \mathbf{x} \in A - B\}.$$

We see that the distance can be defined as the length of the shortest relative translation that brings the objects into contact. The shortest relative translation is unique, although a pair of closest points is not necessarily unique. For nonintersecting objects, closest points must lie on the boundaries of the respective objects. This is not true for intersecting objects.

There also exists a measure for the amount of penetration. The *penetration depth* is defined as the length of the shortest relative translation that separates two intersecting objects:

$$p(A, B) = \inf\{\|\mathbf{x}\| : \mathbf{x} \notin A - B\}.$$

We use infimum rather than minimum since all objects, including CSOs, are considered to be closed sets. As with closest points, witness points of a positive penetration depth must lie on the boundaries of the respective objects.

Note that for computing a pair of closest points, or a pair of witness points of the penetration depth, the CSO offers insufficient information, since the CSO reflects only the relative configuration of objects. This is true for witness points of any type of query on a CSO. If witness points are required, then additional information concerning the actual objects A and B needs to be collected while performing the query, as we shall find out further on.

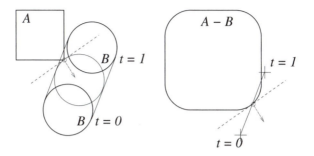

Figure 5.2. Computing a contact point (open dot) and a contact normal (arrow) of a box and a moving sphere (left) by performing a ray test on the CSO of the objects (right).

Computing the time of impact between objects moving under translation boils down to performing a ray cast on the CSO. The relative translation in space-time can be visualized as a point that starts at the origin and moves towards the difference of the target translations of the objects. More formally, let the configuration of objects A and B over a time interval be given by $A + t\mathbf{c}_A$ and $B + t\mathbf{c}_B$, where $t \in [0, 1]$. Here, $\mathbf{c}_A$ and $\mathbf{c}_B$ are the target translations of A and B, respectively. The earliest time the objects come into contact is given by the smallest t for which

$$t(\mathbf{c}_B - \mathbf{c}_A) \in A - B.$$

As can be seen, this expression defines the first intersection of a ray that is cast from the origin towards $\mathbf{c}_B - \mathbf{c}_A$.

Besides the time of impact, we can also compute the point of contact and a contact normal from the ray cast. The contact point corresponds to the point where the ray enters the CSO, and the contact normal is the normal to the boundary of the CSO at this point. Figure 5.2 shows an example of the ray test for a box and a moving sphere.

For many pairs of shape types, the CSO's shape cannot be represented explicitly in a simple way. Fortunately, we do not need an explicit representation of the CSO for performing any of these proximity queries. Instead, we require an implicit representation of the used shapes in terms of their support mappings.

5.3 Support Mappings

The versatility of GJK lies in the fact that it uses support mappings for reading the geometry of convex objects. A *support mapping* for an object C is a function

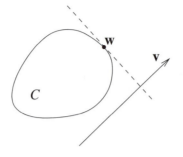

Figure 5.3. Object C is fully contained in the closed negative half-space of the plane defined by normal vector $\mathbf{v}$ and support point $\mathbf{w} = s_C(\mathbf{w})$.

s_C that maps a vector $\mathbf{v}$ to a point of C, according to

$$s_C(\mathbf{v}) \in C \quad \text{such that} \quad \mathbf{v} \cdot s_C(\mathbf{v}) = \max\{\mathbf{v} \cdot \mathbf{x} : \mathbf{x} \in C\}.$$

In plain terms, a support mapping returns a point of an object that lies furthest in the direction of the input vector. We say "a point" since such a point is not necessarily unique. In cases where multiple points yield the maximum dot product, the support mapping may return any of these points. We do not care which point as long as it yields a maximum dot product with the input vector.

The result of a support mapping for a given vector is called a *support point*. A support point $\mathbf{w} = s_C(\mathbf{v})$ together with its input vector $\mathbf{v}$ forms a supporting plane of the object defined by the set of points $\mathbf{x}$ for which $\mathbf{v} \cdot \mathbf{x} = \mathbf{v} \cdot \mathbf{w}$. The object itself is fully contained in the closed negative half-space of this supporting plane, as can be seen in Figure 5.3.

Support mappings can be found for all primitive shape types, such as triangles, spheres, cones, and cylinders. For example, the support mapping of a polytope is simply the support mapping of its set of vertices. Furthermore, support mappings for objects that are obtained from primitive shape types by affine transformation, convex hulls, and Minkowski addition can be constructed using the support mappings of the primitive types. A discussion of support mappings for commonly used shape types falls outside the scope of this chapter. The reader is referred to [van den Bergen 03] for learning more about support mappings. However, it is important to note that the support mapping of the CSO of A and B is given by

$$s_{A-B}(\mathbf{v}) = s_A(\mathbf{v}) - s_B(-\mathbf{v}).$$

A support point of the CSO is simply the vector difference of the support points for the two objects. As can be seen, an explicit representation of the CSO is not required as long as we rely purely on support mappings in our algorithms.

5.4   Overview of GJK

GJK is an iterative method for approximating the distance between two convex objects. The original paper on this topic discussed the use of GJK for polytopes only [Gilbert et al. 88], however, with some minor adaptations of the termination condition, GJK is applicable to convex objects in general [Gilbert and Foo 90]. In this section, we will briefly discuss GJK in order to get us going for the next section. For an in-depth discussion of GJK, the reader is referred to [van den Bergen 03].

GJK essentially approximates the point of the CSO that is closest to the origin. GJK may be used to solve other queries as well, but at its core it remains a method for finding the closest point. GJK approximates the closest point of $A - B$ in the following way. In each iteration, a simplex is constructed that is contained in $A - B$ and that lies closer to the origin than the simplex constructed in the previous iteration. A *simplex* is the convex hull of an affinely independent set of vertices. The simplices can have one to four vertices, so a simplex can be a single point, a line segment, a triangle, or a tetrahedron. We define W_k as the set of vertices of the simplex constructed in the kth iteration and $\mathbf{v}_k$ as the point closest to the origin of the simplex. Initially, we take $W_0 = \emptyset$, and $\mathbf{v}_0$, an arbitrary point in $A - B$. Since the simplex[1] W_k is contained in $A - B$, we see that $\mathbf{v}_k \in A - B$, and thus, the length of $\mathbf{v}_k$ is an upper bound for the distance between A and B.

In each iteration, a new support point $\mathbf{w}_k = s_{A-B}(-\mathbf{v}_k)$ is added as a vertex to the current simplex W_k. Let $Y_k = W_k \cup \{\mathbf{w}_k\}$ be the new simplex. The closest point $\mathbf{v}_{k+1}$ of the new simplex is taken to be the current best approximation of the point closest to the origin of $A - B$. As we keep adding vertices, older vertices that no longer contribute to the closest point are removed. Thus, each new simplex W_{k+1} is taken to be the smallest set $X \subseteq Y_k$, such that $\mathbf{v}_{k+1}$ is contained in the convex hull of X. It can be seen that exactly one such X exists and that it must be affinely independent.

GJK terminates as soon as $\mathbf{v}_k$ is close enough to the closest point of $A - B$. In order to determine the error in the current approximation, we need also a lower bound for the distance. As a lower bound we can use the signed distance of the origin to the supporting plane at $\mathbf{w}_k$, which is

$$\frac{\mathbf{v}_k \cdot \mathbf{w}_k}{\|\mathbf{v}_k\|}.$$

Note that the upper and lower bounds depend on $\|\mathbf{v}_k\|$. Computing the length of a vector involves evaluating a square root, which may hurt performance. A cheaper

---

[1]Formally, we should refer to the simplex as $\mathrm{conv}(W_k)$, the convex hull of W_k, but we often identify a simplex by its vertices.

measure for the error can be found by multiplying the upper and lower bounds by $\|\mathbf{v}_k\|$:

$$\|\mathbf{v}_k\|^2 - \mathbf{v}_k \cdot \mathbf{w}_k.$$

This value is an upper bound for the squared distance between $\mathbf{v}_k$ and the closest point of $A - B$ [Gilbert et al. 88, van den Bergen 03].

For any pair of convex objects A and B, the sequence $\{\mathbf{v}_k\}$ indeed converges to the closest point of $A - B$ [Gilbert et al. 88, van den Bergen 03]. Therefore, Algorithm 1, which describes the GJK distance algorithm in pseudocode, terminates in a finite number of iterations for any positive error tolerance ε.

Algorithm 1 The GJK distance algorithm. Point $\mathbf{v}$ approximates the point closest to the origin of $A - B$ within a distance of ε.

> $\mathbf{v} \leftarrow$ *arbitrary point in* $A - B$;
> $W \leftarrow \emptyset$;
> $\mathbf{w} \leftarrow s_{A-B}(-\mathbf{v})$;
> while $\|\mathbf{v}\|^2 - \mathbf{v} \cdot \mathbf{w} > \varepsilon^2$ do
> begin
> $Y \leftarrow W \cup \{\mathbf{w}\}$;
> $\mathbf{v} \leftarrow$ *point closest to the origin of* $\mathrm{conv}(Y)$;
> $W \leftarrow$ *smallest* $X \subseteq Y$ *such that* $\mathbf{v} \in \mathrm{conv}(X)$;
> $\mathbf{w} \leftarrow s_{A-B}(-\mathbf{v})$;
> end;
> return $\|\mathbf{v}\|$

5.5   Johnson's Algorithm

For computing the point closest to the origin of a simplex, and for determining the smallest subsimplex that contains the closest point, we use a subalgorithm called Johnson's algorithm. Let $Y = \{\mathbf{y}_1, \ldots, \mathbf{y}_n\}$ be the set of vertices of a simplex. Then, any point $\mathbf{x}$ of the simplex may be described as an *affine combination* of Y in the following way:

$$\mathbf{x} = \sum_{i=1}^{n} \lambda_i \mathbf{y}_i, \quad \text{where} \quad \sum_{i=1}^{n} \lambda_i = 1.$$

The coefficients $(\lambda_1, \ldots, \lambda_n)$ are the barycentric coordinates of $\mathbf{x}$ with respect to Y. In order for $\mathbf{x}$ to be contained in $\mathrm{conv}(Y)$, the barycentric coordinates must be non-negative, in which case $\mathbf{x}$ is a *convex combination* of Y. The smallest $X \subseteq Y$ such that $\mathbf{x} \in \text{conv}(X)$ is the set $X = \{\mathbf{y}_i : \lambda_i > 0\}$. In other words, the set X is found by discarding all the points $\mathbf{y}_i$ from Y whose coordinate for $\mathbf{x}$ is zero.

Having to deal with inequality constraints that bound the coordinate domain is quite inconvenient. So as a first step, we seek to compute the closest point of the affine hull rather than the convex hull of a set of vertices. The *affine hull* $\text{aff}(X)$ of a set of points X is the set of affine combinations of X. The affine hull of a set of vertices is a point, a line, a plane, or the whole space. Barycentric coordinates of points on an affine hull still sum to one; however, they can be negative.

The barycentric coordinates of the point $\mathbf{v}$ closest to the origin of an affine hull can be computed by solving a linear system of equations. Let $\mathbf{v} = \lambda_1 \mathbf{y}_1 + \cdots + \lambda_n \mathbf{y}_n$. First of all, the barycentric coordinates need to sum to one, so $\lambda_1 + \cdots + \lambda_n = 1$ is the first equation. Secondly, the vector (from the origin to point) $\mathbf{v}$ is orthogonal to the affine hull. More specifically, $\mathbf{v} \cdot (\mathbf{y}_i - \mathbf{y}_j) = 0$ for any $\mathbf{y}_i, \mathbf{y}_j \in X$. Substituting $\mathbf{v}$ by the expression above yields $n - 1$ linearly independent equations. For example, in order to warrant that a vector is orthogonal to a triangle, the vector must be orthogonal to two edges of the triangle. Thus, for a set of n points, we have n linear equations that uniquely determine the closest point.

Johnson's algorithm uses a recursive formulation for the solution of the system of equations. Each subsimplex X of Y is represented by a set of indices $I_X \subseteq \{1, \ldots, n\}$, where n is the number of vertices in Y. Let $X = \{\mathbf{y}_i : i \in I_X\}$ be a subsimplex. Then, the barycentric coordinates of the closest point of $\text{aff}(X)$ are given by

$$\lambda_i = \frac{\Delta_i^X}{\Delta^X},$$

and Δ_i^X is defined recursively as

$$\Delta_i^{\{\mathbf{y}_i\}} = 1,$$

$$\Delta_j^{X \cup \{\mathbf{y}_j\}} = \sum_{i \in I_X} \Delta_i^X (\mathbf{y}_i \cdot (\mathbf{y}_k - \mathbf{y}_j)) \quad \text{for } j \notin I_X \text{ and any } k \in I_X,$$

and finally, Δ^X is defined as

$$\Delta^X = \sum_{i \in I_X} \Delta_i^X.$$

This recursive solution is obtained by applying Cramer's rule and cofactor expansion [van den Bergen 03].

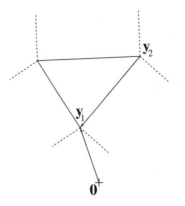

Figure 5.4. The Voronoi regions of the subsimplices of a triangle are bounded by dashed lines. The origin lies in the Voronoi region of $\{\mathbf{y}_1\}$. The plane test for subsimplex $\{\mathbf{y}_1, \mathbf{y}_2\}$ at $\mathbf{y}_1$ is negative, since $\Delta_2^{\{\mathbf{y}_1, \mathbf{y}_2\}} = \mathbf{y}_1 \cdot (\mathbf{y}_1 - \mathbf{y}_2) < 0$.

Now, let $\mathbf{v}$ be the point closest to the origin of the simplex given by Y, and let X be the smallest subsimplex of Y that contains $\mathbf{v}$. It is not very difficult to see that $\mathbf{v}$ is also the closest point of the affine hull of X. So, a naive solution for computing the closest point of a simplex would be to compute the closest point of the affine hull of each subsimplex, reject the subsimplices for which the barycentric coordinates of the closest point are not all positive, and of the remaining subsimplices select the one that is closest to the origin.

However, we can do better than that. There is a cheaper way to determine the closest subsimplex, and for this purpose, we introduce the concept of Voronoi regions. Each subsimplex has a region of space associated with it in which the origin must lie in order for that subsimplex to be the closest one. We call this the *Voronoi region* of the subsimplex. Figure 5.4 shows the Voronoi regions of the subsimplices of a triangle in two dimensions. In three dimensions, the Voronoi regions are bounded by planes. By testing the origin against the planes, we can quickly find the closest subsimplex. The Δ_i^X values tell us on which side of a Voronoi region the origin lies. A positive value indicates that the origin lies on the inside of the associated Voronoi plane. The associated Voronoi plane of Δ_i^X is the plane orthogonal to X *not* containing $\mathbf{y}_i$. For example, in Figure 5.4, the plane orthogonal to the edge $\{\mathbf{y}_1, \mathbf{y}_2\}$ through $\mathbf{y}_1$ is associated with $\Delta_2^{\{\mathbf{y}_1, \mathbf{y}_2\}}$.

The smallest $X \subseteq Y$ such that $\mathbf{v} \in \mathrm{conv}(X)$ can now be characterized as the subset X for which (a) $\Delta_i^X > 0$ for each $i \in I_X$ and (b) $\Delta_j^{X \cup \{\mathbf{y}_j\}} \leq 0$ for all $j \notin I_X$. Thus, the origin lies within the bounds of subsimplex X but not within the bounds of a bigger subsimplex containing X. Johnson's algorithm successively tests each nonempty subset X of Y until it finds one for which (a) and (b) hold.

In theory, we do not need to test all subsimplices, only the ones containing the most recently added vertex [van den Bergen 99, van den Bergen 03]. However, in practice, it often occurs that due to rounding errors, a termination condition of GJK is not met and the last-added vertex is thrown off. So, for the sake of robustness, it is better to check all subsimplices.

Johnson's algorithm has been heavily debated in the game physics community. Admittedly, the formulation is not very intuitive, which may explain why it tends to scare implementors away and makes them look for a solution in more geometrically familiar concepts. This chapter attempts to explain Johnson's algorithm in geometric terms in order to encourage the reader to stay with this formulation. The formulation has a number of advantages over ad hoc solutions for finding the closest point of a simplex.

First of all, the formulation has a lot of opportunities for reuse of intermediate computations. The Δ_i^X values for lower-dimensional subsimplices can be used for computing the values for the higher-dimensional subsimplices. Reuse of these values extends over iterations, since each new simplex is based on the previous one.

Contrary to popular belief [Muratori 06], an abundant amount of reuse from earlier iterations is possible, even if only the subsimplices that contain the last-added support point are tested. Despite the increased importance of data cache coherence and the gain in raw computing power in modern CPU architectures, reuse of earlier computations may still be worthwhile. A caching scheme for the Δ_i^X values as suggested in [van den Bergen 99] requires 512 bytes of storage using double precision and can easily fit in an L1 data cache. Of course, the problem is keeping it there. Timing when to prefetch the data is tricky: too early will get the data trashed back to memory, too late will stall the read.

However, better performance is not our only concern. Caching of intermediate values may result in loss of precision. In the x86 architecture, floating-point registers are 80 bits wide, whereas a double-precision floating-point variable is usually 64 bits wide. Saved values from previous iterations will be rounded down unless they are stored in a type that is wide enough. Unfortunately, not all compilers support storing floating-point numbers at 80-bit precision [Wikipedia 10a].

All things considered, reuse of computations from earlier iterations takes quite some effort to make it pay off. However, reusing computations within a single iteration is much easier and offers a substantial performance gain. Here, the intermedate values do not need to go through memory and often can be kept in floating-point registers. The recursive formulation can be exploited successfully when multiple subsimplices need to be checked in a single iteration. This would be the case for triangles and tetrahedra, which are the common cases in GJK.

Finally, after you get a feel for it, the formulation is actually very simple and offers a clean way to control precision. It is simple, since there is no case distinction. The formula works the same for simplices of any dimension. Of course, we can add case distinction based on the number of vertices, and if we want to maximize reuse within an iteration, that actually would be a smart thing to do. However, the structure of all computations remains the same: we start by computing the Δ_i^X values for edges first, then for triangles, and finally for a tetrahedron, reusing the values from lower-dimensional simplices in the higher-dimensional ones.

Simplicity is also nice for controlling precision. Basically, there are only two places where precision is lost. Cancellation happens in the dot product and in the summation of cofactor terms. We can reduce loss of precision due to cancellation by making sure that the vector $\mathbf{y}_k - \mathbf{y}_j$ that is used as an argument in the dot product is as short as possible [van den Bergen 03]. We have some freedom in the choice of $\mathbf{y}_k$, so we choose the $\mathbf{y}_k \in X$ closest to $\mathbf{y}_j$.

The division by Δ^X can be skipped or at least postponed if we rely on different termination criteria, since only the direction of $\mathbf{v}$ is required for computing the support points [Muratori 06]. This is an interesting idea since it allows us to compute the direction of $\mathbf{v}$ directly from the closest subsimplex without the need to go through barycentric coordinates, potentially giving us better precision. However, for selecting the closest subsimplex, we still need to do the Voronoi plane tests, so the direct approach does not offer us a more reliable closest-subsimplex selection. Furthermore, the need for the (squared) length of $\mathbf{v}$ rises if termination is guarded by testing whether each iteration makes significant progress towards the closest point. Divisions do not reduce precision and since only one is needed per iteration, they take less than five percent of the total computation time, so performance is not harmed too much by keeping the division.

5.6   Continuous Collision Detection

We are now ready to solve the problem of how to perform collision detection in continuous space-time. As mentioned earlier, objects move only by translation between time steps. For each instance of time $t \in [0, 1]$ between two time steps, the configuration of objects A and B is given by $A + t\mathbf{c}_A$ and $B + t\mathbf{c}_B$. Let $\mathbf{r} = \mathbf{c}_B - \mathbf{c}_A$ be the relative target translation over the time interval. Then, the earliest time the objects come in contact is given by the smallest t for which

$$t\mathbf{r} \in A - B.$$

We need to perform a ray cast on the CSO to find the t at the first hit. We will denote this instance of time by t_{hit}. The corresponding point $t_{\text{hit}}\mathbf{r}$ is called the *hit spot*. If the origin is not contained in $A - B$, meaning $t_{\text{hit}} > 0$, then the hit spot must be a point on the boundary of $A - B$. In that case, there exists a proper normal at the hit spot.

A nonzero vector $\mathbf{n}$ and a point $\mathbf{p}$ on the boundary of the CSO define a supporting plane if

$$\mathbf{n} \cdot \mathbf{p} = \max\{\mathbf{n} \cdot \mathbf{x} : \mathbf{x} \in A - B\}.$$

A supporting plane exists for all points on the boundary as long as the CSO is convex. Clearly, any nonzero vector $\mathbf{n}$ is a normal of a supporting plane at $s_{A-B}(\mathbf{n})$.

Let us make a few observations. For a supporting plane with normal $\mathbf{n}$ and point $\mathbf{p}$ on the boundary of $A-B$, we know that all points $\mathbf{x}$ for which $\mathbf{n}\cdot\mathbf{x} > \mathbf{n}\cdot\mathbf{p}$ are not contained in $A - B$. Now, let $\mathbf{x} = t\mathbf{r}$ be a point on the ray. We find that the section of the ray corresponding to

$$t\mathbf{n} \cdot \mathbf{r} > \mathbf{n} \cdot \mathbf{p}$$

is not contained in $A - B$, and thus cannot contain the hit spot. More specifically, for

$$t_{\text{clip}} = \frac{\mathbf{n} \cdot \mathbf{p}}{\mathbf{n} \cdot \mathbf{r}},$$

we know the following:

1. If $\mathbf{n} \cdot \mathbf{r} < 0$, then t_{clip} is a lower bound for t_{hit}. Moreover, if $\mathbf{n} \cdot \mathbf{p} < 0$, then t_{clip} is positive and indeed the ray is clipped.

2. If $\mathbf{n} \cdot \mathbf{r} > 0$, then t_{clip} is an upper bound for t_{hit}. Now, if $\mathbf{n} \cdot \mathbf{p} < 0$, then t_{clip} is negative and the ray can be rejected since it will never hit the CSO.

3. If $\mathbf{n} \cdot \mathbf{r} = 0$, then the ray is not clipped at all. Furthermore, if $\mathbf{n} \cdot \mathbf{p} < 0$, then the ray can be rejected as well, since it completely lies in the positive half-space of the supporting plane.

Note that in all three cases the ray is either clipped by or completely contained in the positive half-space of the supporting plane if $\mathbf{n} \cdot \mathbf{p} < 0$.

Our strategy for computing t_{hit} is to iteratively clip sections of the ray that are guaranteed not to intersect the CSO until we arrive at the hit spot. This approach is generally known as *conservative advancement* [Mirtich and Canny 95];

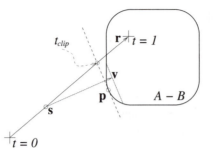

Figure 5.5. A new lower bound t_{clip} is found by clipping the ray $\mathbf{r}$ using the supporting plane at $\mathbf{p} = s_{A-B}(-\mathbf{v})$.

however, in our case, we perform the advancement inside GJK. We do regular GJK iterations and use the supporting planes that are generated in each iteration as clipping planes. Each time we find a new lower bound t_{clip}, time is advanced to this value. In terms of configuration space, we say that the origin is "shifted" to $t_{\text{clip}}\mathbf{r}$. Of course, conceptually the origin does not move along the ray. Instead, the CSO moves in the opposite direction.

Let $\mathbf{s} = t\mathbf{r}$ be the current lower bound for the hit spot. Then the current CSO is $A-B-\mathbf{s}$. In search of the point of the CSO closest to the origin, GJK generates a supporting plane with normal $-\mathbf{v}$ and support point $\mathbf{p} = s_{A-B}(-\mathbf{v})$. We can identify the intersection point of the plane and the ray as

$$t_{\text{clip}} = \frac{\mathbf{v} \cdot \mathbf{p}}{\mathbf{v} \cdot \mathbf{r}}$$

and find the following:

1. If $\mathbf{v} \cdot \mathbf{r} > 0$, then t_{clip} is a lower bound for t_{hit}, and if $\mathbf{v} \cdot \mathbf{p} > t\mathbf{v} \cdot \mathbf{r}$, then $t_{\text{clip}} > t$, which means that we found a better lower bound. See Figure 5.5 for an illustration of this case.

2. If $\mathbf{v} \cdot \mathbf{r} < 0$, then t_{clip} is an upper bound for t_{hit}, and if $\mathbf{v} \cdot \mathbf{p} > t\mathbf{v} \cdot \mathbf{r}$, then $t_{\text{clip}} < t$, which means we have evidence that the ray misses.

3. If $\mathbf{v} \cdot \mathbf{r} = 0$, then the ray is not clipped at all, and if $\mathbf{v} \cdot \mathbf{p} > 0$, then the ray misses as well, since it is completely contained in the positive half-space of the supporting plane.

Again, we see that for all three cases, if $\mathbf{v} \cdot \mathbf{p} > t\mathbf{v} \cdot \mathbf{r}$, then the ray can either be clipped or rejected. As long as this condition is not valid, we continue performing regular GJK iterations. Note that we need to search for the closest point of the translated CSO, so we must add $\mathbf{p} - \mathbf{s}$, rather than $\mathbf{p}$, to the current simplex. Each time a better lower bound is found, the current simplex is flushed and GJK is restarted using the last-found support point as the initial simplex. An alternative to flushing the simplex would be to translate it along with the CSO. However, this approach is not advised since simplices generated from the translated simplex may be close to being affinely dependent, causing all sorts of numerical issues.

Algorithm 2 GJK-based continuous collision test. For positive results, this algorithm terminates with t being the time of impact, $\mathbf{s}$ the hit spot, and $\mathbf{n}$ the normal at $\mathbf{s}$.

$t \leftarrow 0$;
$\mathbf{s} \leftarrow \mathbf{0}$;
$\mathbf{n} \leftarrow \mathbf{0}$;
$\mathbf{v} \leftarrow$ *arbitrary point in* $A - B$;
$W \leftarrow \emptyset$;
while $\|\mathbf{v}\|^2 > \varepsilon^2$ do
begin
    $\mathbf{p} \leftarrow s_{A-B}(-\mathbf{v})$;
    if $\mathbf{v} \cdot \mathbf{p} > t\mathbf{v} \cdot \mathbf{r}$ then
    begin
      if $\mathbf{v} \cdot \mathbf{r} > 0$ then
      begin
        $t = \frac{\mathbf{v} \cdot \mathbf{p}}{\mathbf{v} \cdot \mathbf{r}}$;
        if $t > 1$ then return false;
        $\mathbf{s} \leftarrow t\mathbf{r}$;
        $W \leftarrow \emptyset$;
        $\mathbf{n} \leftarrow -\mathbf{v}$
      end
      else return false;
    end;
    $Y \leftarrow W \cup \{\mathbf{p} - \mathbf{s}\}$;
    $\mathbf{v} \leftarrow$ point closest to the origin of $\text{conv}(Y)$;
    $W \leftarrow$ *smallest* $X \subseteq Y$ *such that* $\mathbf{v} \in \text{conv}(X)$
end;
return true

The algorithm terminates when either $\mathbf{s}$ is close enough to $A - B$ or we find evidence that the ray does not intersect $A - B$. Since the ray has a finite length, we can also return a miss as soon as the lower bound t becomes greater than one. The distance of $\mathbf{s}$ to $A - B$ is approximated by $\|\mathbf{v}\|$, so an obvious termination condition is $\|\mathbf{v}\|^2 \leq \varepsilon^2$, where ε is the set tolerance for the absolute error of the hit spot. Algorithm 2 describes the GJK-based continuous collision test in pseudocode.

As mentioned, we can only progress if $\mathbf{v} \cdot \mathbf{p} > t\mathbf{v} \cdot \mathbf{r}$. Note that the sequence $\{\mathbf{v}_k\}$ generated by GJK can have a wild behavior, especially in the first few iterations, so it is not guaranteed that this condition is immediately met. However, the condition must become valid in a finite number of iterations. This can be shown as follows. First of all, for regular GJK iterations, $\|\mathbf{v}_k\|^2 - \mathbf{v}_k \cdot \mathbf{w}_k$ approaches zero. Since $\|\mathbf{v}_k\|^2 > 0$, we see that $\mathbf{v}_k \cdot \mathbf{w}_k$ must become positive in a finite number of iterations. It follows from

$$
\begin{aligned}
\mathbf{v} \cdot \mathbf{w} &= \mathbf{v} \cdot (\mathbf{p} - \mathbf{s}) \\
&= \mathbf{v} \cdot (\mathbf{p} - t\mathbf{r}) \\
&= \mathbf{v} \cdot \mathbf{p} - t\mathbf{v} \cdot \mathbf{r}
\end{aligned}
$$

that, within a finite number of iterations, our condition must be valid. So, as long as $\mathbf{s}$ is not contained in $A - B$, it takes a finite number of GJK iterations to either get closer to the hit spot or find a condition for rejecting the complete ray. Note that progress along the ray is a necessary yet not sufficient condition for global convergence. The interested reader is referred to [van den Bergen 04] for a proof that Algorithm 2 is indeed guaranteed to terminate at the hit spot, should one exist.

The returned normal at the hit spot is the normal of the last supporting plane that clipped the ray. If the objects A and B are intersecting at time $t = 0$, then of course the ray is never clipped, and the algorithm terminates returning a zero hit spot and normal. This all makes perfect sense since if the objects are already intersecting then the normal at the first time of impact is not defined.

Note that in contrast to the GJK distance algorithm, the CSO may change position during iterations. The CSO is given by $A - B - \mathbf{s}$ and changes position each time $\mathbf{s}$ is updated. These updates result in a behavior that deviates from the normal behavior of GJK. First of all, $\|\mathbf{v}_k\|$ is no longer monotonically decreasing in k. Secondly, the same support point may be returned over multiple iterations.

With the original GJK, generating the same support point twice is theoretically impossible. Since it is a clear sign of numerical problems in a finite-precision implementation of GJK, this property can be exploited to exit gracefully should a support point ever reappear [van den Bergen 99]. For the GJK ray cast, we can still rely on this property for signaling numerical problems; however, we need to take care that the support-point history is flushed along with the simplex whenever $\mathbf{s}$ is updated.

An issue that needs some attention is the choice of error tolerance ε in the termination condition. The relative error in the computed value for $\mathbf{v}$ can be quite large. We have found that the error in the squared length of $\mathbf{v}$ is roughly proportional to the maximum squared length of a vector in Y. So, a robust implementation would use as termination condition

$$\|\mathbf{v}\|^2 \le \varepsilon_{\text{tol}} \max\{\|\mathbf{y}\|^2 : \mathbf{y} \in Y\},$$

where ε_{tol} is an order of magnitude larger than the machine epsilon of the used floating-point format. Choosing a tolerance ε_{tol} that is too small may result in infinite looping, since then the rounding noise in the computation of $\|\mathbf{v}\|^2$ can become greater than ε_{tol} times the maximum squared length of a vector $\mathbf{y} \in Y$.

The convergence speed depends on the used shape types. We have found the worst convergence for quadric shapes such as spheres and cylinders. For a quadric, the average number of iterations is roughly proportional to $-\log(\varepsilon_{\text{tol}})$. For instance, an ε_{tol} of 10^{-6} results in eight iterations on average for random rays with a high hit probability. Polytopes usually take fewer iterations.

For collision detection, the performance of GJK can be boosted by allowing an early out as soon as $\mathbf{v}$ becomes a separating axis [van den Bergen 99]. Frame coherence can be exploited by caching this axis and using it as the initial $\mathbf{v}$ in the next frame. A similar scheme can be used for the GJK ray cast. In case of a miss, $\mathbf{v}$ is a separating axis of the ray and the object CSO. If the configuration of objects does not change a lot over time, then this separating axis is likely to be a separating axis in the next frame as well. By initializing $\mathbf{v}$ with a previously returned separating axis, the number of iterations per frame can be reduced considerably. Note that since this $\mathbf{v}$ may no longer be contained in $A - B$, it is necessary to skip the termination test for the first iteration. Overall, a continuous GJK collision test that exploits earlier separating axes is only slightly more expensive than the static version.

5.7 Contacts

A contact between two objects is defined by a contact point and an orientation of the contact plane. The plane separates the two objects at the contact point. In physics-based simulations, contact constraints should keep the objects from further interpenetrating at the contact point. Usually, a force or impulse along the contact normal is applied in order to take care of this. The objects are, of course, free to move away from each other, so normal forces or impulses act in only one direction. Furthermore, objects in contact usually experience friction. Friction acts laterally, i.e., along the contact plane.

The collision handler should return a contact point and normal for each colliding pair of convex objects. The continuous collision test described in Section 5.6 returns these contact data for the first time of contact. The problem is that if the objects are already interpenetrating at the beginning of the time step, then no normal is defined. For these cases, which generally are resting contacts, we need a different method for computing the proper contact data.

We could compute a pair of witness points to the penetration depth. The penetration-depth vector is orthogonal to the boundaries of the objects and as such is a pretty good approximation of a contact normal. The corresponding witness points could pass as contact points with reasonable fidelity. There are, however, a few issues with using the penetration depth for obtaining contact data.

First of all, computing the penetration depth is often a lot harder than computing the distance. For general convex objects, the penetration depth can be found using the *expanding polytope algorithm* (EPA) [van den Bergen 03]. EPA is computationally a lot more expensive than GJK and has some initialization problems for shallow contacts. If we restrict ourselves to polytopes, we can resort to feature-walking or brute-force approaches, but still, the conclusion would remain that computing penetration depths is harder than computing distances.

Secondly, for triangle meshes, the penetration-depth vectors of the individual triangles that intersect a query object may not be a good representation of the actual contact. The shortest translation that separates the object from a triangle may have a significant lateral component, so an object that intersects an edge between two triangles is likely to collect two "fighting" normals that point towards each other. Figure 5.6 depicts this situation. In any physics system, these fighting normals would show the edge as an obstacle along the path of a sliding or rolling object, making the object bump into the edge and change direction. Obviously, this behavior is not what we want.

It is clear that an algorithm for computing penetration depths, such as EPA, is not our best option for getting contact data, at least not for shallow contacts. For shallow contacts, we are better off computing closest-point pairs. However, in order to return a proper normal from a closest-point pair, the query objects need to have some clearance, since otherwise, the closest points coincide and the normal will be zero.

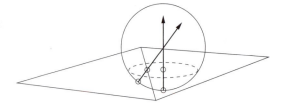

Figure 5.6. Contact normals that are derived from the penetration-depth vectors may cause a sliding or rolling object to bump into an edge of a perfectly flat mesh.

In order to make this possible, we will need to dilate at least one of the objects by a small radius. We will call the part of the object that is formed by dilation the *skin* and the rest of the body the *bone*. If only the skins overlap, then we can compute the contact data using the closest points of the bones. For deeper penetrations, we can fall back to the penetration depth for our contact data.

We combine the collision test of the dilated objects and the computation of the closest points of the bones into a single GJK query rather than perform a separate test for each of the two operations. Of course, it suffices to simply compute the distance between the bones, since the dilated objects intersect only if the distance between the bones is not greater than the sum of the radii of the skins. However, we can do a little better.

Often it is not necessary to compute an accurate distance, since once we have evidence that the distance is greater than the sum of the radii, we can exit early. GJK maintains a lower bound for the distance in the form of

$$\frac{\mathbf{v}_k \cdot \mathbf{w}_k}{\|\mathbf{v}_k\|}.$$

If this value ever gets greater than $\rho_A + \rho_B$, the sum of the radii of objects A and B, then we may exit. Again, we do not like to evaluate $\|\mathbf{v}\|$ since this involves a square root, so we square out both ends of the inequality, but not before checking whether $\mathbf{v}_k \cdot \mathbf{w}_k$ is positive. The added termination condition now becomes

$$\mathbf{v}_k \cdot \mathbf{w}_k > 0 \ \text{ and } \ \frac{(\mathbf{v}_k \cdot \mathbf{w}_k)^2}{\|\mathbf{v}_k\|^2} > (\rho_A + \rho_B)^2.$$

Algorithm 3 describes the hybrid approach in pseudocode.

Falling back to a penetration-depth query should only happen in emergencies. Under normal conditions, the objects should only intersect with their skins. The question remains of how to pick a proper radius for the dilation. Under the assumption that high-velocity impacts are resolved using the contact data from the continuous collision detection algorithm discussed in Section 5.6, it is safe to conclude that the hybrid approach only needs to compute contact data for resting contacts.

Depending on the physics engine's contact solver and the type of application, the dilation radius may vary, but let us assume that the resting object is allowed to drop into the other object by the distance it can move in a single frame due to gravity. If we start with a relative velocity of zero, the traversed distance is $\frac{1}{2}gt^2$, where g is the gravitational acceleration and t is the frame time. For an acceleration[2] of 20 m/s^2 and a frame time of 0.033 seconds, this results in a distance of

---

[2]Games usually have a gravitational acceleration that is greater than 9.8 m/s^2.

Algorithm 3 The hybrid approach to computing contact data using GJK. Objects A and B are dilated by respective radii ρ_A and ρ_B. Here, the contact data are a normal $\mathbf{n}$ and a pair of points $\mathbf{p}_A$ and $\mathbf{p}_B$ on the dilated boundaries of the respective objects. Any distances less than tolerance ε_{tol} are assumed to be zero, which means that contact data need to be obtained from a penetration-depth query.

$\mathbf{v} \leftarrow$ *arbitrary point in* $A - B$;
$W \leftarrow \emptyset$;
$\mathbf{w} \leftarrow s_{A-B}(-\mathbf{v})$;
while $\|\mathbf{v}\|^2 - \mathbf{v} \cdot \mathbf{w} > \varepsilon^2$ do
begin
    if $\mathbf{v} \cdot \mathbf{w} > 0$ and $\frac{(\mathbf{v} \cdot \mathbf{w})^2}{\|\mathbf{v}\|^2} > (\rho_A + \rho_B)^2$ then
        $\{\!\{$ *The dilated objects do not intersect.* $\}\!\}$
        return false
    $Y \leftarrow W \cup \{\mathbf{w}\}$;
    $\mathbf{v} \leftarrow$ *point closest to the origin of* $\mathrm{conv}(Y)$;
    $W \leftarrow$ *smallest* $X \subseteq Y$ *such that* $\mathbf{v} \in \mathrm{conv}(X)$;
    $\mathbf{w} \leftarrow s_{A-B}(-\mathbf{v})$;
end;
if $\|\mathbf{v}\|^2 > \varepsilon^2$ then $\{\!\{$ *Only the skins overlap.* $\}\!\}$
begin
    Compute the closest points $\mathbf{p}_A$ and $\mathbf{p}_B$ of the bones.
    $\{\!\{$ *Move the witness points to the skin boundaries.* $\}\!\}$
    $\mathbf{n} \leftarrow \frac{\mathbf{v}}{\|\mathbf{v}\|}$;
    $\mathbf{p}_A \leftarrow \mathbf{p}_A - \rho_A \mathbf{n}$;
    $\mathbf{p}_B \leftarrow \mathbf{p}_B + \rho_B \mathbf{n}$
end
else $\{\!\{$ *The distance between the bones is (close to) zero.* $\}\!\}$
    Compute contact data from penetration depth.;
return true

---

roughly one centimeter. Under these conditions, a combined radius of one or two centimeters will do.

For computing the closest points $\mathbf{p}_A$ and $\mathbf{p}_B$, additional data concerning the individual objects A and B need to be maintained along with the current simplex. Recall that each vertex of the simplex is obtained from the support mapping s_{A-B}, which is given by

$$s_{A-B}(\mathbf{v}) = s_A(\mathbf{v}) - s_B(-\mathbf{v}).$$

So each $\mathbf{w}_i \in W$ is the vector difference of $\mathbf{a}_i = s_A(\mathbf{v})$ and $\mathbf{b}_i = s_B(-\mathbf{v})$ for some $\mathbf{v}$. Furthermore, recall that at termination the point $\mathbf{v}$ is expressed as an affine combination of W:

$$\mathbf{v} = \lambda_1 \mathbf{w}_1 + \cdots + \lambda_n \mathbf{w}_n.$$

Now, the closest points $\mathbf{p}_A$ and $\mathbf{p}_B$ are computed simply as

$$\begin{aligned}
\mathbf{p}_A &= \lambda_1 \mathbf{a}_1 + \cdots + \lambda_n \mathbf{a}_n, \quad \text{and} \\
\mathbf{p}_B &= \lambda_1 \mathbf{b}_1 + \cdots + \lambda_n \mathbf{b}_n.
\end{aligned}$$

Since the barycentric coordinates λ_i are all positive, $\mathbf{p}_A$ and $\mathbf{p}_B$ must be contained, respectively, by A and B. It is easy to verify that $\mathbf{v} = \mathbf{p}_A - \mathbf{p}_B$, so $\mathbf{p}_A$ and $\mathbf{p}_B$ are indeed closest points of A and B.

The hybrid approach serves as a faster and more robust alternative to a vanilla penetration-depth method, but it still has the same problem when it comes to finding contacts for triangle meshes. When sliding from one triangle to an adjacent one, the normal direction may change dramatically depending on the skin thickness and penetration depth. In order to experience smooth contacts, the mapping of normals to the surface should be continuous.

Smoothly varying surface normals are being used in computer graphics to solve pretty much the same problem: hiding the internal edges of a mesh [Wikipedia 10b]. In a graphical mesh, the normals are usually given only at the vertices. A normal at an arbitrary point in a triangle is computed by interpolating the normals at the triangle's vertices. The easiest interpolation technique that achieves a continuous normal field on the surface is simply a normalized linear interpolation. Here, the normal is computed by adding the vertex normals weighted by the barycentric coordinates of the point in the triangle and normalizing the result. More sophisticated interpolation techniques exist as well [van Overveld and Wyvill 97].

In solving our "bumpy edge" problem, we also apply normal interpolation. We will use the hybrid approach to compute the closest points of the query object and the triangles in the mesh that collide with it. However, instead of using the difference of the closest points, we use the surface normal at the closest point on the mesh as our contact normal. So, we need to have vertex normals for the collision mesh and a way to compute the barycentric coordinates of the closest point in the mesh.

We already have barycentric coordinates for the closest point at termination; however, these are computed for the closest point of the CSO. Although the current simplex W is affinely independent, the associated support points $\mathbf{a}_i$ and $\mathbf{b}_i$ of the individual objects A and B may contain duplicates. Getting the barycentric

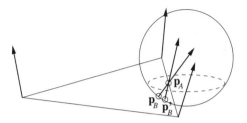

Figure 5.7. Instead of the penetration-depth vector, we use the interpolated surface normal at $\mathbf{p}_A$ for triangle meshes. The contact point $\mathbf{p}_B$ is mapped to $\mathbf{p}'_B$ in order to align it with the surface normal.

coordinates for the point on a triangle is not difficult. We simply need to add the barycentric coordinates of the duplicate vertices to find the coordinates for that vertex. It helps to store a vertex index 0, 1, or 2 with each of the support points to quickly find duplicates and store the barycentric coordinates in the correct order.

After changing the orientation of the contact plane to the interpolated surface normal of the mesh, the closest point on the query object is no longer aligned with the closest point on the mesh and should be remapped. Otherwise, the objects may receive an unwanted torque from the contact solver. A proper contact point on the boundary of the query object can be found by multiplying the interpolated surface normal by the penetration depth and subtracting it from the contact point on the mesh. Let $\mathbf{p}_A$ and $\mathbf{p}_B$ be the closest points on, respectively, the mesh and the query object, and let $\vec{n}$ be the interpolated surface normal. Then, the corrected contact point $\mathbf{p}'_B$ on the query object is computed as

$$\mathbf{p}'_B = \mathbf{p}_A - \mathbf{n}\|\mathbf{p}_A - \mathbf{p}_B\|.$$

Figure 5.7 illustrates the remapping of the contact point. Note that the corrected contact point may not lie perfectly on the boundary of the query object, but for our purposes it is good enough.

Vertex normals are usually created by a content-creation tool and are stored with vertex positions in the mesh. They are not hard to compute, in case they are missing in the collision mesh. A vertex normal is the weighted sum of the face normals of the adjacent triangles. As a weight the angle of the triangle's edges at the vertex should be used. Without the angles as weights, the normals would be pulled too much to where there are many adjacent triangles. The angle defines the amount of "pull" that a triangle can have on a vertex normal.

As in graphics, more detail can be added by using a normal map rather than an interpolated normal. A normal map is a two-dimensional texture image that contains normal x, y, z-coordinates rather than RGB colors. Instead of the vertex normals, the texture coordinates at the vertices are interpolated using barycentric coordinates. The resulting texture coordinates are used for fetching the proper normal from a texture. Normal maps can be used to create bumps on a flat surface, for instance, for modeling metal grating or brick roads. In the future, when haptic feedback takes a more prominent role in the gaming experience, normal maps can help enrich the world perception and are expected to be a common part of any physics system.

5.8   Conclusion

With the addition of the continuous collision test presented in Section 5.6, GJK remains the most versatile algorithm for performing proximity queries. This single algorithm computes space-time collisions, distances, common points, separating axes, and ray casts. Together with the hybrid approach for computing the penetration depth, we have a complete tool set for finding contact data. The beauty of it all is that GJK and EPA are applicable to any combination of convex shape types. The use of support mappings for reading geometry offers new methods for representing shapes in game environments and removes the need for representing convex shapes with polygonal surfaces. Moreover, GJK is one of the fastest algorithms available for collision detection between convex polytopes and offers a smooth tradeoff between accuracy and speed.

The application domain is not restricted to convex shapes: in Section 5.7, we presented a solution for finding contact data between triangle meshes and convex shapes. Even the most basic three-dimensional game will have a convex shape sliding, rolling, or strafing along a triangle mesh, so obtaining smooth contacts for these cases should receive top priority.

Bibliography

[Cameron 85] S. Cameron.   "A Study of the Clash Detection Problem in Robotics." In *Proceedings of the IEEE International Conference on Robotics and Automation*, pp. 488–493. Los Alamitos, CA: IEEE Press, 1985.

[Cameron 90] S. Cameron. "Collision Detection by Four-Dimensional Intersection Testing." *IEEE Transactions on Robotics and Automation* 6:3 (1990), 291–302.

[Canny 86] John Canny. "Collision Detection for Moving Polyhedra." *IEEE Transactions on Pattern Analysis and Machine Intelligence* 8:2 (1986), 200–209.

[Eckstein and Schömer 99] Jens Eckstein and Elmar Schömer. "Dynamic Collision Detection in Virtual Reality Applications." In *Proceedings of the 7th International Conference in Central Europe on Computer Graphics, Visualization, and Interactive Digital Media'99*, pp. 71–78. Winter School of Computer Graphics, 1999.

[Gilbert and Foo 90] E. G. Gilbert and C.-P. Foo. "Computing the Distance between General Convex Objects in Three-Dimensional Space." *IEEE Transactions on Robotics and Automation* 6:1 (1990), 53–61.

[Gilbert et al. 88] E. G. Gilbert, D. W. Johnson, and S. S. Keerthi. "A Fast Procedure for Computing the Distance between Complex Objects in Three-Dimensional Space." *IEEE Journal of Robotics and Automation* 4:2 (1988), 193–203.

[Hubbard 93] P. M. Hubbard. "Space-Time Bounds for Collision Detection." Technical Report CS-93-04, Department of Computer Science, Brown University, 1993.

[Mirtich and Canny 95] Brian Mirtich and John Canny. "Impulse-Based Simulation of Rigid Bodies." In *Proceedings of the 1995 Symposium on Interactive 3D Graphics*, pp. 181–188. New York: ACM Press, 1995.

[Muratori 06] Casey Muratori. "Implementing GJK." 2006. Available at http://mollyrocket.com/849.

[Redon et al. 02] Stéphane Redon, Abderrahmane Kheddar, and Sabine Coquillart. "Fast Continuous Collision Detection between Rigid Bodies." 21:3 (2002), 279–288.

[Schömer and Thiel 95] Elmar Schömer and Christian Thiel. "Efficient Collision Detection for Moving Polyhedra." In *Proceedings of the 11th Annual ACM Symposium on Computational Geometry*, pp. 51–60. New York: ACM Press, 1995.

[van den Bergen 99] Gino van den Bergen. "A Fast and Robust GJK Implementation for Collision Detection of Convex Objects." *Journal of Graphics Tools* 4:2 (1999), 7–25.

[van den Bergen 03] Gino van den Bergen. *Collision Detection in Interactive 3D Environments.* San Francisco: Morgan Kaufmann, 2003.

[van den Bergen 04] Gino van den Bergen. "Ray Casting against General Convex Objects with Application to Continuous Collision Detection." 2004. Available at http://www.dtecta.com/papers/unpublished04raycast.pdf.

[van Overveld and Wyvill 97] C. W. A. M. van Overveld and B. Wyvill. "Phong Normal Interpolation Revisited." *ACM Transactions on Graphics* 16:4 (1997), 397–419.

[Wikipedia 10a] Wikipedia. "Long Double." 2010. Available at http://en.wikipedia.org/wiki/Long_double.

[Wikipedia 10b] Wikipedia. "Phong Shading." 2010. Available at http://en.wikipedia.org/wiki/Phong_shading.

− III −

Particles

– 6 –

Optimized SPH

Kees van Kooten

6.1 Introduction

Smoothed particle hydrodynamics (SPH) [Monaghan 88] is a method for simulating nonrigid substances in real time as clouds of particles, with applications ranging from water to soft bodies and gaseous phenomena. Contrary to fluid simulations based on a fixed Eulerian grid, as treated in [Harlow and Welch 65] and [Stam 99], the particle cloud is free to move anywhere in space and dynamically change the resolution of any area of the simulation to suit its importance to the observer.

The concept of SPH employs smooth scalar functions that map points in space to a mass density. These scalar functions, referred to as *smoothing kernels*, represent point masses that are centered at particle positions and smoothed out over a small volume of space, similar to a Gaussian blur in two-dimensional image processing. The combined set of smoothing kernels defines a density field; the density at a point is the summation over the function of every individual smoothing kernel in the set. The density field is used in the SPH equations to derive a force field, which governs the motion of the particles within the fluid.

SPH can be implemented in many different ways, both as a sequential algorithm running on a CPU [Müller et al. 03] and in parallel on a Cell processor [Hjelte 06] or GPU [Harada et al. 07]. To visualize the state of the simulation, most often the concept of metaballs is employed. This is a type of implicit surface invented by Blinn in the early 1980s [Blinn 82], used to achieve a fluid-like appearance. To approximate the shape of this implicit surface, many different visualization methods have been proposed, ranging from classical methods like marching cubes [Lorensen and Cline 87] to ray tracing [Kanamori et al. 08], point-based visualizations [van Kooten et al. 07], various screen-space methods based on depth field smoothing [van der Laan et al. 09], or screen-space meshes [Müller et al. 07], and combinations of any of the aforementioned techniques [Zhang et al. 08]. The preferred technique for both the simulation and the visualization task depends heavily on the purpose of the simulation and the target platform of the implementation.

This chapter does not focus on the visualization of the metaballs. We will solely focus on the SPH simulation—the algorithms forming the basis of SPH and their implementation. Also, we will not focus on an implementation specific to a particular target platform, as the current emergence of parallel architectures in their multitudinous embodiments advances at a pace that swiftly depreciates any such dedicated implementation effort. Instead, in this chapter we discuss an efficient representation of the SPH equations, followed by an optimization suitable for any target platform. As do many real-time applications, our version of the SPH equations trades in accuracy for performance. Therefore, we also discuss differences in stability and behavior compared to the standard implementation from [Müller et al. 03]. Additionally, we discuss an optimization to the data structure used for evaluation of the SPH equations, along with its performance compared to the original method.

Section 6.2 gives an overview of the basic SPH equations, followed by a description of the basic algorithm used to evaluate these equations in Section 6.3. Section 6.4.1 discusses the choice of data structure used to accelerate the evaluation of the SPH equations, followed by an optimization of the chosen data structure in Section 6.4.2. Section 6.5 introduces an optimization for the SPH algorithm. We evaluate the stability and behavior of the optimized SPH algorithm in Section 6.6 and test the performance of the original and optimized algorithm and data structure in Section 6.7.

6.2   The SPH Equations

In this section, we will briefly describe the SPH model, to establish the definitions and highlight the choices specific to our implementation. We define a set of fluid particles $\{i : 1 \leq i \leq n\}$, with positions x_i, velocities v_i, accelerations a_i, and masses m_i constant over time. Also, every particle has a density ρ_i, which is the fluid density at x_i. SPH consists of a set of equations that ultimately define a force f_i applied to every particle i. The positions and velocities of the fluid particles at any time t can be determined by integration of f_i using an integration scheme, such as the semi-implicit Euler method [Vesely 01].

In general, every particle attribute can be seen as a quantity A defined at the particle positions. The SPH model, as mentioned in Monaghan's original paper [Monaghan 88], states a general equation that can be applied to interpolate any such quantity A at an arbitrary location x from the values of A at all particle locations. This general SPH equation is defined by

$$A(\mathbf{x}) = \sum_{j=1}^{n} \frac{m_j}{\rho_j} A_j W(\mathbf{x} - \mathbf{x_j}, h), \tag{6.1}$$

where $A(\mathbf{x})$ is an arbitrary quantity A evaluated at location $\mathbf{x}$, A_j is the same quantity A evaluated at the location of a particle j, and $W(\mathbf{r}, h)$ is a smoothing kernel. The smoothing kernel is a scalar-valued function that smoothes out as the evaluation position $\mathbf{r}$ moves away from the origin. If $\mathbf{r}$ is within a distance h, called the smoothing radius, the function evaluates to a nonzero value, outside the radius it evaluates to zero. There are many types of smoothing kernels, some of which are mentioned in [Müller et al. 03]. We keep h fixed during our simulation.

One of the quantities that can be interpolated by Equation (6.1) in a straightforward manner is the density ρ_i of a fluid particle i, as defined by the following:

$$\rho_i = \sum_{j=1}^{n} \frac{m_j}{\rho_j} \rho_j W(\mathbf{x_i} - \mathbf{x_j}, h) = \sum_{j=1}^{n} m_j W(\mathbf{x_i} - \mathbf{x_j}, h), \tag{6.2}$$

where we choose W to take the form of $W(\mathbf{r}, h) = \frac{15}{\pi h^3}(1 - \|\mathbf{r}\|/h)^3$, equal to the "spiky" smoothing kernel in [Müller et al. 03]. Note that ρ_i is never zero, as the term of the summation where $j = i$ always evaluates to the *smoothing norm* $15/\pi h^3$.

A nice property of Equation (6.1) is that derivatives of the function $A(\mathbf{x}, h)$ only affect the smoothing kernel, which makes it possible to evaluate derivatives of any quantity A, as shown in Equation (6.3). The same also holds for higher order derivatives, like the Laplacian ∇^2.

$$\nabla A(\mathbf{x}) = \sum_{j=1}^{n} \frac{m_j}{\rho_j} A_j \nabla W(\mathbf{x_i} - \mathbf{x_j}, h). \tag{6.3}$$

Using this property, it is possible to interpolate internal fluid forces anywhere within the fluid. As in [Müller et al. 03], we split the force $\mathbf{f_i}$ acting on particle i into three components,

$$\mathbf{f_i} = \mathbf{f_i^P} + \mathbf{f_i^v} + \mathbf{f_i^{ext}}, \tag{6.4}$$

where $\mathbf{f_i^P}$ is the pressure force, related to the pressure p; $\mathbf{f_i^v}$ is the viscous force, related to the velocity $\mathbf{v}$; and $\mathbf{f_i^{ext}}$ are external forces like gravity, which we will not discuss in this chapter.

The equations for $\mathbf{f^P}(\mathbf{x})$ and $\mathbf{f^v}(\mathbf{x})$—the pressure and viscous forces at any location in the fluid—are derived from the Navier-Stokes equations. Specifically,

$\mathbf{f^P} = -\nabla p$ is the pressure force, and $\mathbf{f^v} = \mu\nabla^2\mathbf{v}$ is the viscous force. Equation (6.1) can be applied to these two quantities to interpolate them at any location in the fluid.

We will first interpolate $\mathbf{f^P(x)}$ in a straightforward manner, as stated by

$$\mathbf{f^P(x)} = -\nabla p(\mathbf{x}) = -\sum_{j=1}^{n} \frac{m_j}{\rho_j} p(\mathbf{x})\nabla W(\mathbf{x} - \mathbf{x_j}, h). \qquad (6.5)$$

To calculate the per-particle force $\mathbf{f_i^P}$, [Müller et al. 03] proposed an adaptation to Equation (6.5) to obtain symmetric pressure forces between any pair of particles i and j, by substituting $(p_i + p_j)/2$ for $p(\mathbf{x})$. Also, the acceleration of the fluid, defined as $\mathbf{a(x)} = \mathbf{f(x)}/\rho(\mathbf{x})$, has to be matched by every fluid particle. Therefore, the pressure force $\mathbf{f^P(x)}$ at an arbitrary location within the fluid defined by Equation (6.5) is multiplied by $\frac{m_i}{\rho_i}$ to get the pressure force $\mathbf{f_i^P}$ acting on a single particle i. The complete definition of $\mathbf{f_i^P}$ is given by

$$\mathbf{f_i^P} = -\nabla p_i = -\frac{m_i}{\rho_i}\sum_{j=1}^{n}\frac{m_j}{\rho_j}\frac{(p_i + p_j)}{2}\nabla W(\mathbf{x_i} - \mathbf{x_j}, h), \qquad (6.6)$$

where according to the ideal gas law $p_j = k\rho_j$, with k being a gas constant that can be used to increase or decrease the compressibility of our simulated fluid. We do not find it necessary to use a rest density as in [Müller et al. 03]. We choose the smoothing kernel $\nabla W(\mathbf{r}, h) = (45/\pi h^4)(1 - \|\mathbf{r}\|/h)^2\frac{\mathbf{r}}{\|\mathbf{r}\|}$, which is the gradient of the spiky kernel used for density computations. Note that $\nabla W(\mathbf{r}, h)$ is undefined when $\mathbf{r} = \mathbf{0}$. Because a particle never exerts a force on itself, we define $W(\mathbf{0}, h) = 0$.

Apart from Equation (6.6), there are other ways in which we can use Equation (6.1) to interpolate a gradient. According to [Colin et al. 06], some of them yield more-accurate approximations of the gradient of a function. For instance, a more-accurate approximation would be obtained by using the difference gradient approximation formula (DGAF), as in [Colin et al. 06]. However, the inaccuracies of Equation (6.6) tend to decrease compressibility for areas with similar but high pressure, while this is not the case for a DGAF approximation. Simulating water or other incompressible fluids therefore benefits from using Equation (6.6).

The approximation of the viscous force $\mathbf{f_i^v} = \mu\nabla^2\mathbf{v}$ is similar to the approximation of $\mathbf{f_i^P}$, as the following demonstrates:

$$\mathbf{f_i^v} = \mu\nabla^2\mathbf{v} = \mu\frac{m_i}{\rho_i}\sum_{j=1}^{n}\frac{m_j}{\rho_j}(\mathbf{v_j} - \mathbf{v_i})\nabla^2 W(\mathbf{x_i} - \mathbf{x_j}, h), \qquad (6.7)$$

where μ is the viscosity constant, used to increase or decrease the viscosity of the simulated fluid. Here, we choose the smoothing kernel $\nabla^2 W(\mathbf{r}, h) = (45/\pi h^6)$

$(h - \|\mathbf{r}\|)$, equivalent to the one used for viscosity in [Müller et al. 03]. A more-accurate equation for interpolating a Laplacian is proposed by [Colin et al. 06], but it is significantly more complex to evaluate and therefore not employed by our implementation.

6.3   An Algorithm for SPH Simulation

Given a set of fluid particles, the SPH algorithm that solves the SPH equations yields particle positions $([\mathbf{x_i}]^0, [\mathbf{x_i}]^1, [\mathbf{x_i}]^2, \ldots)$ for consecutive time steps $(t_0, t_1, t_2, \ldots)$. In the remainder of this chapter, we will use the brackets with superscript notation $[A]^0$ to denote the value of an attribute A at a certain time t_0. Starting out with positions $\{[\mathbf{x_i}]^0 : 1 \leq i \leq n\}$, Equation (6.2) is used to calculate densities $\{[\rho_i]^0 : 1 \leq i \leq n\}$. This corresponds to Step 1 in Figure 6.1.

From the definitions of the SPH equations in Section 6.2, it follows that all densities have to be known before any forces are calculated for corresponding time steps, as both Equations (6.6) and (6.7) depend on all the particles' densities. Calculation of $\{[\mathbf{f_i^P}]^0 : 1 \leq i \leq n\}$ therefore takes place after Step 1 and involves the densities and positions of particles, while $\{[\mathbf{f_i^v}]^0 : 1 \leq i \leq n\}$ also involves velocities. Both components of $\mathbf{f_i}$ can be established at the same time, corresponding to Step 2 in Figure 6.1. Through $\mathbf{a_i} = \frac{\mathbf{f_i}}{m_i}$, we implicitly establish $[\mathbf{a_i}]^0$ as well. Step 3 corresponds to integration of $[\mathbf{a_i}]^0$ into $[\mathbf{v_i}]^1$ and $[\mathbf{v_i}]^1$ into

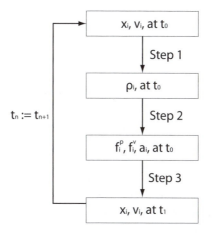

Figure 6.1. The states of the SPH algorithm, represented by boxes. The arrows denote the steps of the algorithm to get from one state to another.

$[\mathbf{x_i}]^1$ using a symplectic Euler integration scheme:

$$[\mathbf{v_i}]^1 = [\mathbf{v_i}]^0 + [\mathbf{a_i}]^0 \triangle t,$$
$$[\mathbf{x_i}]^1 = [\mathbf{x_i}]^0 + [\mathbf{v_i}]^1 \triangle t,$$

where $\triangle t = t_1 - t_0$. We chose a symplectic Euler scheme over normal Euler integration because it has better energy-conservation properties [Ruth 83].

When $[\mathbf{x_i}]^1$ is known, the algorithm repeats itself for the next time step.

6.4   The Choice of Data Structure

6.4.1   Spatial Hashing

The SPH equations that have to be evaluated per fluid particle are defined by Equations (6.2), (6.6) and (6.7) in Section 6.2. Each of these equations is a summation over attributes of every fluid particle in the simulation. Obviously, a full quadratic evaluation is wasteful to perform in practice, as a certain fluid particle only influences other particles within a radius h of its position. Overall, evaluating the SPH equations in Steps 1 and 2 of Figure 6.1 is more expensive than the velocity and position integration in Step 3, which only has a complexity linear in the amount of fluid particles.

The process of finding a particle's neighboring particles can be accelerated by using a data structure. Most SPH simulations employ a spatial hash, as described by [Teschner et al. 03], which can also be used in the case of parallel execution [Green 08]. The structure of a spatial hash is shown in Figure 6.2.

A spatial hash consists of a hash table, with each entry called a hash bucket. Hash buckets are—in the case of an SPH simulation—lists of fluid particles. Fluid particles are mapped to hash buckets based on their position $\mathbf{x_i}$ using a hash function $H(\mathbf{x})$, indexing into the hash table.

A property of the hash function is that it discretizes three-dimensional space into grid cells and maps each grid cell to the limited number of hash buckets available in a uniformly random fashion. So regardless of the spatial configuration of grid cells that participate in the fluid simulation—the ones that contain fluid particles—they are uniformly distributed over the available hash buckets.

Constructing a spatial hash is of time complexity $O(n)$, while a single query is of time complexity $O(q)$, with q being the number of fluid particles mapping to a single hash bucket within the spatial hash. Construction of the hash structure is performed in the *construction phase*, which takes place immediately after the fluid particle locations are known, before Step 1 in Figure 6.1. Querying is performed during Step 2—the density and force calculations—which is referred to as the

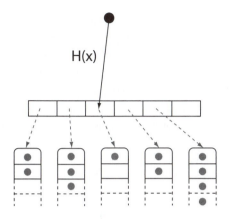

Figure 6.2. The structure of a spatial hash as described by [Teschner et al. 03]. A fluid particle—the black dot at the top—is mapped to a table of hash buckets of fixed size—the grid in the middle—by a hash function $H(\mathbf{x})$. Every hash bucket references a list of fluid particles, which is represented by the bottom layer. Note that this figure shows only the concept of the structure; it is not representative of the memory layout for an optimized implementation.

query phase. This section will focus on the choices that can be made during the design of a spatial hash and their effect on computational efficiency, both in the construction phase and in the query phase.

Hash construction can be performed from scratch each frame or incrementally. In both cases, an efficient implementation keeps particles belonging to the same hash bucket in a contiguous block of memory, to avoid cache misses during a query of the spatial hash. Construction from scratch is possible by placing all fluid particles in a contiguous block of memory and (radix) sorting them based on their hash index. Each particle stores its hash index along with its state, so constructing the hash table only requires an iteration through the list of particles to find the start of each hash bucket. For parallel implementations, a radix sort is suitable as well, and constructing the hash table follows from the sorted list of particles as a compaction step, where each first hash bucket element writes a reference to itself into the corresponding hash bucket of the hash table. Radix sort and compaction for parallel architectures like a GPU is explained in detail by [Harris et al. 07].

To construct the spatial hash incrementally, inserted fluid particles are not removed from the spatial hash at every frame. Instead, particles are relocated whenever they move to another hash bucket. This method performs well if particles do not move around too much between consecutive frames. Ideally, hash buckets are represented by contiguous blocks of memory; each hash bucket is preallocated based on a maximum number of particles per hash bucket. The disadvantage is that the size of a hash bucket can never exceed the maximum number of particles estimated during preallocation. For architectures without a cache, contiguity of hash buckets is not necessary, so a hash bucket can alternatively be represented in a linked-list fashion, where each particle references the previous and next particle of the hash bucket it belongs to. Each particle then updates only these references as it moves around within the fluid simulation, but it does not change its location within the list of particles constituting the spatial hash. This way, restrictions on hash bucket size are avoided. In either case, the incremental solution modifies an existing spatial hash, which makes it less suitable for parallel implementations.

Regardless of the method of construction, the spatial hash structure can be utilized in two different ways. One way is to insert a fluid particle during the construction phase in all the hash buckets that its area of influence maps to and—to find all neighbors of a particle during the query phase—query just the hash bucket that a fluid particle position maps to. The second way is to insert the fluid particle into one hash bucket and query all hash buckets of grid cells intersecting the area of influence of a particle during the neighbor search. The two methods do not differ much in terms of complexity: the first method has c insert operations and one query operation per particle, where c is the number of grid cells intersecting an area of influence defined by the smoothing radius h, and the second method has one insert operation and c query operations per particle.

Still, there are at least three reasons why the latter method is more popular. Firstly, constructing the hash structure is more complex than is querying the hash structure. For every new insertion, data have to be copied around or modified, and some solutions require reservation of space to hold the data. A query operation just reads the data, without modifications to the data structure itself. Secondly, constructing the hash structure is, in essence, a scattering operation, while querying it resembles a gathering operation, which is much better suited to many of today's parallel architectures. Thirdly, using the method with a single insertion operation makes it easier to update the hash structure incrementally as the particles move around within the fluid, instead of reconstructing the hash from scratch at every new iteration of the SPH algorithm.

For querying, a spatial hash structure has to minimize the number of fluid particles mapping to a single hash bucket q, as querying is of time complexity $O(q)$. This is achieved by choosing parameters for the spatial hash structure and the fluid simulation itself. We will highlight three possible choices.

The first choice is to use a larger spatial hash with more buckets. This decreases the chance that two grid cells map to the same hash bucket and, as such,

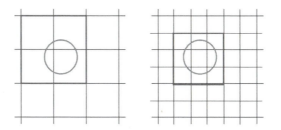

Figure 6.3. The choice of the grid cell size of a spatial hash has implications for the query area of a fluid particle: larger cells (left) versus smaller cells (right). Smaller grid cell sizes imply a smaller search volume, and thus a smaller amount of potential neighbors visited. Note, however, that the amount of grid cells intersecting the volume increases, having a negative impact on efficiency.

minimizes the chance of hash collisions. Choosing a larger number of hash buckets is usually not a problem, as the memory footprint of the hash table is small compared to the footprint of the list of fluid particles in the spatial hash.

The second choice pertains to the resolution of the spatial hash. The higher the resolution of the spatial hash, the smaller the grid cells. This means the total volume of grid cells intersecting the influence area of a particle decreases, so a particle has a smaller volume to search for neighboring particles, as depicted in Figure 6.3. For example, a grid cell size equal to $2h$ means that 8 grid cells per particle are queried for neighbors, with a total volume of $(4h)^3 = 64h^3$, while a grid cell size equal to h implies that 27 grid cells have to be queried, with a total volume of $(3h)^3 = 27h^3$. The trade-off is that the amount of grid cells intersecting the influence area of a particle increases, so the amount of hash indices calculated per particle also increases. Whether the cost of calculating the extra hash indices plus the associated cache misses of retrieving different hash buckets is less than the efficiency gained by visiting a smaller number of potential neighbors depends on the platform and characteristics of the simulated scenario, i.e., the average number of particles residing in a single hash bucket. Therefore, the choice of spatial hash resolution should always be based on performance profiles of the intended target platform.

The third choice that influences q is related to the fluid simulation itself. To minimize q, we can increase the gas constant k used for determining the pressure. This separates the fluid particles as much as possible. The fluid becomes less compressible in central areas, which is beneficial for simulating water, but it decreases the stability of particles on the fluid surface. Decreasing external forces, like gravity pushing down on the fluid, may have a comparable effect, but generally causes a more gaseous behavior of the fluid. We will refrain from making any recommendation on the value of k because of its artistic implications. Instead, we will discuss its effects on stability and behavior in Section 6.6.

6.4.2   Grid-Cell-Based Spatial Hashing

Section 6.4.1 discussed the choice of a spatial hash as data structure for our fluid simulation. It also discussed the choice of spatial hash and fluid-simulation parameters, with their effects on computational efficiency. Section 6.5 will change the structure of the SPH algorithm to decrease the computational burden of finding neighbors and iterating over fluid particles multiple times. Section 6.7 will show that despite these improvements, the majority of the computational burden still falls to the nearest-neighbor search, even more so than in the actual evaluation of the SPH equations.

To decrease the work required for the nearest-neighbor search, we propose a slight change in the structure of the original spatial hash, as described in [Teschner et al. 03]. The change is meant to minimize the number of potential neighbors visited during a spatial hash query.

In the original spatial hash, as shown in Figure 6.2, multiple grid cells map to a single hash bucket, since we have an infinite number of grid cells but only a limited number of hash buckets. If multiple grid cells contain fluid particles, fluid particles from two spatially unrelated grid cells may be inserted into the same hash bucket, causing a hash collision. The number of hash collisions can be minimized by increasing the number of hash buckets. However, hash collisions can rarely be avoided in practice; the fluid-simulation configuration is free to take on any shape, including those producing collisions. As a result, during a query of the hash at a fluid-particle position, all particles in the corresponding hash bucket are visited, including the ones that are spatially unrelated.

The goal of our structural change is to speed up querying: we keep the hash function enabling us to find a list of potential neighbors with $O(1)$ time complexity, while eliminating iteration over particles that do not belong to the grid cell being queried.

Figure 6.4 shows the modified hash structure, which we refer to as a *grid-cell-based spatial hash*. At the topmost level we keep a hash table, but instead of storing a bucket of fluid particles, the bucket now contains a list of grid cells—the middle layer. Every grid cell element consists of its discretized grid cell coordinates and a list of fluid particles belonging to the grid cell. The list of fluid particles is represented by the bottom layer in Figure 6.4.

Insertion of a fluid particle into the grid-cell-based spatial hash proceeds as follows:

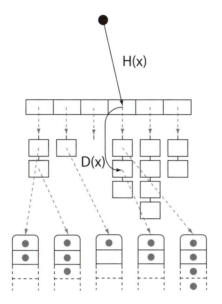

Figure 6.4. The structure of the grid-cell-based spatial hash. The black dot at the top is a fluid particle, which is mapped to hash buckets—the rectangular grid—using the hash function $H(\mathbf{x})$. A hash bucket contains a list of grid cells instead of fluid particles, represented by the variable-length chains of squares. The discretized position $D(\mathbf{x})$ of the fluid particle is used to find the grid cell (if any) it belongs to. Every grid cell references a list of fluid particles located within the grid cell—the bottom layer. Note that this figure shows only the concept of the structure; it is not representative of the memory layout for an optimized implementation.

- Calculate the hash bucket to which the fluid particle maps using the hash function $H(\mathbf{x})$ in the same way as for the original spatial hash. However, keep the discretized fluid-particle position $D(\mathbf{x})$ as its grid cell coordinates.

- Using the hash index and grid cell coordinates, select the grid cell list of the indexed hash bucket and iterate over it to find the grid cell matching the grid cell coordinates.

  - If a grid cell is found, insert the fluid particle into the list of fluid particles referenced by the grid cell.

  - Otherwise, a new grid cell is created and inserted into the hash bucket, after which the fluid particle is inserted into the grid cell.

The complexity of this operation is not constant anymore, as we have to traverse the list of grid cells mapped to the hash bucket. Instead, it is of time complexity

$O(c)$, with c being the number of hash collisions in a hash bucket. However, the number of collisions should always be very small because it is possible to optimize for a limited number of collisions by increasing the number of hash buckets.

To find all neighbors of a fluid particle, we calculate its grid cell and neighboring grid cells. We can then query the hash structure for every one of these grid cells. Querying is performed as follows:

- Calculate the hash bucket the grid cell maps to using its grid cell coordinates. The grid cell coordinates are equal to $D(\mathbf{x})$ for all positions $\mathbf{x}$ within the grid cell.

- Iterate through the hash bucket's list of grid cells.

    - If a grid cell that matches the queried grid cell coordinates is found, search its list of fluid particles to find potential neighbors.

    - If no matching grid cell is found, the query for this grid cell is terminated.

It is possible to construct a grid-cell-based spatial hash from scratch as well as incrementally. To construct from scratch, a contiguous block of particles is sorted based on grid cell coordinates to obtain lists of particles per grid cell, contiguous in memory. From the sorted list of particles, a list of grid cells is extracted. The list of grid cells is sorted based on hash index to obtain lists of grid cells per hash bucket, also contiguous in memory. Based on the sorted list of grid cells, the hash bucket references are constructed.

For incremental construction, particles are relocated between grid cells as they change position, while grid cells are added and removed from the lists of grid cells per hash bucket as particles are added and removed from the grid cells. The lists of grid cells per hash bucket and the lists of particles per grid cell can be preallocated, based on the maximum number of grid cell collisions per hash bucket c and the maximum number of particles per grid cell g, respectively. This allows lists of particles per grid cell as well as lists of grid cells per hash bucket to be contiguous in memory.

Regardless of the method of construction, the grid-cell-based spatial hash structure contains three contiguous lists instead of two: the hash table, a list of grid cells sorted by hash bucket, and a list of fluid particles sorted by grid cell coordinates.

Compared to the original spatial hash structure, one more indirection has been added for querying; instead of immediately iterating through potential neighbors in a hash bucket, we implicitly filter out the potential neighbors belonging to grid cells different from the one that is queried. The disadvantage of the indirection is obvious: per query, there may be one more cache miss. However, a hash query visits only the particles of a single grid cell instead of a whole hash bucket. So, the number of cache misses during traversal of the particle list—the last step in the query algorithm—may be greatly reduced.

A more subtle disadvantage of the original spatial hash is that it requires extra bookkeeping for finding all neighbors of a fluid particle. Multiple neighboring grid cells are queried—27 for a grid cell size of h—and all of these neighboring grid cells may map to the same hash bucket. For the original spatial hash structure, it would be incorrect to traverse the same hash bucket more than once for multiple neighboring grid cells; the fluid particles belonging to this hash bucket would be included as neighbors multiple times. A guard has to be constructed to prevent these superfluous hash bucket traversals. For the grid-cell-based hash, such a guard is not required because a query only visits a single grid cell belonging to a hash bucket. All neighboring grid cells of a fluid particle are distinct, so a single grid cell is never visited twice, even if the same hash bucket is visited twice.

The performance of querying the grid-cell-based hash structure is of time complexity $O(c)+O(g)$, where c is the number of hash collisions in a hash bucket and g is the number of fluid particles in a grid cell. The original hash structure query complexity was of $O(q)$, with q being the number of fluid particles in a hash bucket. As $q = c * g$, the time complexity of a hash query has been improved in the grid-cell-based spatial hash.

For testing performance of the grid-cell-based spatial hash in Section 6.7 on an Intel Xeon W3520, we used an implementation with incremental construction, using preallocated hash buckets and grid cells. Furthermore, this implementation uses a grid cell size equal to h, with a fluid particle inserted into the hash just once, as described in Section 6.4.1.

6.5   Collapsing the SPH Algorithm

In Section 6.3, the basic algorithm for evaluation of the SPH equations was described. The algorithm in its original form is inefficient in a number of ways. These inefficiencies will be described in this section, along with a modified SPH algorithm which eliminates the inefficiencies.

Looking back at the algorithm from Figure 6.1, we can see three dependencies in the form of Step 1 to Step 3. This algorithm can be described by the pseudocode in Algorithm 1.

It is clear that we iterate over all fluid particles thrice. If this algorithm runs sequentially on a CPU, there is an increased chance of cache misses. In a

---

Algorithm 1 SPH algorithm in pseudocode.

$\{\{ \ \{[\mathbf{x_i}]^0 : 1 \leq i \leq n\} \ and \ \{[\mathbf{v_i}]^0 : 1 \leq i \leq n\} \ are \ known \ \}\}$
begin
    construct spatial hash structure using $\{[\mathbf{x_i}]^0 : 1 \leq i \leq n\}$;
    for all *particles* i
    begin
        query spatial hash at $[\mathbf{x_i}]^0$;
        for all *nearby particles* j *from query*
        begin
            accumulate $[\rho_i]^0$ *using* $[\mathbf{x_j}]^0$ *and* m_j;
        end;
    end;
    for all *particles* i
    begin
        query spatial hash at $[\mathbf{x_i}]^0$;
        for all *nearby particles* j *from query*
        begin
            accumulate $[\mathbf{f_i}]^0$ *using* $[\mathbf{x_j}]^0$, $[\mathbf{v_j}]^0$, $[\rho_j]^0$ *and* m_j;
        end;
    end;
    for all *particles* i
    begin
        calculate $[\mathbf{a_i}]^0$ *using* $[\mathbf{f_i}]^0$ *and* m_i;
        integrate $[\mathbf{v_i}]^1$ *using* $[\mathbf{a_i}]^0$;
        integrate $[\mathbf{x_i}]^1$ *using* $[\mathbf{v_i}]^1$;
    end;
end;

---

parallel environment, we would need to run three parallel passes: one for the density update, one for the force update, and one for position integration. Usually this requires sending data like the particle positions, densities and forces to the parallel execution units multiple times, decreasing the effective bandwidth of the system.

Also, the density and force update passes require iterating over all nearby particles—potential neighbors—of the particle that is updated. So, the search for actual neighbors is performed twice. A neighbor list can be used for every particle to alleviate the loss of efficiency caused by performing all distance comparisons twice. The neighbor list keeps the actual neighbor particles determined during the first neighbor search in step 1, where the particle densities are determined.

Subsequent passes then only have to evaluate particles that are actual neighbors instead of evaluating all potential neighbors. However, constructing such a neighbor list costs time, and in parallel execution environments it becomes non-trivial to manage query access patterns of the neighbor list on the different execution units. While efficiency of a neighbor list for parallel execution is shown to be good by [Hjelte 06], the effect of using a neighbor list on the overall performance of the algorithm is difficult to estimate and tune.

Instead, it is an interesting idea to forgo the complexity of multiple passes and neighbor lists by collapsing the three passes into one, possibly at the cost of simulation accuracy. Naively collapsing the three passes gives the algorithm in Algorithm 2.

Algorithm 2 SPH algorithm with the three passes collapsed.

$\{\{ \ \{[\mathbf{x_i}]^0 : 1 \leq i \leq n\}, \ \{[\mathbf{v_i}]^0 : 1 \leq i \leq n\} \ and \ \{[\rho_i]^{-1} : 1 \leq i \leq n\} \ are \ known \ \}\}$
begin
   construct spatial hash structure using $\{[\mathbf{x_i}]^0 : 1 \leq i \leq n\}$;
   for all *particles* i
   begin
     query spatial hash at $[\mathbf{x_i}]^0$;
     for all *nearby particles* j *from query*
     begin
       accumulate $[\rho_i]^0$ *using* $[\mathbf{x_j}]^?$ *and* m_j;
       accumulate $[\mathbf{f_i}]^0$ *using* $[\mathbf{x_j}]^?$, $[\mathbf{v_j}]^?$, $[\rho_j]^?$ *and* m_j;
     end;
     calculate $[\mathbf{a_i}]^0$ *using* $[\mathbf{f_i}]^0$ *and* m_i;
     integrate $[\mathbf{v_i}]^1$ *using* $[\mathbf{a_i}]^0$;
     integrate $[\mathbf{x_i}]^1$ *using* $[\mathbf{v_i}]^1$;
   end;
end;

This algorithm is not complete. It is not clear what the state of $\mathbf{x_j}$ is for every particle j during accumulation of $[\rho_i]^0$, and the same problem presents itself during accumulation of $[\mathbf{f_i}]^0$. The problem is caused by a partially updated state of neighbor particles when a certain particle i is being updated, as some neighbor particles may already have updated their state to time step t_1—in particular, those with indices $j : j < i$. One solution is to simply use the state at t_1 for those particles, but in that case, the state of the particle positions may be inconsistent with the state of the spatial hash, unless we decide to update the spatial hash in between particle updates as well. This may not be such a problem for sequential implementations, but for parallel implementations, the use of particle states at t_1 is more problematic. The main culprit is the synchronization of particle states that are updated, with particle states being read for density and force accumulations. This sort of dependency has been proven to be inefficient even for much simpler cases [Green 08].

Instead, we simply use the "old" state at t_0 for $\mathbf{x_i}$ and $\mathbf{v_i}$ and use t_{-1} for ρ_j, as $[\rho_j]^0$ is not yet determined when positions are updated to time step t_0. The algorithm now has an easy and efficient implementation for both sequential- and parallel-execution environments, at the expense of some accuracy. The full *collapsed SPH algorithm* is presented in Algorithm 3.

Algorithm 3 Full collapsed SPH algorithm.

$\{\{ \ \{[\mathbf{x_i}]^0 : 1 \leq i \leq n\}, \{[\mathbf{v_i}]^0 : 1 \leq i \leq n\} \text{ and } \{[\rho_i]^{-1} : 1 \leq i \leq n\} \text{ are known} \ \}\}$
begin
  construct spatial hash structure using $\{[\mathbf{x_i}]^0 : 1 \leq i \leq n\}$;
  for all *particles* i
  begin
    query spatial hash at $[\mathbf{x_i}]^0$;
    for all *nearby particles* j *from query*
    begin
      accumulate $[\rho_i]^0$ *using* $[\mathbf{x_j}]^0$ *and* m_j;
      accumulate $[\mathbf{f_i}]^0$ *using* $[\mathbf{x_j}]^0$, $[\mathbf{v_j}]^0$, $[\rho_j]^{-1}$ *and* m_j;
    end;
    calculate $[\mathbf{a_i}]^0$ *using* $[\mathbf{f_i}]^0$ *and* m_i;
    integrate $[\mathbf{v_i}]^1$ *using* $[\mathbf{a_i}]^0$;
    integrate $[\mathbf{x_i}]^1$ *using* $[\mathbf{v_i}]^1$;
  end;
end;

Note that this algorithm is almost the same as the original algorithm, apart from using the density at t_{-1} instead of at t_0 for calculating the force at t_1. Using a sufficiently small time step, $[\rho_j]^0 - [\rho_j]^{-1}$ should be small, so the resulting difference in fluid behavior should be small as well. As an aside, we might try to estimate $[\rho_j]^0$ based on $[\rho_j]^{-1}$ and a time derivative of ρ, as defined by

$$\frac{d\rho_i}{dt} = \sum_{j=1}^{n} m_j(\mathbf{v_i} - \mathbf{v_j})\nabla W(\mathbf{x_i} - \mathbf{x_j}, h).$$

We choose not to perform this estimation because it relies on estimating a change in the smoothing kernel based on a first-order derivative, which can lead to large inaccuracies when the derivative is high. Furthermore, to obtain $[d\rho_j/dt]^0$ for all neighbors j of a particle i, $[d\rho_j/dt]^0$ has to be calculated before the update loop at t_0 because it involves a sum over the neighbors of every particle j. However, during the update loop of t_{-1}, the velocities $[\mathbf{v_j}]^0$ have not yet been established for all particles, so $[d\rho_j/dt]^0$ cannot be accurately calculated and has to be estimated itself.

6.6   Stability and Behavior

Within an SPH fluid simulation, many parameters influence the behavior of fluid particles. The behavioral influence can be so large that, in certain cases, adding gravity to a system of particles is enough to keep the particles from moving into a rest state. In other words, the stability of the SPH simulation is easily compromised, even in basic situations. This section will identify the parameters that influence the behavior of an SPH particle system and evaluate the stability and behavior of a particle system under the influence of gravity for different values of selected parameters. The evaluation will be performed for both the original SPH algorithm as discussed in Section 6.3 and the collapsed SPH algorithm optimized for performance from Section 6.5.

First, we will focus on stability under extreme circumstances; for both algorithms, we will try to find parameters for which the SPH simulation becomes too unstable to remain usable. The resulting range of usable parameters will establish whether one algorithm is restricted in the possible selection of parameters compared to the other algorithm. Afterwards, we will evaluate the visual output of both the original and the collapsed SPH simulation. We can thereby verify differences in behavior between both types of algorithms.

To find the range of usable parameters for an SPH fluid simulation, we have to find the parameters that influence the behavior of the simulation. Therefore, we look at the forces acting on a particle, as defined by Equation (6.4). Three forces act on a fluid particle: $\mathbf{f_i^p}$, $\mathbf{f_i^v}$, and $\mathbf{f_i^{ext}}$. In our test scenario, the only external forces are gravity and collision forces produced by static geometry. We will only consider gravity and leave collision forces out of the discussion, as these are very specific to the type of collision response desired. Also, we do not consider viscous forces. Viscous forces dampen the velocity of particles, reducing the effects of instability. As we had to constrain the number of parameters influencing the fluid behavior, we chose to evaluate cases where instability is most prevalent, namely, the ones with zero viscosity.[1]

---

[1] We performed tests to verify that adding viscosity does not affect the collapsed SPH algorithm in ways different from the original algorithm. Both algorithms turned out to be more stable with added viscosity—a larger range of parameters could be chosen—but neither one turned out to be more stable than the other. We therefore chose to omit the results of tests with nonzero viscosity.

So, apart from gravity, we only consider the pressure force term. To evaluate parameters that influence the pressure force term, a simplification of Equation (6.6)—the pressure equation—is presented in Equation (6.8). Instead of showing the definition of $\mathbf{f}_i^P$, we instead choose to show $\mathbf{a}_i^P$, since fluid behavior is equal if particles have the same acceleration. We also make the simplifying assumption that the fluid is homogeneous, so $m_i = m_j = m$ for any two particles i and j:

$$
\begin{aligned}
\mathbf{a}_i^P &= -\frac{1}{\rho_i} \sum_{j=1}^n \frac{m}{\rho_j} \frac{(p_i+p_j)}{2} \nabla W(\mathbf{x_i} - \mathbf{x_j}, h) \\
&= -\sum_{j=1}^n m \frac{(p_i+p_j)}{2\rho_i\rho_j} \nabla W(\mathbf{x_i} - \mathbf{x_j}, h) \\
&= -\sum_{j=1}^n \frac{k}{2}\left(\frac{m}{\rho_j} + \frac{m}{\rho_i}\right) \nabla W(\mathbf{x_i} - \mathbf{x_j}, h) \\
&= -\sum_{j=1}^n \frac{km}{2}\left((mW_l^i(h))^{-1} + (mW_l^j(h))^{-1}\right) \nabla W(\mathbf{x_i} - \mathbf{x_j}, h) \\
&= -\sum_{j=1}^n \frac{k}{2}\left((W_l^i(h))^{-1} + (W_l^j(h))^{-1}\right) \nabla W(\mathbf{x_i} - \mathbf{x_j}, h),
\end{aligned}
$$
(6.8)

where $W_l^i(h) = \sum_{l=1}^n W(\mathbf{x_i} - \mathbf{x_l}, h)$.

From Equation (6.8) it follows that the acceleration of a fluid particle is determined by the pressure constant k and the number of fluid particles—the latter being represented by the summations in the equation. The mass m of a particle turns out to have no influence on the acceleration, so it can be disregarded. The smoothing kernel radius h seems to be of influence, since it determines the evaluation of the various forms of W. However, Section 6.9 shows that scaling h and all fluid particle positions by a factor s also scales all fluid-particle accelerations $\mathbf{a}_i^P$ by a factor s—provided that k scales by a factor s^2. Therefore, the scale of our fluid simulation has no influence on the fluid behavior relative to the scaling factor. Of course, this assumes that the external forces and collision geometry are scaled by s as well. As a result, we keep the smoothing kernel radius fixed and express the pressure constant as a relative pressure constant $k_r = \frac{k}{h^2}$ and gravity as the relative gravity $g_r = \frac{g}{h}$.

To test the stability of an SPH simulation, we measure the average relative velocity $\mathbf{v_r} = \frac{\mathbf{v}}{h}$ of a set of fluid particles over a time period of one second, which will be the measure of stability. We consequently change the time step t, the number of particles n, gravity g_r, and the pressure constant k_r. The test case resembles a nonviscous fluid falling into a glass, where stability is measured after the fluid has had time to move into a resting state. The results are shown in Table 6.1.

As can be observed from Table 6.1, increasing the time step or k_r decreases stability. Increasing the number of fluid particles—translating into more layers of particles on top of each other—decreases stability as well, as the maximum pressure constant for a situation with $8,000$ particles is much lower than it is in the case of $4,000$ particles. Choosing a smaller value for g_r does not seem to

		Scenario A		Scenario B		Scenario C	
		col	ori	col	ori	col	ori
Low k_r	60 Hz	0.250	0.268	0.280	0.306	0.247	0.338
	40 Hz	0.234	0.276	0.281	0.302	0.152	0.178
	30 Hz	0.190	0.240	0.239	0.314	0.151	0.168
	15 Hz	0.461	0.240	0.197	0.215	1.112	0.361
Medium k_r	60 Hz	0.079	0.111	0.086	0.107	0.067	0.091
	40 Hz	0.097	0.122	0.067	0.071	0.121	0.077
	30 Hz	**57.94**	**53.36**	**51.41**	**48.90**	**49.69**	**46.59**
	15 Hz	**71.94**	**68.60**	**66.06**	**64.08**	**58.14**	**56.92**
High k_r	60 Hz	0.101	0.189	2.351	**30.40**	0.200	0.186
	40 Hz	**106.5**	**102.3**	**113.1**	**111.3**	**82.23**	**81.21**
	30 Hz	**108.5**	**107.9**	**114.4**	**114.2**	**86.95**	**85.80**
	15 Hz	**102.5**	**101.2**	**105.7**	**103.3**	**85.73**	**85.73**

Table 6.1. Stability for three scenarios, measured as the average $\mathbf{v_r}$ of all particles over a period of one second for both the original (ori) and the collapsed (col) SPH algorithm. Scenario A models 8,000 particles with $g_r = 100$. Scenario B models 4,000 particles with $g_r = 100$. Scenario C models 8,000 particles with $g_r = 33$. All scenarios use a low, medium and high pressure constant of $k_r = 35$, $k_r = 250$, and $k_r = 750$, respectively, except for scenario B, which allows for a high pressure of $k_r = 1,100$. None of the scenarios incorporate viscosity. Unstable simulation results are marked in bold. All tests were performed on a single core of an Intel Xeon W3520.

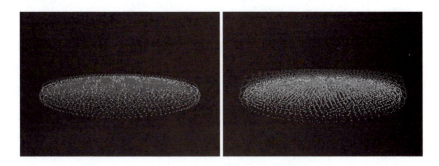

Figure 6.5. Execution of scenario A from Table 6.1. On the left, the simulation with $k_r = 100$. On the right, the simulation with $k_r = 250$. Particle colors range from blue to green to red to denote areas of low, medium, and high density, respectively (see Color Plate I).

influence stability much, but bear in mind that the advantage of decreased gravity is a decreased number of neighbors as the fluid simulation expands, increasing performance. This allows us to obtain more or less the same fluid behavior with a smaller number of fluid particles.

In Figure 6.5, the fluid simulation is shown during execution of scenario A from Table 6.1. The left image shows a pressure constant of $k_r = 100$, while the right image shows a pressure constant of $k_r = 250$. While only the latter image seems to generate a useful fluid simulation without too much compression, the results of the stability test imply that a pressure constant around $k_r = 250$ and upwards already causes too much instability for update rates around 30 Hz. Adding fluid viscosity or overall velocity damping is a requirement in these cases.

We can conclude from the stability test that there is not much difference in terms of stability between the original SPH algorithm and the collapsed algorithm.[2] Observe that at every parameter change that introduces instability, both algorithms show a high (i.e., > 10) average velocity. We tried to find extremes at which the fluid simulation would still behave correctly, both for small and large time steps. We therefore searched for the maximum k_r yielding a stable simulation for the smallest time step and the maximum k_r for the largest time step. For small time steps, the collapsed SPH algorithm allows for the highest pressure constant, while for large time steps, the original SPH algorithm is more stable. However, the maximum pressure constant obtainable for both algorithms is always within five percent of each other, which is not a significant difference.

The similarity in usable parameters for both types of SPH algorithms does not guarantee that both algorithms yield the same fluid behavior. To verify any visual differences between the original and collapsed SPH algorithms, we compare the visualizations of the SPH simulations for all three scenarios in Table 6.1 with low, medium, and high k_r. We look for differences in configuration and movement of the fluid particles, such as the number of layers of fluid particles and their separation. Also, we use an artificial wave running through the glass of water to find differences in behavior when forces are applied to the fluid particles.

The visual output of one of the scenarios is shown in Figure 6.6. The obtained result is typical for the other scenarios as well. In general, the overall configuration of the fluid particles is the same for both SPH algorithms. At rest, the image produced by the original SPH algorithm cannot be distinguished from the image produced by the collapsed SPH algorithm. During application of the wave force, differences between the algorithms are minimal. There is a slight increase of fluid compression at the center of the wave in the image of the collapsed SPH algorithm, but this is unnoticable during movement. Therefore, choosing the collapsed SPH algorithm instead of the original SPH algorithm seems to have a negligible influence on the overall appearance of the fluid.

---

[2]The deviating result from scenario B in Table 6.1 at $k_r = 1100$, 60 Hz is caused by collision forces that are too aggressive. Because the fluid particle velocities have no damping, some keep moving around the cylindrical collision geometry. Particles inside the glass were stable in this particular situation.

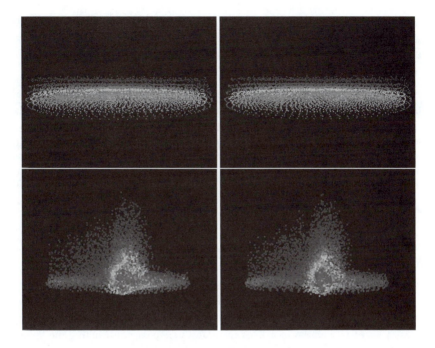

Figure 6.6. Execution of scenario A from Table 6.1 with $k_r = 250$ at 60 Hz. The images on the left correspond to the original SPH algorithm, while the images on the right correspond to the collapsed SPH algorithm. The top images visualize a fluid at rest, while the bottom images show the behavior of the fluid under influence of an artificially generated wave. Particle colors range from blue to green to red to denote areas of low, medium, and high density, respectively (see Color Plate II).

6.7 Performance

In this section, we will evaluate the performance of the original SPH algorithm from Section 6.3, the collapsed SPH algorithm from Section 6.5, and the grid-cell-based spatial hash structure from Section 6.4.2. Also, we will show performance numbers for an SPH implementation based on the homogeneous SPH simplifications presented in Equation (6.8) to test whether the algorithm is bound by the complexity of SPH evaluations or by neighbor searching.

To test the performance, we again use the water-in-a-glass simulation from Section 6.6, with three different sets of parameters. However, we now measure the performance during three stages of the simulation: stage 1, in which water falls and sloshes about; stage 2, in which water stabilizes until it is at rest; and stage 3, in which an artificial wave is generated, compressing the fluid particles against the sides of the glass. For all three parts of the simulation, we measure both

Figure 6.7. The three different stages used for our performance measurements in Table 6.2. From left to right, we have the stage 1 in which fluid particles fall into a glass, stage 2 with fluid particles at rest and stage 3 in which artificial waves are generated. Particle colors range from blue to green to red to denote areas of low, medium and high density respectively (see Color Plate III).

construction time of the spatial hash and evaluation time of the SPH equations. The results are listed in Table 6.2, while the three different stages are visualized in Figure 6.7.

As can be observed from Table 6.2, stage 1 requires a large spatial hash construction effort. Because we incrementally construct the spatial hash for all test cases, a lot of movement translates to more time spent constructing the spatial hash. Particles fly around and change hash buckets often, but as they spread around the glass, the number of neighbors is minimized, reducing the amount of work performed for evaluation of the SPH equations. Table 6.2 shows the highest construction times but the lowest update times during stage 1. Stage 2 requires spending more time on the evaluation of the SPH equations than stage 1, as particles enter the resting state with many neighbors. However, out of all three stages, stage 2 spends the smallest amount of time on constructing the spatial hash, because particles stay in the same hash bucket. The results reflect this, showing an increased evaluation time compared to stage 1, with the lowest hash construction time overall. Stage 3 is the most demanding stage; fluid particles are moving because of the artificial wave and heavily compress at one side of the glass. This is magnified by the fact that the glass is a cylinder. Construction of the spatial hash during stage 3 takes more time than during stage 2. Also, evaluating the SPH equations during stage 3 is more expensive than at any other stage because of an artificially increased number of neighbors.

Overall, it is immediately clear that evaluation of the SPH equations takes much more time than does construction of the spatial hash. Evaluation can last anywhere between 10 and 100 times longer than construction. Also, the two grid-cell-based spatial hash simulations—gcb and hom—require around 10% more construction time than their counterparts with a regular spatial hash, but they perform roughly 20% better during SPH evaluation. Consequently, the time won dur-

		Scenario A		Scenario B		Scenario C	
		cons	upd	cons	upd	cons	upd
Stage 1	ori	0.888	38.6	0.955	29.3	1.017	22.2
	col	0.806	33.2	0.938	25.5	0.974	19.7
	gcb	1.071	28.7	1.169	22.1	1.219	17.6
	hom	1.026	29.5	1.210	21.0	1.300	17.3
Stage 2	ori	0.622	57.1	0.718	36.4	0.910	25.2
	col	0.541	46.8	0.696	31.6	0.857	22.6
	gcb	0.624	40.6	0.740	26.4	0.963	19.2
	hom	0.617	40.0	0.742	26.0	1.107	18.6
Stage 3	ori	0.731	68.2	0.753	38.6	0.813	29.2
	col	0.619	54.0	0.741	33.2	0.801	25.7
	gcb	0.721	37.9	0.819	27.9	0.826	21.6
	hom	0.710	36.9	0.819	27.4	0.912	21.1

Table 6.2. Performance of the original SPH algorithm with neighbor lists (ori), the collapsed SPH algorithm (col), the collapsed algorithm with the grid-cell-based data structure (gcb), and a simulation with all previous improvements and the optimizations for homogeneous fluids (hom). Execution times are measured in milliseconds and split in a spatial hash construction part (cons) and an SPH simulation update part (upd). The evaluation is split in three stages: stages 1 and 2 both last 2 seconds, and stage 3 lasts 16 seconds. Three scenarios are tested at 60 Hz with 8,000 fluid particles; scenario A has parameter values $k_r = 250$, $g_r = 100$, $\mu_r = h\mu = 1.5$; scenario B has parameter values $k_r = 750$ $g_r = 100$, $\mu_r = 1.5$; and scenario C has parameter values $k_r = 250$, $g_r = 33$, $\mu_r = 1.5$. All tests are performed on a single core of an Intel Xeon W3520.

ing evaluation royally outweighs the time lost during construction. These benchmarks suggest that for the chosen target platform, a grid-cell-based spatial hash is a sound choice.

Table 6.2 also shows that the collapsed SPH algorithm—used by col, gcb, and hom—has a much improved evaluation time compared to the original SPH algorithm.

Lastly, the optimizations introduced by simplification of the SPH equations introduced in Section 6.6 hardly pay off. The simulation seems to be bound by the neighbor search, not by the SPH arithmetic.

To give an impression of actual frame rates obtained by the aforementioned methods, we show frame rates of the water-in-a-glass test in five cases: the original two-pass SPH algorithm without neighbor lists, the original algorithm with neighbor lists, the collapsed SPH algorithm, the collapsed algorithm with a grid-cell-based hash structure, and the collapsed algorithm for homogeneous fluids. Between the first and the last case, the difference in frame rate is almost twofold. The frame rates are listed in Table 6.3.

Naive	Neighbor	Collapse	GCB Hash	Homogeneous
19	26	30	36	37

Table 6.3. Actual framerates produced by the original two-pass algorithm (Naive), the original algorithm with neighbor lists (Neighbor), the collapsed SPH algorithm (Collapse), the collapsed algorithm with a grid cell based hash (GCB Hash) and an implementation with all previous improvements and the optimizations for homogeneous fluids (Homogeneous). The simulation consists of 8000 fluid particles at rest in a glass, with $k_r = 750$ $g_r = 100$ and $\mu_r = h\mu = 1.5$. All tests are performed on a single core of an Intel Xeon W3520.

6.8   Conclusion

In this chapter, the elements for constructing an efficient and stable SPH simulation have been discussed, applicable to both sequential and parallel algorithms. This includes optimizing the SPH algorithm and equations, designing an efficient spatial hash for nearest-neighbor searching, and obtaining a stable simulation. Further work can focus on the implementation and optimization of the spatial hash data structure—or other spatial data structures—for specific parallel platforms. For an implementation on multiple processors, one can take a look at Chapter 7, "Parallelizing Particle-Based Simulation on Multiple Processors" by Takahiro Harada. Because current real-time SPH simulations still allow the fluid to compress, another interesting topic of research is incompressible SPH for a more convincing simulation of water, as described in [Koshizuka and Oka 96] and [Edmond and Shao 02]. Lastly, efficient real-time visualization of fluids remains an open problem despite the plethora of methods available and is also a necessity for presenting a believable simulation to the end user.

6.9   Appendix: Scaling the Pressure Force

Scaling the fluid simulation—the fluid-particle positions x and smoothing kernel size h—with a factor s does not necessarily have an influence on fluid behavior. This section shows that for our choice of smoothing kernels, the fluid-particle acceleration a scales linearly with the fluid simulation. Consequently, the fluid behavior resulting from pressure forces does not change relative to the scale of the simulation. The only requirement is that the pressure constant k scale according to s^2. The proof follows from Equation (6.9) below, which defines the acceleration of the scaled fluid particles i_s in terms of the acceleration of the original fluid particles i. The definition of $\mathbf{a}_i^P$ is taken from Equation (6.8):

$$\mathbf{a}_{\mathbf{i}_s}^{\mathbf{P}} = \sum_{j=1}^{n} \frac{s^2 k}{2} ((\sum_{l=1}^{n} W(s\mathbf{r}_{\mathbf{il}}, sh))^{-1} + (\sum_{l=1}^{n} W(s\mathbf{r}_{\mathbf{jl}}, sh))^{-1}) \nabla W(s\mathbf{r}_{\mathbf{ij}}, sh)$$

$$= \sum_{j=1}^{n} \frac{s^2 k}{2} ((\frac{1}{s^3} \sum_{l=1}^{n} W(\mathbf{r}_{\mathbf{il}}, h))^{-1} + (\frac{1}{s^3} \sum_{l=1}^{n} W(\mathbf{r}_{\mathbf{jl}}, h))^{-1}) \frac{1}{s^4} \nabla W(\mathbf{r}_{\mathbf{ij}}, h)$$

$$= \sum_{j=1}^{n} \frac{s^2 k}{2} \frac{s^3}{s^4} ((\sum_{l=1}^{n} W(\mathbf{r}_{\mathbf{il}}, h))^{-1} + (\sum_{l=1}^{n} W(\mathbf{r}_{\mathbf{jl}}, h))^{-1}) \nabla W(\mathbf{r}_{\mathbf{ij}}, h)$$

$$= s \sum_{j=1}^{n} \frac{k}{2} ((\sum_{l=1}^{n} W(\mathbf{r}_{\mathbf{il}}, h))^{-1} + (\sum_{l=1}^{n} W(\mathbf{r}_{\mathbf{jl}}, h))^{-1}) \nabla W(\mathbf{r}_{\mathbf{ij}}, h)$$

$$= \mathbf{a}_{\mathbf{i}}^{\mathbf{P}} s,$$

(6.9)

where (see Section 6.2)

$$W(\mathbf{r}_{\mathbf{ij}}, h) = W(\mathbf{x}_{\mathbf{i}} - \mathbf{x}_{\mathbf{j}}, h),$$

$$W(\mathbf{r}, h) = \frac{15}{\pi h^3} (1 - \|\mathbf{r}\|/h)^3,$$

$$\nabla W(\mathbf{r}, h) = \frac{45}{\pi h^4} (1 - \|\mathbf{r}\|/h)^2 \frac{\mathbf{r}}{\|\mathbf{r}\|}$$

Bibliography

[Blinn 82] James F. Blinn. "A Generalization of Algebraic Surface Drawing." *ACM Transactions on Graphics* 1:3 (1982), 235–256.

[Colin et al. 06] F. Colin, R. Egli, and F. Y. Lin. "Computing a Null Divergence Velocity Field Using Smoothed Particle Hydrodynamics." *Journal of Computational Physics* 217:2 (2006), 680–692.

[Edmond and Shao 02] Y. M. L. Edmond and S. Shao. "Simulation of Near-Shore Solitary Wave Mechanics by an Incompressible SPH Method." *Applied Ocean Research* 24 (2002), 275–286.

[Green 08] Simon Green. "Particle-Based Fluid Simulation." Available at http://developer.download.nvidia.com/presentations/2008/GDC/GDC08_ParticleFluids.pdf, 2008.

[Harada et al. 07] T. Harada, S. Koshizuka, and Y. Kawaguchi. "Smoothed Particle Hydrodynamics on GPUs." Paper presented at Computer Graphics International Conference, Petropolis, Brazil, May 30–June 2, 2007.

[Harlow and Welch 65] Francis H. Harlow and Eddie J. Welch. "Numerical Calculation of Time-Dependent Viscous Incompressible Flow of Fluid with
Free Surface." *Physics of Fluids* 8:12 (1965), 2182–2189.

[Harris et al. 07] Mark Harris, Shubhabrata Sengupta, and John D. Owens. "Parallel Prefix Sum (Scan) with CUDA." In *GPU Gems 3*, edited by Hubert
Nguyen, pp. 851–876. Reading, MA: Addison Wesley, 2007.

[Hjelte 06] N. Hjelte. "Smoothed Particle Hydrodynamics on the Cell Broadband
Engine." Preprint, 2006. Available at http://www.2ld.de/gdc2004/.

[Kanamori et al. 08] Yoshihiro Kanamori, Zoltan Szego, and Tomoyuki Nishita.
"GPU-Based Fast Ray Casting for a Large Number of Metaballs." *Comput.
Graph. Forum* 27:2 (2008), 351–360.

[Koshizuka and Oka 96] S. Koshizuka and Y. Oka.   "Moving-Particle Semi-
implicit Method for Fragmentation of Incompressible Flow." *Nucl. Sci. Eng.*
123 (1996), 421–434.

[Lorensen and Cline 87] William E. Lorensen and Harvey E. Cline.   "Marching Cubes: A High Resolution 3D Surface Construction Algorithm."   In
*SIGGRAPH '87: Proceedings of the 14th Annual Conference on Computer
Graphics and Interactive Techniques*, pp. 163–169. New York: ACM Press,
1987.

[Monaghan 88] J. J. Monaghan. "An Introduction to SPH." *Computer Physics
Communications* 48 (1988), 89–96. Available at http://dx.doi.org/10.1016/
0010-4655(88)90026-4.

[Müller et al. 03] Matthias Müller,   David Charypar,   and Markus Gross.
"Particle-Based Fluid Simulation for Interactive Applications." In *Proceedings of the 2003 ACM SIGGRAPH/Eurographics Symposium on Computer
Animation*, pp. 154–159. Aire-la-Ville, Switzerland: Eurographics Association, 2003.

[Müller et al. 07] Matthias Müller,   Simon Schirm,   and Stephan Duthaler.
"Screen space meshes." In *SCA '07: Proceedings of the 2007 ACM SIG-
GRAPH/Eurographics Symposium on Computer animation*, pp. 9–15. Aire-
la-Ville, Switzerland: Eurographics Association, 2007.

[Ruth 83]   Ronald D. Ruth. "A Canonical Integration Technique." *IEEE Transactions on Nuclear Science* 30 (1983), 2669–2671.

[Stam 99]   Jos Stam. "Stable Fluids." In *SIGGRAPH '99: Proceedings of the 26th Annual Conference on Computer Graphics and Interactive Techniques*, pp. 121–128. New York: ACM Press/Addison-Wesley, 1999.

[Teschner et al. 03]   M. Teschner, B. Heidelberger, M. Mueller, D. Pomeranets, and M.Gross.   "Optimized Spatial Hashing for Collision Detection of Deformable Objects."   In *Proceedings of Vision, Modeling, Visualization VMV'03*, pp. 47–54. Heidelberg: Aka GmbH, 2003.   Available at http://graphics.ethz.ch/~brunoh/download/CollisionDetectionHashing_VMV03.pdf.

[van der Laan et al. 09]   Wladimir J. van der Laan, Simon Green, and Miguel Sainz. "Screen Space Fluid Rendering with Curvature Flow." In *Proceedings of the 2009 Symposium on Interactive 3D Graphics and Games*, pp. 91–98. New York: ACM Press, 2009.

[van Kooten et al. 07]   Kees van Kooten, Gino van den Bergen, and Alex Telea. "Point-Based Visualization of Metaballs on a GPU." In *GPU Gems 3*, edited by Hubert Nguyen, pp. 123–156. Reading, MA: Addison-Wesley, 2007.

[Vesely 01]   Franz J. Vesely. *Computational Physics: An Introduction*, Second edition. New York: Springer, 2001.

[Zhang et al. 08]   Yanci Zhang, Barbara Solenthaler, and Renato Pajarola. "Adaptive Sampling and Rendering of Fluids on the GPU." In *Proceedings of the IEEE/EG International Symposium on Volume and Point-Based Graphics*, pp. 137–146. Aire-la-Ville, Switzerland: Eurographics Association, 2008.

– 7 –

Parallelizing Particle-Based Simulation on Multiple Processors

Takahiro Harada

7.1 Introduction

Particle-based simulation is a method that can simulate liquid without having to use any numerical techniques to track the fluid surfaces. Simulating particle motion gives us not only the information about the fluid surface but also about splashes. Moreover, a particle-based method can be used for a simplified rigid-body simulation as well [Harada 07], and since they can be solved in the same framework, the rigid-body simulation can be coupled with the fluid simulation easily.

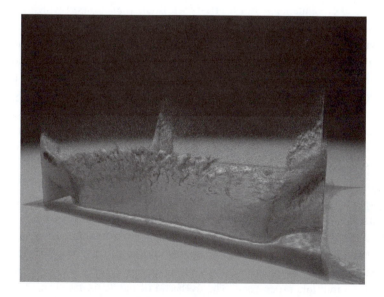

Figure 7.1. Rendered image from a simulation using multiple GPUs (see Color Plate IV).

However, the drawback of particle-based simulation is its computational cost. If the resolution of the simulation is the same as for a grid-based simulation, i.e., the number of particles are the same as the number of grid points in a grid-based simulation, particle-based simulations of fluids are much more expensive because the neighboring particles have to be searched in every time step. In order to get good visual quality, a large number of particles have to be simulated. It depends on the situation, but a simulation with only thousands of particles does not usually give us a satisfactory result.

In this chapter, a method to parallelize particle-based simulation on multiple processors with distributed memory is presented. The method simulates the motion of particles by splitting a simulation into smaller simulations. Using this method, a high-resolution simulation, as shown in Figure 7.1, can be simulated in a few milliseconds per step. GPUs are generally used for parallelizing simulations, but the present method is not limited to GPUs, as it is also applicable to multiple CPUs.

7.2   Dividing Computation

To utilize multiple processors for a simulation, the computation has to be divided into several computations. For a grid-based fluid simulation, in which connectivity among fixed simulation entities is parallelized on multiple processors, the approach we should take is obvious. The simulation domain is divided into subdomains, and a subdomain is assigned to a processor. Because of the fixed connectivity, the decomposition of the simulation domain has to be done once before the simulation starts. To calculate each subdomain, the simulation requires some data from an adjacent subdomain. The elements whose data have to be transferred to an adjacent processor are fixed. Therefore, it is relatively easy to use multiple processors for a grid-based fluid simulation. The overhead of the parallelization is not so large because of the fixed connectivity.

Particle-based simulation, the analogy of the domain decomposition for grid-based simulation, involves dividing particles into sets equal to the number of processors. We quickly realize that this is not a good choice, because particles mix up soon after a simulation starts so that the communication among processors would almost halt the simulation. Thus, it is not obvious how to divide a particle-based simulation in which simulation entities, particles, move freely in the computation domain on multiple processors. The overhead of parallelization can easily kill the benefits of using multiple processors without a carefully designed method, because the simulation data have to be managed at each simulation step.

We chose to use domain decomposition, which is often used in grid-based simulation, for particle-based simulation instead of splitting the particles by their indices. A processor assigned to a subdomain simulates the particles in the subdomain. At first, particle motions are ignored for simplicity. Their motion will be taken into account in the next section.

We first have to consider how to store the particle data. The simplest way would be by employing server–client-type management, in which a server processor containing all the data distributes jobs with data to client processors and retrieves the results in each step. Although this is easy to implement, it requires a large data transfer. This is not efficient when the data transfer between processors is expensive, as with GPUs. Moreover, the clients have to wait while the server is preparing the data to be sent. Therefore, we used another strategy to manage the data that is better suited for parallelizing on multiple processors, and in which each processor manages its own data: peer-to-peer–type management.

To calculate the physical values of a particle, the values of neighboring particles are used: positions of neighbors are used to calculate forces using a distinct element method (DEM) simulation [Mishra 03]; physical values of neighbors are integrated in a smoothed particle hydrodynamics (SPH) simulation (see Chapter 6). Neighbors can be in the adjacent subdomain computed by another processor. In this case, the processor has to ask for the data from the adjacent processor. Accessing the memory of another processor whenever it is necessary, is inefficient because it lowers the granularity of the memory transfer when it is smaller and more frequent. Therefore, we introduce ghost regions to the simulation—the entire computation domain is

$$C = \{x | s < x \le e\},$$

and two processors p_0 and p_1 are used for the simulation. The domain is decomposed at x by a plane perpendicular to the x-axis, so the subdomains for p_0 and p_1 are

$$C_0 = \{x | s < x \le m\},$$
$$C_1 = \{x | m < x \le e\},$$

where $m = (s + e)/2$ is the midpoint of the computation domain in the x-direction. Then, the ghost region for p_0 is the area in C_1 adjacent to C_0, so

$$G_{1 \to 0} = \{x | m < x \le m + g\},$$

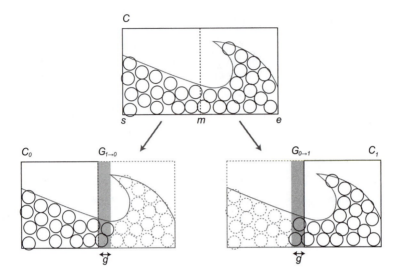

Figure 7.2. Division of a simulation using two processors.

and the ghost region of p_1 is the area in C_0 adjacent to C_1:

$$G_{0 \to 1} = \{x | m - g < x \le m\},$$

where g is the size of the ghost region, as illustrated in Figure 7.2.

When n processors are used, the simulation domain is divided into n domains, and each processor (except for the ones at either end) have two ghost regions, one on each side. Let the effective radius (particle diameter in the case of DEM) be $r_e = g$; then the particles that can be the neighbors of the particles in C_0 can be found in the area $C_0 \cup G_{1 \to 0}$. Thus, a processor does not have to query for particle values kept by adjacent processors during the computation if the particle data in the ghost region is transferred before the time step (to be precise, this is true for explicit computation but not for implicit computation, like the moving particle semi-implicit (MPS) method, which solves Poisson's equation of pressure on particles [Koshizuka and Oka 96]). We refer to these particles in a ghost region as ghost particles. Processor p_0 updates the particles in C_0 but only reads the values of ghost particles. All the particles are updated because all particles exist in $C_0 \cup C_1$ without any duplications ($G_{1 \to 0} \subset C_1$ and $G_{0 \to 1} \subset C_0$). If particles were static, this would be sufficient—but particles move. In the next section, data management for moving particles is discussed.

7.3 Data Management without Duplication

The motion of particles causes a flow of particles between subdomains; some particles go to and some particles come from an adjacent subdomain. The ghost particles at a time step can change dynamically, so efficient management of particles is necessary.

As discussed above, we have employed peer-to-peer–type management of particle data. Although we chose it, there are still several other choices for how to manage data. The easiest way is as follows: each processor has the data of all the particles (using the same index for each particle) and updates the data of the particles belonging to its particular subdomain. However, this is not memory efficient, because all the processors have to have all the particle data. In the following subsections, we are going to describe a method in which a processor only keeps the data of particles in its own subdomain. Therefore, there is no processor that holds the data of all the particles.

7.3.1 Sending Data

As discussed above, data from a neighboring processor is necessary for the computation of particles at a boundary of a subdomain. Also, particles that move out of a subdomain have to be passed to an adjacent processor. Therefore, the particles that have to be sent to an adjacent processor are the particles that move from their subdomain to an adjacent subdomain and also the ghost particles in the subdomain. Let x_i^t be the x-coordinate of particle i at time t calculated by processor p_0, which calculates subdomain C_0. Particle i is in the subdomain of p_0 if $x_i^t < m$. The particles that move out from C_0 to C_1 are

$$EP_{0 \to 1}^{t + \Delta t} = \{i | m < x_i^{t + \Delta t}, x_i^t \le m\}. \tag{7.1}$$

The ghost particles of p_1 in the subdomain of C_0 that come from p_0 are

$$GP_{0 \to 1}^{t + \Delta t} = \{i | m - g < x_i^{t + \Delta t} \le m, x_i^t \le m\}. \tag{7.2}$$

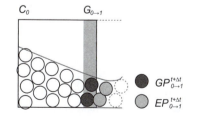

Figure 7.3. Particles sent from p_0 to p_1.

Note that this does not include the ghost particles of p_1 from p_1. From Equations (7.1) and (7.2), the particles that have to be sent to p_1 are

$$
\begin{aligned}
SP_{0\to1}^{t+\Delta t} &= EP_{0\to1}^{t+\Delta t} + GP_{0\to1}^{t+\Delta t} \\
&= \{i|x_i^{t+\Delta t} > m - g, x_i^t \le m\},
\end{aligned}
$$

as shown in Figure 7.3.

To send the data, $SP_{0\to1}^{t+\Delta t}$ has to be selected from all the particles in the memory of a processor. Flagging particles in the region and using prefix sums, which is often used in algorithms on the GPU [Harris et al. 07] to compact them to a dense memory, adds some computation cost which may seem negligible, but not for high-frequency applications like our problem. Most of the processors have to select two sets of particles on each sides for two neighbors if more than two processors are used. This means we have to run these kernels twice.

Instead, the grid constructed for efficient neighbor search is reused to select the particles in our implementation. The data can be directly used to select the particles so that we can avoid increasing the cost. The particles that have to be sent to C_0 are particles in voxels with $x_v > m - g$. However, the grid constructed in this simulation step cannot be used directly because particles have changed their positions in the time step. To avoid the full build of the grid, we used a simulation condition to restrict the particles we want to find. We used the distinct element method (DEM) to calculate force on a particle by placing springs and dampers. DEM is an explicit method but is not unconditionally stable. It has to restrict the size of the time step according to the velocity to maintain stability. Thus, we need $v\Delta t/l_0 < c$, where $v, \Delta t, l_0$, and c are particle velocity, time-step size, particle diameter, and Caulant number, respectively, which have to be less than one. This condition guarantees that the motion of any particle is below its diameter. Since we set the side length of a voxel equal to the particle diameter, particles do not move more than l_0, which is the side length of a voxel. From these conditions, we find $SP_{0\to1}^{t+\Delta t}$ in simulation time t are the particles (let the x-coordinate of this be x) in

$$
S'_{0\to1} = \{m - d - l_0 < x \le m\},
$$

and especially when $d = r_e$,

$$
S'_{0\to1} = \{m - 2d < x \le m\}.
$$

A buffer has to be prepared to store these selected particles. When a uniform grid is used and $g = r_e$, two voxel widths in the direction of the space split have to be sent. The buffer size can be calculated from the configuration of the grid.

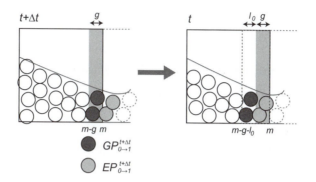

Figure 7.4. Particles to be sent at $t + \Delta t$ (left) and their configuration at t (right).

Actually, we are not using a uniform grid but rather a sliced grid, which has a much tighter fit to particle distribution, as will be described in Section 7.4.

7.3.2 Receiving Data

If all the processors are using the same indices for particles, all we have to do is update the values of these particles after receiving the data from other processors. However, in our approach, each processor manages its own data and does not have a unique index for a particle in all of the particles of the simulation. Thus, the index of a particle at a boundary of a subdomain does not necessarily agree between the two processors sharing the boundary. When one processor receives particles from another, it adds them to its own particle list. We have to be careful about the duplication of particles. If we cannot guarantee that the particle sent from a neighbor does not already exist in the list, all the particles have to be scanned to find the entry—something we do not want to do.

However, what we have to do is delete the particles in the ghost region that were received in the previous time step. For example, p_0 received a set of particles from p_1 at time t. The set of particles consists of particles in $x^{t+\Delta t} > m$ and $x^{t+\Delta t} \leq m$. So after deleting particles in $x^{t+\Delta t} > m$, only particles in $x^{t+\Delta t} \leq m$ remain. Note that this is not the same as the set of particles in the ghost region after updating the particle positions. This can be proved by the following two propositions:

1. A set of particles $GP_{1 \to 0}^{t}$ that is in $G_{1 \to 0}$ at time t is included in the set of particles $SP_{1 \to 0}^{t+\Delta t}$, which will be sent from the adjacent subdomain at time $t + \Delta t$ (see Figure 7.4).

2. A set of particles $EP_{0 \to 1}^{t+\Delta t}$ that is in C_0 at time t and will be in $G_{1 \to 0}$ at time $t + \Delta t$ will not be included in $SP_{1 \to 0}^{t+\Delta t}$.

For the first proposition, because $SP_{1 \to 0}^{t+\Delta t}$ is created by reading the grid at time t,

$$SP_{1 \to 0}^{t+\Delta t} = \{i | m < x_i^t \le m + d + l_0\},$$

$$GP_{1 \to 0}^t = \{i | m < x_i^t \le m + d, x^{t-\Delta t} > m\}.$$

These equations lead to $GP_{1 \to 0}^t \subset SP_{1 \to 0}^{t+\Delta t}$, which proves that ghost particles at time t will be sent from the neighbor at time $t + \Delta t$. Therefore, ghost particles at time t have to be deleted before the processor receives the particles coming from adjacent subdomains.

For the second proposition,

$$EP_{0 \to 1}^{t+\Delta t} = \{i | m - d < x_i^t \le m, m < x^{t+\Delta t}\},$$

and

$$SP_{1 \to 0}^{t+\Delta t} = \{i | m < x_i^t \le m + d + l_0\}.$$

These equations lead to $EP_{0 \to 1}^{t+\Delta t} \notin SP_{1 \to 0}^{t+\Delta t}$. Thus, particles in a ghost region at time $t + \Delta t$ should not be deleted. We can also see that the particles coming from a neighbor have no duplication of particles in its subdomain. So the received data can just be added at the end of the particles of the processor.

If a grid is used to select the particles to be sent, there are several voxels that are not fully saturated to the maximum capacity of a voxel. If sent data kept being added, invalid entries would accumulate. To prevent this, the array is compacted by using a prefix sum after receiving neighbors.

7.4   Choosing an Acceleration Structure

So far, we have discussed how to manage the data on multiple processors. As neighboring-particle search is expensive, acceleration data structures have to be introduced. In this section, we first discuss the requirements for a particle-based simulation and then present the sliced grid, which we used for our simulation. It not only has several advantages as an acceleration structure, but is also well suited for parallelized particle-based simulation using domain decomposition.

7.4.1 Requirements for Particle-Based Simulation

The data structures introduced to make neighboring-particle search efficient are classified into three categories: uniform grids, hash grids, and hierarchical grids, all illustrated in Figure 7.5. There are two major requirements for a grid used in particle-based simulations. The first is that the construction cost is low enough to be reconstructed at every time step. The other requirement is that it should be easy to access the memory of the voxel to which a particle belongs, because the data stored in the memory is frequently referred to in a simulation. There is actually another condition—although it is not necessarily required, but is preferable—a smaller memory footprint. In the following, we discuss these points in the three grids: uniform grid, hash grid, and hierarchical grid.

The uniform grid allocates the memory for all the voxels in the computation domain whether it is occupied by particles or not. This simple nature keeps the construction and access costs low. Although the uniform grid satisfies the two requirements, it needs a large memory to hold the data for all the voxels in the computation domain. There can be a large number of empty voxels, storing no particles, which is nothing but a waste of memory.

The hash grid improves on the uniform grid by not allocating all the voxels. Instead, it maps the voxels to a fixed-sized array by using the hash function. It looks to be a good candidate, but it suffers from hash collision, in which several voxels are mapped to the same location because the hash grid cannot guarantee a perfect hash. When the grid is accessed, the stored values have to be checked to see whether they are in the same voxel or not. So the access cost is more than it is in the uniform grid.

The hierarchical grid improves the memory efficiency a lot. Figure 7.5 (right) shows a quad tree (correspondence to the three-dimensional case is octree), which divides a cell with a valid entry. The top level of the tree is the bounding box of the input data. A node with an entry will be divided into four nodes; this is done recursively when the criteria are met. It avoids allocation of memory for empty space by using hierarchical representation. The drawback of the hierarchy is the access cost of a leaf node. Unlike the uniform grid, it cannot calculate the memory address directly from the position of the query. Instead, it has to traverse the tree structure from the root of the tree.

We now parallelize particle-based simulations on multiple processors, which has some additional requirements. One requirement is that all the computations are parallelized. Especially when using a GPU, the entire algorithm should be performed on the GPU; otherwise, data have to be transferred between the GPU and the CPU. Another consideration is that a uniform computation burden is preferred to keep the load balance uniform. To summarize this discussion, a uniform

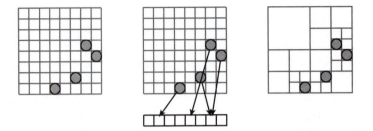

Figure 7.5. Uniform grid (left), hash grid (middle), and hierarchical grid (right). The uniform grid allocates memory for an entire domain. The hash grid maps a voxel to a memory array using the hash function. The hierarchical grid only subdivides voxels containing particles.

grid is memory inefficient and a hash grid is not suited for implementation on the GPU because of the hash collision. Construction of a grid and accessing a voxel is computationally expensive in a hierarchical grid.

The sliced grid, developed by [Harada et al. 07], is another option. This is a grid whose construction cost is low, has easy access to a voxel, and requires a small footprint. So we chose the sliced grid for the acceleration structure for our neighboring-particle search. In the following, a short introduction of the sliced grid is presented, followed by an implementation on the GPU using CUDA.

7.4.2 Sliced Grid

When a uniform grid is used, a bounding box is defined to enclose the computational domain, and memory for the voxels inside of the bounding box is allocated whether a voxel is occupied or not by a particle, as shown in Figure 7.6 (left). We can see that a large amount of memory is wasted because it allocates memory for unused voxels. However, the sliced grid allocates memory, as shown in Figure 7.6 (right). The procedure to build a grid starts by scanning the space for the grid cells filled with particles. Of course, it is possible to identify voxels containing particles by scanning the whole space, but there is a cost for that. The sliced grid increases the memory efficiency by adding a little computation.

First of all, orthogonal basis vectors (e^x, e^y, e^z) and a uniform grid along the bases in the computational domain are prepared. Note that the grid is not allocated in the memory at this time. The first step is the scanning of the number of voxels required to store the data.

An axis is chosen from the bases, and the grid in the domain is divided into slices perpendicular to the axis. Each slice has a one-voxel thickness in the direction of the axis. Thus, the slices have one dimension less than the spatial dimension of the computation domain. A sliced grid allocates memory for the two-dimensional bounding boxes for each slice. By not excluding empty voxels completely, it keeps the computation cost low. When $\mathbf{e}^x$ is chosen as the axis, the slice is spread over the space of the bases $\mathbf{e}^y$ and $\mathbf{e}^z$. The following explanation assumes that the coordinate in the grid space of a point $\mathbf{x} = (x, y, z)$ is $\mathbf{b} = (b^x, b^y, b^x) = (\mathbf{x} \cdot \mathbf{e}^x, \mathbf{x} \cdot \mathbf{e}^y, \mathbf{x} \cdot \mathbf{e}^z)$. After dividing the computational space into slices, the bounding box (two-dimensional in this case) for each slice is calculated by scanning the grid coordinates of all the particles. The maximum and minimum of y and z of slice i are

$$B^y_{i,\max} = \max_{j \in P_i}\{b^y_j\}, \quad B^y_{i,\min} = \min_{j \in P_i}\{b^y_j\},$$
$$B^z_{i,\max} = \max_{j \in P_i}\{b^z_j\}, \quad B^z_{i,\min} = \min_{j \in P_i}\{b^z_j\},$$

where $P_i = \{j | b^x_j = i\}$.

With these values, the number of voxels in the y- and z-directions are computed as

$$n^y_i = \frac{B^y_{i,\max} - B^y_{i,\min}}{d} + 1,$$
$$n^z_i = \frac{B^z_{i,\max} - B^z_{i,\min}}{d} + 1,$$

where d is the side length of the voxels. This bounding box with $n_i = n^y_i n^z_i$ voxels in a slice is allocated in memory. This is much more efficient than using the uniform grid, although it still has some empty voxels. The index of a voxel at (x, y, z) at slice i can be calculated by

$$v_i(x, y, z) = \left\lceil (y - B^y_{i,\min})/d \right\rceil + \left\lceil (z - B^z_{i,\min})/d \right\rceil n^y_i. \tag{7.3}$$

Placing the memory for slices in a contiguous memory requires the offsets or the indices of the first voxels of the slices. Let the index of the first voxel of slice i be

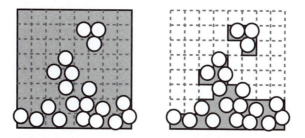

Figure 7.6. Uniform grid (left) and sliced grid(sliced in the x-direction) (right).

p_i. It is calculated as the summation of the number of voxels from the first slice S_0 to slice S_{i-1}. Thus, $p_i = \sum_{i<j} n_j$. Taking the prefix sum of the number of voxels in the slices gives us the indices of the first voxels.

We are now ready to store the data in the grid. The index of the voxel to which a point (x, y, z) belongs is calculated in two steps. The first step is the computation of the slice the point is on. It can be calculated by $i = [(b^x - B^x_{\min})]$, where $B^x_{\min}$ is the minimum coordinate of the slices in the x-direction. By using the index of the slice, the first voxel of the slice stored in the table calculated in the preprocessing step is read. From the index and Equation (7.3), the index of the voxel is calculated as follows:

$$v(x, y, z) = p_i + \left(\frac{y - B^y_{i,\min}}{d} + \frac{z - B^z_{i,\min}}{d} n^y_i \right).$$

Of course, we can push this slicing concept to another dimension to remove more empty voxels, i.e., by slicing in the x-direction before slicing in the y-direction. However, this is a tradeoff between memory saving and computation; it adds much more overhead for real-time applications.

Implementation on the GPU. Before storing particle indices to memory, the bounding box and the first index of the voxel in each slice have to be calculated. Although these computations are trivial on a sequential processor, it requires some effort to perform these on multiple processors. The GPU implementation is explained in the following paragraphs.

Calculating the bounding box and the first voxel index of every slice is performed in several steps. The first step is the computation of the bounding boxes in which memory will be allocated. The grid coordinate calculated from the particle position is inserted in the bounding box of the slice on which the particle is located. Although the flexibility of current GPUs makes the serial version of the computation possible on the GPU, it cannot exploit the power of the GPU. For efficiency reasons, the computation is divided into two stages. The particles are divided into several sets, and bounding boxes for these sets are computed in parallel. If there are m slices and the particles are divided into n sets, n sets of m bounding boxes are calculated in parallel. (Of course, this is also effective on other multiple processors.) Then, the results are merged into a set of bounding boxes. This reduction step can also be parallelized on the GPU.

Here we assume that the x-axis is taken as the slicing axis. Then, what we have to compute are $B^y_{i,\max}, B^y_{i,\min}, B^z_{i,\max}$, and $B^z_{i,\min}$, which are the maximum and the minimum values for the y- and z-directions on ith slice of the x-direction. Let n and m be the total number of particles and the number of the small computations (we will call them jobs from now on). The ith job is responsible for particles whose indices are in $n/m \leq a < (i+1)n/m$. Then the bounding box of the jth slice in the ith job is

$$B^y_{ij,\max} = \max_{a \in P_{ij}}\{b^y_a\}, \quad B^y_{ij,\min} = \min_{a \in P_{ij}}\{b^y_a\},$$
$$B^z_{ij,\max} = \max_{a \in P_{ij}}\{b^z_a\}, \quad B^z_{ij,\min} = \min_{a \in P_{ij}}\{b^z_a\},$$

where $P_{ij} = \{a | b^x_a = j, n/m \leq a < (i+1)n/m\}$. One job is processed by a block of threads on CUDA. Since the bounding values are frequently read and updated, they can be stored quickly on chip memory if available. On CUDA, shared memory is used for their storage.

However, the updating of the bounding values has to be serialized in case of write conflicts among threads. Therefore, whenever a thread updates a bounding volume, it has to be locked. This kills the performance when a large number of threads are running at the same time. To increase the efficiency of the computation, one job is split into smaller jobs and threads in a block are also divided into smaller thread groups. The computation can be much more efficient because these smaller thread groups calculate their own bounding volume data by synchronizing fewer numbers of threads. Figure 7.7 illustrates a three-step computation of the bounding volumes.

We will look more closely at the implementation of this computation on a current GPU. Reducing the size of data is a good idea in most cases because the latency of the memory access is much higher than are the arithmetic instructions. Also, the chip resources that can be used in computation are limited. To maximize the efficiency of the GPU, the register and shared-memory usage should be kept to a minimum. The size of the shared memory on an NVIDIA G80 is 16 KB per

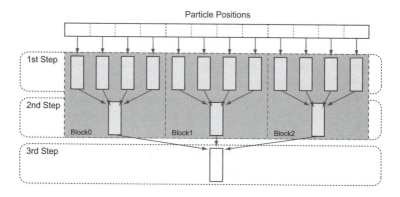

Figure 7.7. Computation of bounding volumes.

multiprocessor. If eight bits are used for the bounding values, and assuming there are 256 cells in each direction at most, a set of bounding boxes requires 1 KB of storage. (Of course we can use 32 bits for a bounding value, but it strains the local resources and results in less usage of hardware threads.) Therefore, we can calculate at most 16 sets of bounding boxes by the same number of small thread groups in a block at the same time. The computation of the bounding volumes is done by reading particle values from main memory with aligned memory access and updating the values using synchronization in the thread group. This corresponds to the first step in Figure 7.7. The next step is reduction of these sets of values. These outputs are still placed in shared memory, and one set of bounding boxes is calculated from in the same kernel by assigning a thread to a bounding box that reads all the bounding values from the smaller groups. In short, we have 256 slices, 256 threads run at the merge step, and thread i assigned to the ith slice compares all the values of the slices from all the small groups. Then threads write the values to the global memory at the last merge step.

The last merge step runs in another kernel. This step is almost the same as the previous merge except for reading the values off chip memory this time. Instead of using a thread to reduce a slice, tree-shaped reduction, in which $n/2$ threads are assigned to a slice (n is the number of bounding boxes) and reduce two values to one in a step is used; it has an advantage in performance. This is the third step in Figure 7.7. In this way, a set of bounding boxes is calculated from all the particles.

When using CUDA for the computation, the number of real threads running is not equal to the width of a kernel. In most cases, it is smaller than the kernel width. Although we can make the kernel the same block size as the number of real threads, increasing the size of blocks makes the computation much more efficient because it makes the threads switch between work groups (like multithreading on the CPU when a work group is stalled).

Now that we have the bounding boxes for all the slices, the number of voxels in a slice is calculated. This computation is tricky when using shaders, but with the function of synchronization among threads in a block, it has become easier. The prefix sum of the array is calculated in parallel to get the indices of the first voxels. For this parallel reduction, a method presented in [Harris et al. 07] is used.

Figure 7.8 shows how much the sliced grid improves the memory efficiency in a test simulation. It compares the memory consumption of the uniform grid, octree, and sliced grid in a DEM simulation. We can see that the sliced grid can reduce the memory consumption greatly over the uniform grid, and the efficiency is close to the octree. Moreover, the cost of accessing the voxel data is at least as cheap as the uniform grid, and can be much better, as will be shown later.

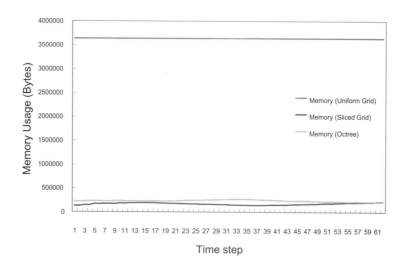

Figure 7.8. Memory consumptions when using uniform grid, sliced grid, and octree (see Color Plate V).

7.4.3 Introducing Sort

Introduction of the sliced grid not only improves the memory efficiency but also improves the performance thanks to the dense voxel data, which will be shown later. This section discusses how to improve the performance from the perspective of cache efficiency. A simple implementation of a particle-based simulation is accompanied by random access of the data. The random-access pattern of the memory reduces the performance. If the particle data are also arranged in the order of the spatial distribution of particles, the cache hit-rate of accessing the particle data increases as well. However, because particles not having any fixed connectivity move freely, the memory location of spatially close particles becomes random as the simulation proceeds. This reduces the memory locality and results in the slowdown of a simulation. An idea to improve the simulation performance is to sort the particle data by the spatial order of particles. We have to be careful in the selection of the sort algorithm used, especially for real-time applications, because the speedup from the ordering of the particle data has to be greater than the cost of the sorting. Otherwise, it just slows the simulation down.

Researchers have been studying sorting on the GPU. However, the best algorithm for sequential processors is not always the best for parallel processors. For example, quick sort, which is one of the most efficient sorts on the CPU, does not perform well on the GPU. Instead, sorting networks, such as bitonic merge sort, are preferred because of their parallel nature [Kipfer and Westermann 05]. However, the drawback of sorting networks is that they require lots of passes to complete the sorting. Recently, the functionality of the GPU has made it possible to implement radix sort, which requires fewer passes [Grand 07].

Although the radix sort runs quickly on the GPU, the sorting cost of the radix sort is prohibitively expensive for the sole purpose of improving cache efficiency. Actually, it took more than the computation of one step on DEM simulation in our experiment. So it does not meet our goal. There are several sorting algorithms suited for a nearly sorted list, such as insertion sort. They are good for situations with temporal coherency between frames, like our simulation. But the problem here is that an insertion sort is a completely sequential algorithm, which is not good for multiple processors, such as GPUs. But what we want is not a completion of a sort in a frame because the sort is used just to increase the spatial coherency of the data. Even if a sort in a time step improves the order of the lists more or less, it would improve the cache efficiency.

7.4.4   Block Transition Sort

Among sorting networks, we have chosen an odd-even transition sort, a sorting network that completes a sort by repeating two simple operations: comparing adjacent odd-even index pairs and flipping them if they are in the wrong order, then comparing adjacent even-odd index pairs. If blocks with an arrow in Figure 7.9 are thought of as two adjacent elements, it shows how the sorting works. Odd-even transition sort is good for a nearly sorted list but is pretty poor when it is applied to a random list. If only two adjacent elements are flipped, it can complete the sort in one or two steps. But if they are arranged in the reverse order, it takes n steps to move them to the correct order.

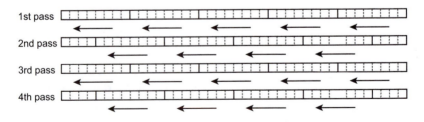

Figure 7.9. Block transition sort. An array is divided into blocks, and two adjacent blocks are sorted in a pass.

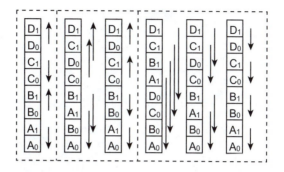

Figure 7.10. Bitonic merge sort. Thread A compares A_0 and A_1, and so on.

We generalize the idea of an odd-even transition sort to develop our block transition sort, which is suited for architectures like the GPU that have a fast local memory for a set of threads. Instead of comparing two adjacent index pairs, it compares two adjacent blocks consisting of several elements. Precisely, it sorts two adjacent blocks in a step. Figure 7.9 illustrates how the block transition sort works. Block transition sort is good for a GPU, which has fast local memory for each processor, because partitioning the computation into small problems lets threads sort two adjacent blocks only on the fast local memory without writing back to the slower global memory. Also, the memory-access pattern is preferable, because all the random access can be done on the chip memory so that all the read and write operations can be aligned memory accesses.

In our implementation, we used bitonic merge sort for sorting two adjacent blocks. As shown in Figure 7.10, bitonic merge sort always compares $n/2$ sets of entries in a pass, where n is the total number of elements. So $n/2$ threads are executed, and each of them reads two elements to shared memory. Then it repeats comparison and synchronization until sorting is done. It is important to set the size of a block such that two blocks can fit in shared memory.

If we have more budget for the sorting, the two adjacent sorted chunks of data could be merged by using merge sort to make it much more efficient.

7.4.5 Performance

Figure 7.11 shows a simulation that sorts particle values. A box half-filled with particles is rotated. To make the effect of sorting illustrative, particles are colored by their indices. We can see that these colors do not mix up, although particles are mixed up. This is because of the renumbering of particles. The simulation times on a GPU are shown in Figure 7.12. The figure shows total computation time of a

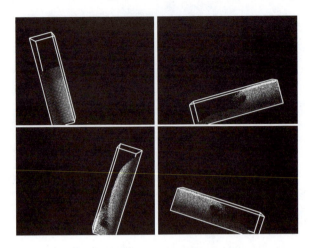

Figure 7.11. Simulation result with sorting (see Color Plate VI).

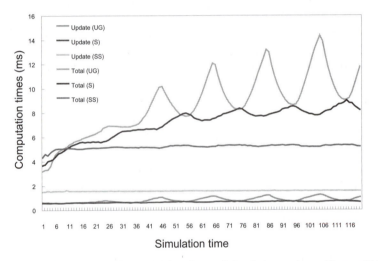

Figure 7.12. Comparison of computation times of simulations using uniform grid (UG), sliced grid (S), and sliced grid with sorting (SS) (see Color Plate VII).

time step and update of the particle values. When sorting is used for a sliced grid, particles are sorted at the update. Concretely, particle indices are sorted using the grid coordinates as keys. Then updated velocities and positions are written to the new memory locations. This timing also includes the time for sorting. We can see that total time with sorting does not spike when sorting is introduced, although update with sorting does takes some time.

7.5 Data Transfer Using Grids

The sliced grid in which the computation domain is sliced by the x-axis is used by the acceleration structure to search for neighboring particles. The data that have to be sent to an adjacent processor are two contiguous slices when the side length of voxels equals the particle diameter. Generally, the data to be sent is smaller than using a uniform grid although efficiency depends on the distribution of particles.

Sending the data between GPUs cannot be done directly at the moment. Therefore, the data have to be sent via main memory in two steps: first, send the data from a GPU to main memory, then the second GPU reads the data from main memory. Because the neighbors of GPUs do not change, the destination of the memory to which a GPU writes the data and the memory a GPU reads from is defined at spatial decomposition. Figure 7.13 illustrates how this works when using four GPUs for a simulation. Each GPU computes a subdomain, and they each have one or two ghost regions. After the computation of a time step, all the GPUs send the data to the predefined location in main memory. GPUs at both ends write particle data to one buffer and other GPUs write to two buffers. To make sure that all the data are ready, all of the threads are synchronized after the send. Then the reading from the defined memory location finishes the transfer. As you can see, these threads run completely in parallel except for one synchronization per time step.

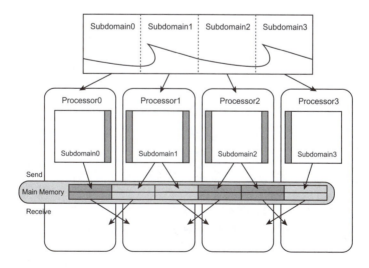

Figure 7.13. Overview of a simulation using four GPUs.

7.6   Results

Our method was implemented using C++ and NVIDIA CUDA 1.1 on a PC equipped with an Intel Core2 Q6600 CPU, a GeForce8800GT GPU, and Tesla S870 GPUs. The program executes five CPU threads: it uses one GPU for rendering and the other four GPUs for the computation of the particle-based simulation. A CPU thread managing a GPU executes kernels for the GPU.

Figure 7.14 is a comparison of the computation times of the simulation shown in Figure 7.15, changing the number of GPUs. A simulation using one million particles takes about 95 ms for a simulation step using one GPU, while the same simulation takes about 40 ms and 25 ms on two GPUs and four GPUs, respectively. Although these timings include the management of particles and the data transfer time between GPUs, they are nearly scaling to the number of processors. The efficiency of parallelization decreases for the simulation on four GPUs compared to the simulation on two GPUs. This is because it is necessary to communicate with one other GPU when using two GPUs, but communication with two adjacent GPUs is necessary when using four GPUs. The timing, excluding the time for data transfer, are also shown in Figure 7.14. These time only exclude the actual data transfer between processors but include the time to manage data. From this figure, we can see that the overhead of data management is small enough that the performance is scaling well to the number of GPUs.

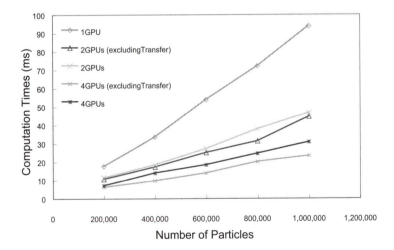

Figure 7.14. Comparison of simulation times using up to four GPUs (see Color Plate VIII).

Figure 7.15. A screenshot from a real-time simulation using 500,000 particles on four GPUs. The simulation domain is split by planes perpendicular to the x-axis. The different particle colors show on which GPU they are calculated (see Color Plate IX).

7.7 Conclusion

In this chapter, we have discussed techniques to use multiple processors with distributed memory for a particle-based simulation. The performance of the method scales well to the number of processors when particles are distributed evenly on each computation domain. However, the performance is not good when the particle distribution is not uniform because it uses a fixed decomposition of the computation domain. Dynamic load balancing is something to be considered in future work, but it would be possible by using the data calculated for the sliced grid because it has histograms of the particle distribution in the sliced direction.

Bibliography

[Grand 07] S. L. Grand. "Broad-Phase Collision Detection with CUDA."" In *GPU Gems 3*, edited by Herbert Nguyen, pp. 697–722. Reading, MA: Addison-Wesley, 2007.

[Harada et al. 07] T. Harada, S. Koshizuka, and Y. Kawaguchi. "Slided Data Structure for Particle-based Simulations on GPUs." In *Proc. of GRAPHITE*, pp. 55–62. New York: ACM, 2007.

[Harada 07] T. Harada. "Real-Time Rigid Body Simulation on GPUs." In *GPU Gems 3*, edited by Herbert Nguyen, pp. 611-632. Reading, MA: Addison-Wesley, 2007.

[Harris et al. 07] M. Harris, S. Segupta, and J.D. Owens. "Parallel Prefix Sum (Scan) with CUDA." In *GPU Gems 3*, edited by Herbert Nguyen, pp. 851–876. Reading, MA: Addison-Wesley, 2007.

[Kipfer and Westermann 05] Peter Kipfer and Rüdiger Westermann. "Improved GPU Sorting." In *GPU Gems 2*, edited by Matt Pharr, pp. 733–746. Reading, MA: Addison-Wesley, 2005.

[Koshizuka and Oka 96] S. Koshizuka and Y. Oka. "Moving-Particle Semi-Implicit Method for Fragmentation of Incompressible Flow." *Nucl. Sci. Eng.* 123 (1996), 421–434.

[Mishra 03] B. K. Mishra. "A Review of Computer Simulation of Tumbling Mills by the Discrete Element Method: Part I—Contact Mechanics." *International Journal of Mineral Processing* 71:1 (2003), 73–93.

- IV -

Constraint Solving

– 8 –

Ropes as Constraints

Anton Knyazyev

8.1 Introduction

Ropes are often considered to be a fairly trivial game-code gimmick and not really a part of a physics engine proper. In this article, I'll try to show that it might be beneficial to have a low-level rope implementation, which can look past the surface and treat a rope for what it is—a complex dynamic constraint rather than a general set of connected points that apply impulses. Which also means that ropes—or chains!—are some of the most gameplay-friendly physics features, since gameplay at its core is a collection of constraints (in the most general sense).

You open your eyes. You are in a spacious white room with a high ceiling. There are two levels; you are on the upper one, next to a heavy-looking metal box with a hook on its top. One wall is made of reflective glass, but you can make out several figures behind it, dressed in lab coats. One feeling overwhelms you: hunger.
> save
game saved
> look
On the lower floor, opposite to you but on the ground level there is a compartment in a wall, covered by a glass pane. Inside you can see a large bunch of bananas, a dozen or two. Your hunger immediately gets stronger, pulsating inside you. There is a rope hanging from the ceiling, right next to the compartment. In a far corner of the room you notice a smaller bunch of bananas.
> take large bunch
They are behind a glass pane.
> hit pane
You smash the pane, but it doesn't look like you can break it. If it wasn't for the hunger, your hand would really hurt now.
> take small bunch
You take the small bunch; there are three bananas in it. You can barely control yourself.

THE DEVIL .

> eat bananas

You hastily eat the bananas you have, which appeases the hunger... but only momentarily. If anything, it seems to have stirred it up instead. You notice two figures behind the glass wall talking to each other. One of them seems to shake his head.

> take rope

You grab the rope's end, hanging next to the glass pane.

> throw rope to box

You try to throw the rope so that it lands next to the metal box, but it immediately slides back.

> load

Game loaded

> take small bunch

You take the small bunch; there are three bananas in it. You can barely control yourself.

> tie bunch to rope

You tie the bananas you have to the free end of the rope, desperately fighting off the hunger.

> throw bananas to box

You try to throw the bananas so that they land next to the metal box. It takes a couple of tries, but you succeed eventually. You can see the people behind the glass wall talking. They seem rather excited.

> tie rope to box

The rope is still tied to the bananas.

> untie rope

Done

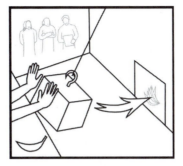

> eat bananas

You greedily eat the small bunch of bananas, which appeases the hunger, but only momentarily. It comes back almost immediately, stronger than before. As you let loose the rope end, it slides back to the lower level.

> undo

Last action ("eat bananas") reverted.

> tie rope to box

You tie the rope to the hook on the top of the metal box.

> push box

The box is quite heavy, but you manage to push it off the edge. It swings reluctantly, but quickly gains momentum and smashes right into the glass pane, shattering it completely. You can see a lot of reaction from the people behind the reflective wall. You *think* you see one of them handing money to another.

> eat bananas

You take the large banana bunch and eat it quickly, to your great satisfaction. This seems to have driven off the hunger, and you feel pleasant dizziness and comfort. You fall asleep.

8.2   Free-Hanging Ropes

First, let's talk a bit about free-hanging ropes, which are, in fact, just general sets of connected points that apply impulses to each other. Ok, not *quite* general, since linearity enables a lot of optimizations. For instance, ropes can be made entirely unstretchable by just applying positional segment-length enforcement starting from the connected end (see Figure 8.1). It's a bit harder if both ends are connected—one approach is to apply the enforcement several times, alternating the ends.

Another observation is that it's also possible to have a "perfect" solution for the rope's points' velocities in linear time. Here we are solving for contact

Figure 8.1. Sequential segment length enforcement. Here, black vertices represent the
initial state, and gray ones represent the state after length enforcement.

impulses applied along the rope segments to keep the relative vertex velocities
along these directions zero (we are assuming the rope has no contacts for now,
and also that it resists compressing as well as stretching—to make the problem
just linear instead of linear complementary):

$$\mathbf{v}'_i = \mathbf{v}_i + \frac{\mathbf{d}_i \mathrm{P}_i}{\mathrm{m}_i},$$

$$\mathbf{v}'_{i+1} = \mathbf{v}_{i+1} - \frac{\mathbf{d}_i \mathrm{P}_i}{\mathrm{m}_{i+1}},$$

$$(\mathbf{v}'_{i+1} - \mathbf{v}'_i) \cdot \mathbf{d}_i = 0.$$

Here, $\mathbf{v}_i$ is vertex i's current velocity, $\mathbf{v}'_i$ is its updated velocity, $\mathbf{d}_i$ is its
normalized direction from vertex i to vertex $i+1$, P_i is the (scalar) impulse applied
to $\mathbf{v}_i$ and $\mathbf{v}_{i+1}$ along $\mathbf{d}_i$, and m_i is the vertex i's mass.

We can see that each impulse P_i participates in only three neighboring equations (except for the border ones):

$$(\mathbf{v}'_i - \mathbf{v}'_{i-1}) \cdot \mathbf{d}_{i-1} = 0,$$

which expands to

$$(\mathbf{v}_i - \mathbf{v}_{i-1})\mathbf{d}_{i-1} + \mathrm{P}_i \frac{\mathbf{d}_i \cdot \mathbf{d}_{i-1}}{\mathrm{m}_i} - \mathrm{P}_i \left(\frac{1}{\mathrm{m}_i} + \frac{1}{\mathrm{m}_{i-1}}\right) + \mathrm{P}_{i-2} \frac{\mathbf{d}_{i-2} \cdot \mathbf{d}_{i-1}}{\mathrm{m}_{i-1}} = 0.$$

$$(\mathbf{v}'_{i+1} - \mathbf{v}'_i) \cdot \mathbf{d}_i = 0,$$

which expands to

$$(\mathbf{v}_{i+1} - \mathbf{v}_i)\mathbf{d}_i + \mathrm{P}_{i+1} \frac{\mathbf{d}_{i+1} \cdot \mathbf{d}_i}{\mathrm{m}_{i+1}} - \mathrm{P}_i \left(\frac{1}{\mathrm{m}_{i+1}} + \frac{1}{\mathrm{m}_i}\right) + \mathrm{P}_{i-1} \frac{\mathbf{d}_{i-1} \cdot \mathbf{d}_i}{\mathrm{m}_i} = 0.$$

$$(\mathbf{v}'_{i+2} - \mathbf{v}'_i) \cdot \mathbf{d}_i = 0,$$

which expands to

$$(\mathbf{v}_{i+2} - \mathbf{v}_{i+1})\mathbf{d}_{i+1} + \mathrm{P}_{i+2}\frac{\mathbf{d}_{i+2} \cdot \mathbf{d}_{i+1}}{\mathrm{m}_{i+2}} - \mathrm{P}_{i+1}\left(\frac{1}{\mathrm{m}_{i+2}} + \frac{1}{\mathrm{m}_{i+1}}\right)$$
$$+ \mathrm{P}_i\frac{\mathbf{d}_{i-2} \cdot \mathbf{d}_{i-1}}{\mathrm{m}_i} = 0.$$

This makes the equation system tridiagonal, and such systems happen to have a linear time-exact solution [Wiki 10a]. Collisions can be handled in this method by just projecting contact vertices' velocities to the contact plane whenever they occur in equations.

Of course, this again requires cheating one's way around the inherent complementarity of the problem (since separating velocities don't need to be projected back to the plane). It gets worse when friction, especially static, is introduced (dynamic friction can just be applied independently before the solver). One standard solution is to make an assessment of how a vertex will behave after the solver pass based on its initial condition and then solve a respective linear problem (namely— no constraints for would-be separating vertices, plane projection for sliding, and full lock for those held by static friction). Naturally, it's possible to make several iterations of this step. In general though, for shorter (10–20 segment) ropes it might be advisable to use a simple iterative linear complementarity problem (LCP) solver instead (which can have correct friction and separation), and switch to the direct method for longer ones, where artifacts in individual vertex motion are less visible and vertex behavior can be better predicted based on the current state of it and its neighbors.

Another interesting point about free-hanging ropes is that it's possible to calculate the final resting pose if the endpoints and the total length are known. This can be very useful when placing things like power cables on a game level, since knowing the exact resting pose means the rope will not suddenly start swaying when the player comes close. Despite a moderately common misconception that this slack curve is a parabola, in actuality, it's a special curve type, called "the catenary" [Wiki 10b]. It does look similar to a parabola, but if we want a perfectly still resting pose, we'd better use the real thing. An interesting side note about the catenary is that it is also (unsurprisingly) shaped as an arch that can support its weight with no sliding forces between the stones (which means no cement is needed). Once we know the shape's parameters, we can place the vertices at equal distances with this formula:

$$x_i = a \sinh^{-1}\left(\frac{[\text{desired\_segment\_length}]}{a} + \sinh\frac{x_{i-1}}{a} \right),$$

$$y_i = a \cosh\frac{x_i}{a},$$

where x is the horizontal coordinate, y is the vertical coordinate (i.e., the one aligned with the gravity), and a is the curve's parameter. To find it, we must solve this equation:

$$2a \sinh\frac{s}{2a} = \frac{h}{\sinh\left(\tanh^{-1}\frac{h}{L}\right)}$$

where s is the horizontal distance between the endpoints, h is the vertical distance, and L is the desired rope length. Unfortunately, it doesn't have an analytical solution and has to be solved numerically. Small price for an ability to just *know* the end result, though!

8.3   Strained Ropes

Now, what about strained ropes? We may notice that when a rope gets strained along a line, it in essence creates a temporary constraint between the objects it's tied to, one that is very similar to a frictionless contact (with the rope's direction serving as a surface normal), with only two differences:

- Each object has its own application point.

- Instead of preventing the bodies from going towards each other, rope prevents them from separating, which can be easily achieved by just choosing the normal's direction appropriately (for instance, if contacts expect the normal to go inside the first body, then the rope should have its "normal" going outside).

The good thing here is that the rope can use a very large number of simulation segments—they will never slow down the solver because it will never know about them in the first place. Even if the number of segments is small, if they are simulated as separate rigid bodies, they can still present a difficult heavy-light-heavy scenario (unless they are not actually light compared to the other objects, in which case it'll likely look wrong)—not the case with a dedicated constraint.

An obvious restriction is, of course, that this method cannot handle ropes that wrap around other objects in a strained state. Or can it?

A familiar feeling wakes you up. Hunger. You get up, but something feels unusual; it is as if some force pushed you down, making you use your arms to support yourself. Your arms... they are covered with fur. What is going on here? Were you always like this? You try to remember, but your past, which you thought was clear and full with details, eludes you the moment you try to focus on any particular piece; it feels like trying to recall a fleeting dream. And who are those people behind the glass wall?

> look around

You are in a large room, divided into two parts by a tall thick wall. There's a wide doorway in it. On the top of the wall, in a long groove, lies a transparent plexiglass cylinder. It has bananas inside. Next to you there's another plexiglass crate with bananas and a coil of rope.

> open crate

Surprisingly, the crate on the floor opens freely. The bananas are yours to grab now. But it can't be that easy, can it? Something is not right here.

> save

Game saved

> eat bananas

You gorge on the bananas. It feels almost like a small nuclear explosion when their soft sweet pulp and your hunger meet inside you, annihilating each other. A familiar dizziness overwhelms you. But there's still a crate on top of the wall. You know you must get it and fight the sleep off.

> throw crate at cylinder

You try to hit the cylinder with the crate, but the crate's still too heavy for you to throw hard enough. It barely touches the cylinder and slides back.

> load

Game loaded

> put rope end into crate

You take a loose rope end and put it inside the open crate.

> close crate

The lid snaps into place, firmly trapping the rope end inside the crate. You see some movement behind the glass wall with your peripheral vision. Do they do that when you do something right?

> throw rope above cylinder

You throw the rest of the rope above the wall so that it lands on top of the cylinder and then falls down on the other side of the wall. Luckily, the rope is long enough. Those bastards behind the wall might not be as cruel as you thought.

> `go to other side`

You go to the other side of the room. The rope is hanging down from the cylinder, within your grasp.

> `pull rope`

As you slowly pull the rope, it locks with the cylinder, making it roll toward you. Eventually it gets out of the groove and slumps down. It is full with bananas.

> `open cylinder`

You inspect the cylinder, but it looks like it's welded shut. What kind of a sadistic joke is this?! The figures behind the glass wall seem to be almost as excited as you. You wish you could kill them.

> `open crate`

You return to the other side of the room and try to open the crate. Unfortunately, the lid is stuck now because of the rope. Your hunger reaches its peak and suddenly fully transforms into something much stronger, much more powerful. Rage. You *must* kill those people.

> `smash glass wall`

You smash the glass wall as hard as you can. The people behind it back off a bit, but the wall shows no signs of yielding. The pain only fuels your rage.

> `repeat`

("smash glass wall") You hit the wall again and again, exhausting yourself completely. Suddenly, the rage leaves you, leaving a gaping empty hole that sucks your consciousness in. You pass out.

The short version of the answer is "yes it can." Let's start going through the long version by discussing collisions. While free-hanging (and obviously those strained along a line) ropes have the liberty of being able to try different collision methods (such as vertex-only and "rigid sticks"), these new ropes need a system that will allow them to quickly wrap around objects and form sharp cor-

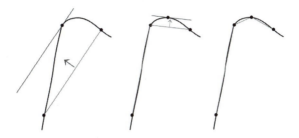

Figure 8.2. Collision-based dynamic subdivision.

ners in appropriate places when needed. An approach that seems to have worked reasonably well is to keep a set of (initially) fixed-length segments that can form temporary inner vertices based on the current frame's collisions.

Segment ends test collisions as independent particles (and their main concern is to stay outside any potentially colliding geometry, which is not a terribly hard thing to do for a point). Segment bodies are first traced as rays, and if such a ray goes through something, it gets unprojected to the state where it touches the geometry at a single point (the direction can be chosen using some heuristic magic, based on the contact normal, neighboring-segments directions, and the last frame's state). A new temporary vertex is created at this point, and the procedure is repeated for the two new edges that connect it to the original segment's ends (see Figure 8.2). The process can stop when either the amount of subvertices reaches a limit or a subsegment length becomes short enough.

The next step is finding out whether the rope is actually strained, and this is obviously not as straightforward as in the case of a straight rope (apologies for the pun). First thing to think about here is friction. In a frictionless case, the rope won't be able to apply any force on the objects it collides with while it's "tilted" relative to the surface normal since any pull force will be fully transferred to the rope's lateral sliding motion (we are making an assumption that the rope is infinitesimally light compared to the rigid bodies it interacts with—an assumption that, perhaps, hasn't been postulated sufficiently clearly so far).

Such perfect alignment will obviously not happen during a discrete simulation, so a tilt tolerance will be required. In practice, it makes sense to have two separate and independent frictions, in lateral and pull directions. The former would simply define a maximum tilt angle that keeps the rope in a strained state. If all noncontacting fragments of the rope are sufficiently close to a straight line and all contacts are within the friction-allowed tilt range, the entire rope can be considered strained, and we can proceed. Unfortunately, as with a depressingly

Figure 8.3. Collision normals. Here, gray lines define the surface normal at the contact vertex, and thick solid lines represent the rope and its "collision normal," which forms an angle with the surface normal.

large amount of things in a physics simulation, this test requires its fair share of tolerances and tweaks to make it work in a plausible way. Nevertheless, now we have a strained, frictionless rope; let's see how it can apply impulses to all objects at once, within a single constraint.

These observations allow us to build the final equation (see Figure 8.4):

- Normals here are not the surface contact normal but just the bisectors of the incoming and outgoing rope directions at a contact vertex.

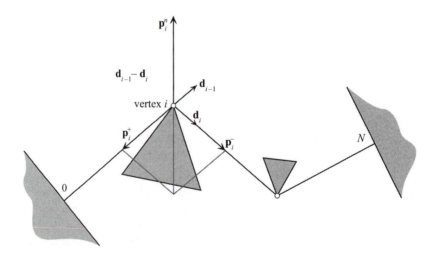

Figure 8.4. Impulses at contact points (frictionless case).

- The sum of all impulses applied to a contacting rope vertex must be zero (otherwise it'll gain infinite velocity, since the impulses have dimensions relative to the main set of bodies, which is infinitely heavier than the rope). Thus, $\mathbf{P}_i^+$ must be equal in length to $\mathbf{P}_i^-$, and their vector sum must be equal to $\mathbf{P}_i^n$ (applied from the contacting body along the normal).

- Impulses don't change along straight fragments, so $\mathbf{P}_i^- = -\mathbf{P}_{i+1}^n$.

- There should be no relative movement between the rope vertices along the rope direction, also, no relative movement between the contacting vertices and the corresponding point on the body. These last two conditions are only active while the rope remains strained (note that this state can alternate during the solving process). This gives us

$$\mathbf{v}_i \cdot \mathbf{d}_i = \mathbf{v}_{i+1} \cdot \mathbf{d}_i \tag{8.1}$$

$$\mathbf{v}_i \cdot (\mathbf{d}_{i-1} - \mathbf{d}_i) = \mathbf{v}_i^n \cdot (\mathbf{d}_{i-1} - \mathbf{d}_i)$$

$$\mathbf{v}_i \cdot \mathbf{d}_i = \mathbf{v}_i \cdot \mathbf{d}_{i-1} - \mathbf{v}_i^n \cdot (\mathbf{d}_{i-1} - \mathbf{d}_i) \tag{8.2}$$

Since we know $\mathbf{v}_0 \cdot \mathbf{d}_0$, we can use Equation (8.1) to compute $\mathbf{v}_1 \cdot \mathbf{d}_0$, then use $\mathbf{v}_1^n$ and Equation (8.2) to compute $\mathbf{v}_1 \cdot \mathbf{d}_1$, and so on, until we reach the last segment, for which we can now write the dynamic contact inequality:

$$\mathbf{v}_N \cdot \mathbf{d}_N - \mathbf{v}_0 \cdot \mathbf{d}_0 + \sum_{i=1}^{N-1} \mathbf{v}_i^n \cdot (\mathbf{d}_{i-1} - \mathbf{d}_i) < 0. \tag{8.3}$$

The zero on the right-hand side can of course be replaced by a desired "penalty" velocity that will pull the rope ends together if the total length after simulation exceeds the target one.

Now we need to compute how applying an impulse will affect this inequality. To do that, we apply a test impulse with magnitude one to the two end bodies and along all contact normals (in the latter case multiplied by $(\mathbf{d}_i - \mathbf{d}_{i-1})$ since it's being applied from both sides) and measure the changes in velocities, summing them in accordance with Equation (8.3). Let's denote this change $\mathbf{d}_v$. Resolving this contact is now simple: whenever the inequality in Equation (8.3) becomes violated by v, we apply an impulse $v/\mathbf{d}_v$ to the rope (which means applying it to all affected bodies). It's also quite straightforward to use it in a direct-ish solver, since those usually just need to know the dot product between the contact impulse and the resulting velocity changes.

The following pseudocode shows the two core steps of the procedure— applying an impulse at all contact points and measuring velocity response.

```
ApplyRopeImpulse(float P) {
   bodies[0].ApplyImpulse(d[0]*P);
   for(int i=1; i<N; i++)
      bodies[i].ApplyImpulse((d[i]−d[i−1])*P);
   bodies[N].ApplyImpulse(d[N−1]*−P);
   }
   // same procedure is used for applying test impulse,
   // except body impulses are accumulated in a special set of P,L

   float MeasureVelocityResponse() {
      ApplyTestImpulse(1.0f);
      // compute v_test and w_test for each body as velocity changes
      // due to test impulses
      // compute v[i] = bodies[i].v_test + (bodies[i].w_test ^
      //                      // pt[i]−bodies[i].center)
      float dv = v[N]*d[N] − v[0]*d[0];
      for(int i=1; i<N; i++)
         dv += v[i]*(d[i−1]−d[i]);
      return dv; //now 1/dv can be precomputed
}
```

The final push will be to add friction in the pull direction (see Figure 8.5).

The first thing to do is separate contact vertices with static and dynamic friction. It would make sense to assume that all contacts with $\tan(\alpha) < \mu$ (the friction coefficient) are static and the rest are dynamic, applying friction impulse in the direction opposite to the current slide velocity, in accordance with the Coulomb law (in reality some of the latter might actually become static during the solving process, but not addressing that immediately in the same frame sounds like a reasonable approximation).

Static friction contacts can be handled by simply splitting the rope constraint into several parts so that each one has no static contacts in the middle (series of consecutive static contacts with the same object can be merged).

For the dynamic sliding contacts, the velocity Equation (8.3) thankfully remains the same. To find the impulses, we'll use the same idea that impulses applied to each contact vertex sum up to zero. Assuming that P_i^+ and P_i^- are the (scalar) impulses that pull a vertex towards its left and right neighbors, respectively, and P_i^n is the normal impulse from the object, we can write the following:

$$(P_i^+ + P_i^-) \cos \alpha = P_i^n, \tag{8.4}$$

$$(P_i^+ + P_i^-) \sin \alpha = \mu P_i^n.$$

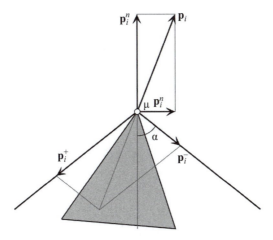

Figure 8.5. Impulses at contact points (with friction).

Here μ can be negative, depending on the initial rope-slide direction; Figure 8.5 assumes that the rope slides from right to left. This yields

$$P_i^- = P_i^+ \frac{\sin \alpha - \mu \cos \alpha}{\sin \alpha + \mu \cos \alpha}. \tag{8.5}$$

Thus, for each vertex we get the "outgoing" impulse from the "incoming" one. Expressing P_i^- and P_i^n through P_i^+ and substituting the results into Equation (8.4), we get the vector impulse applied by each body to the corresponding rope vertex (the impulse applied by the rope to each body will be its opposite):

$$\mathbf{P}_i = ((\mathbf{d}_{i-1} - \mathbf{d}_i) \sin \alpha + (\mathbf{d}_{i-1} + \mathbf{d}_i)\mu \cos \alpha) \frac{P_i^+}{\sin \alpha + \mu \cos \alpha}.$$

Now we can use the same approach as before, which is to apply a test impulse to the contact sequence, measure the velocity response, and then do the same during the solving with a real impulse (of course, the impulse will no longer stay constant from vertex to vertex—it will be changed according to Equation (8.5) after each one).

The following pseudocode shows an updated version of the impulse-application routine.

```
ApplyRopeImpulse(float P) {
  bodies[0].ApplyImpulse(d[0]*P);
  for(int i=1; i<N; i++) {
    // most of the math here should of course be computed
    // only once and stored
    float cos2a = −(d[i]*d[i−1]);
    float cosa = sqrt((1+cos2a)*0.5);
    float sina = sqrt((1−cos2a)*0.5);
    P /= sina+mue*cosa;
    bodies[i].ApplyImpulse(
      ((d[i]−d[i−1])*sina + (d[i−1]+d[i])*mue*cosa)*P);
    P *= sina−mue*cosa;
  }
  bodies[N].ApplyImpulse(d[N−1]*−P);
}
```

As tempted as I am to use the word "voila," I'll refrain and will instead just casually note that this is pretty much everything needed to efficiently simulate a rope that can wrap around objects (I'll also refrain from calling this rope "advanced," since the word quickly lost its value after a couple of iterations of engine marketing). Now it's time to put it to good use. Or bad—the choice is yours, as it always is.

You are in a room larger than the first two. Although it may just seem larger because you can no longer stand upright. The hunger is excruciating—no wonder, since you didn't eat the last time. You are standing—or rather crouching—close to an edge, with a rope hanging from the ceiling next to you. Down below you see several crates of different sizes.

> look at crates > wrap rope around neck

You quickly wrap the rope around your neck. This seems to have drawn the attention of your captors, and a lot of it.

> jump down

As you jump down the edge, you see the figures running out of their room. Bright lights turn on with distinct loud cracks, doors open on what seemed to be perfectly smooth walls, and several people run toward you. As your vision fades, you move your hands away from your neck and look at them. They are human.

THE FOOL.

Bibliography

[Wiki 10a] "Tridiagonal Matrix Algorithm." *Wikipedia*. Available at http://en.
wikipedia.org/wiki/Tridiagonal_matrix_algorithm, 2010.

[Wiki 10b] "Catenary." *Wikipedia*. Available at http://en.wikipedia.org/wiki/
Catenary, 2010.

– 9 –

Quaternion-Based Constraints

Claude Lacoursière

9.1 Introduction

The content in the present chapter will help us define rotational constraints between rigid bodies that are never unstable and that always return to the correct
configuration. This means, in particular, that a hinge joint defined the way I explain below will *never* stabilize in an antiparallel configuration, no matter how
much abuse it is subjected to. There is also a true constant velocity joint that
we can use to replace our Hooke joints. This is in fact more useful since it truly
transmits the rotational motion faithfully. There is a lot of mathematics involved,
but the final results are easy to implement. If you get lost or impatient, just look
at the pictures and jump to the last few paragraphs of each section.

9.2 Notation and Definitions

In what follows, I will write about indicator functions $\mathbf{c}(\mathbf{x})$—indicator for short—
such that a geometric constraint is satisfied when $\mathbf{c}(\mathbf{x}) = 0$ and violated otherwise. Here, $\mathbf{x}$ is the generalized coordinate vector that contains information about
the positions and orientations of all bodies. Indicators are then vector functions
of a vector argument because we often consider multiple indicators to be a single
object. We need two scalar indicators to define a hinge, for instance. When I say
constraint, I mean a hinge joint.

When I write $y^{(x)}$, I mean quantity y in body x. Subscripts are reserved
for components of vectors. Quaternions are written as $\mathbf{q}$, and the components
are written $\mathbf{q} = [q_s, q_1, q_2, q_3]^{\mathrm{T}}$ and in block form as $\mathbf{q} = [q_s, \mathbf{q}_v]^{\mathrm{T}}$. Here, q_s
stands for the scalar part. The complex conjugates are written as $\mathbf{q}^\dagger$. Vectors are
written as $\mathbf{x}$, and *most* matrices are written with bold upper-case letters, such as $\mathbf{A}$.
But I also use certain special parametric matrices that are written as $\mathcal{G}(\mathbf{q})$, $\mathcal{E}(\mathbf{q})$,
$\mathcal{Q}(\mathbf{q})$, and $\mathcal{P}(\mathbf{q})$, which are defined from a quaternion $\mathbf{q} \in \mathbb{H}$ in Section 9.5. I
write $\mathbb{P}$ for projection operators. The vectors are always *columns* unless explicitly

transposed. The matrix vector multiplication is $\mathbf{Ax}$. Quaternions $\mathbf{q} \in \mathbb{H}$ behave as vectors with respect to addition and scalar multiplication. What makes them a useful algebra is the product operation, which we write as $\mathbf{qp}$. We will use the right-hand convention for this, as is defined in Chapter 1. A three-dimensional vector $\mathbf{x}$ can be promoted to a quaternion $\mathbf{p} = \mathbf{q}(\mathbf{x})$ by writing $p_s = 0$ and $\mathbf{p}_v = \mathbf{x}$. That is a purely imaginary quaternion since $\mathbf{p}^\dagger = -\mathbf{p}$. If I forget to tell you in a particular set of equations, I always use $\mathbf{u}$, $\mathbf{v}$, and $\mathbf{n}$ to denote right handed orthogonal systems, which are rotations of the references $\mathbf{x}$, $\mathbf{y}$, and $\mathbf{z}$ with the exact correspondence.

Credit where credit is due. My initial inspiration came after reading [Serban and Haug 98] and [Haug 89]. I then found results similar to what is below in [Tasora and Righettini 99]. The matrix formulation of quaternion algebra is already in the graphics literature [Shoemake 91, Shoemake 10] but is not widely used. There is a whole chapter about details of this matrix representation in my PhD thesis [Lacoursière 07a] for those who may be interested.

And now, let's begin.

9.3   The Problem

Rotational constraints between rigid bodies are problematic when they are defined using dot product indicators. This makes them bistable since obviously $\mathbf{x} \cdot \mathbf{y} = 0$ implies that $-\mathbf{x} \cdot \mathbf{y} = 0$ as well. Take, for instance, the rotational part of a hinge joint between bodies 1 and 2 that have right-handed orthonormal frames defined with $\mathbf{u}^{(1)}, \mathbf{v}^{(1)}, \mathbf{n}^{(1)}$ and $\mathbf{u}^{(2)}, \mathbf{v}^{(2)}, \mathbf{n}^{(2)}$, respectively. Taking $\mathbf{n}^{(1)}$ as the normal axis of the hinge attached on body 1, the hinge indicator is defined as the set of the two conditions

$$\mathbf{n}^{(1)} \cdot \mathbf{u}^{(2)} = 0 \quad \text{and} \quad \mathbf{n}^{(1)} \cdot \mathbf{v}^{(2)} = 0. \tag{9.1}$$

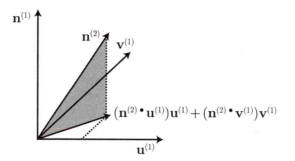

Figure 9.1. The hinge definition.

When these are satisfied, the vector $\mathbf{n}^{(1)}$ has no projection in the $\mathbf{u}^{(2)}$–$\mathbf{v}^{(2)}$ plane, as shown in Figure 9.1.

The content of the constraint is that $\mathbf{n}^{(1)}$ *and* $\mathbf{n}^{(2)}$ are both normal to the $\mathbf{u}^{(2)}$–$\mathbf{v}^{(2)}$ plane, which means they are parallel, and thus, by transitivity, $\mathbf{n}^{(2)}$ is a normal to the $\mathbf{u}^{(1)}$–$\mathbf{v}^{(1)}$ plane as well. But the indicator function in Equation (9.1) is satisfied simultaneously for both $\mathbf{n}^{(1)} = \mathbf{n}^{(2)}$ and $\mathbf{n}^{(1)} = -\mathbf{n}^{(2)}$, i.e., the antiparallel case. But we usually want the first of the two options. This is shown below in Figure 9.2.

It is possible to flip between one and the other by wrenching the two bodies hard enough, irrespective of our numerical method of choice. In addition, the constraint weakens as it gets further and further away from the desired configuration. It is, in fact, metastable when vector $\mathbf{n}^{(1)}$ lies in the $\mathbf{u}^{(2)}$–$\mathbf{v}^{(2)}$ plane since the Jacobian vanishes there, and so it might stabilize either the right way or the wrong way. That makes them easy to flip since the constraint force starts to weaken at $\pi/4$, and it starts to point the wrong way after $\pi/2$. We could avoid such headaches using reduced coordinate formulations, as is common in robotics, but that will cause other types of pain. As an aside, we might think that the indicator $\mathbf{n}^{(1)} \cdot \mathbf{n}^{(2)} = \cos\theta = 0$, which is a single equation, is equally good as the two equations in Equation (9.1). The problem is that this single equation is, in fact, quadratic, i.e., it behaves as θ^2 near $\theta = 0$, which means that the Jacobian vanishes.

The remedy to that is to construct indicators with a unique zero, and this can be done using quaternions. These indicators have extreme values ± 1 precisely when one of the normal vectors used in the dot product definition is flipped by $180°$. One problem remains though. The Jacobians still vanish at the maximum constraint violation, and that means they weaken on the way there. It is possible to add nonlinear terms to the indicator functions to fix this problem. But that's

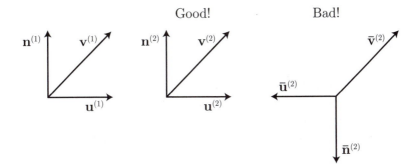

Figure 9.2. Axis flip.

beyond our scope here, and I think we can manage better with good logic code to catch the problem cases.

The theory below is an overkill, but the results are easy to implement and not much more expensive computationally than the standard dot product versions. Three constraints are analyzed in detail, namely, the lock joint, the hinge joint, and the homokinetic joint. This last one is also known as the constant velocity joint, CV for short. It is much like the Hooke or universal joint but without the problems. The Hooke joint is easy to define as a bistable constraint in dot product form. It seems that it is not possible to define a monostable version without introducing a third body that is hinged to the other two. If we look at a good diagram and animations of the Hooke joint [Wikipedia 10b], we will see clearly why a third body is needed. But more to the point, the CV joint is the one we see in our front traction cars, since otherwise, the wheels would not move at constant rotational velocity. Curiously, though it is an engineering puzzle to construct a CV joint [Wikipedia 10a] that is not fragile, it is dead easy to define the geometry using quaternions. A homokinetic joint can be constructed using two hinges, and this makes the analysis much more complicated [Masarati and Morandini 08] than the quaternion definition given below.

These three rotational joints are used in combination with positional constraints to produce all other joints, namely, the "real" hinge, the prismatic of the sliding joint that requires the full lock constraint, the cylindrical joint that requires the hinge constraint, etc. A robust Hooke joint can also be built out of three bodies using two hinges.

In what follows, I will first explain the indicators themselves by looking at special quaternions and the geometry of the resulting kinematics. Then, I will explain how to construct the Jacobians for these.

9.4   Constraint Definitions

It is enough to consider just one quaternion $\mathbf{q}$ describing the orientation of one rigid body with respect to the inertial frame to start with. This is because, in the end, the quaternion used in the constraint will be the *relative* rotation going from body 1 to body 2. That will simplify things and save our time. Also note that in this first stage, I assume that both our hinge and CV axes are aligned along z in each body. Generalizations are provided below.

The quaternion that corresponds to no rotation at all is just the unit quaternion, i.e.,

$$q_s = 1, \quad \mathbf{q}_v{}^{\mathrm{T}} = [0,0,0]^{\mathrm{T}}.$$

The indicator is easy to define here:

$$c_{\text{lock}} = \mathbf{q}_v = \mathbb{P}\mathbf{q} = \mathbf{P}_{\text{lock}}\mathbf{q} = 0, \tag{9.2}$$

where $\mathbb{P} = \mathbf{P}_{\text{lock}}$ is the projection operator

$$\mathbb{P} = \begin{bmatrix} 0 & 1 & 0 & 0 \\ 0 & 0 & 1 & 0 \\ 0 & 0 & 0 & 1 \end{bmatrix}$$

so that

$$\mathbb{P}\mathbf{q} = \mathbf{q}_v.$$

There is still an ambiguity since the constraint is satisfied by both $\pm\mathbf{q}$. But that is of no consequence since both cases correspond to a unit rotation. Remember that quaternions cover the rotation group twice. The lock constraint is thus a simple linear projection of the relative quaternion. That will hold for all the other constraints.

The hinge constraint requires that the original and transformed frame share a common axis. This is set to the axis $\mathbf{z}$ arbitrarily, and thus the allowed rotations have the form

$$q_s = \cos(\phi/2) \quad \text{and} \quad \mathbf{q}_v = [0, 0, \sin(\phi/2)]^{\mathrm{T}}, \tag{9.3}$$

which gives the two equations we want:

$$c_{\text{hinge}} = \begin{bmatrix} \mathbf{x} \cdot \mathbf{q}_v \\ \mathbf{y} \cdot \mathbf{q}_v \end{bmatrix} = \begin{bmatrix} \mathbf{x}^{\mathrm{T}} \\ \mathbf{y}^{\mathrm{T}} \end{bmatrix} \mathbb{P}\mathbf{q} = \mathbf{P}_{\text{hinge}}\mathbf{q} = \begin{bmatrix} 0 \\ 0 \end{bmatrix}, \tag{9.4}$$

where

$$\mathbf{P}_{\text{hinge}} = \begin{bmatrix} \mathbf{x}^{\mathrm{T}} \\ \mathbf{y}^{\mathrm{T}} \end{bmatrix} \mathbb{P} = \begin{bmatrix} 0 & 1 & 0 & 0 \\ 0 & 0 & 1 & 0 \end{bmatrix}$$

is the hinge projection operator. We'll see in Section 9.8 how to define this for axes other than $\mathbf{z}$.

And now comes the CV joint. The kinematic constraint we want to create here is such that the rotational motion along the axis $\mathbf{n}^{(1)}$ of an object produces an identical rotation about the axis $\mathbf{n}^{(2)}$ of another. That is precisely the relationship between the plate of a turntable and the disc sitting on it, although these two objects share the same longitudinal plane. But the idea is the same: we want a driver that produces a constant rotational velocity in a secondary body about some axis fixed in that body.

Let's now visualize a perfect CV joint using two pens with longitudinal axes $\mathbf{n}^{(1)}$ and $\mathbf{n}^{(2)}$, respectively, each with a longitudinal reference line drawn on the

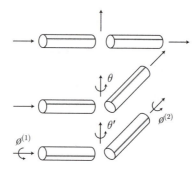

Figure 9.3. An illustration of the CV coupling.

circumference. Hold the pens 1 and 2 in your left and right hands, respectively, and align the axes and the reference lines so that they face up. Now, rotate pen 2 by some angle θ about the vertical axis $\mathbf{z}$ away from you. Choosing $\theta \approx 45°$ will make things obvious. The two pens lie in the horizontal plane, with an angle θ between $\mathbf{n}^{(1)}$ and $\mathbf{n}^{(2)}$. Now, realign the two pens and rotate them about their common longitudinal axes by 90°. Keep the reference lines aligned but make them face you. Then rotate pen 2 by the same angle θ as before about the axis $\mathbf{z}$. Clearly, the axis of rotation $\mathbf{r}$ is still perpendicular to $\mathbf{n}^{(1)}$ but is not the same as before. If you had done this in small increments, you would have seen the CV joint at work. You would probably scratch your head wondering how you would actually construct something that worked like that. You can even change the angle θ as you move along, keeping perfect alignment between the reference lines. One thing is constant though: relative rotation between pens 1 and 2, as seen from pen 1, is about an axis $\mathbf{r}$ that is perpendicular to $\mathbf{n}^{(1)}$. This axis $\mathbf{r}$ is not fixed, however. This is what I've sketched in Figure 9.3.

Let's get rid of all the indices now. The conclusion from the experiment above is that a rotation by any angle θ about any axis $\mathbf{r}$ such that $\mathbf{r} \cdot \mathbf{z} = 0$ always, will not rotate the transformed $\mathbf{x}'$–$\mathbf{y}'$ plane about the transformed axis $\mathbf{z}'$. Mathematically, this implies that the relative quaternion $\mathbf{q}$ satisfies

$$q_s = \cos(\theta/2) \quad \text{and} \quad \mathbf{q}_v = \sin(\theta/2)\mathbf{r}, \quad \text{where } \mathbf{r} \cdot \mathbf{z} = 0. \tag{9.5}$$

Therefore,

$$\mathbf{c}_{\mathrm{CV}} = \mathbf{z} \cdot \mathbf{q}_v = \mathbf{z}^{\mathrm{T}}\mathbb{P}\mathbf{q} = \mathbf{P}_{\mathrm{CV}}\mathbf{q} = 0, \tag{9.6}$$

where

$$\mathbf{P}_{\mathrm{CV}} = \mathbf{z}^{\mathrm{T}}\mathbb{P} = [0, 0, 0, 1].$$

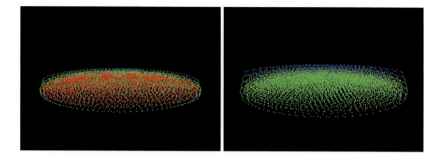

Plate I. Execution of scenario A from Table 6.1. On the left, the simulation with $k_r = 100$. On the right, the simulation with $k_r = 250$. Particle colors range from blue to green to red to denote areas of low, medium, and high density, respectively (see page 145).

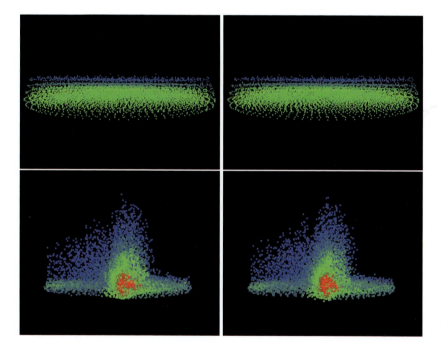

Plate II. Execution of scenario A from Table 6.1 with $k_r = 250$ at 60 Hz. The images on the left correspond to the original SPH algorithm, while the images on the right correspond to the collapsed SPH algorithm. The top images visualize a fluid at rest, while the bottom images show the behavior of the fluid under influence of an artificially generated wave. Particle colors range from blue to green to red to denote areas of low, medium, and high density, respectively (see page 147).

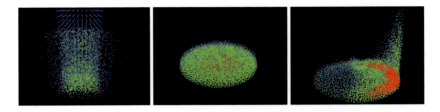

Plate III. The three different stages used for our performance measurements in Table 6.2. From left to right, we have the stage 1 in which fluid particles fall into a glass, stage 2 with fluid particles at rest and stage 3 in which artificial waves are generated. Particle colors range from blue to green to red to denote areas of low, medium and high density respectively (see page 148).

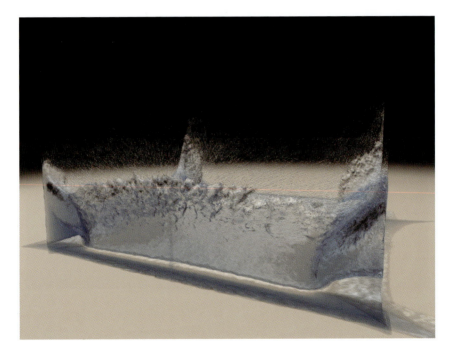

Plate IV. Rendered image from a simulation using multiple GPUs (see page 155).

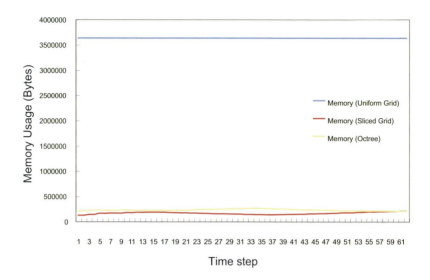

Plate V. Memory consumptions when using uniform grid, sliced grid, and octree (see page 169).

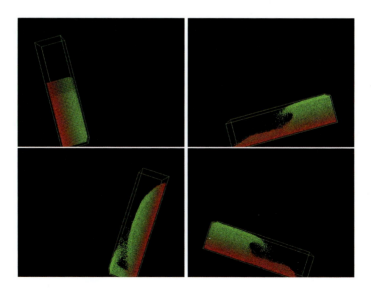

Plate VI. Simulation result with sorting (see page 172).

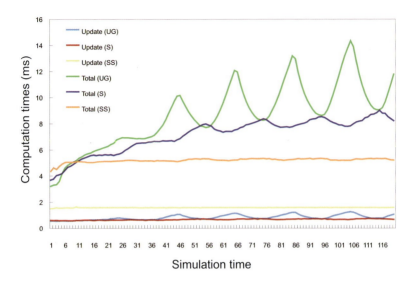

Plate VII. Comparison of computation times of simulations using uniform grid (UG), sliced grid (S), and sliced grid with sorting (SS) (see page 172).

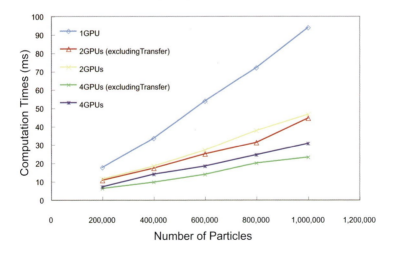

Plate VIII. Comparison of simulation times using up to four GPUs (see page 174).

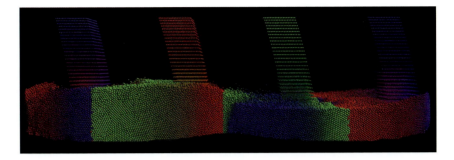

Plate IX. A screenshot from a real-time simulation using 500,000 particles on four GPUs. The simulation domain is split by planes perpendicular to the x-axis. The different particle colors show on which GPU they are calculated (see page 175).

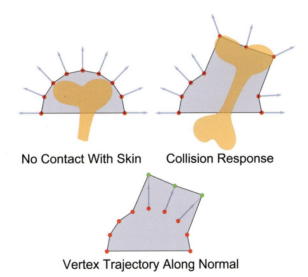

No Contact With Skin   Collision Response

Vertex Trajectory Along Normal

Plate X. Skin with nicely contained collision geometry (bone). Arrows represent vertex normals (top left). The collision bone has moved. Ray casting for each vertex has found their new positions "outside" the bone. New vertex normals are also computed (top right). The displacement vectors for the vertices that were "pushed" by the collision geometry (bottom) (see page 294).

Plate XI. Simulation examples. The top row shows the rest positions, and the bottom row shows the deformed positions (see page 238).

Plate XII. The two figures on the right show an example of surface mesh, and the two figures on the left show the associated volumetric mesh (see page 247).

Plate XIII. From left to right: a bone model, a skeleton-driven (kinematically deformed) mesh, and an animated mesh with secondary, dynamic deformation. Derivation from the primary positions is indicated by a red color (see page 305).

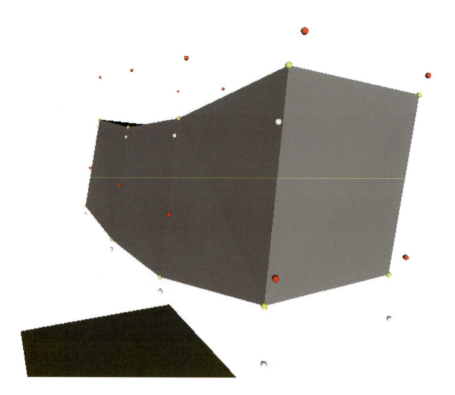

Plate XIV. Driven deformation of a simple mesh geometry (see page 318).

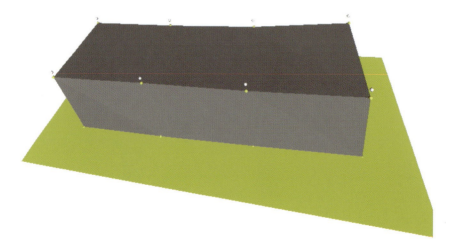

Plate XV. Under the influence of gravity, the geometry stays in shape just by means of shape matching of the local neighborhoods (see page 318).

Now that we have constraint definitions, we need Jacobians. But to get that right, I need to tell you a bit more about how I manipulate quaternion expressions.

9.5 Matrix-Based Quaternion Algebra

The quaternion algebra is covered in Chapter 1, so this section is just a simple translation into language I find useful. The format I use here should help you implement what is described in this chapter.

First, note that any quaternion $\mathbf{q}, \mathbf{p} \in \mathbb{H}$ can be represented as a simple four-dimensional vector. That works for addition and subtraction, obviously. The only thing needed to make the correspondence complete is to define the quaternion product in terms of matrix-vector operations, as I do now. Since the quaternion product of $\mathbf{q}, \mathbf{p} \in \mathbb{H}$ is linear in both $\mathbf{q}, \mathbf{p} \in \mathbb{R}^4$, we can write it as the matrix-vector product

$$\mathbf{qp} = \mathcal{Q}(\mathbf{q})\mathbf{p} = \mathcal{P}(\mathbf{p})\mathbf{q},$$

corresponding to the right and left products, respectively, with the definitions

$$\mathcal{Q}(\mathbf{q}) = \begin{bmatrix} q_s & -q_1 & -q_2 & -q_3 \\ q_1 & q_s & -q_3 & q_2 \\ q_2 & q_3 & q_s & -q_1 \\ q_3 & -q_2 & q_1 & q_s \end{bmatrix} = \begin{bmatrix} q_s & -\mathbf{q}_v^T \\ \mathbf{q}_v & q_s I_3 + [\mathbf{q}_v]_\times \end{bmatrix} = \begin{bmatrix} \mathbf{q} & \mathcal{G}^T(\mathbf{q}) \end{bmatrix},$$

$$\mathcal{P}(\mathbf{q}) = \begin{bmatrix} q_s & -q_1 & -q_2 & -q_3 \\ q_1 & q_s & q_3 & -q_2 \\ q_2 & -q_3 & q_s & q_1 \\ q_3 & q_2 & -q_1 & q_s \end{bmatrix} = \begin{bmatrix} q_s & -\mathbf{q}_v^T \\ \mathbf{q}_v & q_s I_3 - [\mathbf{q}_v]_\times \end{bmatrix} = \begin{bmatrix} \mathbf{q} & \mathcal{E}^T(\mathbf{q}) \end{bmatrix},$$

where

$$\mathcal{G}(\mathbf{q}) = \begin{bmatrix} -\mathbf{q}_v & q_s I_3 - [\mathbf{q}_v]_\times \end{bmatrix}, \qquad \mathcal{E}(\mathbf{q}) = \begin{bmatrix} -\mathbf{q}_v & q_s I_3 + [\mathbf{q}_v]_\times \end{bmatrix},$$

$$[\mathbf{x}]_\times = \begin{bmatrix} 0 & -x_3 & x_2 \\ x_3 & 0 & -x_1 \\ -x_2 & x_1 & 0 \end{bmatrix}.$$

For the last definition, this means that $[\mathbf{x}]_\times \mathbf{y} = \mathbf{x} \times \mathbf{y}$. For completeness, the complex conjugation matrix is

$$\mathcal{C} = \begin{bmatrix} 1 & 0 & 0 & 0 \\ 0 & -1 & 0 & 0 \\ 0 & 0 & -1 & 0 \\ 0 & 0 & 0 & -1 \end{bmatrix} = \begin{bmatrix} 1 & 0 \\ 0 & -I \end{bmatrix}, \text{ so } \mathbf{q}^\dagger = \mathcal{C}\mathbf{q}.$$

The correspondence to the quaternion algebra is then

$$\mathcal{Q}(\mathbf{p})\mathcal{Q}(\mathbf{q}) = \mathcal{Q}(\mathbf{pq}) \quad \text{and} \quad \mathcal{P}(\mathbf{p})\mathcal{P}(\mathbf{q}) = \mathcal{P}(\mathbf{qp}),$$

as well as

$$\mathcal{Q}(\mathbf{q}^\dagger) = \mathcal{Q}(\mathbf{q})^\mathrm{T} \quad \text{and} \quad \mathcal{P}(\mathbf{q}^\dagger) = \mathcal{P}(\mathbf{q})^\mathrm{T}.$$

The two matrices $\mathcal{Q}(\mathbf{q})$ and $\mathcal{P}(\mathbf{q})$ also commute so that

$$\mathcal{Q}(\mathbf{p})\mathcal{P}(\mathbf{q}) = \mathcal{P}(\mathbf{q})\mathcal{Q}(\mathbf{p}),$$

as we can easily verify. This representation makes it easy to compute the Jacobian matrices related to quaternion constraints.

We need an expression for $\dot{\mathbf{q}}\mathbf{q}^\dagger$ for unit quaternions $\langle\langle\mathbf{q}\rangle\rangle = 1$, which are the ones corresponding to orthonormal transforms, i.e., rotations. That will connect the changes in the relative quaternions to the angular velocities of the connected rigid bodies. Since $\mathbf{q}^\dagger\mathbf{q} = 1$ always, we have

$$\frac{d}{dt}\left(\mathbf{q}^\dagger\mathbf{q}\right) = 0 = \dot{\mathbf{q}}\mathbf{q}^\dagger + \mathbf{q}\dot{\mathbf{q}}^\dagger$$
$$= \dot{\mathbf{q}}\mathbf{q}^\dagger + \left(\dot{\mathbf{q}}\mathbf{q}^\dagger\right)^\dagger,$$

and therefore

$$\mathbf{w} = \frac{1}{2}\dot{\mathbf{q}}\mathbf{q}^\dagger = -\mathbf{w}^\dagger$$

is purely imaginary and so

$$\mathbf{w} = \begin{bmatrix} 0 \\ \omega \end{bmatrix} = \mathbb{P}^\mathrm{T}\omega,$$

where $\omega \in \mathbb{R}^3$ is the angular velocity expressed in the inertial frame. So now, we have

$$\mathbf{q}^\dagger\dot{\mathbf{q}} = \mathcal{Q}(\mathbf{q})^\mathrm{T}\dot{\mathbf{q}} = \frac{1}{2}\mathbb{P}^\mathrm{T}\omega = \frac{1}{2}\mathcal{G}^\mathrm{T}(\mathbf{q})\omega \quad \text{and}$$
$$\dot{\mathbf{q}}^\dagger\mathbf{q} = \mathcal{P}(\mathbf{q})\dot{\mathbf{q}}^\dagger = -\frac{1}{2}\mathbb{P}^\mathrm{T}\omega = -\frac{1}{2}\mathcal{E}^\mathrm{T}(\mathbf{q})\omega. \tag{9.7}$$

These identities are usually summarized as

$$\dot{\mathbf{q}} = \frac{1}{2}\mathbf{q}\mathbf{w}. \tag{9.8}$$

Note that the definition in Equation (9.8) is sometimes written the other way round, as is the case when defining the angular velocity vector in the body frame or when using left-handed multiplication, which is often used in three-dimensional graphics. Beware.

9.6 A New Take on Quaternion-Based Constraints

The Jacobians of any quaternion-based constraint can be computed using just one master Jacobian matrix and various projections. This is done using the matrix representation described in Section 9.5. Consider two rigid bodies with quaternions $\mathbf{r}, \mathbf{s} \in \mathbb{H}$ and angular velocities $\omega^{(1)}$ and $\omega^{(2)}$, respectively. The definition of the relative quaternion is $\mathbf{q} \in \mathbb{H}$. The first task is to relate the rate of change of $\mathbf{q}$ to the angular velocities $\omega^{(1)}$ and $\omega^{(2)}$. The time derivative of $\mathbf{q}$ is

$$\dot{\mathbf{q}} = \dot{\mathbf{r}}^\dagger \mathbf{s} + \mathbf{r}^\dagger \dot{\mathbf{s}} = (\dot{\mathbf{r}}^\dagger \mathbf{r})\mathbf{r}^\dagger \mathbf{s} + \mathbf{r}^\dagger \mathbf{s}(\mathbf{s}^\dagger \dot{\mathbf{s}})$$
$$= (\dot{\mathbf{r}}^\dagger \mathbf{r})\mathbf{q} + \mathbf{q}(\mathbf{s}^\dagger \dot{\mathbf{s}}). \tag{9.9}$$

So now, using the matrix representation of the quaternion product, taking the left product using $\mathcal{P}(\mathbf{q})$ on the first term and the right product using $\mathcal{Q}(\mathbf{q})$ on the second, and substituting the identities in Equation (9.7), we have

$$\dot{\mathbf{q}} = -\frac{1}{2}\mathcal{P}(\mathbf{q})\mathbb{P}^\mathrm{T}\omega^{(1)} + \frac{1}{2}\mathcal{Q}(\mathbf{q})\mathbb{P}^\mathrm{T}\omega^{(2)}$$
$$= -\frac{1}{2}\mathcal{E}(\mathbf{q})^\mathrm{T}\omega^{(1)} + \frac{1}{2}\mathcal{G}(\mathbf{q})^\mathrm{T}\omega^{(2)}. \tag{9.10}$$

The only Jacobians you need for all three quaternion constraints defined here are these. It might seem that we took a very long detour to arrive at Equation (9.10), which is very simple since we just need matrices $\mathcal{E}(\mathbf{q})$ and $G(\mathbf{q})$ in the end.

Looking at the indicators defined above in Equations (9.2), (9.4), and (9.6), the different Jacobians are simply different projections of the same proto-Jacobian, namely,

$$\mathbf{G}_{\mathrm{lock}}^{(1)} = -\frac{1}{2}\mathbb{P}\mathcal{E}(\mathbf{q})^\mathrm{T}, \qquad \mathbf{G}_{\mathrm{lock}}^{(2)} = \frac{1}{2}\mathbb{P}\mathcal{G}(\mathbf{q})^\mathrm{T},$$
$$\mathbf{G}_{\mathrm{hinge}}^{(1)} = -\frac{1}{2}\mathbf{P}_{\mathrm{hinge}}\mathcal{E}(\mathbf{q})^\mathrm{T}, \qquad \mathbf{G}_{\mathrm{hinge}}^{(2)} = \frac{1}{2}\mathbf{P}_{\mathrm{hinge}}\mathcal{G}(\mathbf{q})^\mathrm{T}, \tag{9.11}$$
$$\mathbf{G}_{\mathrm{CV}}^{(1)} = -\frac{1}{2}\mathbf{P}_{\mathrm{CV}}\mathcal{E}(\mathbf{q})^\mathrm{T}, \qquad \mathbf{G}_{\mathrm{CV}}^{(2)} = \frac{1}{2}\mathbf{P}_{\mathrm{CV}}\mathcal{G}(\mathbf{q})^\mathrm{T}.$$

9.7 Why It Works

The dot product representation of the indicators for rotational constraints is as follows:

$$\mathbf{c}_{\mathrm{dlock}} = \begin{bmatrix} \mathbf{n}^{(1)} \cdot \mathbf{u}^{(2)} \\ \mathbf{n}^{(1)} \cdot \mathbf{v}^{(2)} \\ \mathbf{u}^{(1)} \cdot \mathbf{n}^{(2)} \end{bmatrix} = \begin{bmatrix} 0 \\ 0 \\ 0 \end{bmatrix},$$

$$c_{dhinge} = \begin{bmatrix} \mathbf{u}^{(1)} \cdot \mathbf{n}^{(2)} \\ \mathbf{v}^{(1)} \cdot \mathbf{n}^{(2)} \end{bmatrix} = \begin{bmatrix} 0 \\ 0 \end{bmatrix},$$

$$c_{dhooke} = \mathbf{u}^{(1)} \cdot \mathbf{v}^{(2)} = 0.$$

We use the Hooke joint here for rough comparison since it is not practical to define the CV joint with dot products. Now, choose body 2 to be the universe and rotate body 1 about $\mathbf{u}^{(2)}$ by π so both the new $\mathbf{v}^{(2)}$ and $\mathbf{n}^{(2)}$ axes have reversed signs. Clearly, all three constraints are now violated geometrically, despite the fact that the indicator functions are still 0.

This is not the case with the quaternion-based constraints defined in Equations (9.2) and (9.4) since for a rotation that flips the axis $\mathbf{z}$ by $180°$—$\mathbf{q}^{(2)} = [0, 1, 0, 0]^{T}$, say—the indicators are then $c_{lock} = [1, 0, 0]^{T}$ and $c_{hinge} = [1, 0]^{T}$, respectively. For the CV joint, the rotation that flips the axis $\mathbf{x}$ corresponds to $\mathbf{q} = [\cos(\pi/2), 0, 0, \sin(\pi/2)]^{T} = [0, 0, 0, 1]^{T}$, giving $c_{CV} = 1$. These are all maximum violation given that all constraints correspond to components of unit quaternions. Thus, the Jacobians at these points are then

$$\mathbf{G}^{(2)}_{dlock} = \begin{bmatrix} 0 & 0 & 0 \\ 0 & 0 & -1 \\ 0 & 1 & 0 \end{bmatrix},$$

$$\mathbf{G}^{(2)}_{dhinge} = \begin{bmatrix} 0 & 0 & -1 \\ 0 & 0 & 0 \end{bmatrix},$$

$$\mathbf{G}^{(2)}_{dhk} = \begin{bmatrix} 0 & 0 & 0 \end{bmatrix},$$

respectively, and so the restoration force vanishes at maximum violation. Since the Jacobians have full row rank when the constraints are satisfied, some of the rows must decrease gradually on the path to maximal constraint violation and so the constraint weakens. This problem can be addressed by adding nonlinear terms in the constraint definitions. That's beyond the present scope, however.

9.8   More General Frames

Of course, we may not always have hinge joints that align the axis $\mathbf{z}$ of body 1 with the axis $\mathbf{z}$ of body 2. Changing that is quite easy to do in the dot product version, but there are a few additional tricks for the quaternion counterpart, as I now show.

Assume now that the body-fixed reference frames in which the joints are defined have quaternions $\mathbf{e}, \mathbf{f} \in \mathbb{H}$, respectively. Figure 9.4 demonstrates the situation for body 1 and transform $\mathbf{e}$.

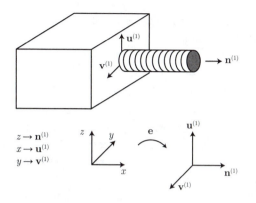

Figure 9.4. Attachment frames.

The quaternions that map vectors defined in these frames to the global frames are then in world frame, so we have

$$\mathbf{re} \text{ and } \mathbf{sf},$$

respectively. This changes the definition of the relative quaternion in Equation (9.9) to

$$\mathbf{p} = \mathbf{e}^\dagger \mathbf{r}^\dagger \mathbf{sf}.$$

Following the steps in Equations (9.9) and (9.10), we get

$$\dot{\mathbf{p}} = \mathbf{e}^\dagger \dot{\mathbf{q}} \mathbf{f}$$
$$= \mathcal{P}(\mathbf{f})\mathcal{Q}(\mathbf{e})^\mathrm{T}\dot{\mathbf{q}}.$$

Everything else follows. To define a hinge joint, for instance, we can either specify the quaternion transforms $\mathbf{e}$ and $\mathbf{f}$ directly or provide a hinge frame containing at least the axis of rotation in world coordinates. If we have a full frame of reference for the hinge definition, it is possible to define the reference joint angle also. Otherwise, the orthogonal complement of the axis must be computed and the quaternions $\mathbf{e}, \mathbf{f}$ extracted from the frame.

Once we have a full frame defining the hinge geometry in world coordinates with three orthogonal axes, $\mathbf{u}, \mathbf{v}, \mathbf{n}$, forming an orthonormal basis in which $\mathbf{n}$ is the axis of rotation, we build the matrix

$$\mathbf{R} = \begin{bmatrix} \mathbf{u} & \mathbf{v} & \mathbf{n} \end{bmatrix}$$

and extract the quaternion $\mathbf{t}$ from it using well-known techniques [Shoemake 10]. Once you have that, you compute

$$\mathbf{e} = \mathbf{r}^\dagger \mathbf{t} \quad \text{and}$$
$$\mathbf{f} = \mathbf{s}^\dagger \mathbf{t}, \tag{9.12}$$

where $\mathbf{r}$ and $\mathbf{s}$ are the orientation quaternions of body 1 and 2, respectively.

For the CV joint, the axis of rotation may be different in each body. For that case, we need two axes or two frames, as before. A full frame helps to define the zero reference, as for the hinge case. The computations are the same as in Equation (9.12).

Putting everything together, we can now define the general constraints and constraint Jacobians in a unified way using three different projection operators $\mathbf{P}$ acting on the relative quaternion $\mathbf{q}$. The meta definition is this:

$$\mathbf{c}(\mathbf{x}) = \mathbf{P}\mathbf{q},$$
$$\mathbf{G}^{(1)} = -\frac{1}{2}\mathbf{P}\mathcal{E}^\mathrm{T}(\mathbf{q}),$$
$$\mathbf{G}^{(2)} = \frac{1}{2}\mathbf{P}\mathcal{G}^\mathrm{T}(\mathbf{q}).$$

In turn, the different constraints have the following projection operators:

$$\mathbf{P}_{\text{lock}} = \mathbb{P},$$
$$\mathbf{P}_{\text{hinge}} = \begin{bmatrix} \mathbf{x}^\mathrm{T} \\ \mathbf{y}^\mathrm{T} \end{bmatrix} \mathbb{P}\mathcal{P}(\mathbf{f})\mathcal{Q}(\mathbf{e}), \tag{9.13}$$
$$\mathbf{P}_{\text{CV}} = \mathbf{z}^\mathrm{T}\mathbb{P}\mathcal{P}(\mathbf{f})\mathcal{Q}(\mathbf{e}).$$

These projection matrices need to be computed only once, unless we have limits and drivers, as I explain in the next section.

9.9   Limits and Drivers

The hinge joint leaves one degree of freedom. Good or bad, even this freedom is sometimes taken away with joint limits, locks, or drivers. Going back to the definitions in Equations (9.4) and (9.3), we can compute the angle from

$$\theta = 2\operatorname{atan}(q_s/q_3).$$

This is now a scalar function of the vector argument $\mathbf{q}$,

$$\theta = 2f(g(\mathbf{q})),$$

and we can follow the chain rule to get

$$\dot{\theta} = f' \nabla g \dot{\mathbf{q}}$$

and then expand $\dot{\mathbf{q}}$.

First, observe that $f' = q_s^2/(q_s^2 + q_3^2) \approx q_s^2$ near constraint satisfaction, so that one is easy. For the rest, we have

$$\nabla(q_3/q_s) = \frac{1}{q_s^2} \begin{bmatrix} -q_3 & 0 & 0 & q_s \end{bmatrix}.$$

When all is said and done, we have to add an additional row to the projection operator in Equation (9.13):

$$\mathbf{P}_{\text{hingec}} = \begin{bmatrix} 0 & 1 & 0 & 0 \\ 0 & 0 & 1 & 0 \\ -q_3 & 0 & 0 & q_s \end{bmatrix} \mathcal{P}(\mathbf{f})\mathcal{Q}(\mathbf{e}).$$

The subscript "hingec" now stands for controlled hinge.

The case for the CV joint is similar. Start from the definition of the polar angle

$$\theta = 2\operatorname{atan}(\langle\langle \mathbf{q}_v \rangle\rangle/q_s)$$

using Equation (9.5). The chain rule essentially provides the same results as before, namely,

$$\mathbf{p}^{\text{T}} = \nabla(\langle\langle \mathbf{q}_v \rangle\rangle/q_s) = \begin{bmatrix} -\langle\langle \mathbf{q}_v \rangle\rangle & \frac{q_s}{\langle\langle \mathbf{q}_v \rangle\rangle}\mathbf{q}_v^T \end{bmatrix},$$

and so, as in the case of the hinge constraint, the control part augments the projection defined in Equation (9.13) to

$$\mathbf{P}_{\text{CVc}} = \begin{bmatrix} \mathbf{P}_{\text{CV}} \\ \mathbf{p}^{\text{T}} \end{bmatrix}, \text{ where } \mathbf{P}_{\text{CV}} = \begin{bmatrix} 0 & 0 & 0 & 1 \end{bmatrix}^{\text{T}}, \tag{9.14}$$

as before in Equation (9.11). And now we are all set to control anything we like, or almost anything.

9.10 Examples

What follows are simple illustrations of the constraints in action. One single rigid body is attached to the inertial frame following the logic explained in the main text, i.e., only the relative quaternion is of relevance.

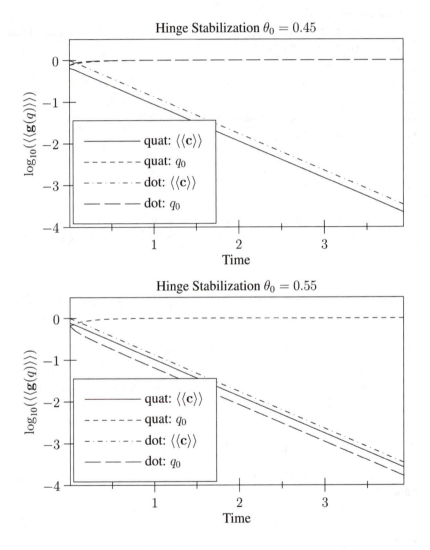

Figure 9.5. The hinge joint defined using either quaternions (top) or dot constraints (bottom).

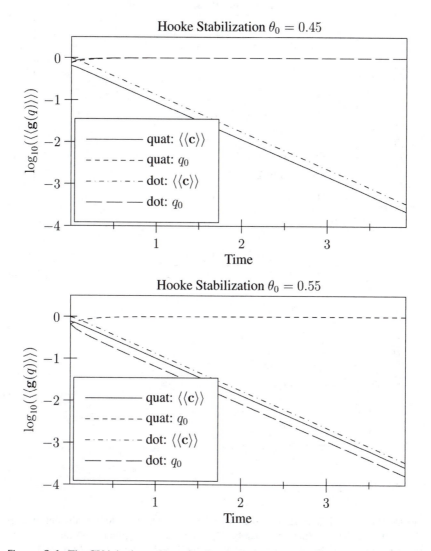

Figure 9.6. The CV joint is used here for the quaternion formulation (top), and the Hooke joint is used for the dot product one (bottom).

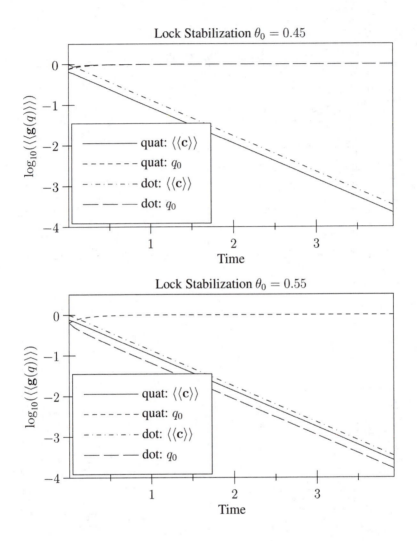

Figure 9.7. A lock joint simulated using either the quaternion (top) or the dot product (bottom) formulation. Starting at nearly $90°$ from the vertical, both constraints relax to the correct position, in which $q_s = 1$. When the initial angle is slightly over $90°$, the quaternion formulation finds its way back to the correct configuration, but the dot product version goes the wrong way, stabilizing at the wrong zero of the indicator.

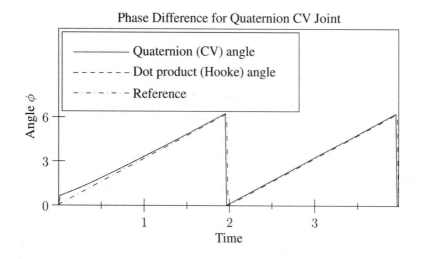

Figure 9.8. Constraint violation and phase difference between input driver and driven body. This is done for a moderate joint angle of $5°$. Both constraint definitions introduce only a small phase difference.

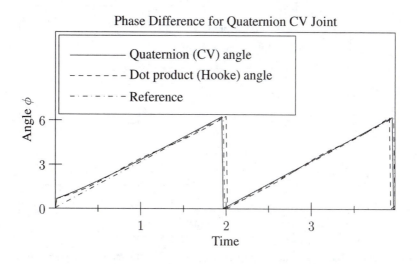

Figure 9.9. Constraint violation and phase difference between input driver and driven body. Here, the angle is more pronounced at $20°$. The result is that the CV joint does still follow the driver with a small phase difference. The Hooke joint deviates significantly from the input driver.

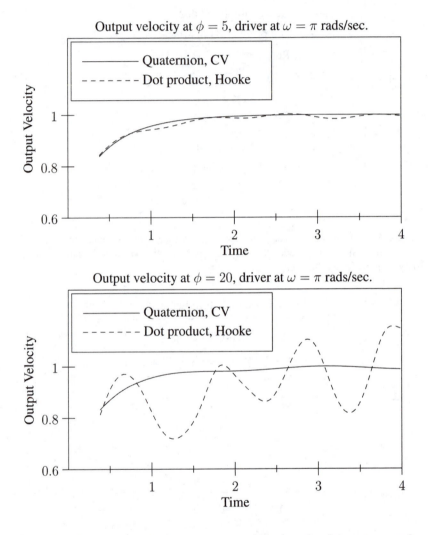

Figure 9.10. These two graphs illustrate more precisely the ratio of the output angular velocity to the driver for the quaternion (top) and the dot product (bottom) formulations. The CV joint does follow at both 5° and 20°, but the Hooke joint shows large deviations.

What is illustrated is very simple indeed: the simulation starts with a large constraint violation. Only two cases are considered, namely, one in which the initial configuration produces a little less than 50% of the way toward maximal constraint violation, the other of which is just over 50%. As expected, all the dot product–based constraints stabilize at the "good" zero of the indicator for the first case and at the bad zero for the second. But not so for the quaternion constraints. In Figures 9.5–9.10, I plot both the constraint violation and the value of q_s for the body. We have $q_s = 1$ at both the "good" zero and the "bad" zero of the dot product indicator.

A further comparison is made between the *driven* Hooke and CV joints. The pictures demonstrate the wobbling of the Hooke joint, i.e., the difference between the input rotational velocity and the output. This joint also appears to be unstable over long periods of time.

For all the examples, I have used the SPOOK integrator [Lacoursière 07b], which I derived in my PhD thesis [Lacoursière 07a]. It is an extension of the Verlet integrator for constrained systems. This is very stable and provably so. But you can use any technique that you feel comfortable with.

9.11 Conclusion

A quaternion-based representation of rotational constraints can add much stability to simulations of many things, cars for instance. They are not difficult to implement because the three different constraints amount to the selection of rows in a master lock constraint. In addition, the universal joint that is natural in the quaternion representation is better than the well-known Hooke joint, which is equally natural in the dot product representation because it exactly transfers the rotation of one body into the other. This is different from the Hooke joint, which loses efficiency at moderate angles already and is more closely related to the real drive trains found in front traction cars.

9.12 Acknowledgments

This research was supported by High Performance Computing Center North (HPC2N), Swedish Foundation for Strategic Research grant (A3 02:128), and EU Mål 2 Structural Funds (UMIT-project).

Bibliography

[Haug 89] Edward J. Haug. *Computer Aided Kinematics and Dynamics of Mechanical Systems, vol 1; Basic Methods.* Allyn and Bacon Series in Engineering, Upper Saddle River, NJ: Prentice Hall, 1989.

[Lacoursière 07a] Claude Lacoursière. "Ghosts and Machines: Regularized Variational Methods for Interactive Simulations of Multibodies with Dry Frictional Contacts." PhD thesis, Department of Computing Science, Umeå University, 2007.

[Lacoursière 07b] Claude Lacoursière. "Regularized, Stabilized, Variational Methods for Multibodies." In *The 48th Scandinavian Conference on Simulation and Modeling (SIMS 2007), 30–31 October, 2007, Göteborg (Särö), Sweden*, edited by Peter Bunus, Dag Fritzson, and Claus Führer, pp. 40–48. Linköping: Linköping University Electronic Press, 2007.

[Masarati and Morandini 08] Pierrangelo Masarati and Marco Morandini. "An Ideal Homokinetic Joint Formulation for General-Purpose Multibody Real-Time Simulation." *Multibody Syst Dyn* 20 (2008), 251–270.

[Serban and Haug 98] R. Serban and E. J. Haug. "Kinematic and Kinetic Derivatives in Multibody System Analysis." *Mechanics Structures Machines* 26:2 (1998), 145–173.

[Shoemake 91] Ken Shoemake. "Quaternions and 4×4 Matrices." In *Graphics Gem 2*, edited by Jim Arvo, pp. 352–354. San Francisco: Morgan Kaufmann, 1991.

[Shoemake 10] Ken Shoemake. "Quaterions." Unknown. Available at ftp://ftp.cis.upenn.edu/pub/graphics/shoemake/quatut.ps.Z, accessed June 12, 2010.

[Tasora and Righettini 99] Alessandro Tasora and Paolo Righettini. "Application of the Quaternion Algebra to the Efficient Computation of Jacobians for Holonomic Rheonomic-Constraints." In *Proc. of the EUROMECH Colloquium: Advances in Computational Multibody Dynamics*, edited by Jorge A. C. Ambrósio and Werner O. Schielen, IDMEC/IST Euromech Colloquium 404, pp. 75–92. Lisbon: European Mechanics Society, 1999.

[Wikipedia 10a] Wikipedia. "Constant-Velocity Joint." 2010. *Wikipedia*. Available at http://en.wikipedia.org/w/index.php?title=Constant-velocity_joint&oldid=351128343, accessed April 27, 2010.

[Wikipedia 10b] Wikipedia. "Universal Joint." 2010. *Wikipedia*. Available at http://en.wikipedia.org/w/index.php?title=Universal_joint&oldid=356595941, accessed April 27, 2010.

- V -

Soft Body

– 10 –

Soft Bodies Using Finite Elements

Cesar Mendoza and Marcos Garcia

10.1   Introduction

Much of the physics in three-dimensional game engines is still based on rigid-body dynamics. Effects such as cloth or soft bodies are rarely used, and only some basic precalculated approaches are usually applied. However, the increasing demand for realism in the video game industry has started to change this, and a different approach is required for the underlying real-time algorithms to simulate deformable bodies. With this trend, the latest video games and real-time graphics applications have started to simulate soft bodies based on their real physical behavior. Including physically based soft bodies into a computer game enhances the realism, but it also poses a great challenge to the game developers since the algorithms are more complex, slower, and less controllable.

Nowadays, many of the techniques used to simulate physically based soft bodies rely on mass-spring systems. They are the simplest, the easiest to implement, and the most computationally efficient if used together with an explicit integration scheme. The general idea is to represent the vertices of the mesh as mass points, governed by Newton's second law, and the edges as elastic massless links (springs). Hence, the object is deformed when the lengths of the elastic links (relative to the resting length) change. This happens when the relative position of the mass points changes due to external forces, such as friction, gravity, and object collisions. However, these models have some important drawbacks. In the first place, the motion of the mass points depends on the direction of their connecting links, i.e., they are topology dependant, which in most cases is not the best behavior. Moreover, selecting the parameters of the springs, such as the stiffness and damping, to simulate a particular material is not trivial, and generally, these parameters are chosen arbitrarily. Evidently, despite the nice features of mass-spring models, they are not very accurate since they are not based on the elasticity theory and are strongly topology dependent.

On the other hand, finite element models (FEM) are based on elasticity theory, in which physical material properties can be described using only some parameters obtained from textbooks. Unlike mass-spring models, finite element methods model soft bodies in a more accurate manner, and they make it easy to simulate any particular material. This fact makes things easier for game artists in charge of modeling different types of soft bodies.

In the past, finite element models have been used very little in computer games and in real-time applications since they have been considered to be computationally expensive and complex to implement. This has changed, and today's new hardware power and new researches allow real-time applications. The purpose of this chapter is to describe the implementation of real-time finite element models from an implementation point of view, trying to keep mathematics as basic as possible. We start by giving a short introduction to continuum mechanics, which is important to understanding the basic concepts of elasticity. Next, in Section 10.3, we explain how we translate these concepts into a discretized soft-body model, also known as the finite element method. Within this section, we provide pseudocode listings of some key parts to help programmers implement the model. In Section 10.4, we describe some techniques to accelerate the resolution of the model and achieve real-time simulations. We also provide some pseudocode listings that will help in the understanding of the solutions. Finally, we explain how to link the soft-body model to the mesh resource used for the graphical rendering.

10.2   Continuum Mechanics

Continuum mechanics is used to model the kinematics and the mechanical behavior of objects on the macroscopic scale such as solids and fluids (e.g., liquids and gases). It ignores the fact that matter is made of atoms and molecules and treats objects as if their matter were continuously distributed throughout the space it occupies. The continuum concept allows us to approximate physical quantities, such as energy and momentum, to describe the mechanical behavior of a given object. Based on this, continuum mechanics defines the governing equations of an object based on its material properties, or more generally, on its constitutive laws.

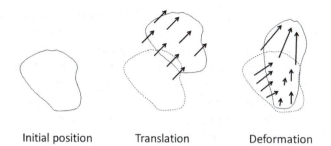

| Initial position | Translation | Deformation |

Figure 10.1. On the left, the object at its rest position. In the middle, the arrows show a constant displacement field. On the right, the fields are more complex due to deformations of the object.

The mathematical modeling of a continuum object consists of analyzing the behavior of a set of infinitesimal volumetric elements, known as material points. The positions of these material points at time t defines the *configuration*, or geometrical state, of the body at that time t. Hence, the behavior of any object can be described by analyzing the evolution of its configuration throughout time. Often, the undeformed body is considered to be the configuration at $t = 0$ (also known as the equilibrium or reference configuration, or initial or rest shape). This initial configuration is used as a reference for all the subsequent configurations that represent the deformations of the body. The coordinates, or position $\vec{x}_0 \in \mathbb{R}^3$, of a point in the undeformed shape of the object are called *material coordinates*.

When forces are applied, the body deforms, changing its configuration; in other words, any given point $\vec{x}_0$ moves to a new location $\vec{x} \in \mathbb{R}^3$. The new location in the deformed configuration is known as the *spatial* or *world coordinates* of the object, and the displacement of the point is given by the vector

$$\vec{u} = \vec{x} - \vec{x}_0.$$

The displacements of all the points of the continuum body represent the displacement field of the body. A pure translation of the body, also known as a rigid body translation, creates a constant displacement field, while a complex deformation creates an arbitrary field (see Figure 10.1). It would be impossible to simulate the displacements of all the points of the continuum body. Instead, as will be shown later in Section 10.3.1, we discretize the object into a set of finite adjacent elements, normally tetrahedrons or hexahedrons, and map the displacement field to their corners. Thus, we don't simulate the displacements of all the points of the continuum body, we only compute the vertices' displacements of a finite element set, as we will see in Section 10.3.

When the external forces are removed, the object pops back to its original configuration if it is a pure and perfect elastic body. The speed at which it returns to its rest position depends on the physical properties of the object material. In some cases, after applying and removing forces, the resistance to deformations may vary due to the fatigue or weakening of the object (e.g., human tissue). It is not in the scope of this chapter to deal with these types of cases, however it is important to introduce some basic concepts of elasticity in order to relate object deformations to its material properties.

10.2.1 Strain

The elastic strain ε is a dimensionless measure of deformation. In the one-dimensional case, e.g., a line element or a fiber being deformed, the strain is simply $\delta l/l_0$, where δl is the increment of the rest length l and represents the compression or stretching of the fiber. In the three-dimensional case, the strain represents changes in length in three directions and hence is expressed as a 3×3 symmetric matrix. In the linear case, we can use the *Cauchy strain* represented by

$$\varepsilon = \begin{bmatrix} \varepsilon_{11} & \varepsilon_{12} & \varepsilon_{13} \\ \varepsilon_{21} & \varepsilon_{22} & \varepsilon_{23} \\ \varepsilon_{31} & \varepsilon_{32} & \varepsilon_{33} \end{bmatrix} , \qquad (10.1)$$

where each entry of the matrix is given by

$$\varepsilon_{ij} = \frac{1}{2} \left[\frac{\partial u_i}{\partial x_j} + \frac{\partial u_j}{\partial x_i} \right] ,$$

with $i = 1, 2, 3$ and $j = 1, 2, 3$. Partial derivatives may create a sensation of complexity to the reader, and unfortunately, they are unavoidable. However, as we will see later in this chapter, most of them can be easily and explicitly solved before writing the respective code, as shown, for example, in Equation (10.10).

Linear strains are suitable for measuring small deformations, but when the object is subjected to large rotational deformations, its original volume increases unrealistically since the Cauchy strain is not invariant to rotations. Although non-linear strains, such as the Green-Lagrange strain, model large deformations more accurately, they are computationally more expensive since they have to evaluate quadratic terms. Fortunately, as we will explain later in this chapter, using a corotational formulation [Muller and Gross 04, Etzmuss et al. 03, Garcia et al. 06] allows the use of the linear strain without artifacts, keeping plausible soft body simulations.

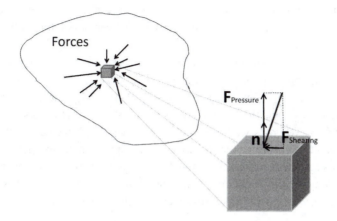

Figure 10.2. Forces acting around an infinitesimal volumetric mass element.

10.2.2 Stress

The notion of stress was introduced by Cauchy around 1822. Intuitively, the stress combines strains and physical material properties to determine the internal forces of the object. In fact, when external forces are applied to the object, these are transmitted from point to point within the material body, leading to the generation of internal forces; any small element of matter of the continuum object receives forces from all around. One way to describe the surrounding internal forces acting locally is to evaluate the force, $\vec{F}$, acting on a given surface element of an infinitesimal element (see Figure 10.2). The component of $\vec{F}$ along the normal $\vec{n}$ is analogous to a pressure applied to a small element of matter of the object. Note that the stress has the same units as the pressure (pascal (Pa) in SI). The orthogonal component of $\vec{F}$ with respect to $\vec{n}$ is the force that makes parallel internal surfaces slide past one another, and it is normally known as the shearing force. Cauchy extrapolated this idea to the three-dimensional case to define the stress per volume unit acting on the continuum object as the second-order tensor σ, known as the Cauchy stress tensor, which is defined as

$$\sigma = \begin{bmatrix} \sigma_{11} & \sigma_{12} & \sigma_{13} \\ \sigma_{21} & \sigma_{22} & \sigma_{23} \\ \sigma_{31} & \sigma_{32} & \sigma_{33} \end{bmatrix},$$

where σ_{11}, σ_{22}, and σ_{33} are normal stresses, and σ_{12}, σ_{13}, σ_{21}, σ_{23}, σ_{31}, and σ_{32} are shear stresses.

The first index i indicates that the stress acts on a plane normal to the x_i axis, and the second index j denotes the direction in which the stress acts. A stress component is positive if it acts in the positive direction of the coordinate axes and the plane where it acts has an outward normal vector pointing in the positive coordinate direction.

It is important to note that the Cauchy stress has been obtained considering objects that experience small deformations. For large deformations, other measures of stress are required, such as the first and second Piola-Kirchoff stress tensors, the Biot stress tensor, and the Kirchoff stress tensors that accurately model nonlinear elasticity. However, as we have mentioned previously, large deformations lead to less-intuitive equations that are, besides, computationally expensive. Muller and Gross have shown accurate results for soft body simulation using simply linear elasticity [Muller and Gross 04]. Their approach is based on a corotational formulation, which we will describe later in Section 10.3.4.

10.2.3   Linear Elasticity

According to the principle of conservation of linear and angular momentum, equilibrium requires that the addition of moments with respect to an arbitrary point is zero, which leads to the fact that the stress tensor is symmetric. Therefore, instead of using nine stress components, we can reduce the stress to only six independent stress components. Similarly, the strain assumes orthogonal infinitesimal displacements, which allow us to reduce its nine components to only six. This symmetry property is very convenient, since it allows us to reduce memory consumption during the simulation.

The relationship between the strain and the stress is defined by the constitutive equations of the object, which in the simplest case is defined by Hooke's law, where such relationship is linear. This is known as linear elasticity and can be expressed as

$$\vec{\sigma} = \mathbf{E}\vec{\varepsilon},$$

where $\mathbf{E}$ is a tensor of 81 experimental elastic constants that are independent of stress or strain. Since the strain and the stress can be represented using only six independent components, we can reduce the elasticity matrix to only 36 constants. We can simplify further the elasticity matrix if we make the following assumptions:

1. We consider that the constitutive equations of the object are the same for any point within the object. This is usually known as the *homogeneous property*.

2. The elastic properties are independent of temperature changes.

3. The behavior of the object is symmetric in all directions at any point, i.e., we assume that the object is *isotropic*.

These assumptions lead to a simpler version of the elasticity matrix that only depends on two independent values, Poisson's ratio ν and Young's modulus Y:

$$\mathbf{E} = \begin{bmatrix} \lambda + 2\mu & \lambda & \lambda & 0 & 0 & 0 \\ \lambda & \lambda + 2\mu & \lambda & 0 & 0 & 0 \\ \lambda & \lambda & \lambda + 2\mu & 0 & 0 & 0 \\ 0 & 0 & 0 & \mu & 0 & 0 \\ 0 & 0 & 0 & 0 & \mu & 0 \\ 0 & 0 & 0 & 0 & 0 & \mu \end{bmatrix},$$

where

$$\lambda = \frac{\nu Y}{(1 + \nu)(1 - 2\nu)}$$

and

$$\mu = \frac{Y}{2(1 + \nu)}.$$

The symbols λ and μ are known as the Lamé constants of the material. Poisson's ratio controls the conservation of the volume of the object, and its values are normally between 0.0 for nonvolume preservation (in practice, it is usually 0.25) and 0.5 for a perfect incompressible object. Young's module represents the resistance to stretching, which can intuitively be stated as the stiffness of the material. These values can be obtained from the mechanics literature. However, Young's module values for soft bodies may be sometimes more difficult to find than values for hard materials. This is not really a big issue since it is, in fact, the game artist who chooses the right value for specific soft bodies. The programmer can help the game artist by providing a manner in which to vary Young's modulus values (e.g., with sliders). In any case, a first coarse approximation can be found in books.

10.3   Linear FEM

The finite element method is an analytical tool for stress, thermal, and fluid analyses of systems and structures. We use it here to describe the deformations of objects due to external loads. The finite element method is probably the most physically correct model among all the methods used in computer graphics to simulate deformations, however, its use has not been spread out in the video game community due to its complex and lengthy simulations. We show how to simulate soft bodies in real-time using finite elements, keeping a high degree of realism.

The key is to use linear elasticity, as we explained in the previous section, and handle the artifacts that may arise from its use to keep accurate, fast, and robust simulations. Finite element methods that assume linear elasticity are usually known as *linear FEM*. In this section we describe all the needed theory to easily implement a type of linear FEM and show how to prevent linear-elasticity-related inaccuracy issues.

10.3.1 Discretization

In order to simulate the deformations of the continuum object, we need to represent the constitutive equations of the object in a way that the computer can solve numerically; in other words, we need to discretize the continuum object. There exist several techniques to this end, but the most widely used is the finite element method due to its accuracy in modeling deformations on complex bodies.

The idea behind the finite element method is to discretize the object into a finite set of adjacent and nonoverlapping subdomains that are, in general, either four-node tetrahedrons or eight-node hexahedrons. The displacement fields of the continuum matter within the tetrahedrons or hexahedrons are mapped to their vertices, allowing us to approximate the constitutive equation laws of the object using the displacements of their nodes. The whole set of finite elements is usually known as a tetrahedral or hexahedral mesh.

Tetrahedrons are the usual choice for representing finite elements since they can be constructed from triangular meshes, and they are arguably the best choice. Hexahedral meshes are, however, more accurate but require more memory resources (information on eight nodes instead of four) and are obviously more computationally expensive, but on the other hand, hexahedral meshes can represent objects with less elements than can tetrahedral meshes.

We use tetrahedrons in this chapter. Describing the techniques used to generate tetrahedral meshes are out of the scope of this chapter. The reader can refer to these works for further details [Spillman et al. 06, Muller and Teschner 03]. Alternatively, there exists a well-documented and simple open-source library known as TetGen [Si 09]. It is, however, important to remark that the construction of the tetrahedral mesh is a crucial step since the quality of the tetrahedron, and their distribution within the object may vary the complexity of the system. Badly distributed tetrahedral meshes or almost flat tetrahedrons may lead to complex and harder-to-solve systems.

In order to replace the continuous displacement field with the displacement of the tetrahedron vertex we use what we call *shape functions*, which in general, for a tetrahedron, are based on its barycentric coordinates (see Figure 10.3). Let the displacement field over the tetrahedron be defined as $\hat{\vec{u}} = [u_x, u_y, u_z]$, which are

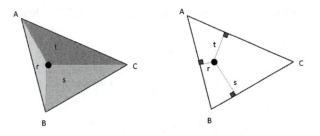

Figure 10.3. Barycentric coordinates of a triangle, where $\xi_1 = \frac{r}{r+s+t}$, $\xi_2 = \frac{s}{r+s+t}$, and $\xi_3 = \frac{t}{r+s+t}$. This representation can be extended for tetrahedral elements. Barycentric coordinates can be described from areas (left) or from distances (right).

obtained by linear interpolations of the tetrahedron nodal displacements. We can write this as

$$\hat{\vec{u}} = \xi_1 \vec{u}_1 + \xi_2 \vec{u}_2 + \xi_3 \vec{u}_3 + \xi_4 \vec{u}_4, \qquad (10.2)$$

where ξ_i are the shape functions and $\vec{u}_i$ are the displacements of the four nodes of the tetrahedron. We can rewrite this using the components of each displacement as

$$\hat{\vec{u}} = \begin{bmatrix} \xi_1 & 0 & 0 & \xi_2 & 0 & 0 & \xi_3 & 0 & 0 & \xi_4 & 0 & 0 \\ 0 & \xi_1 & 0 & 0 & \xi_2 & 0 & 0 & \xi_3 & 0 & 0 & \xi_4 & 0 \\ 0 & 0 & \xi_1 & 0 & 0 & \xi_2 & 0 & 0 & \xi_3 & 0 & 0 & \xi_4 \end{bmatrix} \begin{bmatrix} u_{1x} \\ u_{1y} \\ u_{1z} \\ u_{2x} \\ u_{2y} \\ u_{2z} \\ u_{3x} \\ u_{3y} \\ u_{3z} \\ u_{4x} \\ u_{4y} \\ u_{4z} \end{bmatrix}$$

or simply

$$\hat{\vec{u}} = \mathbf{H}_e \vec{u}, \qquad (10.3)$$

where $\mathbf{H}_e$ is a 3×12 matrix containing the shape functions.

Let us now describe how to relate the displacements to the strains. From the definition of the linear strain, we can explicitly write Equation (10.1) as

$$\varepsilon = \begin{bmatrix} \frac{1}{2}\left(\frac{\partial u_x}{\partial x} + \frac{\partial u_x}{\partial x}\right) & \frac{1}{2}\left(\frac{\partial u_x}{\partial y} + \frac{\partial u_y}{\partial x}\right) & \frac{1}{2}\left(\frac{\partial u_x}{\partial z} + \frac{\partial u_z}{\partial x}\right) \\ \frac{1}{2}\left(\frac{\partial u_y}{\partial x} + \frac{\partial u_x}{\partial y}\right) & \frac{1}{2}\left(\frac{\partial u_y}{\partial y} + \frac{\partial u_y}{\partial y}\right) & \frac{1}{2}\left(\frac{\partial u_y}{\partial z} + \frac{\partial u_z}{\partial y}\right) \\ \frac{1}{2}\left(\frac{\partial u_z}{\partial x} + \frac{\partial u_x}{\partial z}\right) & \frac{1}{2}\left(\frac{\partial u_z}{\partial y} + \frac{\partial u_y}{\partial z}\right) & \frac{1}{2}\left(\frac{\partial u_z}{\partial z} + \frac{\partial u_z}{\partial z}\right) \end{bmatrix},$$

and as we said previously, the strain can be described using only its six indepen-
dents components. We can re-arrange this as

$$
\begin{bmatrix} \varepsilon_{xx} \\ \varepsilon_{yy} \\ \varepsilon_{zz} \\ \varepsilon_{yz} \\ \varepsilon_{zx} \\ \varepsilon_{xy} \end{bmatrix} = \begin{bmatrix} \frac{\partial}{\partial x} & 0 & 0 \\ 0 & \frac{\partial}{\partial y} & 0 \\ 0 & 0 & \frac{\partial}{\partial z} \\ \frac{\partial}{2\partial y} & \frac{\partial}{2\partial x} & 0 \\ 0 & \frac{\partial}{2\partial z} & \frac{\partial}{2\partial y} \\ \frac{\partial}{2\partial z} & 0 & \frac{\partial}{2\partial x} \end{bmatrix} \begin{bmatrix} u_x \\ u_y \\ u_z \end{bmatrix} = \mathbf{D}\vec{u}_e.
$$

Replacing the displacement field by its nodal description of Equation (10.3), we
have

$$
\hat{\vec{\varepsilon}} = \mathbf{D}\mathbf{H}_e \vec{u}_e. \tag{10.4}
$$

Hence, we can deduce the displacement-deformation matrix to be $\mathbf{B}_e = \mathbf{D}\mathbf{H}_e$,
which written explicitly is

$$
\mathbf{B}_e = \begin{bmatrix}
\frac{\partial \xi_1}{\partial x} & 0 & 0 & \frac{\partial \xi_2}{\partial x} & 0 & 0 & \frac{\partial \xi_3}{\partial x} & 0 & 0 & \frac{\partial \xi_4}{\partial x} & 0 & 0 \\
0 & \frac{\partial \xi_1}{\partial y} & 0 & 0 & \frac{\partial \xi_2}{\partial y} & 0 & 0 & \frac{\partial \xi_3}{\partial y} & 0 & 0 & \frac{\partial \xi_4}{\partial y} & 0 \\
0 & 0 & \frac{\partial \xi_1}{\partial z} & 0 & 0 & \frac{\partial \xi_2}{\partial z} & 0 & 0 & \frac{\partial \xi_3}{\partial z} & 0 & 0 & \frac{\partial \xi_4}{\partial z} \\
\frac{\partial \xi_1}{\partial y} & \frac{\partial \xi_1}{\partial x} & 0 & \frac{\partial \xi_2}{\partial y} & \frac{\partial \xi_2}{\partial x} & 0 & \frac{\partial \xi_3}{\partial y} & \frac{\partial \xi_3}{\partial x} & 0 & \frac{\partial \xi_4}{\partial y} & \frac{\partial \xi_4}{\partial x} & 0 \\
0 & \frac{\partial \xi_1}{\partial z} & \frac{\partial \xi_1}{\partial y} & 0 & \frac{\partial \xi_2}{\partial z} & \frac{\partial \xi_2}{\partial y} & 0 & \frac{\partial \xi_3}{\partial z} & \frac{\partial \xi_3}{\partial y} & 0 & \frac{\partial \xi_4}{\partial z} & \frac{\partial \xi_4}{\partial y} \\
\frac{\partial \xi_1}{\partial z} & 0 & \frac{\partial \xi_1}{\partial x} & \frac{\partial \xi_2}{\partial z} & 0 & \frac{\partial \xi_2}{\partial x} & \frac{\partial \xi_3}{\partial z} & 0 & \frac{\partial \xi_3}{\partial x} & \frac{\partial \xi_4}{\partial z} & 0 & \frac{\partial \xi_4}{\partial x}
\end{bmatrix}.
$$
$$\tag{10.5}$$

To compute the partial derivatives of Equation (10.5), we need to further analyze the tetrahedron geometry. Let us remember the geometric definition of a
tetrahedron in terms of its barycentric coordinates and the position $\vec{p}_i$ of its four
nodes:

$$
\begin{bmatrix} 1 \\ p_x \\ p_y \\ p_z \end{bmatrix} = \begin{bmatrix} 1 & 1 & 1 & 1 \\ p_{1,x} & p_{2,x} & p_{3,x} & p_{4,x} \\ p_{1,y} & p_{2,y} & p_{3,y} & p_{4,y} \\ p_{1,z} & p_{2,z} & p_{3,z} & p_{4,z} \end{bmatrix} \begin{bmatrix} \xi_1 \\ \xi_2 \\ \xi_3 \\ \xi_4 \end{bmatrix}. \tag{10.6}
$$

Therefore, the barycentric coordinates can be found by inverting the matrix:

$$
\begin{bmatrix} \xi_1 \\ \xi_2 \\ \xi_3 \\ \xi_4 \end{bmatrix} = \begin{bmatrix} \alpha_1 & \alpha_2 & \alpha_3 & \alpha_4 \\ \beta_1 & \beta_2 & \beta_3 & \beta_4 \\ \gamma_1 & \gamma_2 & \gamma_3 & \gamma_4 \\ \delta_1 & \delta_2 & \delta_3 & \delta_4 \end{bmatrix} \begin{bmatrix} 1 \\ p_x \\ p_y \\ p_z \end{bmatrix}, \tag{10.7}
$$

where

$$
\begin{bmatrix} \alpha_1 & \alpha_2 & \alpha_3 & \alpha_4 \\ \beta_1 & \beta_2 & \beta_3 & \beta_4 \\ \gamma_1 & \gamma_2 & \gamma_3 & \gamma_4 \\ \delta_1 & \delta_2 & \delta_3 & \delta_4 \end{bmatrix} = \begin{bmatrix} 1 & 1 & 1 & 1 \\ p_{1,x} & p_{2,x} & p_{3,x} & p_{4,x} \\ p_{1,y} & p_{2,y} & p_{3,y} & p_{4,y} \\ p_{1,z} & p_{2,z} & p_{3,z} & p_{4,z} \end{bmatrix}^{-1}. \tag{10.8}
$$

We show in Listing 10.1 a pseudocode of how to build this barycentric matrix. Then, we can easily compute the barycentric coordinates; for example, the first barycentric coordinate ξ_1 is computed as

$$\xi_1 = \alpha_1 + \alpha_2 p_{1,x} + \alpha_3 p_{2,y} + \alpha_4 p_{3,z}, \tag{10.9}$$

and therefore its partial derivative, required to compute one of the entries of $\mathbf{B}_e$, is simply

$$\frac{\partial \xi_1}{\partial x} = \alpha_2, \tag{10.10}$$

since the element's shape functions are linear and constant. Thus, all the entries in the displacement-deformation matrix of Equation (10.5) are computed similarly given the following constant matrix:

$$\mathbf{B}_e = \begin{bmatrix} \alpha_2 & 0 & 0 & \beta_2 & 0 & 0 & \gamma_2 & 0 & 0 & \delta_2 & 0 & 0 \\ 0 & \alpha_3 & 0 & 0 & \beta_3 & 0 & 0 & \gamma_3 & 0 & 0 & \delta_3 & 0 \\ 0 & 0 & \alpha_4 & 0 & 0 & \beta_4 & 0 & 0 & \gamma_4 & 0 & 0 & \delta_4 \\ \alpha_3 & \alpha_2 & 0 & \beta_3 & \beta_2 & 0 & \gamma_2 & \gamma_3 & 0 & \delta_2 & \delta_3 & 0 \\ 0 & \alpha_4 & \alpha_3 & 0 & \beta_4 & \beta_3 & 0 & \gamma_4 & \gamma_3 & 0 & \delta_4 & \delta_3 \\ \alpha_4 & 0 & \alpha_2 & \beta_4 & 0 & \beta_2 & \gamma_4 & 0 & \gamma_2 & \delta_4 & 0 & \delta_2 \end{bmatrix}.$$

Finally, substituting $\mathbf{B}_e$ into Equation (10.4), we obtain

$$\hat{\vec{\varepsilon}} = \mathbf{B}_e \vec{u}_e.$$

Refer to Listing 10.2 for the corresponding pseudocode.

10.3.2 Static System

When an elastic object is deformed by stretching it or compressing it, it stores an energy that tries to restore the object to its original shape. One way to describe this behavior is by seeking the mechanical equilibrium of the object. Recall that the object has been discretized into many subregions, in our case tetrahedrons, and that for each tetrahedron the displacement field has been written in terms of the nodal values, which we have used to find the linear relationship between the stress and the strains. Introducing this into the strain-energy function restricted to the node displacements, we get the static equilibrium given by

$$\vec{f}_{\text{ext}} = \mathbf{K}_e \vec{u}_e,$$

where $\vec{f}_{\text{ext}}$ are the external forces applied to the nodes of the tetrahedron and $\vec{u}_e$ the displacements of the nodes. The matrix $\mathbf{K}_e$ is known as the *stiffness matrix* of the tetrahedron element, which generalizes the stiffness of Hooke's law to a matrix.

Let us now explain how to compute the stiffness matrix that arises from assuming that the work done by the applied forces is transformed into strain (potential) energy and that it is completely recoverable. The strain energy in the form of elastic deformation is mostly recoverable in the form of mechanical work. The definition of the elastic potential energy is given by

$$\Pi = U - W,$$

where U is the strain energy and W is the work done by external forces. The object is in a stable equilibrium when the potential energy reaches a minimum, which happens when

$$\frac{\partial \Pi}{\partial \vec{u}_e} = 0. \tag{10.11}$$

The work W is defined as

$$W = \vec{u}_e^{\mathrm{T}} \vec{f}_{\text{ext}},$$

and the strain energy of the elastic linear body is defined as

$$U = \frac{1}{2} \int_{\text{vol}_e} \varepsilon^{\mathrm{T}} \sigma dV. \tag{10.12}$$

Replacing the values of the strain with $\vec{\varepsilon} = \mathbf{B}_e \vec{u}_e$ and $\sigma = \mathbf{E}\varepsilon$, we get

$$\Pi = \frac{1}{2} \int_{\text{vol}_e} \vec{u}_e^{\mathrm{T}} \mathbf{B}_e^{\mathrm{T}} \mathbf{E} \mathbf{B}_e \vec{u}_e dV + \vec{u}_e^{\mathrm{T}} \vec{f}_{\text{ext}}.$$

Noting that none of the quantities inside the integral terms depend on the position of the coordinates, we have for the total potential

$$\Pi = \frac{1}{2} \text{vol}_e \vec{u}_e^{\mathrm{T}} \mathbf{B}_e^{\mathrm{T}} \mathbf{E} \mathbf{B}_e \vec{u}_e + \vec{u}_e^{\mathrm{T}} \vec{f}_{e_{\text{ext}}},$$

and taking the derivative with respect to $\vec{u}_e$ to seek the static equilibrium, as required in Equation (10.11), we obtain:

$$\vec{f}_{\text{ext}} = \text{vol}_e \mathbf{B}_e^{\mathrm{T}} \mathbf{E} \mathbf{B}_e \vec{u}_e,$$

hence

$$\mathbf{K} = \text{vol}_e \mathbf{B}_e^{\mathrm{T}} \mathbf{E} \vec{B}_e.$$

In general, instead of solving each element separately, we group all the external forces into one global vector and the stiffness matrix into a larger-dimension global matrix:

$$\vec{F}_{\text{ext}} = \sum_e \vec{f}_e$$

and

$$\mathbf{K} = \begin{bmatrix} \sum_e \mathbf{K}_{e,1,1} & \sum_e \mathbf{K}_{e,1,2} & \cdots & \sum_e \mathbf{K}_{e,1,n} \\ \vdots & & \ddots & \\ \sum_e \mathbf{K}_{e,n,1} & \sum \mathbf{K}_{e,n,2} & \cdots & \sum \mathbf{K}_{e,n,n} \end{bmatrix},$$

where $\sum_e \mathbf{K}_{e,i,j}$ is the stiffness matrix of the tetrahedron e that relates node i to node j. Note that the global matrix is sparse and symmetric semipositive-semidefinite.

$$\mathbf{K}\vec{u} = \vec{F}_{\text{ext}}.$$

We show how to build the barycentric matrix of a tetrahedron and its displacement-deformation matrix $\mathbf{B}_e$ in Listings 10.1 and 10.2, respectively. These functions

```
void buildBarycentric (CMatrix &Pe, //Stiffness matrix (out)
                       CPoint3d const& x1, //Tetra vertex (in)
                       CPoint3d const& x2, //Tetra vertex (in)
                       CPoint3d const& x3, //Tetra vertex (in)
                       CPoint3d const& x4) //Tetra vertex (in)
{
    for (int i=0; i<4; i++)
        Pe(0,i)= 1;

    for (int i=1; i<4; i++)
        Pe(i,0) = x1[i−1];

    for (int i=1; i<4; i++)
        Pe(i,1) = x2[i−1];

    for (int i=1; i<4; i++)
        Pe(i,2) = x3[i−1];

    for (int i=1; i<4; i++)
        Pe(i,3) = x4[i−1];

    Pe = Pe.invert();
}
```

Listing 10.1. Building a barycentric matrix.

```
void buildBe(CMatrix &Be, //Strain−displacement matrix (out)
             CMatrix const& Pe) //Barycentric matrix (in)
{
    Be.loadZero();

    //First row
    Be(0,0) = Pe(0,1); Be(0,3) = Pe (1,1);
    Be(0,6) = Pe(2,1); Be(0,9) = Pe (3,1);

    //Second row
    Be(1,1) = Pe(0,2); Be(1,4) = Pe (1,2);
    Be(1,7) = Pe(2,2); Be(1,10) = Pe (3,2);

    //Third row
    Be(2,2) = Pe(0,3); Be(2,5) = Pe (1,3);
    Be(2,8) = Pe(2,3); Be(2,11) = Pe (3,3);

    //Fourth row
    Be(3,0) = 0.5 * Pe(0,2); Be(3,1) = 0.5 * Pe (0,1);
    Be(3,3) = 0.5 * Pe(1,2); Be(3,4) = 0.5 * Pe (1,1);
    Be(3,6) = 0.5 * Pe(2,2); Be(3,7) = 0.5 * Pe (2,1);
    Be(3,9) = 0.5 * Pe(3,2); Be(3,10) = 0.5 * Pe (3,1);

    //Fifth row
    Be(4,1) = 0.5 * Pe(0,3); Be(4,2) = 0.5 * Pe (0,2);
    Be(4,4) = 0.5 * Pe(1,3); Be(4,5) = 0.5 * Pe (1,2);
    Be(4,7) = 0.5 * Pe(2,3); Be(4,8) = 0.5 * Pe (2,2);
    Be(4,10) = 0.5 * Pe(3,3); Be(4,11) = 0.5 * Pe (3,2);

    //Sixth row
    Be(5,0) = 0.5 * Pe(0,3); Be(5,2) = 0.5 * Pe (0,1);
    Be(5,3) = 0.5 * Pe(1,3); Be(5,5) = 0.5 * Pe (1,1);
    Be(5,6) = 0.5 * Pe(2,3); Be(5,8) = 0.5 * Pe (2,1);
    Be(5,9) = 0.5 * Pe(3,3); Be(5,11) = 0.5 * Pe (3,1);
}
```

Listing 10.2. Building matrix $\mathbf{B_e}$.

can be used to compute the stiffness matrix of the tetrahedron $\mathbf{K}_e$, as shown in the code in Listing 10.3. Finally, we show how to assemble the global matrix $\mathbf{K}$ in Listing 10.4. These algorithms are useful for the general case, but when we are modeling a linear and isotropic material, we can simplify the algorithm using Listing 10.5.

We can obtain the displacement of the nodes under external forces by inverting the stiffness matrix as follows:

$$\vec{u} = \mathbf{K}^{-1} \vec{F}_{\text{ext}}. \tag{10.13}$$

```
void buildKe(CMatrix &Ke, //Stiffness matrix (out)
               CPoint3d const& x1, //Element vertex (in)
               CPoint3d const& x2, //Element vertex (in)
               CPoint3d const& x3, //Element vertex (in)
               CPoint3d const& x4, //Element vertex (in)
               float mu, //Physical parameter (in)
               float lambda) //Physical parameter (in)
{
    CMatrix Be(6,12),E(6,6),Pe(4,4);
    float vol,mr; //Element volume

    buildBarycentric(Pe, x1, x2, x3, x4);
    vol = 1.0/(Pe.det()*6);

    buildBe(Be,Pe);

    E.loadZero();
    mr=2*mu+lambda;
    E(0,0) = mr; E(0,1) = lambda; E(0,2) = lambda;
    E(1,0) = lambda; E(1,1) = mr; E(1,2) = lambda;
    E(2,0) = lambda; E(2,1) = lambda; E(2,2) = mr;
    E(3,3) = mu; E(4,4) = mu; E(5,5) = mu;

    Ke= vol*Be.transpose()*E*Be;
}
```

Listing 10.3. Building matrix $\mathbf{K_e}$.

A range of standard methods exist to solve this system: Gauss elimination, Cholesky factorization, and conjugate gradient, to name just a few. In Section 10.4, we briefly describe some of them.

An important requirement to solve the static system in Equation (10.13) and find the displacements is to fix and keep hold of at least three nodes (or nine degrees of freedom), otherwise the system is singular, meaning that no unique solution exists. This can be intuitively explained by the fact that without any boundary conditions or prescribed positions, the body has no unique position in space, and because there is no unique position, there is no unique deformation. Boundary conditions are also used as a manner of applying external loads to the body. Refer to Section 10.3.5 for more details on this subject.

Note that the system does not depend on time, meaning that if we simulate it, the object *jumps* from one configuration to another without taking into account any previous configuration. The deformed shape of the body is defined exclusively by the material properties of the object and the applied forces at that instant. If the applied forces are removed, the object returns instantaneously to its rest position; there are no dynamics on the system.

```
void assembleK(CSparseMatrix &K, //Stiffness matrix (out)
                CTetraArray tList, //Tetrahedron list (in)
                CVertexArray vList, //Vertex list (in)
                float mu, //Physical parameter (in)
                float lambda) //Physical parameter (in)
{
    int vSize = vList.size();
    int tList = tList.size();
    K.resize (3*vSize,3*viSize);
    K.loadZero ();

    for (tIdx = 0; iIdxt < tSize; tSize++)
    {
        //pIdx contain the index of the tetrahedron nodes.
        int pIdx[4];
        pIdx[0]=tList[tIdx].p1Idx;
        pIdx[1]=tList[tIdx].p2Idx;
        pIdx[2]=tList[tIdx].p3Idx;
        pIdx[3]=tList[tIdx].p4Idx;

        //We build a 12 by 12 matrix
        CMatrix Ke(12,12);
        buildKe(Ke,
                vList[pIdx[0]],
                vList[pIdx[1]],
                vList[pIdx[2]],
                vList[pIdx[3]],
                mu,lambda);

        for (i=0; i<4; i++)
        for (j=0; j<4; j++)
        {
            int orgX,orgY,destX,destY;
            destI=pIdX[i]*3;
            destJ=vector[j]*3;

            for (t=0; t<3; t++)
            for (m=0; m<3; m++)
                K(destI+t,destJ+m)+=Ke(i*3+t,j*3);
        }
    }
}
```

Listing 10.4. Building a global matrix **K**.

```
void buildKe(CMatrix &Ke, //Stiffness matrix (out)
             CPoint3d const& x1, //Element vertex (in)
             CPoint3d const& x2, //Element vertex (in)
             CPoint3d const& x3, //Element vertex (in)
             CPoint3d const& x4, //Element vertex (in)
             float mu, //Physical parameter (in)
             float lambda) //Physical parameter (in)
{
    CMatrix Pe(4,4);
    float sigma,tr,vol;

    buildBarycentric(Pe, x1, x2, x3, x4);
    vol = 1.0/(Pe.det()*6);

    Ke.loadZero();
    for (int i=0;i<4;i++)
    for (int j=0;j<4;j++)
    {
        int i3=3*i-1,j3=3*j-1;

        for(int a=1;a<4;a++)
        for(int b=1;b<4;b++)
            Ke(i3+a,j3+b) = 0.5*vol*
                (lambda*Pe(i,a)*Pe(j,b) + mu*Pe(i,b)*Pe(j,a));

        i3++;j3++;

        sigma = Pe(i,1) * Pe(j,1) +
                Pe(i,2) * Pe(j,2) +
                Pe(i,3) * Pe(j,3);

        tr = mu*0.5*vol*sigma;
        K(i3, j3) += tr;
        K(i3+1, j3+1) += tr;
        K(i3+2, j3+2) += tr;
    }
}
```

Listing 10.5. Building the matrix K_e optimization.

10.3.3 Dynamic System

In order to simulate dynamic deformations of an object, we need to make the position coordinates a function of time. For linear elasticity, we can use the Lagrange equations of motion, which involve kinematic and potential energies and have the form

$$\mathbf{M}\ddot{\vec{u}} + \mathbf{D}\dot{\vec{u}} + \mathbf{K}\vec{u},$$

where the mass matrix $\mathbf{M}$ and the damping matrix $\mathbf{D}$ are constant (recall that $\vec{u} = \vec{x} - \vec{x}_0$). The stiffness matrix $\mathbf{K}$ is the same one that we computed in the previous section. To compute the displacement of the nodes of the tetrahedral mesh, i.e., to isolate the vector of displacements $\vec{u}$, we will need to invert the mass and damping matrices. Although these matrices are sparse, their inverse may result in a dense matrix that can require more memory storage and processing time. To avoid this, we consider, in general, the damping matrix $\mathbf{D}$ to be a simple diagonal matrix that can be written as $\mu\mathbf{I}$. Similarly, the mass matrix is diagonalized using mass-lumping methods. There are a variety of methods to perform mass lumping; among the most frequently used, we found the following:

- Dividing the total mass into the number of nodes and assigning the result to each node.

- Assuming that the density of the object is homogeneous, use the volume of the tetrahedron to compute its mass. Then assign to each node the mass of the tetrahedron divided by four.

Hence, the mass and damping matrices can be precomputed to accelerate the simulation.

To solve Equation (10.12), we transform it into a set of $2 \times 3n$ equations of first derivatives and replace $\vec{u} = \vec{x} - \vec{x}_0$:

$$\vec{v} = \dot{\vec{x}},$$
$$\mathbf{M}\dot{\vec{v}} = -\mathbf{D}\vec{v} - \mathbf{K}\left(\vec{x} - \vec{x}_0\right) + \vec{f}_{\text{ext}}.$$

There exists a variety of methods to solve this system of equations and find the displacement vector $\vec{x}$; however, we recommend the implicit Euler's method. Although other methods provide faster numerical resolutions, the implicit approach is largely more robust. Euler's implicit resolution method can be stated as follows:

$$\vec{x}(t+h) = \vec{x}(t) + h\vec{v}(t+h), \tag{10.14}$$
$$\mathbf{M}\vec{v}(t+h) = \mathbf{M}\vec{v}(t) + h\mathbf{M}\dot{\vec{v}}(t+h) \tag{10.15}$$

and

$$\mathbf{M}\vec{v}(t+h) = \mathbf{M}\vec{v}(t) + h\left[-\mathbf{D}\vec{v}(t+h) - \mathbf{K}(\vec{x}(t+h) - \vec{x}_0) + \vec{f}_{\text{ext}}\right],$$
(10.16)

where h is the time step of the simulation. Note that the position at time $t + h$ should be implicitly computed from the velocity at time $t + h$, unlike in explicit methods where the velocity is available at time t. In order to find a way to solve the previous equations we need to rearrange them. Thus, replacing $\vec{x}(t + h)$ of Equation (10.15) into Equation (10.16) and grouping terms, we obtain

$$\left[\mathbf{M} + h\mathbf{D} + h^2\mathbf{K}\right]\vec{v}(t+h) = \mathbf{M}\vec{v}(t) + h\left[\mathbf{K}(\vec{x}(t) - \vec{x}_0) - \vec{f}_{\text{ext}}\right]. \quad (10.17)$$

Therefore, to solve the dynamic-system description of a deformable body using an implicit form, we simply have to invert the matrix,

$$\mathbf{S} = \mathbf{M} + h\mathbf{D} + h^2\mathbf{K}, \quad (10.18)$$

and multiply both sides of Equation (10.17) to obtain $\vec{v}(t + h)$ and posteriorly $\vec{x}(t + h)$.

10.3.4 Corotational Formulation

The fact that we are using the finite element model based on linear elasticity has several advantages. First of all, the matrices $\mathbf{K}$, $\mathbf{D}$, and $\mathbf{M}$ are constant at any time t, hence the system matrix $\mathbf{S}$ of Equation (10.18) will also be constant during the simulation, unless a topology change is executed on the object. However, since the linear elasticity formulation is based on the Cauchy strain tensor, which is not invariant under rotations, the model is only accurate for small deformations, i.e., deformations where rotations can be neglected. If the object undergoes large deformations, rotations will appear and make the model inaccurate or even invalid. This leads to an unrealistic increment of the volume of the object. To handle this, nonlinear strains (e.g., Green-Lagrange strain) are used in mechanics to model large deformations with rotations, but this leads to more-complex equations and, therefore, to more computationally expensive simulations. For video games, a good trade-off between the Cauchy strain and nonlinear strains is achieved by using a *corotational* formulation of the finite element method. Although the theory of using a corotational formulation is not new in the mechanics field, it was recently introduced in computer graphics [Muller and Gross 04, Etzmuss et al. 03, Garcia et al. 06]. The development that we have presented through Section 10.3.3 does not change much since it only affects the way of dealing with rotations. The general idea is based on computing the forces applied to the nodes

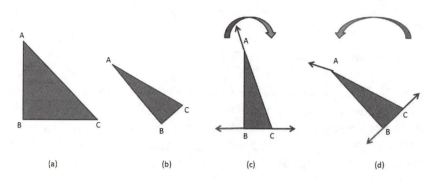

Figure 10.4. Internal force computation. (a) Rest position. (b) Deformed configuration. (c) Unrotated configuration. (d) Final internal forces. This illustration can be extended to tetrahedral elements.

of the tetrahedron by splitting the deformation into translations and rotations. We sketch the method as in [Muller and Gross 04] (see Figure 10.4):

1. The coordinates $\vec{x}$ of the object at the deformed state are rotated back to an unrotated state using $\mathbf{R}_e^{-1}\vec{x}$, where $\mathbf{R}_e$ is the rotation of the tetrahedron given by

$$\mathbf{R}_{e,12\times12}(t) = \begin{bmatrix} \mathbf{R}_e(t) & \mathbf{0}_{3\times3} & \mathbf{0}_{3\times3} & \mathbf{0}_{3\times3} \\ \mathbf{0}_{3\times3} & \mathbf{R}_e(t) & \mathbf{0}_{3\times3} & \mathbf{0}_{3\times3} \\ \mathbf{0}_{3\times3} & \mathbf{0}_{3\times3} & \mathbf{R}_e(t) & \mathbf{0}_{3\times3} \\ \mathbf{0}_{3\times3} & \mathbf{0}_{3\times3} & \mathbf{0}_{3\times3} & \mathbf{R}_e(t) \end{bmatrix}.$$

2. In the unrotated state the displacements are given by $\vec{u}_e = \mathbf{R}_e^{-1}\vec{x}_e - \vec{x}_e(t_0)$. Hence, the forces in the unrotated state are given by

$$\vec{f}_{e_{\text{unrotated}}} = \mathbf{K}_e\left[\mathbf{R}_e^{-1}\vec{x} - \vec{x}_0\right].$$

3. Finally, the forces in the unrotated state are rotated back to the deformed state, i.e.,

$$\vec{f}_e = \mathbf{R}_e\mathbf{K}_e\left[\mathbf{R}_e^{-1}\vec{x} - \vec{x}_0\right]$$
$$= \mathbf{R}_e\mathbf{K}_e\mathbf{R}_e^{-1}\vec{x} - \mathbf{R}_e\mathbf{K}_e\vec{x}_0.$$

Note that $\mathbf{K}_e\vec{x}_0$ can be precomputed since $\vec{K}_e$ is constant during the simulation, allowing us to accelerate the simulation. For the entire object, we get

$$\mathbf{f} = \mathbf{K}_g\vec{x} + \vec{f}_{g_0},$$

where $\mathbf{K}_g$ is the global stiffness matrix that is built by summing up all the stiffness matrices of the tetrahedron. Although $\mathbf{K}_e$ is built only at the beginning, the global matrix has to be built each time the object is deformed. Similarly, the forces at the tetrahedron nodes are summed up to compute the global vector $\vec{f}_{g0}$.

Therefore, at each time step, we need to solve the system given by Equation (10.17), where we have to invert the matrix $\mathbf{S} = \mathbf{M} + h\mathbf{D} + h^2\mathbf{K}$ by

$$\mathbf{K}_g(t) = \begin{bmatrix} \sum_e \mathbf{R}_e(t)\mathbf{K}_{e,1,1}\mathbf{R}_e(t)^{-1} & \cdots & \sum_e \mathbf{R}_e(t)\mathbf{K}_{e,1,n}\mathbf{R}_e(t)^{-1} \\ \vdots & \ddots & \\ \sum_e \mathbf{R}_e(t)\mathbf{K}_{e,n,1}\mathbf{R}_e(t)^{-1} & \cdots & \sum_e \mathbf{R}_e(t)\mathbf{K}_{e,n,n}\mathbf{R}_e(t)^{-1} \end{bmatrix}$$

and

$$\vec{f}_{g0}(t) = \begin{bmatrix} \sum_e \vec{f}_{e,1} \\ \vdots \\ \sum_e \vec{f}_{e,n} \end{bmatrix}.$$

Remember that we can accelerate the simulation by precomputing the stiffness matrices $\mathbf{K}_e$.

Computing the tetrahedron rotation. The corotational formulation algorithm needs to compute the rotations of the mesh elements in each simulation step. Before showing how to obtain the rotations of the elements, we need to know how to compute the transformation $T(\vec{p})$ of the four nodes of the tetrahedron. Hence, let $\mathbf{P}_e$ be the matrix made by the position of the nodes in the tetrahedron e at its rest position:

$$\mathbf{P}_e = \begin{bmatrix} 1 & 1 & 1 & 1 \\ p_{1,x} & p_{2,x} & p_{3,x} & p_{4,x} \\ p_{1,y} & p_{2,y} & p_{3,y} & p_{4,y} \\ p_{1,z} & p_{2,z} & p_{3,z} & p_{4,z} \end{bmatrix},$$

and similarly, let $\mathbf{C}_e$ be the matrix made up of the tetrahedron nodes in the deformed positions. Then, using Equations (10.6), (10.7), (10.8), and (10.9), we can obtain

$$T(\vec{p}) = \mathbf{C}_e\mathbf{P}_e^{-1}\vec{p} = \mathbf{T}\vec{p}, \tag{10.19}$$

where $\mathbf{T} = \mathbf{C}_e\mathbf{P}_e^{-1}$ is the transformation matrix.

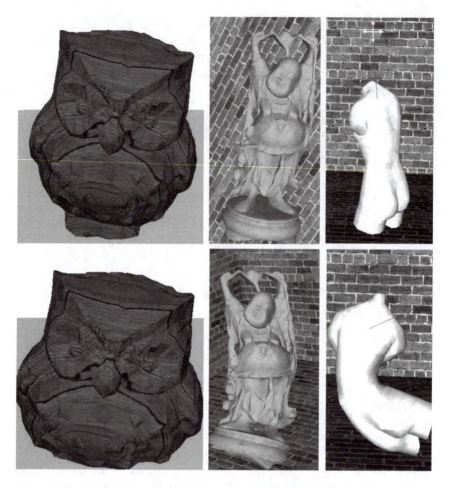

Figure 10.5. Simulation examples. The top row shows the rest positions, and the bottom row shows the deformed positions (see Color Plate XI).

Let us now define the deformation gradient $\mathbf{F}$ as

$$\mathbf{F} = \nabla T(\vec{p}) = \begin{bmatrix} \frac{\partial T(\vec{p})_x}{\partial x} & \frac{\partial T(\vec{p})_x}{\partial y} & \frac{\partial T(\vec{p})_x}{\partial z} \\ \frac{\partial T(\vec{p})_y}{\partial x} & \frac{\partial T(\vec{p})_y}{\partial y} & \frac{\partial T(\vec{p})_y}{\partial z} \\ \frac{\partial T(\vec{p})_z}{\partial x} & \frac{\partial T(\vec{p})_z}{\partial y} & \frac{\partial T(\vec{p})_z}{\partial z} \end{bmatrix}, \qquad (10.20)$$

where $T(\vec{p})$ is the transformation applied to the homogeneous coordinates $\vec{p}$ of a point. The deformation gradient is used to compute the rotation of the tetrahedron.

Hence, after computing Equation (10.20), we obtain

$$\mathbf{F} = \begin{bmatrix} T_{2,2}, T_{2,3}, T_{2,4} \\ T_{3,2}, T_{3,3}, T_{3,4} \\ T_{4,2}, T_{4,3}, T_{4,4} \end{bmatrix}, \tag{10.21}$$

where $T_{i,j}$ are the matrix $\mathbf{T}$ elements and $i, j \in \{1, 2, 3, 4\}$.

This technique requires storing $\mathbf{P}_e^{-1}$ (see Equation (10.19)), i.e., 16 floating-point numbers. Storing this matrix is useful when we have a detailed surface mesh driven by the tetrahedral mesh, as we will show in Section 10.5.

Alternatively, we can compute the gradient $\mathbf{F}$ using the following, less-memory-consuming technique, which requires only nine floats per element.

Let the matrix $\mathbf{D}_e$ of an element e be

$$\mathbf{D}_e = \begin{bmatrix} p_{1,x} - p_{4,x} & p_{2,x} - p_{4,x} & p_{3,x} - p_{4,x} \\ p_{1,y} - p_{4,y} & p_{2,y} - p_{4,y} & p_{3,y} - p_{4,y} \\ p_{1,z} - p_{4,z} & p_{2,z} - p_{4,z} & p_{3,z} - p_{4,z} \end{bmatrix},$$

where its elements are made by the element e nodes in their rest positions. Similarly, we can build $\mathbf{G}_e$ using the nodes of the tetrahedron e in its deformed position. Hence, the deformation gradient of the tetrahedron e can be defined as

$$\mathbf{F} = \mathbf{G}_e \mathbf{D}_e^{-1}.$$

Note that $\mathbf{G}_e$ changes in every iteration but $\mathbf{D}_e^{-1}$ remains constant, so it can be precomputed and stored using nine floating-point numbers.

Once we have computed $\mathbf{F}$, we can extract the rotation using a polar decomposition technique. The polar decomposition technique factorizes $\mathbf{F}$ in two matrices: a rotation $\mathbf{R}$ and a positive definite symmetric matrix $\mathbf{U}$. The polar decomposition computes the nearest unitary basis to the column axes. This ensures that the $\mathbf{U}$ contains the smallest deformation. The method initially computes $\mathbf{U}^2$ as $\mathbf{F}\mathbf{F}^{\mathrm{T}}$. Then we compute $\mathbf{U}$ as

$$\mathbf{U} = \sqrt{\mathbf{U}^2} = \sqrt{\lambda_1} \vec{v}_1 \cdot \vec{v}_1^{\mathrm{T}} + \sqrt{\lambda_2} \vec{v}_2 \cdot \vec{v}_2^{\mathrm{T}} + \sqrt{\lambda_3} \vec{v}_3 \cdot \vec{v}_3^{\mathrm{T}},$$

where $\{v_1, v_2, v_3\}$ are the eigenvectors of $\mathbf{U}^2$ and $\{\lambda_1, \lambda_2, \lambda_3\}$ are its associated eigenvalues. Both $\{v_1, v_2, v_3\}$ and $\{\lambda_1, \lambda_2, \lambda_3\}$ can be calculated using the Jacobi transformations of a symmetric matrix. Describing this method is outside the scope of this chapter, but the reader can refer to [Press et al. 07] for sample code and further information. Finally, we can compute the tetrahedron rotation $\mathbf{R}$ from $\mathbf{R} = \mathbf{F}\mathbf{U}^{-1}$.

10.3.5   Boundary Conditions

As we explained in Section 10.3.2, we need to fix some nodes to find a unique solution for a static finite element formulation. Additionally, in the dynamic system,
we may also need to constrain the movement of one or several points. In order
to interact and explicitly control the object, we might need to force the object to
reach some given displacement.

Fixing or moving a soft body means to fix or move a set of its nodes; this is
usually known as the process of applying boundary conditions.

Fixing nodes. Freezing a node implies that the node is conditioned to a zero displacement. In order to do this, we apply the following simple algorithm:

- From our system matrix, temporarily remove all the rows and columns of
  the node or nodes that we wish to fix, including those of the force vector.

- Fill the values of the known forces among the remaining rows in $\vec{F}$ and set
  the rest of its terms to zero.

- Solve the system for the unknown displacements.

Moving the nodes. In order to explicitly move some mesh nodes to any desired
position, we need to compute the forces that will appear due to the known displacements of these nodes. In this case, the desired displacement (i.e., the displacement boundary condition) is $\vec{u}_i \neq 0$, while the other displacements are unknown. There are two major approaches to carrying this out : the *elimination* and
the *penalty* approaches. Although the elimination approach is more accurate and
efficient, we will describe only the penalty approach, which is a good approximation to an accurate solution and, most importantly, is less cumbersome to handle
in computer programs. The general idea is to solve and compute the displacements of a modified version of the system. This modification consists of adding a
very stiff element to the entries associated to the specified nodes that we wish to
move. Here is the penalty approach:

- Find the largest element of the **K** matrix, and multiply it by a large number,
  say 10,000. Let this number be n.

- Add this new value to the diagonal elements corresponding to the nodes we
  wish to move.

- Modify $\vec{f}$: for each specified node, add the product nu_{desired} to the corresponding row of $\vec{f}$.

- Solve the modified system to find the unknown $\vec{u}$. At this stage, we know
  all the displacements.

External forces. Soft bodies are also exposed to external forces due to collisions. It is not in the scope of this chapter to deal with all the theory of collision response. We will briefly mention some of the approaches to computing forces due to collision. The most common approach is to apply *penalty forces*. By definition, the computed force depends on the penetration depth information between two colliding objects. The resulting force tries to minimize or reduce such penetration. Usually, a skin depth is added to the objects so there is always a virtual penetration. Thus, the force f is usually computed using the penetration distance d and the velocity of the object's penetration $\dot{v}$ in a mass-spring model: $f = kd + b\dot{v}$, where k and b are respectively the stiffness and damping of the spring. This way of computing forces is fast and straightforward, but as in all mass-spring systems, it is difficult to choose its parameters and even more difficult to relate them to the real elasticity of the object. Furthermore, the forces are locally applied, ignoring the inertia of the object.

The other approach is based on a constraint scheme. The approach is commonly used in rigid-body dynamics, where no penetrations are formulated as a linear complementary problem (LCP). The general idea is to identify the contact points between two objects; for example, a box colliding with another box will have four pairs of contact points, one for each corner. Each corner contact defines a constraint where we want to keep a zero penetration distance. This is known as a constrained optimization problem. Some commercial software use this approach combined with impulses to skip one level of integration, but its use with soft bodies might become very lengthy. This is because the inherent nature of a deformable body may lead to an excessive number of constraints.

10.4   Solving the Linear System

In the previous sections, we have seen how to build a linear system using the finite element method (see Equation (10.17)). That system has to be solved in every iteration. In this section, we will propose different ways to solve that linear system. It is not our intention to describe all these methods deeply; instead, we are going to propose some well-known techniques and give cues about when and how to use them.

Before choosing a method to solve our linear system, we need to know its properties. Our equation system has the following form:

$$\mathbf{S}\vec{x} = \vec{b}, \tag{10.22}$$

where $\mathbf{S}$ is the coefficient matrix, $\vec{x}$ is the unknown vector and $\vec{b}$ is the constant terms vector. Matrix $\mathbf{S}$ is symmetric, positive definite, and sparse. We recommend two methods that best fit real-time requirements, taking into account the properties of **S**, the performance, and the memory used:

- the conjugate gradient (CG) method,

- the Cholesky factorization, combined with the Gauss elimination.

The first one is more general and can be used when **S** changes its value in every iteration (see Section 10.3.4), whereas if **S** remains constant (see Sections 10.3.2 and 10.3.4), the second solution achieves better performance.

10.4.1   The Conjugate Gradient Method

The CG method can be used if the coefficient matrix **S** is symmetric and positive definite. This method achieves good performance when **S** is sparse, since the most complex operation required is the multiplication of a vector by **S**. There exist variations of the CG method that deal with nonsymmetric systems and even nonsquare matrices, but fortunately, our coefficient matrix fits with the requirements described above.

Listing 10.6 shows an example of a CG method implementation. The CG method is an iterative algorithm where an initial solution is refined until archiving the correct result. This method reaches the right solution in N iterations, where N is the dimension of **S**. In practical terms, we will never let the algorithm run N iterations. We will stop it when it converges to an acceptable solution. The error of the solution can be estimated using the following expression:

$$\vec{r} = \mathbf{S}\hat{\vec{x}} - \vec{b},$$

where $\vec{r}$ is the error estimation and $\hat{\vec{x}}$ is the estimated solution. The algorithm stops when $|\vec{r}|$ is below a threshold ϵ.

When the solution does not reach this threshold error, we will stop the CG method after a small number of iterations in order to obtain a good performance. In our experience, a value between 30 and 100 (depending on the size of **S**) is good enough. Obviously, it is desirable to compute a good approximation in only a few iterations, i.e., we want to improve the CG convergency by

- providing a good initial solution;

- reducing the matrix condition number,

  - using a good quality mesh,

  - using a preconditioner.

```
void preCGM(CSparseMatrix &S, //Coefficient matrix (in)
           CVector &b, //Constant terms vector(in)
           CVector &x, //System solution and
                              //initial solution (in−out)
           CPreconditioner &P, //Preconditioner (in)
           int iter, //Number of iterations (in)
           float epsilon) //Maximum error tolerance (in)
{
    CVector r,d,q,s;
    double sigmaOld,sigmaNew,alfa,beta,tol;

    r.resize(b.size()); d.resize(b.size());
    q.resize(b.size()); s.resize(b.size());

    //Initialization.
    r = b − S*x;

    // The preconditioner class solves: Pd=r
    P.solve(r,d);

    sigmaNew = dot(r,d);

    for (int i=0; i<iter && epsilon<sigmaNew; i++)
    {
        q = S * d;
        alfa = sigmaNew / dot (d,q);

        //Solution refinement
        x += afla*d;
        r −= alfa*q;

        //The preconditioner class solves: Ps=r
        P.solve(r,s);

        sigmaOld = sigmaNew;
        sigmaNew = dot(r,s);

        beta = sigmaNew/sigmaOld;
        d = s + beta*d;
    }
}
```

Listing 10.6. Preconditioned conjugate-gradient method implementation.

The convergency of the method can be improved by using a good initial solution. Generally, the position computed in the last simulation step is used.

The condition number $\kappa(\mathbf{S})$ of $\mathbf{S}$ also influences the convergency. The smaller it is, the faster the convergency. If $\kappa(\mathbf{S}) = 1$, the solution is achieved in only one

```
class Preconditioner
{
    public:
        //Solves the system Px=b
        virtual void solve
                (Matrix &P, const Vector &b, Vector &x) const;

    //We ensure that this class cannot be instantiate
    protected:
        Preconditioner(void);
        virtual ~Preconditioner(void);
};
```

Listing 10.7. The preconditioner class is just a virtual interface.

iteration. The condition number $\kappa(\mathbf{S})$ can be defined as

$$\kappa(\mathbf{S}) = \lambda_{\max}/\lambda_{\min},$$

where $\lambda_{\max}$ and $\lambda_{\min}$ are the maximum and the minimum eigenvalues of $\mathbf{S}$. Note that $\kappa(\mathbf{S})$ depends on $\mathbf{S}$ and $\mathbf{S}$ depends on the mesh elements. When the mesh elements are regular, the condition number is smaller. Hence, generating good-quality meshes is important to obtain the best performance.

Alternatively, we can also reduce the condition number by using a preconditioner $\mathbf{P}$ (see Listing 10.7). Now, instead of solving Equation (10.22), we compute

$$\mathbf{P}^{-1}\mathbf{S}\vec{x} = \mathbf{P}^{-1}\vec{b},$$

where

$$\kappa(\mathbf{P}^{-1}\mathbf{S}) \ll \kappa(\mathbf{S}).$$

The product $\mathbf{P}^{-1}\mathbf{S}$ is not computed explicitly. Alternatively, in each iteration step we solve the system

$$\mathbf{P}\vec{x'} = \vec{b'}, \tag{10.23}$$

as is shown in Listing 10.8. Thus, $\mathbf{P}$ has to be defined in such a way that Equation (10.23) can be solved easily. Many preconditioners can be found in the literature. Normally, the condition number of $\mathbf{S}$ is not very high, although a simple preconditioner can significantly speed up the system. Therefore, we recommend

```
class JacobiPrecon:public Preconditioner
{
    public:
        //Solves the system P_J*x = b
        virtual void solve
                (Matrix &P, const Vector &b, Vector &x) const;

        JacobiPrecon(void);
        virtual ~JacobiPrecon(void);
};

void JacobiPrecon::solve
                (Matrix &P, const Vector &b, Vector &x) const
{
    for (int k=0;k<b.size();k++)
        x[k]=b[k]/P(k,k);
}
```

Listing 10.8. Implementation of the Jacobi preconditioner class.

the use of the *Jacobi preconditioner* P_J, which is a diagonal matrix made by the diagonal elements of S. Now, solving Equation (10.23) has the same cost as multiplying two N-dimensional vectors. And there is no need for extra memory space, because P_J can be stored in S. More-complex preconditioners can reduce the number of iterations, but their associated cost does not usually lead to any improvement.

Note that Young's modulus values are relatively small for soft bodies when compared with hard materials. For example, the Young's modulus of hard rubber (with small strain) is about 20,000 times smaller than the Young's modulus of steel. Softer bodies will have even smaller values, which is good for 32-bit floating-point accuracy. On this, the accuracy of the CG method is affected when using 32-bit floating-point precision, which is not really an issue since the simulation will be only an approximate solution leading to a plausible simulation only and not to an unstable simulation. Therefore, instead of stopping the CG method using a threshold error, it is better to use a fixed number of 20 iterations, which gives, in general, good approximations. More information about the CG method can be found in [Shewchuk 94] and [Press et al. 07].

10.4.2   Cholesky Factorization and Gauss Elimination

When S does not change during the simulation, the first solution that comes to mind to improve performance would be to precompute S^{-1} to solve

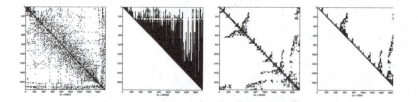

Figure 10.6. Minimizing the number of nonzero elements. The first plot shows **S** without ordering. The second plot shows **L** without ordering. The third plot shows **S** after ordering. And the last plot shows **L** after ordering **S**.

Equation (10.22) as

$$\vec{x} = \mathbf{S}^{-1}\vec{b}.$$

Unfortunately, that leads to no improvement. The main drawback is that although **S** is symmetric, $\mathbf{S}^{-1}$ is not, and $\mathbf{S}^{-1}\vec{b}$ would have an $O(n^2)$ complexity.

Instead, it is better to precompute the Cholesky factorization of **S**:

$$\mathbf{S} = \mathbf{L}\mathbf{L}^{\mathrm{T}},$$

where **L** is a lower triangular matrix. Then, solve Equation (10.22) using the Gauss elimination method.

The Cholesky factorization is performed in a precomputation stage. Much literature exists on this subject, which we are not going to describe here. We do know that the number of zero elements in **L** must be maximized. A good way of maximizing the number of zeroes is ordering the system matrix **S** beforehand. We recommend the use of the *minimum degree algorithm*. Figure 10.6 shows the nonzero elements in **S** and **L** for a particular model. The dots show the nonzero elements. It can be appreciated that the minimum degree algorithm drastically reduces the number of nonzero elements in the Cholesky factorization. We suggest looking at [Press et al. 07] to learn more about Cholesky factorization and [Tinney and Walker 67] to learn more about the minimum degree algorithm.

10.5   Surface-Mesh Update

A coarse mesh implies a faster simulation but it also implies less appeal. To keep real-time simulations, two meshes are built for each object (see Figure 10.7):

- a volumetric coarse representation made of tetrahedrons and used only for the physical simulation,

Figure 10.7. The two figures on the right show an example of surface mesh, and the two figures on the left show the associated volumetric mesh (see Color Plate XII).

- a highly detailed surface representation of the object, usually provided by the game artist and used for the graphical rendering.

The surface mesh is driven by the tetrahedral mesh, i.e., the vertices of the surface mesh are displaced following the underlying tetrahedral mesh, creating a deformation visual effect. This process can be done very efficiently using the barycentric coordinates described in Equations (10.6), (10.7), (10.8), and (10.9).

The surface-mesh update algorithm needs to link each surface-mesh vertex with a volumetric-mesh element in a preprocessing stage. All the vertices inside a tetrahedron are linked to that tetrahedron. An easy way to test whether a vertex $\vec{p}$ is inside tetrahedron e is to compute its barycentric coordinates using Equations (10.7) and (10.8). Once $\vec{\xi} = [\xi_1, \xi_2, \xi_3, \xi_4]$ is calculated, $\vec{p}$ is inside e if and only if the following two constraints are satisfied:

1. $x_i \geq 0 \, \forall i \in \{1, 2, 3, 4\}$,

2. $x_i \leq 1 \, \forall i \in \{1, 2, 3, 4\}$.

If a vertex is not inside any tetrahedron, it will be linked to the closest one.

We store the barycentric coordinates $\vec{\xi}$ of each vertex with respect to its linked tetrahedron. When the surface mesh is rendered, we can update the vertex position using $\vec{\xi}$ and its linked tetrahedron node displacements, as shown in Equation (10.2). Note that the simulation usually runs at higher frequencies than does the renderer. Therefore, we do not need to update the surface mesh each time we update the volumetric mesh.

Storing $\vec{\xi}$ requires four floating-point values per surface-mesh vertex. If the surface mesh is dense, a tetrahedron may have many associated vertices. In this case, we can save memory by computing the transformation $T(\vec{p})$ of a point $\vec{p}$, as shown in Equation (10.19).

Therefore, each time we want to update the surface mesh, we compute $\mathbf{T}$ once for each tetrahedron e and the new position $T(\vec{p})$ of all the surface vertices associated with e using Equation (10.19). It should be noticed that $\mathbf{C}_e$ changes in every iteration step and $\mathbf{P}_e^{-1}$ can be precomputed and stored. Now we have to save 16 floating-point values per tetrahedron instead of four values per surface vertex.

Thanks to the nature of the operations used by the two processes described above, we can dramatically speed-up our system if we perform all the operations in the GPU. Due to space constraints, we are not going to describe the GPU algorithm, but it can be obtained quite straightforwardly from the description made in this section.

Bibliography

[Etzmuss et al. 03] O. Etzmuss, M. Keckeisen, and W. Strasser. "A Fast Finite Element Solution for Cloth Modelling." In *Proceedings of 11th Pacific Conference on Computer Graphics and Applications*, pp. 244–251. Washington, DC: IEEE Computer Society, 2003.

[Garcia et al. 06] M. Garcia, C. Mendoza, A. Rodriguez, and L. Pastor. "Optimized Linear FEM for Modeling Deformable Objects." *Comput. Animat. Virtual Worlds* 17: 3–4 (2006), 393–402.

[Muller and Gross 04] M. Muller and M. Gross. "Interactive Virtual Materials." In *Proceedings of Graphics Interface 2004*, pp. 239–246. Waterloo, Ontario: Canadian Human-Computer Communications Society, 2004.

[Muller and Teschner 03] M. Muller and M. Teschner. "Volumetric Meshes for Real-Time Medical Simulations." In *Bildverarbeitung für die Medizin 2003*, CEUR Workshop Proceedings, 80, pp. 279–283. Aachen, Germany: CEUR-WS.org, 2003.

[Press et al. 07] William H. Press, Saul A. Teukolsky, William T. Vetterling, and Brian P. Flannery. *Numerical Recipes: The Art of Sientific Computing*. New York: Cambridge University Press, 2007.

[Shewchuk 94] Jonathan R. Shewchuk. "An Introduction to the Conjugate Gradient Method Without the Agonizing Pain." 1994. Available at http://www.cs.cmu.edu/~quake-papers/painless-conjugate-gradient.pdf.

[Si 09] Hang Si. "TetGen: A Quality Tetrahedral Mesh Generator and a 3D Delaunay Triangulator." 2009. Available at http://tetgen.berlios.de/.

[Spillman et al. 06] J. Spillman, M. Becker, and M. Teschner. "Robust Tetrahedral Meshing of Triangle Soups." In *Vision, Modeling, and Visualizaton 2006*, pp. 9–16. Berlin: Akademische Verlagsgesellschaft, 2006.

[Tinney and Walker 67] W. F. Tinney and J. W. Walker. "Direct Solutions of Sparse Network Equations by Optimally Ordered Triangular Factorization." *Proceedings of IEEE* 55:11 (1967), 1801–1809.

– 11 –

Particle-Based Simulation Using Verlet Integration

Thomas Jakobsen

11.1   Introduction

This pearl explains a technique that I developed in 1999 for the *Hitman* game series to simulate falling (and usually very dead) people, a method of animation now colloquially known as the ragdoll effect. The algorithm is also useful for simulating cloth, hair, rigid objects, soft bodies, etc.

At the heart of the algorithm lies the so-called Verlet[1] technique for numerical integration coupled with a particle-based body representation and the use of relaxation to solve systems of equations. Together with a nice square root optimization, the combined method has several advantages, most notably speed of execution, stability, and simplicity.

While today's much-faster hardware platforms allow for more advanced and more realistic approaches to physics simulation, there are still situations where a particle-based Verlet approach, like the one presented here, is preferable, either due to speed of execution or because of its simplicity. Verlet-based schemes are especially useful for real-time cloth simulation, for use on low-spec hardware, for two-dimensional games, and as an easy introduction to the world of physically based animation. The mathematics behind the technique is fairly easy to understand, and once you reach the limits of the technique, the underlying ideas of semi-implicit integration and relaxation carry over to more advanced state representations, constraints, and interactions. As such, Verlet integration is not only a good starting point for the beginner, but it also forms the basis for physics simulation in many existing commercial games, and it is a good stepping-stone to more advanced approaches.

---

[1]French, pronounced with a silent *t*: [veʁ'le].

11.1.1 Background

Hitman: Codename 47 was one of the very first games to feature articulate rag-dolls, and as such, the physics simulation ran on much slower hardware than what is common today. I was assigned the task of developing the physics system for *Hitman*, and I threw myself at the various methods for physically based animation that were popular at that time. Most of these, however, either suffered from elastical-looking behavior originating from the use of penalty-based schemes or they had very bad real-time performance for various different reasons.

At some point I remembered the old "demo scene" effect for simulating ripples in water that always had me fascinated. It had all the nice features I was looking for, including stability and speed of execution. Except it simulated water, neither cloth nor hard nor soft bodies. It relied on a velocity-less representation of the system state by using the previous position of the water surface to update the current one. What I came up with for *Hitman* was a technique that also features a velocity-less representation of the system state, yielding a high amount of stability. As it turned out, almost the same technique had been used for years to simulate molecular dynamics (under names such as SHAKE and RATTLE, see [Forester and Smith 98]).

I will now continue with a short review of existing methods for numerical integration, explaining their differences and drawbacks, with a focus on semi-implicit methods and Verlet integration. The remainder of the chapter explains how to apply the Verlet method to interactive physics simulation and goes through some of the related subtleties.

11.2 Techniques for Numerical Integration

For our purposes, the subject of numerical integration deals with how to advance a simulation from one time step to the next, updating the system state by solving an underlying ordinary differential equation (ODE). An introduction to numerical integration has already been given in Chapter 1; please refer to this for additional details.

11.2.1 Forward Euler Integration

When experimenting with cloth simulation for the first time, many developers choose a basic Euler integration as their initial method for time stepping a mass-spring system. But we realized pretty quickly that the technique is far from sufficient: cloth tends to vibrate and even "explode" when moved around too much.

The thing is, basic (forward) Euler integration has a hard time dealing with stiff springs. This is the major drawback of forward Euler integration, and often a showstopper. The problem is that particle positions and velocities come out of sync when time steps are too large. This in turn leads to instabilities, which lead to pain and suffering.

11.2.2   Backward Euler Integration

A way to make up for this is to use implicit integration. The method of backward Euler integration belongs to the family of implicit-integration methods. The members of this family all provide more stability in situations with stiff equations and generally let us use larger time steps without the risk of the system blowing up.

With backward Euler integration, we update the current position, not with the current velocity and acceleration vectors (as was the case with basic Euler integration) but with the resulting velocity vector $\mathbf{v}(t + \Delta t)$ and the resulting acceleration vector $\mathbf{a}(t + \Delta t)$. The problem with this approach, however, is that the acceleration and velocity at time $t + \Delta t$ are unknown, and therein lies the problem with backward Euler integration: as we cannot directly evaluate the update velocity and acceleration, we need to solve for the unknowns. The resulting set of equations can be rather large if there are many particles. This calls for (usually slow) numerical methods for solving equations. This means that in their basic forms, neither backward nor forward Euler integration is immediately useful for our purpose.

11.2.3   Other Approaches

Experimenting with other approaches, such as adaptive integration or higher-order integration methods such as Runge-Kutta, may bring you closer to the desired result, but these methods, too, are not ideal choices for real-time, interactive use for the same reasons: they are basically either slow or unstable. So what does an intelligent game physics programmer do? It seems we cannot escape either having to deal with instability or too much elasticity in the case of explicit integration methods or being forced to solve unwieldy systems of equations in the case of implicit integration methods—or, alternatively, waiting an eternity for adaptive methods to finish.

Luckily, as it turns out, we can have the best of two worlds. The so-called semi-implicit methods (also known as semi-explicit methods) are both simple *and* stable. And while we may lose some accuracy in some cases, it doesn't really matter in the case of game simulation. Who cares if the dead body flies ten percent too far or too short? We're not sending a (real) rocket to the moon. On the other hand, we do care about visual quality and stability, and we do care whether our software runs fast or slow—and semi-implicit methods are usually fast.

The semi-implicit version of Euler integration goes like this:

$$\mathbf{v}(t + \Delta t) = \mathbf{v}(t) + \mathbf{a}\Delta t,$$
$$\mathbf{x}(t + \Delta t) = \mathbf{x}(t) + \mathbf{v}(t + \Delta t)\Delta t.$$

By substitution, the second equation is equivalent to $\mathbf{x}(t) = \mathbf{x}(t - \Delta t) + \mathbf{v}(t)\Delta t$, a fact that together with the above leads us to the Verlet formulation.

11.2.4   Verlet Integration

As mentioned, Verlet integration is an example of a semi-implicit integration method. The Verlet integration update step is just a reformulation of the expressions given in the previous subsection:

$$\mathbf{x}(t + \Delta t) = 2\mathbf{x}(t) - \mathbf{x}(t - \Delta t) + \mathbf{a}(t)(\Delta t)^2.$$

Instead of storing the particles' positions $\mathbf{x}$ and velocities $\mathbf{v}$ as before, it suffices to store the current position $\mathbf{x}(t)$ and the previous position $\mathbf{x}(t - \Delta t)$. Velocities can then be calculated on the fly from $\mathbf{x}(t)$ and $\mathbf{x}(t - \Delta t)$ (if needed at all):

$$\mathbf{v}(t + \Delta t) = (\mathbf{x}(t + \Delta t) - \mathbf{x}(t))/\Delta t.$$

This relation means that positions and velocities are always in sync.

Since $\mathbf{x}(t) - \mathbf{x}(t - \Delta t)$ is just the change in position from the last time frame, the Verlet formula can be interpreted as follows:

1. Add to the current position the distance we just moved in the previous time step.

2. Adjust the position to account for gravity and other forces.

3. The new velocity is directly proportional to the total step we just moved.

Be aware that because velocity is now given only implicitly by using the previous positions of the particles, the time step needs to be kept constant between each call to the numerical integrator. While it is possible to develop formulas that take changing time steps into account, in my experience, the best way to handle larger time steps is to simply call the integrator multiple times.

Velocity Verlet integration. A variant of Verlet integration that is sometimes used is the velocity Verlet algorithm (also called Leapfrog integration):

$$\mathbf{x}(t + \Delta t) = \mathbf{x}(t) + \mathbf{v}(t)\Delta t + \mathbf{a}(t)(\Delta t)^2/2,$$
$$\mathbf{v}(t + \Delta t/2) = \mathbf{v}(t) + \mathbf{a}(t)\Delta t/2,$$
$$\mathbf{a}(t + \Delta t) = f(\mathbf{x}(t + \Delta t), \mathbf{v}(t + \Delta t/2)),$$
$$\mathbf{v}(t + \Delta t) = \mathbf{v}(t + \Delta t/2) + \mathbf{a}(t + \Delta t)\Delta t/2,$$

where f is a function of position and velocity that yields the acceleration given by the current context.

The physics engine in *Hitman* relies on basic Verlet integration only, but in situations that call for higher accuracy or additional robustness, velocity Verlet integration may sometimes be more suitable.

Using Verlet integration in a physics simulation. It is easy to implement the results of the above section in a function that updates a set of unconstrained particles.

```
// Use Verlet integration to advance an array of particles
// t: Size of time step
// x: Array of current positions of particles
// x_prev: Array of previous positions of particles
// a: Current acceleration of each particle
// n: Total number of particle coordinates
//
void VerletTimeStep(double t, double* x, double* x_prev,
                    double* a, int n)
{
    double x_old;
    for(int i=0; i<n; i++) {
        x_old = *x;
        *x = 1.99 * *x − 0.99 * *x_prev + *a * t * t;
        *x_prev = x_old;
        x++;
        x_prev++;
        a++;
    }
}
```

The above code has been written for clarity, not speed. Note that it is possible to save memory transfers with a double-buffering approach by alternating between two arrays. Note also that the Verlet formula has been changed slightly to include the two factors 1.99 and 0.99 in order to introduce a small amount of drag in the system for further stabilization.

11.3 Using Relaxation to Solve Systems of Equations

Verlet integration in itself, as described above, provides a good foundation for, say, an unconstrained particle system. But how do we go about handling more complex restrictions or constraints on the movements of the particles? How should interconnected particles be handled, for example? And how do we keep particles from penetrating a surface? As for the latter, we choose to simply project offending particles out of obstacles. By projection, loosely speaking, we mean moving the point as little as possible until it is free of the obstacle. Normally, this means moving the point perpendicularly out towards the collision surface.

11.3.1 Handling Collisions and Penetrations

Let's look at a simple example. Assume that our world is the inside of the cube $(0, 0, 0) - (1000, 1000, 1000)$ and assume furthermore that the particles' restitution coefficient is zero (that is, particles do not bounce off surfaces when colliding). To keep all particle positions inside the valid interval, the corresponding projection code would be as follows:

```
// Keeps particles in a box
void SatisfyBoxConstraints(double* x, int n) {
    for(int i=0; i<n; i++) { // For all particle coordinates
        *x = min(max(*x, 0.0), 1000.0);
        x++;
    }
}
```

This keeps all particle positions inside the cube and handles both collisions and resting contact. The beauty of the Verlet integration scheme is that the corresponding changes in velocity are handled automatically. Thus, after calling `SatisfyBoxConstraints()` and `VerletTimeStep()` a number of times, the velocity vector will contain no components in the normal direction of the surface (corresponding to a restitution coefficient of zero). The update loop is then:

```
void UpdateLoop() {
    VerletTimeStep();
    SatisfyBoxConstraints();
}
```

Try it out—there is no need to directly cancel the velocity in the normal direction. While the above might seem somewhat trivial when looking at particles, the strength of the Verlet integration scheme is now beginning to shine through and should really become apparent when introducing constraints and coupled rigid bodies in a moment.

11.3.2 Handling Constraints

We now describe by example how more complex constraints can be implemented.

Assume that we have two particles that we wish to keep at a fixed distance from each other, in effect simulating a stick. Just as in the above case, where collisions were handled by projecting the particles in question out of the offending obstacles, we carry out a similar procedure here: if a particle invalidates a constraint after the Verlet time step routine has been called, we simply move the particle by as little as possible in order to satisfy the constraint once again. In the case of the stick this means pulling or pushing the particles directly towards or away from each other (depending on whether their distance is too large or too small; see Figure 11.1).

For each pair of constrained particle positions $\mathbf{x_i^*}$ and $\mathbf{x_j^*}$, the following calculations must be carried out:

$$\mathbf{d} = \mathbf{x}_j - \mathbf{x}_i, \tag{11.1}$$

$$\mathbf{u} = \left(\frac{r}{||\mathbf{d}||} - 1.0 \right) \mathbf{d}, \tag{11.2}$$

$$\mathbf{x_i^*} = \mathbf{x}_i - \frac{1}{2}\mathbf{u}, \tag{11.3}$$

$$\mathbf{x_j^*} = \mathbf{x}_j + \frac{1}{2}\mathbf{u}, \tag{11.4}$$

where r is the rest length of the stick and $\mathbf{u}$ is the missing displacement between the two particles.

Assume now that we also want the particles to satisfy the cube constraints discussed in the previous subsection. By running the above code to fix the stick

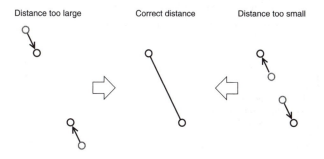

Figure 11.1. Moving the particles to fix an invalid distance.

constraint, however, we may have invalidated one or more of the cube constraints by pushing a particle out of the cube. This situation can be remedied by immediately projecting the offending particle's position back onto the cube surface once more—but then we end up invalidating the stick constraint once again.

Really, what we should do is solve for all constraints at once, both the box and the stick constraints. This would be a matter of solving a system of equations. But instead of explicitly forming the system and solving it with a separate algorithm for solving systems of equations, we choose to do it indirectly by local iteration. We simply repeat the two pieces of code a number of times after each other in the hope that the result is useful. This yields the following code:

```
void TimeStep_StickInBox()
{
    VerletTimeStep();
    while(notConverged) {
        SatisfyBoxConstraints()
        SatisfyStickConstraints()
    }
}
```

While this approach of pure repetition might appear somewhat naive, it turns out that it actually converges to the solution that we are looking for! The method is called relaxation (or Jacobi or Gauss-Seidel iteration depending on how you do it exactly, see [Press et al. 92]). It works by consecutively satisfying various local constraints and then repeating; if the conditions are right, this will converge to a global configuration that satisfies all constraints at the same time. It is useful in many other situations where several interdependent constraints must hold simultaneously. As a general algorithm for solving equations, the method doesn't converge as fast as other approaches do, but for interactive physics simulation it is often an excellent choice.

We get the following overall simulation algorithm (in pseudocode):

```
void TimeStep()
{
    VerletTimeStep();
    // Relaxation step
    iterate until convergence {
        for each constraint (incl. collisions) {
            satisfy constraint
        }
    }
}
```

The number of necessary iterations varies depending on the physical system simulated and the amount of motion. The relaxation can be made adaptive by measuring the change from the last iteration. If we stop the iterations early, the result
might not end up being quite valid but because of the Verlet scheme, in the next
frame it will probably be better, the next frame even more so, etc. This means that
stopping early will not ruin everything, although the resulting animation might
appear somewhat sloppier.

11.3.3 Cloth Simulation

The fact that a stick constraint can be thought of as a really hard spring should
underline its usefulness for cloth simulation. Assume, for example, that a hexag-
onal mesh of triangles describing the cloth has been constructed. For each vertex
a particle is created, and for each edge a stick constraint between the two corresponding particles is initialized (with the constraint's "rest length" simply being
the initial distance between the two vertices).

To solve for these constraints, we use relaxation as described above. The
relaxation loop could be iterated several times. However, to obtain nice-looking
animations for most pieces of cloth, only one iteration is necessary! This means
that the time usage in the cloth simulation depends mostly on the N square root
operations and the N divisions performed (where N denotes the number of edges
in the cloth mesh). As we shall see, a clever trick makes it possible to reduce this
to just N divisions per frame update—this is really fast, and some might argue
that it probably can't get much faster.

Optimizing away the square root. We now discuss how to get rid of the square
root operation. If the constraints are all satisfied (which they should be, at least almost), we already know what the result of the square root operation in a particular
constraint expression ought to be, namely, the rest length r of the corresponding
stick. We can use this fact to approximate the square root function.

Mathematically, what we do is approximate the square root function by its
first-order Taylor expansion at a neighborhood of the squared rest length r^2 (this
is equivalent to one Newton-Raphson iteration with initial guess r). A real-valued
function f may be approximated around a neighborhood a by using its Taylor
series:

$$f(x) = f(a) + \frac{f'(a)}{1!}(x - a) + \frac{f''(a)}{2!}(x - a)^2 + \dots .$$

In the case of the square root function $f(x) = \sqrt{x}$ around $a = r^2$, we get the
following:

$$\sqrt{x} \approx f(r^2) + f'(r^2)(x - r^2) = \sqrt{r^2} + \frac{1}{2\sqrt{r^2}}(x - r^2) = \frac{r^2 + x}{2r}.$$

As expected, for $x = r^2$, we get $\sqrt{x} \approx r$. Using the above approximation to rewrite Equations (11.1)–(11.4), we end up with the following pseudocode:

```
// Pseudo-code for satisfying a stick constraint
// using sqrt approximation
d = x2 - x1; // OBS: vector operation; d, x1 and x2 are vectors
d *= r * r / (dotprod(d, d) + r * r) - 0.5;
x1 += d;
x2 -= d;
```

Notice that if the distance is already correct (that is, if $\|x_2 - x_1\| = r$), then we get $d = (0, 0, 0)$, and no change is going to happen.

Per constraint we now use zero square roots, one division only, and the squared value r^2 can even be precalculated! The usage of time-consuming operations is now down to N divisions per frame (and the corresponding memory accesses)—it can't be done much faster than that, and the result even looks quite nice. The constraints are not guaranteed to be satisfied after one iteration only, but because of the Verlet integration scheme, the system will quickly converge to the correct state over some frames. In fact, using only one iteration and approximating the square root removes the stiffness that appears otherwise when the sticks are perfectly stiff.

By placing support sticks between strategically chosen couples of vertices sharing a neighbor, the cloth algorithm can be extended to simulate bending objects, such as plants. Again, in *Hitman*, only one pass through the relaxation loop was enough (in fact, the low number gave the plants exactly the right amount of bending behavior).

The code and the equations covered in this section assume that all particles have identical mass. Of course, it is possible to model particles with different masses; the equations only get a little more complex. To satisfy constraints while respecting particle masses, use the following code:

```
// Pseudo-code to satisfy a stick \index{stick constraint}constraint with particle masses
d = x2 - x1;
dlen = sqrt(dotprod(d,d));
f = (dlen - r) / (dl * (invmass1 + invmass2));
x1 += invmass1 * d * f;
x2 -= invmass2 * d * f;
```

Here, `invmass1` and `invmass2` are the numerical inverses of the two masses. If we want a particle to be immovable, simply set `invmass=` 0 for that particle (corresponding to an infinite mass). Of course, in the above case, the square root can also be approximated for a speed-up.

11.4   Rigid Bodies

The equations governing motion of rigid bodies were discovered long before the invention of modern computers. To be able to say anything useful at that time, mathematicians needed the ability to manipulate expressions symbolically. In the theory of rigid bodies, this led to useful notions and tools such as inertia tensors, angular momentum, torque, quaternions for representing orientations, etc. However, with the current ability to process huge amounts of data numerically, it has become feasible and in some cases even advantageous to break down calculations to simpler elements when running a simulation. In the case of three-dimensional rigid bodies, this could mean modeling a rigid body by four particles and six constraints (giving the correct amount of degrees of freedom, $4 \times 3 - 6 = 6$). This simplifies many things.

Consider a tetrahedron and place a particle at each of its four vertices. In addition, for each of the tetrahedron's six edges, create a distance constraint like the stick constraint discussed in the previous section. This configuration suffices to simulate a rigid body. The tetrahedron can be let loose inside the cube world from earlier, and the Verlet integrator will then move it correctly. The function `SatisfyConstraints()` should take care of two things: (1) that particles are kept inside the cube (like previously) and (2) that the six distance constraints are satisfied. Again, this can be done using the relaxation approach; three or four iterations should be enough with optional square root approximation.

Inside the cube world, collisions are handled simply by moving offending particles (those placed at the tetrahedron vertices) such that they do not intersect with obstacles. In a more complex setting than the cube world, however, the sides of the tetrahedron may also intersect with obstacles without the particles at the vertices themselves being in invalid positions (see Figure 11.2).

In this case, the vertex particles of the tetrahedron, which describe the position of the rigid body, must be moved proportionally to how near they are to the actual point of collision. If, for example, a collision occurs exactly halfway between particles x_1 and x_2, then both these particles should both be moved by the same amount along the collision surface normal until the collision point (which is halfway between the two particles) has been moved out of the obstacle (see Figures 11.3 and 11.4).

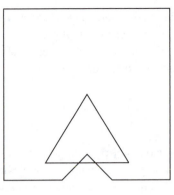

Figure 11.2. Tetrahedron (triangle) intersecting the world geometry.

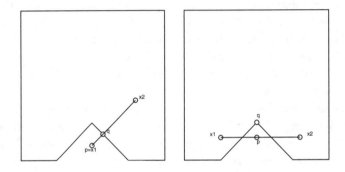

Figure 11.3. Stick intersecting the world geometry in two different ways.

In an analogous way, collisions that take place on a face of the tetrahedrons or even inside the tetrahedron will require moving three or all four particles to fix the penetration. Let $\mathbf{p}$ be the penetration point on the tetrahedron and $\mathbf{q}$ be the one on the obstacle. To handle any type of collision, follow the procedure described below.

First, express $\mathbf{p}$ as a linear combination of the four particles that make up the tetrahedron: $\mathbf{p} = c_1\mathbf{x_1} + c_2\mathbf{x_2} + c_3\mathbf{x_3} + c_4\mathbf{x_4}$ such that the weights sum to one: $c_1 + c_2 + c_3 + c_4 = 1$ (this calls for solving a small system of linear equations). After finding $\mathbf{d} = \mathbf{q} - \mathbf{p}$, compute the value

$$\lambda = \frac{1}{c_1^2 + c_2^2 + c_3^2 + c_4^2}$$

(λ is a so-called Lagrange multiplier). The new particle positions are then given

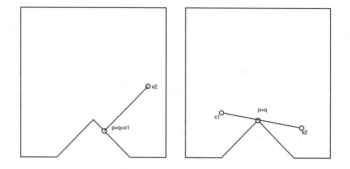

Figure 11.4. Resolved stick collisions.

by

$$x_1^* = x_1 + c_1 \lambda d,$$
$$x_2^* = x_2 + c_2 \lambda d,$$
$$x_3^* = x_3 + c_3 \lambda d,$$
$$x_4^* = x_4 + c_4 \lambda d.$$

The new position of the tetrahedron's penetration point $p^* = c_1 x_1^* + c_2 x_2^* + c_3 x_3^* + c_4 x_4^*$ will coincide with q. For details on the derivation of the above equations, see [Jakobsen 01]. The above equations can also be used to embed the tetrahedron inside another shape, which is then used for collision purposes. In this case, p will be a point on the surface of this shape (See Figure 11.5).

Figure 11.5. Tetrahedron (triangle) embedded in arbitrary object geometry touching the world geometry.

In the above case, the rigid body collided with an immovable world, but the method generalizes to handle collisions of several (movable) rigid bodies. The collisions are processed for one pair of bodies at a time. Instead of moving only p, in this case, both p and q should be moved towards one another.

In the relaxation loop, just like earlier, after adjusting the particle positions such that nonpenetration constraints are satisfied, the six distance constraints that make up the rigid body should be taken care of (since they may have been invalidated by the process), and the whole procedure is then iterated. Three to four relaxation iterations are usually enough. The bodies will not behave as if they were completely rigid since the relaxation iterations are stopped prematurely, but this is mostly a nice feature, actually, as there is no such thing as perfectly rigid bodies—especially not human bodies. It also makes the system more stable.

By rearranging the positions and masses of the particles that make up the tetrahedron, the physical properties can be changed accordingly (mathematically, the inertia tensor changes as the positions and masses of the particles are altered).

11.5   Articulated Bodies

It is possible to connect multiple rigid bodies by hinges, pin joints, and so on. Simply let two rigid bodies share a particle, and they will be connected by a pin joint. Share two particles, and they are connected by a hinge (see Figure 11.6).

It is also possible to connect two rigid bodies by a stick constraint or any other kind of constraint—in order to do so, one simply adds the corresponding constraint-handling code to the relaxation loop.

This approach makes it possible to construct a complete model of an articulated human body. For additional realism, various angular constraints will have to be implemented as well. There are different ways to accomplish this. A simple way is to use stick constraints that are enforced only if the distance between two particles falls below some threshold (mathematically, we have a unilateral [inequality] distance constraint, $||x_2 - x_1|| > 100$). As a direct result, the two particles will never come too close to each other (see Figure 11.7).

Particles can also be restricted to move, for example, in certain planes only. Once again, particles with positions not satisfying the above-mentioned constraints should be moved—deciding exactly how is slightly more complicated than with the stick constraints.

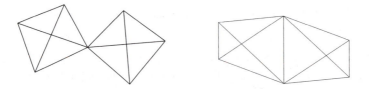

Figure 11.6. Pin joint and hinge joint using particles and sticks.

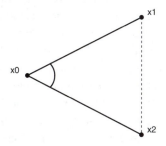

Figure 11.7. Two stick constraints and an inequality constraint (dotted) modeling, e.g., an arm.

Actually, in *Hitman*, corpses aren't composed of rigid bodies modeled by tetrahedrons. They are simpler yet, as they consist of particles connected by stick constraints, in effect forming stick figures (see Figure 11.8). The position and orientation of each limb (a vector and a matrix) are then derived for rendering purposes from the particle positions using various cross-products and vector normalizations (making certain that knees and elbows bend naturally).

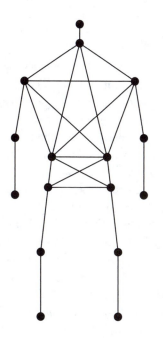

Figure 11.8. Ragdoll model using particles and sticks (used in *Hitman: Codename 47*).

In other words, seen isolated, each limb is not a rigid body with the usual six degrees of freedom. This means that the physics of rotation around the length axis of a limb is not simulated. Instead, the skeletal animation system used to set up the polygonal mesh of the character is forced to orient the leg, for instance, such that the knee appears to bend naturally. Since rotation of legs and arms around the length axis does not comprise the essential motion of a falling human body, this works out okay and actually optimizes speed by a great deal.

Angular constraints are implemented to enforce limitations of the human anatomy. Simple self-collision is taken care of by strategically introducing inequality distance constraints as discussed above, for example, between the two knees—making sure that the legs never cross.

For collision with the environment, which consists of triangles, each stick is modeled as a capped cylinder. Somewhere in the collision system, a subroutine handles collisions between capped cylinders and triangles. When a collision is found, the penetration depth and points are extracted, and the collision is then handled for the offending stick in question exactly as described earlier. Naturally, a lot of additional tweaking was necessary to get the result just right.

11.6   Miscellaneous

11.6.1   Motion Control

To influence the motion of a simulated object, we simply move the particles correspondingly. If a person is hit in the shoulder, move the shoulder particle backwards over a distance proportional to the strength of the blow. The Verlet integrator will then automatically set the shoulder in motion.

This also makes it easy for the simulation to "inherit" velocities from an underlying traditional animation system. Simply record the positions of the particles for two frames and then give them to the Verlet integrator, which then automatically continues the motion. Bombs can be implemented by pushing each particle in the system away from the explosion over a distance inversely proportional to the squared distance between the particle and the bomb center.

It is possible to constrain a specific limb, say the hand, to a fixed position in space. In this way, we can implement inverse kinematics (IK): inside the relaxation loop, keep setting the position of a specific particle (or several particles) to the position(s) wanted. Giving the particle infinite mass (invmass=0) helps make it immovable to the physics system. In *Hitman*, this strategy is used when dragging corpses; the hand (or neck or foot) of the corpse is constrained to follow the hand of the player.

11.6.2 Friction

Friction has not been taken care of yet. This means that unless we do something more, particles will slide along the floor as if it were made of ice. According to the Coulomb friction model, friction force depends on the size of the normal force between the objects in contact. To implement this, we measure the penetration depth d_p when a penetration has occurred (before projecting the penetration point out of the obstacle). After projecting the particle onto the surface, the tangential velocity $\mathbf{v}_t$ is then reduced by an amount proportional to d_p (the proportion factor being the friction constant). This is done by appropriately modifying $\mathbf{x}(t - \Delta t)$ (see Figure 11.9). Care should be taken that the tangential velocity does not reverse its direction—in this case, it should simply be set to zero since this indicates that the penetration point has ceased to move tangentially.

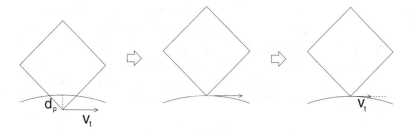

Figure 11.9. Collision handling with friction.

11.6.3 Collision Response

To prevent objects that are moving really fast from passing through other obstacles (because of too-large time steps), a simple test is performed. Imagine the line (or a capped cylinder of proper radius) beginning at the position of the object's midpoint last frame and ending at the position of the object's midpoint at the current frame. If this line hits anything, then the object position is set to the point of collision. Though this can theoretically give problems, in practice it works fine.

Another collision "cheat" was used for dead bodies. If the unusual thing happens that a fast-moving limb ends up being placed with the ends of the capped cylinder on each side of a wall, the cylinder is projected to the side of the wall where the cylinder is connected to the torso.

11.6.4 Relaxation

The number of relaxation iterations used in *Hitman* varies between one and ten with the kind of object simulated. Although this is not enough to accurately solve the global system of constraints, it is sufficient to make motion seem natural. The nice thing about this scheme is that inaccuracies do not accumulate or persist visually in the system causing object drift or the like—in some sense, the combination of projection and the Verlet scheme manages to distribute complex calculations over several frames. Fortunately, the inaccuracies are smallest or even nonexistent when there is little motion and greatest when there is heavy motion—this is nice since fast or complex motion somewhat masks small inaccuracies for the human eye.

A kind of soft body can also be implemented by using "soft" constraints, i.e., constraints that are allowed to have only a certain percentage of the deviation "repaired" each frame (i.e., if the rest length of a stick between two particles is 100 but the actual distance is 60, the relaxation code could first set the distance to 80 instead of 100, next frame to 90, then 95, 97.5, etc.). Varying this relaxation coefficient may in fact be necessary in certain situations to enable convergence. Similarly, over-relaxation (using a coefficient larger than one) may also successfully speed up convergence, but take care not to overdo this, especially if the number of iterations is low, as it may cause instabilities.

Singularities (divisions by zero usually brought about by coinciding particles) can be handled by slightly dislocating particles at random.

11.6.5   Extending the Verlet Approach

There are several ways to extend the Verlet approach to allow for more advanced representations and features. For one thing, it is possible to represent rigid bodies by quaternions and use inertial tensors to better model the properties of objects. The main idea of the Verlet integration of using the previous positions instead of velocities carries over, only the equations get a bit more complex.

Constraints that are more general than the stick constraint may be implemented by computing appropriate constraint Jacobians, finding Lagrange multipliers, etc.

Instead of using relaxation to solve for constraints, it is possible to use more-precise algorithms for solving systems of equations, such as conjugate gradient methods or Newton methods, but this is outside the scope of this chapter.

11.7   Conclusion

This pearl has described how a physics system was implemented in *Hitman: Codename 47* running on a low-spec platform. The underlying philosophy of combining iterative methods with a stable integrator proved to be successful and is very useful for implementation in computer games. Most notably, the unified particle-based framework, which handles both collisions and contact, and the ability to trade off speed versus accuracy without accumulating visually obvious errors are powerful features.

Bibliography

[Forester and Smith 98] T. R. Forester and W. Smith. "SHAKE, Rattle, and Roll: Efficient Constraint Algorithms for Linked Rigid Bodies." *Journal of Computational Chemistry* 19 (1998): 102-111.

[Jakobsen 01] T. Jakobsen. "Advanced Character Physics." Paper presented at Game Developers Conference, 2001.

[Press et al. 92] W. H. Press, S.A. Teukolsky, W.T. Vetterling, and B.P. Flannery. *Numerical Recipes in C: The Art of Scientific Computing.* Second edition. New York: Cambridge University Press, 1992.

– 12 –

Keep Yer Shirt On

Michael Alexander Ewert

12.1 Introduction

Implementing cloth simulation in real-time interactive environments is well understood and is a common sight in modern video games. The types of cloth simulated are often limited to flat, square patches. Clothing for characters is normally skinned and unsimulated. This pearl will demonstrate a way to simulate interesting clothing types on animated characters by building upon previously established simulation techniques. The enhancements presented here are fairly simple and, in many cases common sense, but these make all the difference between a visually pleasing simulation and an uncontrollable mess.

12.2 Stable Real-Time Cloth

The best-known method for implementing stable real-time cloth is by modeling the cloth as a collection of particles linked via distance constraints and integrated forward in time using a first-order Verlet integration scheme. The constraints are solved with a relaxation solver. Collision constraints are enforced by projecting the particle's position to a non-penetrating location [Jakobsen 03].

12.2.1 Verlet Integrator

The Verlet integrator is used because it is extremely stable. In the Verlet integration scheme, velocity is not explicitly represented. Velocity is implicitly encoded as the difference between the previous position and the current position. Integrating a particle forward in time is accomplished by leapfrogging the previous position over the current position, as follows:

$$x_{i+1} = x_i + x_i - x_{i-1}. \tag{12.1}$$

The system's state variables are more in sync this way, which accounts for the superior stability.

12.2.2   Constraint Solver

The threads of the cloth are modeled as distance constraints. An individual constraint strives to maintain a constant distance between two particles. A particle typically has more than one constraint attached to it. This network of constraints is solved with a relaxation solver.

A relaxation solver simply solves each individual constraint independently of the other constraints in the system. Solving one constraint will potentially violate the other connected constraints. However, each time we iterate over all the constraints in the system, the overall global error is reduced. Given enough time, the system converges to a solution.

To solve an individual constraint, we directly update the positions of the attached particles [Provot 95].

```
Vector3 pa = constraint.m_particleA.currentPosition;
Vector3 pb = constraint.m_particleB.currentPosition;
float targetDistance = constraint.m_restingDistance;

Vector3 dp = pa−pb;
distance = dp.length();
float derr = (distance − targetDistance)/distance;

pa += dp*0.5*derr;
pb −= dp*0.5*derr;
```

Often, the rate of convergence for a relaxation solver can be improved slightly by using a technique called over-relaxation. With over-relaxation, we simply overshoot our target by a percentage of the existing error. This technique can cause unwelcome artifacts, so use with caution. In the context of character cloth, I have found that a value of 1.15 allows us to perform 10% fewer iterations while remaining artifact free. This makes some intuitive sense. Since the cloth tends to have more stretching along the longer noncyclical paths during the course of a simulation, over-shooting helps accelerate the global shrinking in those directions, i.e., hanging capes or shirts have their bottoms pulled up quicker.

```
float relaxationFactor = 1.15;
pa += dp*0.5*derr*relaxationFactor;
pb −= dp*0.5*derr*relaxationFactor;
```

12.3   Modeling Real Fabrics

Unmodified, the simulation technique outlined so far produces clothing that looks like a light rubbery silk. Fashionistas typically turn up their noses at such attire, while gamers dream of the comfort such clothing would bestow upon the wearer. Gamers desire to play neither a comfortable gamer nor a fashionista during their gaming sessions. Therefore, this fabric is irrelevant, and we must try to improve the visual appeal.

The application of internal damping helps make the cloth look like it is made of a more natural material. This is done by projecting the particle velocities on the distance constraints. For the best effect, it can be applied every iteration.

```
Vector3 paPrev = constraint.m_particleA.previousPosition;
Vector3 pbPrev = constraint.m_particleB.previousPosition;

float dampingFactor = 0.3f;

Vector3 va = pa − paPrev;
Vector3 vb = pb − pbPrev;
Vector3 vab = va − vb;

Vector3 v = vab.dot( dp );

float damping = v*dampingFactor;

pa += dp*0.5*damping;
pb −= dp*0.5*damping;
```

There is a performance cost here, but the improvement to the visual quality of the material is significant.

Real fabrics buckle much more easily in comparison to their resistance to stretching. Ideally, this would be modeled by using a very high-resolution set of particles. Even then a stiff buckling resistance will be present, although at a higher frequency and less noticeable scale.

An alternative is to weaken the constraints' resistance to compression up to a certain limit. This also helps alleviate the jagged bunching and jittering of cloth that can occur at character joints. Visually we lose some creasing and folding, but the motion looks more convincing. As an example, around the shoulder joint of a character, we will most likely see popping and jagged cloth mesh artifacts. To fix this problem, we can tune the constraints in this area to not respond to compression:

```
float derr = (distance − targetDistance )/distance;
derr = ( derr < 0 ) ? 0.0f : derr;
```

This technique of modeling cloth, and indeed most known cloth simulators, tends to smooth out smaller wrinkles [Bridson et al. 03]. The wrinkles are the most noticeable feature of cloth, since they form dark shadowed valleys against peaks that catch much of the light. We can add wrinkles back in as a rendering effect by using wrinkle maps driven by compression values.

Friction forces are needed to model the contact between cloth and skin in a believable manner. The most basic and performant friction model is to modify the effective velocity of a particle when it experiences a collision. We do so by moving the previous particle position towards the current one by the velocity scaled by the friction coefficient:

```
Vector3 v = p − pPrevious;
v = v − normal*dot(v, normal);
pPrevious += v*mu;
```

Friction between cloth and skin is a fairly complicated interaction. We could make the friction strength depend on the depth of the collision. This is only a rough approximation of the contact force, and given the complicated nature of the situation, we can choose to leave it out. Another choice is when to apply friction. Applying friction with every collision is an option, or only applying it once, either at the start or the end of the solver loop. It is best to experiment to find the right look for each simulation.

12.3.1   Character Cloth Constraint

Attaching simulated cloth to an animated character requires a special type of constraint. A character bone may rotate and translate very large distances in a single frame. Keeping the cloth on the correct side of a bone's collision geometry is a challenge.

The simplest constraint that will keep a particle from passing through collision geometry is to skin it rigidly to the bone. This isn't a very interesting way of doing things. We'll call this the pinning constraint, or just pinning. If we have pinning that makes sure a given particle can never move more than halfway through the collision geometry, then, providing the geometry is convex, the collision response will push the particle out to the side it came from. This can be done with a unilateral distance constraint between the particle and an anchor position. The anchor positions used are the skinned positions for the particle on the character rig. These data should easily be made available, since most game engines will already have a skinning system in place. As a bonus, bone weightings should be authored so the anchor points are in natural locations. This is what would be used for the cloth verts, if there was no simulation.

It is useful to have a hard, immovable constraint where it is not possible to move the cloth particle. Essentially, we don't simulate this particle at all so it doesn't belong with the list of simulated particles, but it will exist as the member of a constraint. A nice way to implement this is to move all those hard-pinned particles to the end of the particle list and then terminate any particle update loops early. During constraint updates, we don't want to update the position of any hard-pinned vert.

We can vary the pinning strength. The pinning strength is a value we use to apply only a portion of the constraint correction. With a value of 1.0, we would move the particle all the way back to its anchor position. Applying a pinning strength that is proportional to the distance from the skinned position helps make it less apparent that there is a hard distance constraint being applied. Such a distance-proportional pinning strength can be applied before and after a set pinning radius. This gives a good deal of control. The pinning function now appears as in Figure 12.1. As long as the pinning strength hits the maximum value of 1.0 before it moves over half the radius of the collision geometry, we can be confident it is doing its job. Since the pinning strength reduces the constraint error by a proportional amount each iteration, the effective strength is much more pronounced

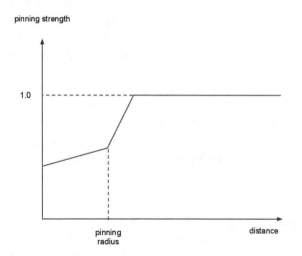

Figure 12.1. Pinning function.

than a linear effect. So, if we want a subtle effect, we need to use quite a small value for the pinning strength.

It is important to have a flexible pinning function because different sections of a piece of clothing require different pinning values. The bottom of a shirt can move large distances, while the areas under an armpit need tighter control. Arms of a shirt are especially tricky to tune because we want both dramatic simulation and control. The radius for the collision geometry representing arms is relatively small. What works well in practice for maximum visual effect is to have a pinning strength of 0 and a radius of under half of the bone's collision radius. Then apply a distance-proportional pinning strength after the radius has been exceeded. This softens the constraint, while providing good control. An easy-to-use interface that allows the character team to paint pinning values on a cloth mesh is a very useful thing.

12.3.2   Collisions

Spheres and capsules are easy-to-use collision geometries and are a fair representation of character limbs. To respond to collisions, we simply push the position of any interpenetrating particle via the shortest path to the surface. This path points along the vector formed from the position of the particle and the center of the collision object.

For a high-resolution cloth mesh, the torso of a character's body is too complicated to model with spheres and capsules. Unless we are using a very large number of capsules and spheres, the way the cloth rests on the character will betray the underlying geometric approximations we used. A triangle mesh can yield good performance by utilizing a caching optimization. Each particle should keep track of which triangle it collided with in the last frame. Check to see whether a particle is within the edge boundaries of its cached triangle (the triangle's extruded wedge). If so, collide with that triangle. If not, use an edge-walking algorithm to find the new triangle whose extruded wedge contains the particle. Typically, the particle will be in the bounds of its cached triangle or have moved to a directly neighboring triangle. Performance is actually quite good. For best results, the mesh should be closed and convex. Responding to the collision is simply a matter of pushing the particle's position out to the surface of the triangle along its normal.

12.4   Performance

By far, the most expensive part of the simulation is the collision detection. Since the constraints directly and immediately update the positions of the particles, we need to perform collision checks, if not for every iteration of the relaxation solver then for every two or three iterations. A final collision pass should be done after all other constraints. This is required to avoid having any geometry lying under the cloth show through.

Determining which collision objects need to collide against which particles can be expensive. To ameliorate this problem, we can group particles with specific collision objects, e.g., the left sleeve only needs to collide with the left arm.

Modern consoles are very sensitive to memory access and cache performance. Avoiding the load-hit-store [Heineman 08] is important. This can be done by ordering the list of constraints so that those that update a common particle are spaced apart. By spacing them apart, a particle's write will hopefully be completed before its data are needed by the next constraint that uses it. At least we will reduce the time the next constraint must wait.

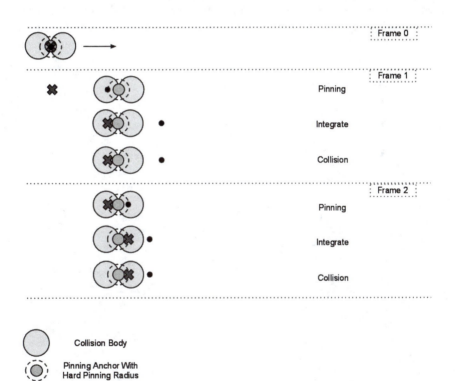

Figure 12.2. Cloth update: wrong ordering.

12.5   Order of Cloth Update Stages

Ordering what parts of the simulation happen when is critically important for minimizing simulation artifacts. When coding, good engineering practices say that we should not have direct coupling between the character animation system and the cloth simulator. The skinning data represent a significant amount of data to hold on to for any length of time. We will want to use it immediately after we have calculated it. Since the skinning data are updated by the character animation system and we have efficiency in mind, the natural thinking is to apply the pinning constraint as the very first thing we do in our update. This is the wrong order. Looking at Figure 12.2 shows why. This figure shows a particle anchored between two collision spheres. The spheres translate a large distance in the first frame. This is not a configuration we would see in practice, but it serves our instructional purposes here. During the render phase (right after the frame boundaries), we are able to see the cloth particle on the wrong side of a collision body. A better ordering is to apply the pinning constraint after integration and before collision

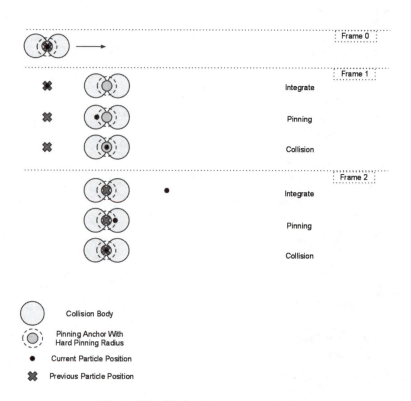

Figure 12.3. Cloth update: correct ordering.

response. Figure 12.3 demonstrates this. This is a more consistent treatment of the different types of constraints. Since it is a constraint, it feels right to group it with the collision and distance constraints. A cache-friendly way of implementing this is via a callback.

12.6 Conclusion, Results, and Future

This technique has been successfully used to simulate character's articles of clothing, from shirts to skirts, at real-time rates. With modern consoles, simulating clothing composed of particles spaced two to four centimeters apart at interactive rates is achievable, given a reasonable computational budget.

There are two major drawbacks to this simulation technique: the limited range of materials it is possible to simulate and the high CPU cost. More sophisticated cloth solvers can model a wider range of cloth with superior fidelity [Baraff and Witkin 98]. However, their performance is orders of magnitude worse and the stability characteristics are not able to handle the stresses of a fast-moving computer game.

Collision detection is the performance bottleneck of our system. If a stable integration technique that worked on the velocity level could be utilized, the performance problems with our system would disappear. An integrator that allowed us to change velocity rather than position during our constraint update would only require one collision pass each frame rather than several, as we currently must do. Research into such a system may yield a better solution than has been previously presented.

This article should be viewed not as the best way to simulate real-time cloth but as a collection of suggestions you can take and expand upon.

Bibliography

[Baraff and Witkin 98] D. Baraff and A. Witkin. "Large Steps in Cloth Simulation." In *Proceedings of the 25th Annual Conference on Computer Graphics and Interactive Techniques*, pp. 43–54. New York: ACM Press, 1998.

[Bridson et al. 03] R. Bridson, S. Marino, and R. Fedkiw. "Simulation of Clothing with Folds and Wrinkles." In *Proceedings of the 2003 ACM SIGGRAPH/Eurographics Symposium on Computer Animation*, pp. 28–36. Aire-la-Ville, Switzerland: Eurographics Association, 2003.

[Heineman 08] Becky Heineman. "Sponsored Feature: Common Performance Issues in Game Programming." *Gamasutra*. Available at http://www .gamasutra.com/view/feature/3687/sponsored_feature_common_.php, 2008.

[Jakobsen 03] Thomas Jakobsen. "Advanced Character Physics.", 2003. *Gamasutra*. Available at http://www.gamasutra.com/resource_guide/20030121/ jacobson_01.shtml.

[Provot 95] Xavier Provot. "Deformation Constraints in a Mass-Spring Model to Describe Rigid Cloth Behavior." In *Graphics Interface '95*, pp. 147–155. Quebec: Graphics Interface, 1995.

– VI –

Skinning

– 13 –

Layered Skin Simulation

Kiaran Ritchie

13.1 Introduction

This article proposes a multilayered, artist-controlled, modular approach to the problem of creating believable mesh-based skin deformations. The general idea is to create a chain of layered deformations, the result of which approximates the behavior of skin. It is well known that traditional smooth skinning produces unsightly artifacts and fails to capture the full range of desired effects, namely, skin sliding, volume preservation, and jiggling.

To fix this, volume preservation is enforced as a postprocess by forcing collision between the deformed skin and an artist-built underlying polygonal anatomy using an optimized ray-casting technique. The resulting mesh is passed to a relaxation phase that enforces an elastic behavior using a modified Jakobsen constraint solver. The relaxed vertex positions are sent to the final phase, where a jiggle effect is added to the skin. This phase computes a per-vertex force vector and uses a simple Euler-integration step to provide some temporal coherence.

I will show that a layered combination of simple modules is sufficient in reproducing the macroscale volume changes observed in moving creatures. Due to the rapid advancement of many-core CPU/GPGPU architectures, these techniques will soon be applicable to real-time environments. It is encouraging that these algorithms are simple to implement, intuitive to work with, and trivially optimized for parallel processors.

13.2 Layered Deformation Architecture

In this article, I would like to introduce physics and animation programmers to the concept of layered deformations. The aim of this section is to convince you that a slight shift in the way we organize our deformation pipelines could usher in a floodgate of much-needed improvements in the fidelity of real-time character animation.

Most modern engine architectures do not support or utilize layered mesh deformations. Typically, character meshes are modified with a single smooth skinning algorithm. Occasionally, this is supplemented with morph target animation applied directly to the vertices prior to skinning. These two deformation methods are hitting a ceiling in terms of their ability to keep pace with audience expectations.

Advancements in shading and lighting have accelerated to the point where real-time characters look remarkably lifelike. That is, until they move. The canned animation and rubber hose deformations in modern video games destroy the illusion created by a modern renderer.

When characters are rendered with full subsurface scattering, ambient occlusion, and high-resolution textures, the disparity between rendering and motion quality becomes even more apparent. Believable deformations, combined with plausible animation synthesis, are the only way we're going to fix this troubling discontinuity.

13.2.1   A Deformer Base Class

From here on, I will refer to a deformer (to use Maya parlance) as a literal C++ function (or vertex shader, compute shader, CUDA kernel, etc.) that takes a polygon mesh as input (complete with connectivity/edge data), modifies the vertex positions according to some formula, and outputs new vertex positions.

Layered deformers are commonly employed in film and television animation. Commercial animation packages like Maya and 3ds Max use a stack of deformers to compute the final vertex positions. For simple deformations, this stack may have only one deformer (usually one that calculates smooth skinning), but for more complex animations, it's not uncommon to see five or more deformations stacked on each other.

A good deformer base class should be designed in such a way to allow for the concatenation of multiple types of deformers into a stack. In this arrangement, each deformer in the stack operates on the output of the previous deformer. This can easily be implemented using something like a linked-list data structure, where each deformer has a pointer to the next.

When the Update() function of the first deformer is finished, it calls the Update() function of the next deformer in the list (provided it's not at the end of the chain), the result being that the mesh is passed through a linear series of modifications (deformations), each of which adds some contribution to the position of the final vertices. Conceptually, this is all very simple, but it's an important change in the way we think about deforming meshes.

The following C++ code demonstrates one method of creating a stackable deformer. This base case could be directly extended through inheritance to create any type of deformer we could dream of (see Listing 13.1).

```cpp
class PolyMesh; //our engine's mesh class
//A pure—virtual base class template for making deformers.
class BaseDeformer
{
public:
    BaseDeformer();
    //Calls Destroy()
    virtual ~BaseDeformer() { Destroy(); }

    //Pure virtual, must be implemented in subclass
    virtual void Deform()=0;

    //Called on root of deformer stack,
    //recursively evaluates entire chain
    void Update()
    {
        Deform();
        if (nextDeformer) nextDeformer->Update();
    }

    //Called on root of deformer stack,
    //recursively destroys entire chain
    void Destroy()
    {
        if (nextDeformer) nextDeformer->Release();
        Release();
    }
    void Release() { delete this; }

protected:
    //Pointer to next deformer
    BaseDeformer *nextDeformer;
    //The mesh we are operating on prior to rendering
    PolyMesh *mesh;
};

//Example subclass of BaseDeformer for doing cloth simulation.
class ClothDeformer: public BaseDeformer
{
public:
    //Pass it a mesh pointer
    ClothDeformer(PolyMesh *inMesh);
    //Base class destructor will be called implicitly.
    ~ClothDeformer(){};

    //Override virtual function
    void Deform()
    {
```

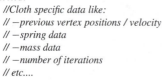

```
    //Do cloth simulation here
    }

protected:
    //Cloth specific data like:
    // −previous vertex positions / velocity
    // −spring data
    // −mass data
    // −number of iterations
    // etc....

}
```

Listing 13.1. A sample pure-virtual base class for creating different kinds of "stack-able" deformers. Update() is called on the base of the stack, which cascades down the chain until all the deformers are computed.

If implemented in an extensible manner, new deformer types can be developed and integrated into our animation system as time permits. The actual guts of the deformer can be any function of the input mesh but may include other generic inputs from our animation system. Common inputs include joints/bones, time, other geometry, implicit surfaces/curves and weight maps.

13.2.2 Layering Deformers Using Weights

It's not uncommon for a deformer to require additional input data in the form of per-vertex weights. These are usually normalized float values that provide the artist with local control over the behavior of the mesh. Artists are familiar with the process of assigning per-vertex values from their experience with smooth skinning.

In this paradigm, it would be useful to consider cloth simulation as just another type of deformer. With the addition of per-vertex weighting, the cloth simulator can interpret a per-vertex float value as the strength of a spring (with zero length) that connects that particle/vertex to its prior position (the position being passed into the cloth deformer).

In this way, the cloth simulation can be layered and combined with any other deformations. To see why this might be useful, consider the example of rigging a dragon wing. For the sake of argument, the wing has a thin membrane of skin stretched between several bony fingers. It would be nice if we could use cloth simulation on the skin membrane and *combine* that with skeletal skinning on the fingers.

With the addition of per-vertex normalized deformer weights, we can create a seamless transition from simulated vertices to those being controlled by the skinning algorithm.

13.2.3   Creating a Deformation Stack

A chain of deformers (or a stack) is a powerful thing. With it, artists are free to create a flexible combination of deformations to achieve almost any desired effect. This simple approach is what has enabled the amazing advances in offline character deformations we see in films and television.

There are two hurdles that prevent this paradigm from being adopted into real-time graphics architectures. First is the problem of finding the extra compute cycles needed by per-point calculations on high-resolution meshes. Due to the rapid advancement of many-core processors, this limitation should soon vanish.

The second impediment comes from a lack of understanding exactly how to construct such a system and what advantages this system might provide to a modern animation pipeline. The remainder of this article is an attempt to demystify these algorithms for programmers who would like to transition from simple smooth skinning, to more advanced filmlike creature effects.

13.3   Smooth Skinning

Smooth skinning (sometimes called *matrix palette* skinning, *enveloping*, *skeletal subspace* deformation, or simply *skinning*) is a staple algorithm in computer graphics. It is in use in almost every contemporary real-time graphics environment. As a means of articulating models with skeletal animation, skinning is unrivaled in its simplicity and, subsequently, its adoption. What follows is a review of the algorithm, its limitations, and suggestions for improvements. For a more in-depth discussion of the classical skinning algorithm, see [LAR01].

13.3.1   The Algorithm

We take as input a point cloud (skinning has no use for edge data) M with vertices $v \in \{1, \ldots i\}$, a set of joints in a reference pose $R \in \{1, \ldots j\}$, and a set of joints in the current pose $P \in \{1, \ldots j\}$. The goal of the skinning algorithm is to compute new vertex positions $v' \in \{1, \ldots i\}$, given a matrix of weights W, where the ijth entry in W represents the amount of influence from the jth joint on the ith vertex.

There are a few typical conventions with regards to how the input data are formatted. Most importantly, the weights in W are normalized in the sense that the sum of the weights W_{ij} for all j will always equal one for any vertex i. The input joints R and P are typically represented as four-by-four matrices. Consequently, the input points v are put in homogeneous form so they can be multiplied directly.

Given our point positions v, our reference joints R, posed joints P, and matrix of weights W, we can compute the deformed vertex positions v' according to the following equation:

$$v_i' = \sum_{j=1}^{n} W_{ij} \cdot P_j \cdot R_j^{-1} \cdot v_i.$$

In practice, the matrix W is sparse since it rarely makes sense to attach a vertex to more than four joints. Knowing that, it's a good idea to check W_{ij} to see if it is zero, and if so, that joint is skipped in the summation. Additionally, the matrix R remains constant so its inverse is also constant and can safely be pre-computed.

13.3.2   Understanding Skinning

Skinning can be understood on an intuitive level. The product of $P_j R_j^{-1} v_i$ results in a vector that translates our input vertex as though it were attached to the single joint j. To prevent a double transformation, we only want the difference between the reference pose R and the current pose P, which is why we multiply P_j by the inverse of R_j (effectively subtracting the rest pose from the final pose, giving us a delta transformation).

This delta matrix records how much the joint has moved/rotated/scaled from its original pose. The delta transformation $P_j R_j^{-1}$ is then applied to the original vertex v, resulting in a new position that represents how that joint would affect v if it had 100% influence over it.

But this is *smooth* skinning, not *rigid* binding. So we need to scale this vector by W_{ij} and sum it with the contributions from all the other joints. Think of the final vertex v' as being the *weighted sum of a series of delta transformations*. Technically, this is a weighted linear interpolation of intermediate points, each of which is generated by a single influencing joint.

13.3.3   The Problem with Smooth Skinning

Everyone who has used smooth skinning knows that if we twist a joint towards 180°, we get the infamous candy wrapper deformation. If we can picture this algorithm as blending transformed points together (as described in the previous section), we will immediately understand where this problem comes from.

Imagine a vertex weighted between just two joints. The resulting blended position lies somewhere on a line that passes through two points, each point coming from the transformation of one of the influencing joints (see Figure 13.1). So a weight of 0.5 to each joint with a 180 degree twist (along the length of the bone) would have the final blended position lying at the halfway point on the line between the twisted point (from the twisted joint) and the original point (from the

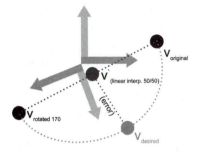

Figure 13.1. With 0.5 weighting to two bones and a rotation approaching 180 degrees, the resulting vertex collapses to the center. The error between the desired position (along the arc) and the actual position is quite noticeable. This error starts off negligible, but increases significantly as the rotation approaches 180 degrees.

joint that is left at its rest pose). This line passes through the axis of rotation, which means our point has completely collapsed.

But long before we get to 180° (an arguably extreme rotation), the point has already begun to deviate from the natural arc we would prefer it to take. So limiting rotations to within some safe range is not really a solution.

This natural arc has been the subject of a lot of research. It is clear that the naive way in which we blend matrices with the smooth skinning algorithm results in a transformation that is no longer rigid, even if the input transformations were themselves rigid. The loss of rigidity means that we are left with a transformation that includes some amount of scaling, when what we really wanted was an orthonormal matrix. This would give us a nice arc under twisting motions, rather than an ugly linear interpolation (resulting in the candy wrapper).

13.3.4 Alternatives to Smooth Skinning

So the question becomes, how do we blend rigid transformations without introducing scaling? There have been several proposed methods in academic papers, including log-matrix blending, decomposition into quaternions (and blending them instead), and most recently, a promising technique based on geometric algebra called dual quaternions (DQ). I will refer interested readers to the excellent treatment of this problem found in [Kavan et al. 07].

All of these methods have their own pitfalls; some require a computationally expensive singular value decomposition, while others result in unacceptable skinning artifacts under certain conditions.

Undoubtedly, the one that has received the most attention from real developers is the dual quaternion approach. This one has the advantage of maintaining

rigid transformations while being computationally competitive and easy to implement. Its only downside is that it does not *directly* support the blending of joints
with scaling. That said, scaling can be done in a separate pass and added after
the DQ deformation. The newest version of Maya does exactly this in its DQ
implementation. Readers interested in implimenting DQ skinning in their own
engine (as several studios already have) will find sample source codes available
from Ladislav Kavan's website: http://isg.cs.tcd.ie/projects/DualQuaternions/.

Spline skinning. Another interesting extension of smooth skinning comes from
the paper titled "Fast Skeletal Animation by Skinned Arc-Spline Based Deformation" [Forstmann and Ohya 06]. This paper contains what I believe to be the best
solution for character skinning. For whatever reason, it has received very little
attention from industry professionals (that I am aware of). What follows is a brief
description of how it can fix the problems with smooth skinning.

The technique involves the creation of spline curves that run through the skeleton, giving it a sense of connectivity. Control points of the spline are placed along
the lengths of the bones. This results in a smooth curve that runs *through* the
skeleton. After the joints are animated, the curve's control points are updated to
lie along the new bone positions (point positions are implicitly defined as a percentage along the length between two joints). New control-point positions are
then used to recompute the curve itself each frame.

13.3.5   Deforming with Splines

Mesh vertices are then attached to a parameterized position, $u(t)$, along the length
of the skeleton curve. The parameter $u(t)$ can be automatically precomputed as
the closest point on the curve, making attachment automatic (and far easier than
the comparatively laborious task of painting weights).

To compute the deformed vertex positions, a new transformation is computed
on-the-fly at the curve position $u(t)$. This transform matrix is positioned at $u(t)$
with the x-axis pointing down the curve and the y-axis aligned with the twist of
the parent joint. The z-axis is computed as the cross-product of the other axes:

$$
\begin{array}{cccc}
X.x & X.y & X.z & 0 \\
Y.x & Y.y & Y.z & 0 \\
(Y \times X).x & (Y \times X).y & (Y \times X).z & 0 \\
u(t).x & u(t).y & u(t).z & 1
\end{array}
$$

Twisting can be added by taking a percentage of the child joint's twisting
rotation and applying that down the length of the parameterized curve using a
linear or exponential falloff. Scaling can be applied similarly.

I have implemented this approach inside the commercial modeling package, Maya. It has several advantages over other techniques I am aware of. The cost of recomputing the spline curve is very minimal and only done once per frame (the curve can be sampled at a constant density so that $u(t)$ can be computed as the weighted blend of neighboring points).

The matrix-blending equation in smooth skinning is replaced with the creation of a single transformation matrix centered at $u(t)$ for each vertex. This is generally faster and involves computing the position on the curve at $u(t)$, its first derivative $u'(t)$, and a cross-product.

The results under twisting deformations are impressive. The mesh vertices remain at a fixed distance from the bones and will never form a candy wrapper. Adjusting the positions of the control points of the curve (sliding them along the length of the bones) can be done to create longer or tighter bending between joints. Additionally, there is nothing preventing you from treating the curve as just another joint so that contributions from the curve may be blended with other joints in the smooth skinning algorithm.

Beyond skinning.... I think spline-skinning is an exciting and remarkably simple way of resolving the problems inherent in the smooth skinning algorithm. It is likely that some variant of the smooth skinning process will be in use long into the future. It is worth investing the time and resources to augment or extend the algorithm so that it works the way artists expect it to, that is, without collapsing into a rubber hose.

That said, this deformation method alone will never be sufficient in capturing all of the subtleties of a creature's skin. Fortunately, we can use it as a base upon further deformations may be added to account for things like skin stretching, wrinkles, and collisions with underlying bones or muscles.

13.4   Anatomical Collisions

One of the greatest problems in designing creature deformations is that of maintaining volume. We don't need to measure the exact volume and literally maintain this over time; that would be overkill. Instead, it is sufficient to create the impression that there is flesh, muscle, and bone underneath a creature's skin.

A limb that bends like a rubber hose is very alarming to human eyes. A limb that shows compression and bulging will immediately give the impression of underlying mass. There are existing techniques that create an inner scaffolding of springs that resist compression to maintain volume. Interested readers should see [ZHO] for an excellent introduction to these interior lattice methods. The method proposed here differs in the sense that the interior is explicitly created by an artist. This gives you the flexibility of creating anatomically correct deformations, but at the cost of additional setup work.

13.4.1   Muscles and Bones the Old Way

The previous section described ways of resolving the volume problem as it arises in the skinning process. Unfortunately, avoidance of rubber hose skinning is only half the battle. Additionally, non-linear volume changes can be observed in living creatures as their skin collides with underlying anatomy.

This other type of volume change (we'll call it *anatomical collision*) can be approximated by simply adding more joints. These muscle joints are then manually animated to bulge and flex. While this is a common contemporary method, there are two major issues with it:

- The additional joints needed to simulate muscle bulging can severely clutter the animation skeleton. It becomes much more time consuming to balance the weighting between limbs and muscles.

- These additional joints only provide *bulging* deformations. They completely lack the ability to give the impression of bone sliding under skin (the bug-under-the-rug effect). This section describes a way to model this behavior in a semiprocedural way.

13.4.2   Interior Collision Geometry

To capture the skin sliding over bones/muscles behavior, we start by creating some geometry to represent the muscles and bones. Then after applying the skinning algorithm, we loop through each vertex and check whether or not a collision has occurred. If it has, we simply push the skin vertices outwards along their normal such that they envelop the entire model.

Modeling anatomy is not a typical requirement of character rigs, but it's essential if we want to simulate this effect. It's never necessary to have a biologically correct representation of muscles and bones. This is where artistic sensibilities become integral to the successful implementation of an advanced character rig.

Typically, major muscle groups can be safely approximated by a single surface. It may even be sufficient to model the radius/ulna as a single capsule. Having the ability to collide with an arbitrary triangular mesh will enable artists to create any desirable sub-skin collision shape.

That said, implicitly defined surfaces work well here and may be significantly faster to compute collisions against. These collision shapes should be parented to the skeleton, and their transformations must be updated prior to calculating the deformation. Needless to say, this geometry is purely for collision purposes and should not be rendered.

13.4.3 Ray-Casting Collisions

Given a well-constructed anatomical model and a mesh wrapping over it with smooth skinning, how do we ensure the vertices collide properly? As is usually the case, these things can be simplified if we make some assumptions. The core assumption here is that vertices only need to adjust to collisions by moving along their normal (i.e., being pushed inwards or outwards). This is a fair assumption if you recall that we are looking for a bug-under-the-rug effect where the bug only pushes the carpet up/down and does not *pull* it tangentially to the surface normal.

With this in mind, calculating the offset is a matter of *finding the furthest point along the vertex normal that touches a collision surface.* If there are multiple surfaces, we must be careful to choose the point that is furthest away.

I must stress here that this is *not* a way of doing general *physical* soft-body collisions. Ray-casting collision response will not prevent the skin mesh from self-intersecting. What it does do is help prevent a loss of volume by keeping the surface of the skin outside the collision geometry.

To do this, create a ray with an origin at the vertex and direction equal to the vertex normal. Cast this ray at the collision geometry and record the point furthest along the ray that intersects with the collision geometry. Now move the vertex to this furthest point of intersection (see Figure 13.2). This is best demonstrated with pseudocode, as shown in Listing 13.2.

```
class PolyMesh; //your engine's mesh class
PolyMesh mesh; //this particular mesh
...

for (eachVertex)
{
    //Create a ray from this vertex
    3dRay ray;
    ray.pos = vertex.pos;
    ray.direction = vertex.normal;

    //Furthest point
    3dPoint furthestPoint=vertex.pos;
    float furthestDist = 0.0;
    for (eachCollisionMesh)
    {
        if ( vertex not attached to this collision mesh )
            return;
```

```
// store the furthest intersection point from castRay()
3dPoint intersectPoint;

//castRay() returns true if ray intersects mesh
if ( collisionMesh.castRay(ray,intersectPoint) )
{
    //Check if this is the furthest
    //collision point yet found
    3dVector vertexToIntersect;
    vertexToIntersect = vertex.pos − intersectPoint.pos;
    if ( vertexToIntersect.length() > furthestDist)
    {
        furthestDist = vertexToIntersect.length();
        furthestPoint = intersectPoint;
    }
}

//Move the vertex to the further point of intersection
vertex.pos = furthestPoint;
}
```

Listing 13.2. The `Deform()` function for a ray-cast collision response (in pseudocode). Each vertex is compared against each collision object and then pushed along its normal to contain or "envelop" the collision object.

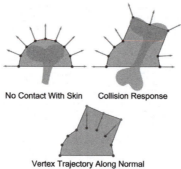

No Contact With Skin   Collision Response

Vertex Trajectory Along Normal

Figure 13.2. Skin with nicely contained collision geometry (bone). Arrows represent vertex normals (top left). The collision bone has moved. Ray casting for each vertex has found their new positions "outside" the bone. New vertex normals are also computed (top right). The displacement vectors for the vertices that were "pushed" by the collision geometry (bottom) (see Color Plate X).

13.4.4   Optimizing and Extending

The details of ray casting itself are beyond the scope of this article (see [Amantides and Choi 97] for details on highly optimized ray-triangle intersection testing). Suffice to say that the `castRay()` function should be highly optimized since it may be called several times for each vertex. Fortunately, the collision geometry is usually very simple and so these ray-casts are not as terribly costly as it might sound.

It is necessary to compile a list of collision geometries to test for each vertex. This not only avoids wasted ray-casting calculations, but it also prevents a vertex on the finger, for example, from flying across the body should its normal intersect a ribcage, skull, or ankle. For this reason, it is wise to assign a limit on the length of the ray (effectively making it a directed line segment).

It is also worth mentioning that this same technique may be trivially extended to include deformations that push the skin from the outside. Imagine the effect of a finger being pushed into a soft belly. In this case, the collision geometry should be specified as a pusher so that vertices that test against it use their negated vertex normal. In this way, the vertex will push inwards if the inverse normal intersects the collision geometry.

13.4.5   Results

This type of pseudo-collision deformation looks remarkably realistic when applied to regions of the body that exhibit a sliding effect. The jaw, biceps, clavicle, knee, and elbow are perhaps the most obvious candidates for bone/muscle collisions. It must be noted, however, that this deformation on its own can lead to some vertex popping across frames.

To understand why, we only have to remember that we are forcibly moving the vertex to the point of collision. This can result in snapping behavior. To combat this issue, collision should be accompanied by some sort of smoothing in order to avoid jarring temporal and spacial discontinuities. Relaxation is one such smoothing algorithm that works beautifully in conjunction with anatomical collisions.

13.5   Relaxation

Any simulation of skin behavior would be woefully inadequate if it didn't include some sense of elasticity. Place your finger on your knuckle and push the skin upwards. Notice the skin at the base of your wrist (a good 10 cm away), stretches in reaction to this small deformation. This type of interconnected elasticity is what a relaxation deformer attempts to replicate.

To do this, we will borrow (or steal) concepts from cloth simulation. The mesh relaxation algorithm described here is almost identical to Thomas Jakobsen's constraint solver as described in his seminal paper, *Advanced Character Physics 2003* [Jakobsen 03]. See Section 11.3 for details on solving constraints with relaxation.

As in Jakobsen's cloth simulation, distance constraints are created between neighboring (in his case) particles (in our case, vertices). These distance constraints are solved by projection for a number of iterations, yielding a solution that approximately satisfies them all. By building distance constraints (we can think of them as springs), we are effectively constructing a linkage between neighboring vertices such that a deformation on one vertex is imparted to its neighbors *through* the constraints. For a very readable introduction to position-based constraint solvers, please see [Müller et al. 06].

13.5.1 Building Edge Constraints

I have experimented with various methods of creating constraints (Euclidian proximity, edge distance, across faces, etc). In my experience, the best behavior is obtained by simply using the edges of the mesh itself. So there will be the same number of constraints as there are edges. A constraint, therefore, contains the index to both vertices, as well as the initial distance between them (see Listing 13.3).

```
struct edgeConstraint
{
    Vertex* vertexA; //Pointer to vertex
    Vertex* vertexB; //Pointer to vertex
    float restLength;
}
```

Listing 13.3. A distance constraint ensures that the distance between two vetices, A and B, remains as close as possible to the original distance (rest length).

13.5.2 Solving Constraints

Once we have a list of constraints, solving them is done by iterating over all of them a set number of times (I've found five to ten iterations is usually plenty), adjusting the position of each vertex accordingly. When the constraints have been sufficiently solved, local deformation on the mesh will be *distributed* across the surface, giving it a very convincing sense of elasticity.

As with Jakobsen, we solve the constraints directly by projecting the vertices to positions that satisfy the constraints. To satisfy the constraint, the distance between the vertices must be the same as it was initially (`currentLength` = `restLength`).

So we compare the current length to the initial length. We find the delta and divide it by two. Each vertex then receives a portion of this delta in the direction that would bring the vertices closer together or further apart depending on if the constraint is stretched or compressed. Because the results of the last iteration are fed into the current iteration, the mesh *evolves* into a smooth shape. Listing 13.4 shows this is in pseudocode.

```
float pushStrength = 0.1;
float pullStrength = 0.5;
int iterations = 10;

for (eachIteration)
{
    for (eachConstraint)
    {
        //Calculate vector from vertex A to vertex B
        vector3d AB;
        AB = constraint.vertexA.pos − constraint.vertexB.pos;
        //Calculate delta and divide in half
        delta = ( constraint.restLength − AB.length() ) * 0.5;

        //Factor in push/pull strength parameters
        if (delta > 0)
            delta *= pushStrength;
        else
            delta *= pullStrength;

        //Add the deltas for point A and point B
        AB.normalize();
        constraint.vertexA.pos += AB*delta;
        constraint.vertexB.pos −= AB*delta;
    }
}
```

Listing 13.4. This is the `Deform()` function of a relaxation deformer. We are solving position constraints by projecting positions for each constraint individually. Doing several iterations smooths out the errors and approaches a stable solution.

You will notice two additional parameters, `pushStrength` and `pullStrength`, which describe how much of the delta to correct with each iteration. As can be seen, the `pushStrength` parameter describes how much to correct deformations that involve compression and `pullStrength` is applied only to those constraints that are stretched. Together, they can be tuned to create the desired behavior.

A large push strength (0.6–1.0) will result in the mesh forming wrinkles when under compression. This may or may not be desirable, but having the ability to tune these parameters is highly recommended.

13.5.3 Laplacian Smoothing

In addition to relaxation, it may sometimes be necessary to aggressively smooth areas of extreme deformation. Because this type of aggressive smoothing generally tends towards a noticeable loss of volume, it must be applied locally and sparingly.

Experience shows that areas at high risk of becoming tangled include, for example, the armpits, corners of the mouth, inside of elbows, or any region with a relatively high amount of curvature coupled with large deformations. Applying several iterations of Laplacian smoothing to these areas can quickly restore order and untangle a mess of polygons.

As the number of iterations increases, the mesh tends towards its so-called Laplacian shape, beyond which additional smoothing has no effect. This is analogous to the limit shape of a subdivision surface.

The Laplacian smoothing operation works by moving each vertex to the average position of its neighbors (those vertices sharing an edge). The new position of a vertex v is defined as

$$v_i' = \frac{1}{n_i} \sum_{j=0}^{n_i} v_j,$$

with vertex v_i having n_i neighbors. Listing 13.5 shows this in pseudocode.

```
//Fetch neighbor vertices for each vertex
PreCalculateNeighbors(mesh);
//Now each vertex has pointers to its neighbors
// ie. vertex.neighbors[i] returns pointer to ith neighbor
...

//Now inside the deform function
for (eachIteration)
{
    for (each vertex in mesh)
    {
        3dPoint averagePos = (0,0);
        float numNeighbors = vertex.neighbors.length();
        for (i=0; i<numNeighbors; i++)
            averagePos += vertex.neighbors[i].pos;
        vertex.newPos = averagePos / vertex.numNeighbors;
    }
}
```

```
//Now we can overwrite original positions
for (eachVertex)
    vertex.pos = vertex.newPos;
}
```

Listing 13.5. In a preprocessing step we compile a list of neighbor vertices for each vertex in the mesh. Then we iterate over the vertices and move each to the average position of its neighbors. Sufficient iterations of the outer loop will deform the mesh into its Laplacian shape.

In practice, three to five iterations of this algorithm is sufficient to approach the limit shape. This algorithm can destroy fine detail and works best on meshes that have relatively evenly distributed edge loops at rest pose (a generally favorable property for most deformation algorithms).

Because it is destructive, in the sense that it will smooth away detail in the rest pose, Laplacian smoothing must be supplied with per-vertex weights to limit its influence on locally defined regions. With the addition of a per-vertex weight, where $\{w \in \mathbb{R} | 0 \le w \le 1\}$, the final vertex position is calculated as

$$v_i' = v_i + w_i \left(v_i - \frac{1}{n_i} \sum_{j=0}^{n_i} v_j \right).$$

13.5.4   Results

When used in conjunction with the anatomical collisions described earlier, mesh relaxation can give very pleasing results. Relaxation with small amounts of Laplacian smoothing is sufficient for smoothing out uneven deformations. These unwanted artifacts can arise from discontinuities in the gradient of the skinning weights, extreme deformations, or sometimes competing deformations (especially in the case of multiple morph targets additively affecting a single vertex).

A solid implementation of this technique should include the ability to assign per-vertex weights to describe what percentage of relaxation/smoothing to apply per vertex. This is necessary to prevent the deformer from smoothing solid parts of the mesh (e.g., buttons or fingernails).

13.6   Jiggle

The final deformation algorithm I will describe here is jiggle. This is fairly self-explanatory: we want the mesh to react to motion and exhibit some sense of

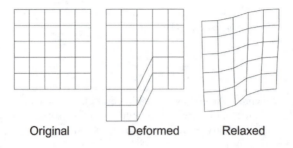

Figure 13.3. Pre-deformation (left). Mesh after a sharp deformation resulting in unnatural stretching (center). The deformed mesh after several iterations of solving the position constraints (right).

inertia. The jiggle deformer is the temporal memory that records the previous positions/velocities of the vertices and ensures that subsequent positions follow a trajectory that mitigates any visible popping artifacts (which are common amongst the outputs from relaxation and collision deformers).

Just like all the other deformers described in this chapter, the input to this function is a mesh from a previous deformer. The input mesh acts as an attractor that the jiggle deformer tries to mimic. The strength of the attraction is defined in the `springk` parameter. Lower values create more floppy skin.

Each time the jiggle deformer is evaluated, it records the last position and velocity of each vertex. To create the smooth attraction behavior, we assume that each vertex is connected to its corresponding input vertex by a spring. The rest length of this spring is always zero so that it acts by pulling the vertex to be coincident with the input position. The force of the attraction is proportional to the length of the spring according to Hooke's Law.

To integrate the position ahead in time, we use the force from the spring as an acceleration that is applied directly to the velocity from the previous time step. Then we do a Euler-integration step to find the final output position. This is shown in the pseudocode in Listing 13.6.

```
//Typical values
float damping = 0.6;
float springk = 25.0;
float timeStep = 1.0 / 24.0;

for (eachVertex)
{
    //Calculate the acceleration
    Vector3d a = (vertex.inputPos − vertex.lastPos) * springk;
    //Calculate new velocity
```

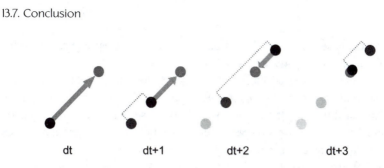

Figure 13.4. Three iterations of the jiggle deformer. The spring imparts a velocity on the vertex that may allow it to overshoot and (thanks to the damping coefficient) eventually come to rest. The result is jiggly-looking skin and eliminates single-frame popping artifacts.

```
vertex.lastVelocity = (vertex.lastVelocity + a) * damping;
//Calculate new position
vertex.lastPos += (vertex.lastVelocity * timeStep);
}
```

Listing 13.6. A simple Hookean spring and Euler integration are all that is needed to smooth out temporal discontinuities in a deformation stack.

Figure 13.4 shows three iterations of the jiggle deformer on a single vertex. The green point is the input vertex that the black dot is attempting to match. The blue arrows show the force vector that acts to bring the vertices together. Notice the vertex can overshoot and come back to the final position; this is the jiggle effect we are going for.

13.7 Conclusion

The deformation system proposed in this article extends existing deformation techniques to include better preservation of volume, skin sliding over bone, elasticity, and jiggle. It is my opinion that these are the major visual elements needed to overcome the stiffness of contemporary deformation methods. Rather than being a disruptive new paradigm, the proposed deformation system is a natural evolution of existing techniques.

13.7.1 Deformer Weights

There are a few nontrivial hurdles to overcome in the successful application of these ideas in a real-world production. Most importantly, there is the problem of authoring the necessary input data. I have implemented these algorithms in the commercial animation software, Maya.

Maya uses a brush-based interface for painting per-vertex weight maps. Sometimes the accuracy obtained by manually assigning vertex weights is preferable, but artists usually prefer the more natural brush-based interface. All common three-dimensional software provides developers with methods of assigning vertex values, but this remains an area ripe for improvements.

The algorithms presented in this article may be extended with many types of per-vertex weighting schemes. For example, all of them can benefit from a master weight, which simply scales the contribution of the deformation per vertex. For the jiggle deformer, we may want to add per-vertex spring values to create local regions of stiffer/floppier skin. Similarly, we may find the relaxation deformer could benefit from push/pull strength weights. All of these additions would give the artist more refined control, which can make a big difference in the quality of the final deformation.

In addition to this, it is nice to have a method of copying weights between characters both spatially and by vertex identity. In the interest of productivity, these concerns should be given a high priority for any group seriously interested in implementing a deformation system.

13.7.2   Optimization Issues

Aside from workflow and interface issues, there is always the issue of runtime speed and optimization. Because most of these algorithms operate on vertices (the same way a shader operates on pixels), parallelism is a natural fit.

This deformation framework is easily optimized further by employing a simple distance-based level-of-detail (LOD) scheme where all but the basic skinning passes are skipped when the mesh is sufficiently far from the screen. It may be useful to add an LOD parameter to the base deformer class so that the artist can assign a range outside of which the computation is skipped.

13.7.3   Final Thoughts

I have worked as both a tools programmer and character rigger in both film and video games. I am always amazed by the imagery that video game artists and engineers are capable of producing within the constraints of real-time environments. But there is no doubt that the computational horsepower available to film productions provide for images that display a richness and fidelity that real-time graphics can scarcely match.

With the popularization of multicore programming in recent years, many of the techniques previously reserved for offline productions are finding their way into modern game engines. A layered skin-simulation system is one such technique.

My hope is that these ideas find their way into future game engines. Without a new approach to character deformations, the gulf between motion quality and rendering fidelity will continue to widen. This is already a big issue with modern games, so the race is on to find a solution.

Bibliography

[Amantides and Choi 97] John Amanatides and Kia Choi. "Ray Tracing Triangular Meshes." In *Proceedings of the Eighth Western Computer Graphics Symposium*, pp. 43–52. New York: ACM, 1997.

[Forstmann and Ohya 06] Sven Forstmann, Jun Ohya. "Fast Skeletal Animation by Skinned Arc-Spline Based Deformation." Paper presented at Eurographics, Vienna, Austria, 2006.

[Jakobsen 03] Thomas Jakobsen. "Advanced Character Physics." Available at http://www.teknikus.dk/tj/gdc2001.htm, 2003.

[Kavan et al. 07] Ladislav Kavan, Steven Collins, Jiri Zara, and Carol O'Sullivan. "Skinning with Dual Quaternions." In *Proceedings of the 2007 Symposium on Interactive 3D Graphics*, pp. 39–46. New York: ACM, 2007.

[Larsen et al. 01] Bent Dalgaard Larsen, Kim Steen Peterson, and Bjarke Jakobsen. "Deformable Skinning on Bones." Technical Report, Technical University of Denmark, 2001.

[Müller et al. 06] M. Müller, B. Heidelberger, M. Hennix, and J. Ratcliff. "Position Based Dynamics." In *Proceedings of Virtual Reality Interactions and Physical Simulations (VRIPhys)*, pp. 71–80, New York: ACM, 2006.

[Zhou et al. 05] Kun Zhou, Jin Huang, John Snyder, Xinguo Liu, Hunjun Bao, and Heung-Yeung Shum. "Large Mesh Deformation Using the Volumetric Graph Laplacian." *SIGGRAPH 2005*. (2005): 496–503.

– 14 –

Dynamic Secondary Skin Deformations

Benjamin J. Block

14.1   Introduction

Animation in computer games is all about aesthetics. If an animation technique is visually pleasing, it is a good technique.

In current games, animation is still mostly generated procedurally or by interpolation between keyframes. These approaches are computationally cheap and easy to implement. In character animation, bone models (Figure 14.1 (left)) are used to ease the creation of realistic motion. Much effort has been put into developing different skinning techniques to produce surface vertex positions from

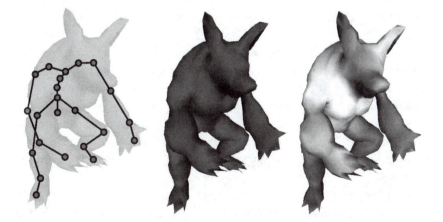

Figure 14.1. From left to right: a bone model, a skeleton-driven (kinematically deformed) mesh, and an animated mesh with secondary, dynamic deformation. Derivation from the primary positions is indicated by a white color (see Color Plate XIII).

the animation of a bone model (for an overview in this field, see, e.g., [Jacka et al. 07]). These techniques work very well in practice, even for challenging regions such as shoulders or heels. They are of a purely kinematic nature and there is no time dependence, so it does not matter if a limb is moved slowly or quickly—the calculated surface vertices are the same.

On the other hand, physics-based simulation has entered computer games, for example, in form of the simulation of ragdolls (a collection of multiple rigid bodies, where each of the bodies is linked to a bone of the skeletal animation system). A famous example is the game *Hitman: Codename 47* by IO Interactive [Jakobsen 01]. Such simulations can be used to model cloth, plants, waving flags, or dying characters.

More advanced physics simulations quickly become computationally intensive and thus not suitable for real-time processing. This is a pity because there are a lot of physical effects that get completely lost even in ragdoll physics—effects that would be stunning if achieved in a real-time simulation. It would be great to realistically simulate the properties of solid materials—watch how they react and deform when applying pressure to the surface—or when under the influence of gravity. Or concerning character animation: animating a character in its low frequency motion using its bone model, defining some material properties, and letting the physics system take care of the small and high-frequency motion—think of the jiggling of fat tissue when an ogre starts to move.

It is this tiny motion that adds most to the realism in a simulation.

Of course, this animation system would have to take care of maintaining surface details, such as the layout of veins on an arm or the wrinkles on an old man's face.

In computer games, performance is very important, and only a small percentage of computation time can be spent on the physics subsystem, but more and more realistic simulations can enter our homes as processors get faster and graphics hardware more programmable.

In this chapter, a physics simulation is developed that can add secondary deformation to a mesh, while the primary deformation can still be driven by a skeleton—the comfort of animating a character by some simple bones will be preserved.

One thing that we have to bear in mind is that for simulation in computer games, we are not ultimately striving for accuracy, as we would in a scientific simulation—but rather, we strive for believability—the programmer is in the position to trick the player into thinking that what the player sees is real.

Such a simulation can dramatically improve the realism of an animation and still be economic in computational effort. In fact, the techniques presented in this chapter take much less computation time than the collision-handling routines that are needed to have different models and geometry applying forces on each other.

The collision handling of deformable bodies has to be more sophisticated than that of rigid bodies, since there is always a certain penetration depth when two deformable objects collide and deform each other, and there is always the possibility of self-penetration (see [Teschner et al. 05] for detailed information).

For simulating the effect of surface connectivity, a technique called "shape matching" [Müller et al. 05] is used, which takes care of maintaining surface details during the simulation.

Several approaches to addressing volumetric effects of a solid material and its applicability are discussed, and the best-fitting technique is used.

If the lack of realism of these techniques is not acceptable, the method presented in Chapter 10 is a much better approach to simulating deformable objects, since it is completely based on a physically correct description.

Throughout this chapter, we are seeking for drop-in solutions that can easily be integrated into an existing simulation.

Objects in current computer games are surface mesh, so our deformable simulation should be surface based while still being able to naturally simulate volumetric behavior. This way, the deformation model can efficiently be integrated into the rendering pipeline, and the computations can even be done on the graphics hardware.

Because of the simplifications made, the simulation will rely on material properties that need to be tuned by a designer during content creation to become realistic.

In this chapter, all the background necessary to understand what is going on in principle is covered, while always focusing on practicability. We will work on an implementation of a deformable mesh simulation that will gradually be extended and can be modified to suit any special purpose in a game.

Section 14.2 will introduce the force model used for the simulation and points out potential pitfalls. Section 14.3 incorporates the effect of surface connectivity in a polygonal mesh in an economical way. The shape-matching algorithm is described. The following section, Section 14.4, accounts for the influences of the volumetric effects on a solid material without an accurate physical simulation of the interior of the mesh.

14.2   The Interaction Model

The starting point of the simulation is a triangle mesh of vertices with positions x_i^0. It can be animated in time (e.g., using keyframes), but it does not have to, for now. We want to enrich this static model with physically motivated motion. There are quite a lot of forces that can be taken into account, so the focus should lie on forces that add most to the felt realism of a simulation. The question then is how to construct them in a computationally economic way.

In the end, the sum of all acting forces is the change in velocity for each vertex at a given time step.

The first extension we make to this basic animated mesh model is to call the vertex positions of the animated mesh model the "rest" positions $(\mathbf{x}_i^0)$ and give our actual positions $(\mathbf{x}_i)$ the freedom to vary from those. They will get a mass to define how they will react on a given force (remember $\mathbf{f} = m\mathbf{a}$?). We also have to keep track of the accumulated forces acting on each vertex. The file structure storing the per-vertex information for now could be something like this:

```
struct Vertex {
    Vector3 pos; // current position
    Vector3 vel; // current velocity
    Vector3 restPos; // position given by data
    Vector3 force; // the total force on a vertex
    real mass;
}
```

The Vector3 data type is a structure holding the three components of a vector; "real" can be either a single- or double-precision floating-point representation.

14.2.1   Numerical Integration

Time is a continuous quantity. When writing down equations for the positions and the velocities of the vertices, they should hold for every time t. In computer simulation, however, we always have to deal with discrete time steps of length h. The introductory chapter of this book (Chapter 1) gives an overview of the most important integration schemes. We update the velocities and positions by the following scheme:

$$\mathbf{v}_i(t + h) = \mathbf{v}_i(t) + h\mathbf{f}_i^{\text{total}}(t),$$
$$\mathbf{x}_i(t + h) = \mathbf{x}_i(t) + h\mathbf{v}_i(t + h).$$

This is the semi-implicit Euler scheme. In contrast to the standard Euler integration, this scheme uses $\mathbf{v}(t + h)$ (implicit) in the equation for $\mathbf{x}(t + h)$ while the standard Euler integration uses $\mathbf{v}(t)$ (explicit). This scheme still commits a global error of the order of h every time step (see [Donelly and Rogers 05] on this matter). If more accuracy is needed, we could consider using higher-order integration schemes, such as the fourth-order Runge-Kutta method [Acton 70].

Numerical solutions of differential equations may be unstable because the problem being solved is unstable or because the numerical method fails. Care has to be taken to construct forces that prevent these instabilities. Additionally, damping can help to get an integration scheme stable.

The next logical step now is to model realistic forces. We will start with a simple force that forms the basis for all other forces we will discuss.

14.2.2 The Spring Force

To get a force that pulls a vertex towards a desired goal position (like its rest position), think of a spring that links the vertex to its goal position. Each spring has a certain constant, which gives us the force driving it to its goal position. When the spring force is too strong compared to the time step, the system will overshoot, which means that it will be driven to the other side of the spring, and even more far away than it was before. This way, the vertex will never reach its goal position, but it will steadily increase its energy. The system "explodes."

The maximum force that will drive an object towards a rest position without overshooting is given by

$$\mathbf{f}_i^{\mathrm{rest}} = \frac{\mathbf{x}_i^0 - \mathbf{x}_i}{h^2}.$$

That this force does not overshoot can be seen by starting off at some time 0 and calculating the succeeding positions and velocities for the next two time steps. The system will "convert" the displacement from the rest position (which means potential energy) into speed (which means kinetic energy), and the speed back into displacement, but the displacement will not get bigger over time, so the total energy will not rise over time. This force can be scaled by a factor smaller than 1 to make the force smaller—this is a first example of a material property that can be tuned by the designer on a per-vertex basis.

When we calculate the force as presented above, it is absolutely necessary that the time step h be fixed to a certain value throughout the simulation and the system be integrated in constant intervals. The physics integration should be run on a dedicated thread, where it updates the positions and velocities at a constant rate, like 30 frames per second (FPS).

With the knowledge of this force, a simple form of secondary motion can be constructed. With the calculated force, we need to update our velocities and the actual positions (that are drawn on the screen) according to the presented integration scheme.

Here is the pseudocode notation:

```
for each vertex v {
    v.force = (v.restPos − v.pos) / (timeStep * timeStep);

    v.vel += v.force * timeStep;
    v.pos += v.vel * timeStep;
}
```

With such a simulation, we would see the vertex positions oscillate about the rest position on and on, for infinity (apart from numerical errors that are introduced in every time step). The contribution of this force can be reduced as more realistic forces are added to the system, but it should still be integrated into the simulation since it helps to keep the system controllable, as there is always a trend to the completely undeformed shape.

14.2.3 Safety Belts

This discussion would be completely out of place in a scientific simulation, but here we are speaking of computer games—we have to deal with a lot of user interaction, collisions, and rapid change of motion. Safety comes first.

Although the algorithms introduced in this chapter provide excellent robustness that should be suitable for computer games, it can always happen that because of some unforeseeable reason, suddenly the system is totally pushed away from its rest position or gets a boost in velocity that will blow up the whole system.

We deal with this in the most straightforward way: we just have to follow the simple principle of "If X hurts, don't do X."

So whenever a vertex is too far away from its rest position, we just have to make sure that it isn't.

Define a radius in which the vertex is allowed to be, and whenever it leaves this sphere, put it back on the surface of the sphere.

The same should be done for the velocities. This is called position and velocity clamping—a quick way to get rid of all possible accidents that can happen to the simulation.

14.2.4 Global Damping

This falls into the same category as position and velocity clamping but it can be motivated on a physical basis. We always want our objects to come to rest at some point in time, so we make sure they do.

Damping can always be used to enforce stability on spring systems, even if the forces are not constructed to be stable with the used integration scheme [Bhasin and Liu 06].

Every system loses energy over time. In a physical sense, the energy is not lost but goes into motion that is not visible to perception, such as heating the materials or the surrounding system. Here, a simple damping model is used that will cause the system to come to rest by just scaling the velocity by a certain factor at every time step.

```
scaleVector(v.vel, v.factorDamping);
```

Damping forces can be constructed to drain energy from the system in a more sophisticated way so global damping can be reduced. But in the end, a form of global damping should still be implemented.

14.3 Neighborhood Interaction

For the following forces, the neighborhood $(\text{nbr}(i))$ of vertex x_i needs to be defined. The neighborhood can be quite a general set of vertices; we just need an applicable definition of it. If we do not have any connectivity information, we can define it to be every vertex that is within a certain radius of another. For vertices that form a lattice, the neighborhood can be the nearest-neighbor lattice sites. A triangle mesh has connectivity information supplied by definition, for example, in the form of a stream of vertices and a stream of triangles that group three vertices into one surface fragment and store additional information that is needed on a per-triangle level. (See Figure 14.2.)

Here, we define the vertex's ring-0 neighbors as its neighborhood. (This equals the vertices that are grouped into one triangle with the vertex!) We also define each vertex as a neighbor of itself, which makes the formalism later simpler.

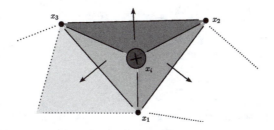

Figure 14.2. A vertex x_i and its local neighborhood.

The representation of the mesh as triangles is optimal for the graphics hardware and the rendering process, but it is unsuited for our algorithms because the neighborhood of a vertex cannot be determined efficiently. If the overhead can be afforded, neighbor lists for all vertices can be created at the beginning:

```
for each triangle t {
  for each pair of vertices v_i, v_j in t {
    v_i.neighborsAdd(v_j); v_j.neighborsAdd(v_i);
  }
}
```

This provides very fast access to the neighborhood of a vertex, but on the downside, it takes a lot of extra memory that can become unacceptable. Since neighborhood access is unlikely to become the bottleneck here, it is advised that we trade some of the access speed for memory—there are way more efficient data structures for this purpose [Campagna et al. 98]. Here, the `DirectedEdge` data structure is used:

```
struct DirectedEdge {
  int vertex; int neighbor; int next; int prev;
};
```

This data structure represents every triangle as three directed edges (see Figure 14.3), where each edge has a reference to the vertex it is directed to, as well as references to its previous, its next, and its "neighbor" edges, saved. When we now give each vertex the reference to just one of the edges that head away from itself, we can restore its whole neighborhood just with the `prev` and the `neighbor` references by the following algorithm:

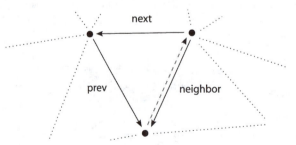

Figure 14.3. A directed edge (dashed) and its previous, its next, and its neighbor edges. To retrieve the whole neighborhood information, we just need to have a pointer to the previous and the neighbor edges of each vertex.

```
int getNeighbors(int vertex, int* neighborList) {
    ee = vertices[vertex].edge;
    neighborList[0] = vertex;
    neighborList[1] = edges[ee].vertex;
    n = 2;
    e = edges[ee].prev; e = edges[e].neighbor;
    while (e != ee) {
        neighborList[n] = edges[e].vertex;
        n++;
        e = edges[e].prev; e = edges[e].neighbor;
    }
    return n;
}
```

Of course, we have to deal with the case where one of these references does not exist—for example, if the triangle has no neighboring triangle. Those references can be set to -1, and the implementation has to handle them with some care.

14.3.1 Viscous Damping

The neighborhood information can be used to construct more sophisticated forces. In a viscous material, two particles in the vicinity of each other feel a pairwise influence if they have a nonzero relative velocity. We use this fact to formulate another form of damping. A vertex should experience resistance when its velocity differs from its neighbors. We sum over all our neighbors and add up the velocity differences between the vertices. In the end, we divide by the amount of neighbors:

$$\mathbf{f}_i^{\text{neigh}} = \frac{1}{h|\text{nbr}(i)|} \sum_{j \in \text{nbr}(i)} \mathbf{v}_j - \mathbf{v}_i,$$

or in pseudocode,

```
for each vertex v in v_i.neighbors {
    sumVel += v.vel;
}
averageVel = sumVel / v_i.numNeighbors;
neighborForce = (averageVel − v_i.vel) / timeStep;
```

This damping model combined with a bit of global damping should be enough to keep the system stable.

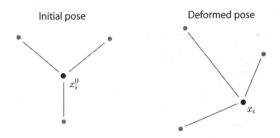

Figure 14.4. Initial ($\mathbf{x}_i^0$ on the left) and deformed ($\mathbf{x}_i$ on the right) positions of a vertex i and its neighbors.

14.3.2   Maintaining Surface Details and Shape Matching

Simulating the effect of surface connectivity based on a physical model is complex. Using the physically correct material laws would not allow for real-time simulation without cutting the geometrical complexity by too much. Fortunately, we are in a lucky position since our simulation does not have to *be* realistic, it just has to *look* realistic. And even most physical models are just approximations of what is really going on. That is the way it works. There are also no rigid bodies in nature, but there are some bodies that look and behave as if they were rigid.

We will use a technique called *shape matching* [Müller et al. 05] that approximates the influence of the neighboring surface vertices for every vertex surprisingly well.

The technique is absolutely nonphysical, but the result looks very realistic, plus it has some important physical properties: it preserves the center of mass and the angular momentum of the matched vertices. This way, it will not introduce any net torque to the system. The basic idea is this: for each vertex, we calculate the least-squares rigid body transformation of its neighbors rest positions and use them as new goal positions. For those not familiar with the topic, this should be explained in a little more detail.

When the mesh gets deformed, the vertex positions are no longer equal to the rest positions of the mesh (see Figure 14.4).

Since the vertices are connected, they should be driven back into their rigid shape by the influence of their nearest neighbors (see Figure 14.5). The rigid shape of the neighborhood does not have to be defined by the rest positions $\mathbf{x}_i^0$ because it is possible to translate and rotate the vertex cloud in whole, without changing the relative shape of it.

Think of a mesh where each vertex has been moved by the same translation—we could just move the rest position by the same translation as the vertices and there will be no forces acting. What if the vertices have been displaced by dif-

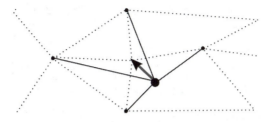

Figure 14.5. A vertex that has been displaced relative to its neighborhood should feel a back-driving force that maintains surface details.

ferent distances? The best translation of the rest positions is the one that matches the centers of mass of the initial (rest) shape and the deformed shape (Figure 14.6 (left)).

This results in the following goal positions:

$$c_i = x_i^0 - \left(x_{cm}^0 - x_{cm}\right).$$

For this quantity, we need to calculate the centers of mass for the original and the deformed shapes:

```
for each vertex v in v_i.neighbors {
    cm += v.pos; cm_0 += v.goalPos;
    masses += v.mass;
}
cm /= masses; cm_0 /= masses;
```

This is still not the optimal solution because the rotational degree of freedom has not yet been used. It is introduced in the form of the matrix $\mathbf{R}$, which represents the optimal rotation of the point cloud around the matched centers of mass (Figure 14.6 (right)).

The optimal rigid transformation

$$c_i = \mathbf{R}(x_i^0 - x_{cm}^0) + x_{cm}$$

has the property that it minimizes the quantity

$$\sum_i m_i \left(c_i - x_i\right)^2.$$

This matches the goal positions and the actual coordinates in the "least-squares sense." Additionally, it takes care of the fact that heavy particles are harder to

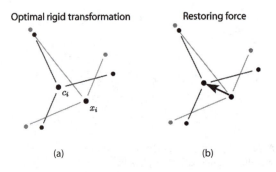

Figure 14.6. The original shape of a vertex i and its neighbors is matched to the deformed shape (x_i) by an optimal rigid transformation. (a) This results in a goal position c_i for vertex i. (b) Then the vertex x_i is pulled towards the goal position c_i.

move than lighter particles—a displacement for a heavy particle should cost more than that of a light particle.

Since the calculation of this rotation is not directly obvious, the derivation of it is put into the appendix for the interested reader.

Now the spring force can be used again to construct a force that pulls the vertex towards the goal positions $\mathbf{c}_i$:

$$\mathbf{f}_i^{\text{detail}} = \frac{\mathbf{c}_i - \mathbf{x}_i}{h^2}.$$

Since the least-squares goal positions were calculated, it should be remarked that these can also be used to build a rigid-body simulator. The goal positions are, of course, the positions of the rigid shape. If we let the actual positions of the vertices directly snap to the goal positions after each integration step, the behavior of a rigid body is mimicked.

The goal positions can also be used to introduce another form of damping: one process [Müller et al. 08] uses the least-squares algorithm to fit an instantaneous rigid motion to the particles. Then at every time step, nonrigid motion is bled off until only the rigid body motion remains.

14.3.3 Deformable Surface Mesh

We have accumulated several forces that can act on every vertex in the mesh. The relative strength of the forces must be defined per material or per vertex. They can be tuned by the designer via an editing interface in the model editor so they end up with a realistic simulation of the material in question. Another method would be to acquire the parameters from example animations that already exist

```
struct Vertex {
    Vector3 pos; Vector3 vel; Vector3 goalPos;

    Vector3 force;

    // force coefficients
    real factorRest;
    real factorDetail;
    real factorNeighbors;
    real factorDamping;

    // one of the edges to retrieve neighborhood
    DirectedEdge edge;

    real mass;
};
```

Listing 14.1. The complete vertex class.

for the model in question. A suitable parameter-fitting algorithm is presented in [Shi et al. 08]. We have to keep in mind that there are limits within which the parameters have to be set for a stable simulation. A complete vertex structure that accumulates the per-vertex information about everything discussed until now could look like Listing 14.1.

We accumulate the forces discussed so far with

$$\mathbf{f}_i^{\text{total}} = \alpha_i^{\text{rest}} \cdot \mathbf{f}_i^{\text{rest}} + \alpha_i^{\text{neigh}} \cdot \mathbf{f}_i^{\text{neigh}} + \alpha_i^{\text{detail}} \cdot \mathbf{f}_i^{\text{detail}}$$

and check whether the calculations work as intended. A block of 16 vertices connected in a simple geometry is defined to test the implementation (see Figure 14.7). The red spheres are the rest positions of the mesh while the white spheres are the goal positions of the shape-matching algorithm. The actual positions are the yellow spheres. First, we can displace every vertex just a bit and watch it go back into its original shape. If we apply a driving force to our block on the right, even the vertices on the other end of the body start to wiggle about. In the demo, we can also switch on a gravitational force (and set `factorRest` to zero) and watch the body hit the ground. The body stays in shape just by means of the shape-matching algorithm (see Figure 14.8). A demo is included with the supplemental materials.

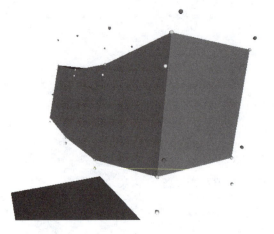

Figure 14.7. Driven deformation of a simple mesh geometry (see Color Plate XIV).

Figure 14.8. Under the influence of gravity, the geometry stays in shape just by means of shape matching of the local neighborhoods (see Color Plate XV).

14.4   Volumetric Effects

While the shape matching of the surface vertices has a huge impact on realism, it still is not a complete solution for our problem, since what we are missing completely is the influence of the interior of the body on the surface of it.

A more practical problem with this is that if only shape matching is used, the surface mesh will not follow the bone motion very well, and too much contribution of $\mathbf{f}^{\text{rest}}$ is needed, which renders the simulation unrealistic. The model we are dealing with is a surface mesh. In a realistic material simulation, the surface vertices should not only experience forces from its neighbors but also forces acting on the surface from the inside. Here we run into a problem. We do not have any information about the inside of the mesh.

Meshless shape matching [Müller et al. 05] discards neighborhood information in whole and performs shape matching on the whole point cloud.

This way, each vertex feels the influence of every other vertex, as would a realistic soft material. The problem with this is that the larger the shape-matching clusters are, the faster deformations are smoothed out, and the shape will return to the rigid shape much sooner. If the algorithm is unaltered, the range of motion is cut drastically. Within the limit of all vertices in one cluster, it will always try to match all particles to the undeformed mesh. Thus, it will only allow small deviations from the rigid shape. This comes in handy for simulating rigid-body dynamics with this algorithm, but this is not in the focus of this chapter.

14.4.1 Extensions to Meshless Shape Matching

Müller [Müller et al. 05] proposes some extensions to the meshless shape-matching algorithm to allow for bigger derivations from the rigid shape. We should look at it for completeness, however it is not that well-suited for character animation.

The idea is to allow the transformation that transforms x_i^0 into c_i,

$$c_i = Rx_i^0 + t,$$

to be more general. Sheer and stretch modes can be accounted for by mixing a bit of the previously calculated linear transformation A into the transformation

$$\beta A + (1 - \beta)R.$$

Here the mixing is controlled by the additional parameter β. The transformation R still ensures that there is a tendency towards the undeformed shape. Volume conservation has to be taken care of by ensuring that $\det(A) = 1$, which is not automatically the case.

This can be extended to include quadratic deformations. We will not use this approach because we will still lose too much realism by discarding the neighborhood information, especially the small, high-frequency modes we want to achieve. Extending the range of motion for the shape matching of the neighborhood clusters is not necessary.

14.4.2 Lattice-Based Shape Matching

Another way of simulating volumetric effects is to turn to discrete approximations of the inside of the mesh. The general idea is to fill the inside with a lattice of evenly spaced vertices, let them take care of the physics, and reconstruct the deformed surface mesh from the deformed lattice after. Unfortunately, these discrete approximations can be very expensive to simulate. Simple lattice deformers have been around for a while—like ChainMail (see [Gibson and Mittrich 97] again), which, although providing speed and robustness suitable for interactive processing, suffers from limited realism.

Here again, shape matching can come to our help. In [Rivers and James 07], an algorithm is presented to efficiently calculate the shape matching of a cubic lattice.

The idea is to voxelize the mesh and flood the inside of the mesh with solid objects in a cubic lattice. Steinemann [Steinemann et al. 08] uses an octree-based hierarchical sampling instead of an evenly spaced lattice. The original mesh is then deformed using trilinear interpolation of the vertex positions in the lattice. Although this approach results (depending on the resolution of the lattice) in interactive rates, we will use a much more simple approach to account for volumetric effects that is more suited to character animation. It is presented in the next paragraph.

14.4.3   A Link to the Bone

When there is a bone model that drives the mesh, another simplified model can be used that mimics the real situation quite well [Shi et al. 08]. We apply yet another spring to our surface vertex for each bone and link it to the bones they are assigned to. But we do not fix the end at a certain position along the bone, allowing it to slide freely along the bone. This way, the force tries to maintain the original distance from the bone. Before constructing this force, a bone model is defined that assigns each vertex just one bone. This will be extended to a model that assigns more than one bone to a vertex for smooth skinning. Here, the calculated force will be the (weighted) sum of the contributions of each bone.

A basic bone model. We start with a simple bone model to discuss the basic structure. The bone model will be built up from the joints, where each joint has a position, an orientation, and a parent. A joint without a parent is called a *root* joint.

---

struct Joint { Quat4 orient; Vector3 pos; **int** parent;};

The link between a joint and its parent is called the *bone*. Each vertex is assigned a joint, and its rest position $\mathbf{x}_i^0$ is calculated by

$$\mathbf{x}_i^0 = \hat{\mathbf{q}}\mathbf{x}_i^{\text{rel}}\hat{\mathbf{q}}^{-1} + \mathbf{j}_i,$$

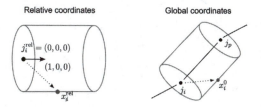

Figure 14.9. Transforming a relative coordinate $\mathbf{x}_i^{\text{rel}}$ (left) to global coordinates $\mathbf{x}_i^0$ (right) using the positions of its joint $\mathbf{j}_i$ and the joint's parent $\mathbf{j}_p$.

where $\hat{\mathbf{q}}$ is the rotation quaternion and $\mathbf{j}_i$ is the position of the joint. Quaternions are explained in the introductory chapter (Chapter 1), since they are quite useful for the representation of rotations in computer graphics—especially character animation.

The vertex positions are relative to its supporting joint and have to be transformed into global space (see Figure 14.9).

The vertex structure is extended by a vector called `relPos`, which is the position of a vertex relative to its supporting joint. This is the only coordinate the designer has to supply; the `restPos` is calculated from this coordinate using the above formula.

```
for each joint j {
    v = j.pos − j.parent.pos;
    normalize(v);
    j−>orient = rotationQuaternion(u, v);
}
for each vertex v {
    j = v.joint;
    tempPos = rotateVector(v.relPos, j.orient)
    v.goalPos = tempPos + j.pos;
}
```

In the first loop, we calculate the rotation quaternion of the joint as described above. In the second loop, we use the calculated quaternion to transform our `relPos` coordinates into global space (`restPos`). These are again the positions that are used by all the force calculations we discussed before.

Calculating the force. We need a force that maintains the distance to the bone for each vertex. For this, we compare the actual distance to the desired distance.

We have to calculate the distance from the bone to the actual positions $\mathbf{x}_i$ and the distance to the rest positions $\mathbf{x}_i^0$.

First, the unit vector in the direction of the joint's parent is obtained by

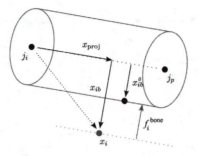

Figure 14.10. The projection $\mathbf{x}_{\text{proj}}$ of the vertex $\mathbf{x}_i$ on the bone is used to construct the distance $\mathbf{x}_{ib}$ from the bone for vertex $\mathbf{x}_i$. The distance is compared to the distance of the rest position $\mathbf{x}_i^0$ to construct a force $\mathbf{f}_i^{\text{bone}}$ that maintains the distance to the bone.

```
axis = joint.pos − parentJoint.pos;
normalize(axis);
```

From this, the part of the vertex position that points in the direction of the joint's parent can be calculated by taking the dot product, and the projection $\mathbf{x}_{\text{proj}}$ of $\mathbf{x}_i$ on the bone can be calculated by multiplying the unit vector in the direction of the bone with this quantity.

```
projection = dotProduct(axis, v.pos);
projVector = scaledVector(axis, projection);
```

The vector that points from the nearest point on the bone to the vertex $\mathbf{x}_i$ is now just the difference between $\mathbf{x}_i$ and $\mathbf{x}_{\text{proj}}$. We call it $\mathbf{x}_{ib}$ for the actual positions and $\mathbf{x}_{ib}^0$ for the goal positions. This is shown graphically in Figure 14.10.

With these two quantities, a force that pulls the vertex to the desired distance from the bone can be constructed:

$$\mathbf{f}_i^{\text{bone}} = \frac{\left(\frac{|\mathbf{x}_{ib}^0|}{|\mathbf{x}_{ib}|} - 1\right)\mathbf{x}_{ib}}{h^2},$$

where $|\mathbf{x}_{ib}|$ is the length of $\mathbf{x}_{ib}$. Whenever $\mathbf{x}_{ib}^0$ is longer than $\mathbf{x}_{ib}$, the force is directed away from the bone (in the direction of $\mathbf{x}_{ib}$), and if $\mathbf{x}_{ib}^0$ is shorter than $\mathbf{x}_{ib}$, the force is directed towards the bone, as is needed.

Figure 14.11. A tube, supported by three joints.

In our variable names, the calculation looks like this:

```
preFactor = (distanceVectorAbs0 / distanceVectorAbs − 1)
    /(timeStep * timeStep);
scale(distanceVector, preFactor);
```

14.4.4 Skeleton-Driven Mesh

We now have a detailed force model consisting of several forces that can be added:

$$\mathbf{f}_i^{\text{total}} = \alpha_i^{\text{rest}} \cdot \mathbf{f}_i^{\text{rest}} + \alpha_i^{\text{neigh}} \cdot \mathbf{f}_i^{\text{neigh}} + \alpha_i^{\text{detail}} \cdot \mathbf{f}_i^{\text{detail}} + \alpha_i^{\text{bone}} \cdot \mathbf{f}_i^{\text{bone}}.$$

We can apply this model to a geometry with two bones connected by a joint, with a cylindrical mesh around each bone (see Figure 14.11). The joints can be moved freely by selecting them with the mouse and moving them around—this causes kinematic deformation of the goal positions. The surface geometry follows the positions of the joints while experiencing secondary deformation. (See Figure 14.1 (middle and right).)

14.4.5 Application to Smooth Skinning

This basic bone model works very badly, especially in joint regions where each vertex should feel the influence of more than one bone. This is addressed by *smooth skinning* (as opposed to rigid skinning, used before) techniques such as *skeleton-subspace deformation* (SSD), which has been around in computer graphics for quite a while [Magnenat-Thalmann et al. 88]. This is used, for example, in the MD5 model format that comes from id Software's *Doom 3* first-person shooter. Vertex positions are not given explicitly but must be calculated by the contributions of multiple weights that are assigned to joints. Here, the weights have relative positions to the bones, not the vertices, so these weight positions get transformed according to their assigned bone. The position of a vertex is a weighted sum of these transformed weight positions. The Internet provides a lot of detailed documentation on this format.

Geometry produced from this specification works well as a kinematic basis for the secondary deformations presented here.

The vertices in the MD5 format are given implicitly as a sum of weights:

```
struct ModelVertex { int start; int count; };
```

Here, start defines the first weight and count the number of weights after the starting weights that belong to this vertex:

```
struct ModelWeight { int joint; float bias; Vector3 pos; };
```

The weight contains the information of how to construct the final vertex positions; pos defines the position of the weight, and bias states how much the weight contributes to the vertex. Using the weight, we can access the bone model information, since joint assigns each weight a joint:

```
struct ModelJoint {
    char name[64];
    int parent;
    Vector3 pos;
    Quat4 orient;
};
```

This is basically the same definition of a joint that was used before. Listings 14.2 and 14.3 show the application of the surface-detail preservation and the bone-distance preservation forces to an actual MD5 model. Since an MD5 model can consist of several independent meshes, we have to specify which one we want to deform. The supplementary material includes an application that demonstrates the interactive deformation of the animated Stanford armadillo model (see Figure 14.12).

```
Vector3 DeformableMD5::detailForce(int mesh, int vertex) {
    int i;
    Vector3 q, p;
    Vertex *vertices = meshes[mesh].finalVertices;

    int neighbors[MAX_NEIGHBORS];
    int numNeighbors = getNeighbors(mesh,vertex,neighbors);
    /* if there are less than 3 particles in the neighborhood,
            the particle is isolated */
    if (numNeighbors < 3) return vecCreate(0.0f,0.0f,0.0f);
    /* calculate centers of mass */
    Vector3 cm = vecZero(); Vector3 cm_0 = vecZero();
    float masses = 0;
    for (i = 0; i < numNeighbors; i++) {
        Vertex * v = &vertices[neighbors[i]];
        vecAdd(cm, v->pos); vecAdd(cm_0, v->restPos);
        masses += v->mass;
    }
    vecScale(&cm, 1.0f/(masses)); vecScale(&cm_0, 1.0f/(masses));
    /* calculate optimal rotation R */
    Matrix3x3 A_pq = matZero();
    for (i = 0; i < numNeighbors; i++) {
        Vertex * v = &vertices[neighbors[i]];
        q = v->restPos - cm_0;
        p = v->pos - cm;
        for (int j = 0; j < 3; j++) for (int k = 0; k < 3; k++) {
            A_pq[j][k] += v->mass * pk * q[j];
        }
    }
    Matrix3x3 R = getRotationalPart(A_pq);

    /* calculate the position that preserves
            best laplacian coordinates */
    Vector3 diff = vertices[vertex].restPos - cm_0;
    matMult(&R, &diff);
    Vector3 force = diff + cm - vertices[vertex].pos;
    vecScale(force, 1/(timeStep * timeStep));
    return force;
}
```

Listing 14.2. The shape-matching algorithm for surface detail preservation on a model definition using SSD.

```
Vector3 DeformableMD5::volumetricForce(int mesh, int vertex) {
  int i;
  ModelMesh *m = &meshes[mesh];
  ModelVertex *mv = &m->vertices[vertex];
  Vertex *v = &m->finalVertices[vertex];
  real totalWeight = 0.0f;
  Vector3 totalForce = vecCreate(0.0f,0.0f,0.0f);

  /* calculate the contribution of one joint */
  for (i = mv->start; i < mv->start + mv->count; i++) {
    ModelWeight *w = &m->weights[i];

    /* from weight, retrieve joint and its parent */
    ModelJoint *j = &skeleton[w->joint];
    ModelJoint *jp = &skeleton[j->parent];

    /* calculate the unit vector in the direction of the bone */
    Vector3 axis = j->pos - &jp->pos;
    vecNormalize(axis);

    /* calculate the force contribution as before */
    Vector3 diffPos = v->pos - j->pos;
    Vector3 diffPos0 = v->restPos - j->pos;
    real projection = vecDot(axis, &diffPos);
    real projection0 = vecDot(axis, &diffPos0);
    Vector3 projVector = vecScaledVector(axis, projection);
    Vector3 projVector0 = vecScaledVector(axis, projection0);
    Vector3 distanceVector = diffPos - projVector;
    Vector3 distanceVector0 = diffPos0 - projVector0;
    real distanceVectorAbs = vecLength(distanceVector);
    real distanceVectorAbs0 = vecLength(distanceVector0);
    if (distanceVectorAbs == 0) return vecCreate(0,0,0);
    real preFactor = (distanceVectorAbs0 /
      distanceVectorAbs - 1.0f) /(timeStep * timeStep);
    Vector3 result = distanceVector;
    vecScale(&result, preFactor * w->bias);
    totalWeight += w->bias;
    vecAdd(&totalForce, &result);
  }

  /* sum over all contributions */
  vecScale(&totalForce, 1.0f/totalWeight);
  return totalForce;
}
```

Listing 14.3. The bone-distance preservation algorithm for a model definition using SSD.

Figure 14.12. The Stanford armadillo model, experiencing secondary deformation—the vertices at the body region deform strongly, giving the experience of fatty tissue.

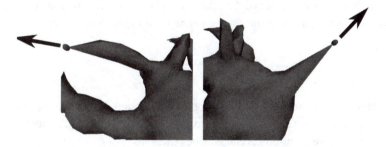

Figure 14.13. The surface vertices can be subject to external forces at runtime, resulting in interactive dynamic deformations.

14.5 Final Remarks

In this chapter, we have managed to bring skeleton-driven animation beyond the purely kinematic approach that is currently used in computer games by developing a dynamic simulation that enriches the visual experience of the animation. Although the simulation is based on forces, it is not exactly physics based since the forces are not modeled on physical laws.

Of course, no technique is suited for all applications—the techniques used here are not suitable when an accurate modeling of the physical situation is needed. This is the weak point of this kind of simulation. But it turns out that the impact on believability in games is immense.

For an accurate (based on the physical definition of the strain tensor) simulation, Chapter 10 provides much better results.

Although the calculations could be applied to the mesh during a preprocessing stage to reduce computational effort, the technique is very well-suited for real-time processing for the benefit of interactivity of the animation. The skeleton-driven vertices can be subject to external forces of any kind (see Figure 14.13). Special collision-detection algorithms might be needed here [Teschner et al. 05], which is unfortunately a lot more computationally intensive. This is beyond the scope of this chapter.

Appendix: Calculating the Optimal Rotation

For the shape-matching algorithm, a rotation is needed that best matches a given set of points to another set of points (with an equal number of points) by minimizing their distance-squares.

Since we already matched the centers of mass (so there is no translation necessary for optimization anymore), we define the relative locations by

$$\mathbf{q}_i = \mathbf{x}_i^0 - \mathbf{x}_{cm}^0$$
$$\mathbf{p}_i = \mathbf{x}_i - \mathbf{x}_{cm}$$

We start off by searching for a linear transformation $\mathbf{A}$ such that $\mathbf{c}_i = \mathbf{A}\mathbf{q}_i + \mathbf{x}_{cm}$ matches $\mathbf{x}_i$ best, and then we try to extract the rotation that $\mathbf{A}$ contains. The quantity we have to minimize can now be written as

$$\sum_i m_i \left(\mathbf{A}\mathbf{q}_i - \mathbf{p}_i\right)^2 .$$

We should now focus on the contribution of one neighbor i and omit the mass for now. We can simplify our notation for the next few calculations to

$$(\mathbf{A}\mathbf{q} - \mathbf{p})^2 = (\mathbf{A}\mathbf{q} - \mathbf{p})(\mathbf{q}^T\mathbf{A}^T - \mathbf{p}^T).$$

Now we write out the multiplications component-wise (take care: u, v, w are matrix and vector entry indices now, not particle indices):

$$\sum_u \left(\sum_v A_{uv}q_v - p_u\right) \left(\sum_k A_{uw}q_w - p_u\right) = \sum_u \left(\sum_v A_{uv}q_v\right)^2$$
$$- 2p_u \sum_v A_{uv}q_v + \sum_u p_u^2.$$

Taking the derivative $\partial/\partial A_{lm}$ to the lm component of the matrix $\mathbf{A}$ yields

$$\frac{\partial \dots}{\partial A_{lm}} = 2A_{lm}q_m q_m - 2p_l q_m.$$

Writing this again in matrix-vector notation, we get

$$2\left((\mathbf{A}\mathbf{q})\mathbf{q}^T - \mathbf{p}\mathbf{q}^T\right),$$

and setting the derivative to zero brings us to

$$\mathbf{A}\mathbf{q}\mathbf{q}^T - \mathbf{p}\mathbf{q}^T = 0$$
$$\rightarrow \mathbf{A} = \mathbf{p}\mathbf{q}^T \cdot (\mathbf{q}\mathbf{q}^T)^{-1}.$$

Doing this calculation with the whole sum and the mass-weights would bring us to

$$\mathbf{A} = \left(\sum_i m_i \mathbf{p}_i \mathbf{q}_i^T\right)\left(\sum_i m_i \mathbf{q}_i \mathbf{q}_i^T\right)^{-1}.$$

This is great because this is a quantity we can actually calculate.

The second part we can throw away because it is symmetric and, thus, cannot contain a rotation. The rest of the expression we call $\mathbf{A}_{pq}$. Just do the math:

```
A_pq = zeroMatrix();
for each vertex v in v_i.neighbors {
    q = v.restPos − cm_0;
    p = v.pos − cm;
    for all entries j, k {
        A_pq[j][k] +=
            v.mass * p[k] * q[j];
    }
}
```

By so-called polar decomposition, we are now able to decompose the matrix $\mathbf{A}_{pq}$ into a rotation $\mathbf{R}$ and a scaling $\mathbf{S}$:

$$\mathbf{A}_{pq} = \mathbf{R}\mathbf{S}.$$

How the scaling can be obtained can be understood intuitively: if we apply $\mathbf{A}_{pq}$ to a unit vector, the rotational part $\mathbf{R}$ will rotate the vector on the unit sphere, but the scaling $\mathbf{S}$ will displace it from the shell of the unit sphere. Now we apply $\mathbf{A}_{pq}^T$: the rotational part $\mathbf{R}^T$ will rotate the vector back to the original position, while the scaling will displace the vector even more from the shell. So the combined operation acts as if we had applied $\mathbf{S}$ twice:

$$\mathbf{A}_{pq}^T \mathbf{A}_{pq} = (\mathbf{RS})^T (\mathbf{RS}) = \mathbf{S}^T \mathbf{R}^T \mathbf{RS} = \mathbf{S}^T \mathbf{S} = \mathbf{S}^2.$$

So, unfortunately, we have to take the square root of this matrix equation to obtain $\mathbf{S}$. As this is a common problem in mathematics and physics, this problem has been addressed a lot and there are good numerical methods to calculate this quantity. The usual approach is to diagonalize the matrix $\mathbf{S}^2$:

$$\mathbf{S}^2 = \mathbf{V} \mathrm{diag}(\lambda) \mathbf{V}^T,$$

where λ are the eigenvalues of the matrix $\mathbf{S}^2$.

A very good overview, as well as some state-of-the-art algorithms for the diagonalization of 3×3 matrices, has been given by [Kopp 06]. Once the matrix is diagonalized, we can take the square root of the diagonal entries.

$$\mathbf{S} = \mathbf{V} \mathrm{diag}(\sqrt{\lambda}) \mathbf{V}^T$$

to obtain the matrix $\mathbf{S}$.

There is also what is called the *Denman–Beavers square root iteration*—this works without diagonalization. It is easy to implement and very robust, although not as efficient (see [Denman and Beavers 76]).

We will use the Jacobi algorithm here, which is the oldest but is also a very robust algorithm. It starts off with the identity matrix for $\mathbf{V}$ and applies so-called Jacobi sweeps on it (see [Kopp 06]).

Since the rotation matrices we are dealing with are "almost diagonal" already, it will take only one to two Jacobi sweeps on the average for each vertex. Since this operation is done very often, we should think about caching the matrix $\mathbf{V}$ from the previous time step instead of starting off with the identity matrix at every time step. This induces further memory usage but reduces computation time.

Using $\mathbf{S}$, we can now calculate the rotational part:

$$\mathbf{R} = \mathbf{A}_{pq} \mathbf{S}^{-1}.$$

Acknowledgments

I want to thank Ury Zhilinsky for his input and support during my work on this chapter. The MD5 model used was built upon polygonal data from the Stanford 3D Scanning Repository.

Bibliography

[Acton 70] F. S. Acton. *Numerical Methods That Work*. New York: Harper and Row, 1970.

[Bhasin and Liu 06] Y. Bhasin and A. Liu. *Bounds for Damping that Guarantee Stability in Mass-Spring Systems*, Studies in Health Technology and Informatics, 119. Amsterdam: IOS Press, 2006.

[Campagna et al. 98] Swen Campagna, Leif Kobbelt, and Hans-Peter Seidel. "Directed Edges—A Scalable Representation for Triangle Meshes." *journal of graphics, gpu, and game tools* 3:4 (1998), 1–12.

[Denman and Beavers 76] E. D. Denman and A. N. Beavers. "The Matrix Sign Function and Computations in Systems." *Applied Mathematics and Computation* 2 (1976), 63–94.

[Donelly and Rogers 05] D. Donelly and E. Rogers. "Symplectic Integrators: An Introduction." *American Journal of Physics* 73 (2005), 938–945.

[Gibson and Mittrich 97] S. F. Gibson and B. Mittrich. "A Survey of Deformable Models in Computer Graphics." Technical Report TR-97-19, Mitsubishi Electric Research Laboratories, Cambridge, MA, 1997.

[Jacka et al. 07] D. Jacka, A. Reid, B. Merry, and J. Gain. "A Comparison of Linear Skinning Techniques for Character Animation." Technical Report CS07-03-00, Department of Computer Science, University of Cape Town, South Africa, 2007.

[Jakobsen 01] T. Jakobsen. "Advanced Character Physics." Available at http://www.teknikus.dk/tj/gdc2001.htm.

[Kopp 06] J. Kopp. "Efficient Numerical Diagonalization of Hermitian 3×3 Matrices." *Int. J. Mod. Phys.* C 19 (2006), 523–548.

[Magnenat-Thalmann et al. 88] N. Magnenat-Thalmann, R. Laperriere, and D. Thalmann. "Joint-Dependent Local Deformations for Hand Animation and Object Grasping." In *Proceedings on Graphics Interface '88*, pp. 26–33. Toronto: Canadian Information Processing Society, 1988.

[Müller et al. 05] M. Müller, B. Heidelberger, M. Teschner, and M. Gross. "Meshless Deformations Based on Shape Matching." *ACM Transactions on Graphics* 24:3 (2005), 471–478.

[Müller et al. 08] M. Müller, B. Heidelberger, M. Hennix, and J. Ratcliff. "Hierarchical Position Based Dynamics." Presentation given at Virtual Reality Interactions and Physical Simulations VIRPhys, Grenoble, November 13–14, 2008.

[Rivers and James 07] A. R. Rivers and D. L. James. "FastLSM: Fast Lattice Shape Matching for Robust Real-Time Deformation." *ACM Transactions on Graphics (SIGGRAPH'07)* 26:3 (2007), Article No. 82.

[Shi et al. 08] X. Shi, K. Zhou, Y. Tong, M. Desbrun, H. Bao, and B. Guo. "Example-Based Dynamic Skinning in Real Time." *ACM Transactions on Graphics (SIGGRAPH'08)* 27:3 (2008), Article No. 29.

[Steinemann et al. 08] D. Steinemann, M. A. Otaduy, and M. Gross. "Fast Adaptive Shape Matching Deformations." In *Proceedings of the 2008 ACM SIGGRAPH/Eurographics Symposium on Computer Animation*, pp. 87–94. Aire-la-Ville, Switzerland: Eurographics Association, 2008.

[Teschner et al. 05] M. Teschner, S. Kimmerle, B. Heidelberger, G. Zachmann, L. Raghupathi, A. Fuhrmann, M.-P. Cani, F. Faure, N. Magnenat-Thalmann, W. Strasser, and P. Volino. "Collision Detection for Deformable Objects." *Computer Graphics Forum* 24:1 (2005), 61–81.

Glossary of Notation

$\mathbf{a}, \mathbf{b}, \mathbf{c}, \ldots$	vectors, points, quaternions
$\mathbf{0}$	zero vector
$\mathbf{e}_i$	ith vector of the standard basis
$\mathbf{v} \cdot \mathbf{w}, \mathbf{v} \times \mathbf{w}$	dot and cross product of vectors $\mathbf{v}$ and $\mathbf{w}$
$\|\mathbf{v}\|, \|\mathbf{v}\|^2$	length and squared length of vector $\mathbf{v}$
$\mathbf{A}, \mathbf{B}, \mathbf{C}, \ldots$	matrices over real numers
$[\alpha_{ij}]$	matrix with element α_{ij} in the ith row and jth column
$[\mathbf{a}_i]$	matrix with vector $\mathbf{a}_i$ as ith column
$\mathbf{A}^{\mathrm{T}}, \mathbf{A}^{-1}$	transpose and inverse of matrix $\mathbf{A}$
$\det(\mathbf{A})$	determinant of matrix $\mathbf{A}$
$\mathbf{E}$	identity matrix
$\mathbf{F}, \tau$	force and torque vector
$\dot{\mathbf{x}}, \ddot{\mathbf{x}}$	first and second time derivatives of $\mathbf{x}$ (velocity and acceleration)
ω, α	angular velocity and angular acceleration
$\mathbf{I}$	inertia tensor
$\sum_{i=1}^{n} a_i$	$a_1 + \cdots + a_n$
$\frac{\partial f}{\partial x}$	partial derivative of multi-variable function f with respect to x
$\nabla f(x_1, \ldots, x_n)$	$(\frac{\partial f}{\partial x_1}, \ldots, \frac{\partial f}{\partial x_n})$, gradient of f
$\nabla^2 f(x_1, \ldots, x_n)$	$\sum_{i=1}^{n} \frac{\partial^2 f}{\partial x_i^2}$, Laplacian of f
$\mathbf{q}^\dagger, \mathbf{q}^{-1}$	conjugate and inverse of quaternion $\mathbf{q}$
$A, B, C, \ldots$	point sets (lines, planes, volumes), or predicates
$\{x_i\}$	set of elements x_i
$\{x : P(x)\}$	set of elements x for which predicate $P(x)$ holds
$\emptyset$	empty set
$A \cup B, A \cap B, A \setminus B$	union, intersection, and set difference of sets A and B
$A \subseteq B$	A is a subset of B and is possibly equal to B
$A + B, A - B$	Minkowski sum and CSO of objects A and B
$[a, b]$	interval of real numbers containing all x for which $a \le x \le b$
$\mathrm{aff}(A), \mathrm{conv}(A)$	affine and convex hull of point set A
$\exists x : P(x)$	there exists an x such that predicate $P(x)$ holds
$\forall x : P(x)$	for all x predicate $P(x)$ holds
$f(n) = O(g(n))$	constants k and c exist such that $f(n) \le cg(n)$ for all $n \ge k$

Contributors

Gino van den Bergen. Gino has been involved professionally with interactive

physics since the beginning of this century. He is the author of the book *Collision Detection in Interactive 3D Environments*. He developed the SOLID collision detection library that has been applied in top-selling game console titles, such as the *Formula One* series for PlayStation®2. Gino holds a PhD in computing science from Eindhoven University of Technology. He currently works as contract programmer and technical director on mostly serious game applications. His pursuits can be traced on www.dtecta.com.

Dirk Gregorius. After studying civil engineering at the RWTH Aachen

and Ruhr-University Bochum, Dirk started his career at Factor 5, where he was responsible for cloth, rigid body physics, and collision detection. He then moved on to work at Havok. Currently Dirk lives in Cologne and works as contractor for game studios, middleware vendors, and publishers.

Benjamin Block. Benjamin Johannes Block graduated in computational physics

at the Johannes Gutenberg University at Mainz in 2010. In his diploma thesis he did research on many particle and lattice physics simulations on the GPU. He is interested in game development, computer graphics, and sound synthesis. As of June 2010 he works for Crytek GmbH, Frankfurt as an R&D Animation Engineer.

Michael Alexander Ewert. As an infant lying under a crystal pyramid in the

frozen tundra outside a small town in the Yukon Territories, Michael Alexander Ewert first learned of the mathematical relationships that governed the universe he had just entered. This knowledge did not seem particularly useful at the time. How to avoid being fed the nastier bits of a freshly killed moose was a more pressing concern. One day in the '90s, after a session of dispatching virtual dinosaurs, the connection between his job as a computer games programmer and the primeval knowledge tucked away in his postnatal memory was made. Since then, Michael has followed the path of an itinerant physics programmer, codifying algorithms that govern Euclidean-space interactions. Michael has done so for a number of computer games and VFX companies in Europe and North America.

Marcos Garca. Marcos Garcia received his degree in Computer Science

and Engineering in 2003 and his PhD in Computer Graphics in 2007, both from the Universidad Politécnica de Madrid. From December 2008 to February 2009 he has worked as a research fellow at the Trinity College Dublin. Currently, he is an assistant professor in the University Rey Juan Carlos (Madrid, Spain). His PhD and his current work is centered on the task of deformable object simulation, and he has published works in the fields of computer graphics and virtual reality.

Dennis Gustafsson. After finishing a master's degree in media technology,

Dennis co-founded Meqon, a Swedish company developing the physics engine selected by clients such as 3D Realms, Black Element, and Saber Interactive. Meqon was acquired by AGEIA Technologies in 2005, where Dennis he worked as software architect for two years, focusing on hardware abstraction and parallel algorithms, but also hands-on integration for specific games, including *Ghost Recon Advanced Warfighter 2*. Dennis is also the developer behind Dresscode, a game engine profiling and tuning tool later acquired by RAD Game Tools. He is currently an independent contractor and working on a new physics engine, which can be followed on his blog: tuxedolabs.blogspot.com.

Takahiro Harada. Takahiro Harada is a GPU Physics Advanced Researcher in

AMD's GPU CTO team, where he is focusing on physics simulation on recent GPU architecture. Before joining AMD, he did R&D on physics simulation at Havok, which is a leading company for real-time physics. Before leaving his country, he was an assistant professor at the University of Tokyo. He earned his PhD in engineering from the University of Tokyo.

Thomas Jakobsen. As former Head of Research at Danish developer Io

Interactive, Thomas Jakobsen created the original physics engine behind the *Hitman* game series. Besides being one of the very first games to use ragdolls, *Hitman* also featured one of the baldest heroes ever (no hair simulation needed!). Thomas earned his MScEng degree and PhD in mathematics from the Technical University of Denmark. At DTU he has also held a position as an assistant professor and did research in cryptanalysis trying to come up with new algorithms with cool names, such as the interpolation attack. When not messing with mobile phones and augmented reality and trying to invent useful devices for magicians, Thomas works as CEO of Q1 Technologies A/S, creating innovative mathematical models for algorithmic trading based on machine learning. Thomas lives in Denmark with his lovely wife, Karin, and their wonderful children, Matilde and Lukas.

Anton Knyazyev. I'm 33 and I've been working as an R&D programmer in the

games industry for the last nine years. If the numbers were of any significance, one would note that it looks like a perfect time for a crucifixion and a Caesarean—though not necessarily in that order. I come from the East,[1] and I live in the West,[2] but belong to neither. I figured a pretentious self-searching bio is still better than a boring one, which it would inevitably have to be otherwise. Oh wait, here's the punchline: my last name is actually easier to pronounce than Eyjafjallajökull.

---

[1] Not the *far* one: just that of Europe.
[2] Footnote 1 still applies.

Claude Lacoursière. After completing his BSc and MSc in physics at McGill

University, Claude joined Lateral Logic in 1996 to develop a
real-time physics engine for a ground vehicle operator train-
ing simulator. He pursued this work as the chief scientist at
MathEngine and CMLabs Simulations until 2003. He then
completed a PhD in this field at Umeå University in 2007. He
now pursues research at the university while serving as chief
scientist at Algoryx. His interests center around discrete-
time variational mechanics applied to multidomain mechanical systems, especially those subject to frictional contacts.
These include rigid and flexible multibodies, fluids, and gran-
ular matter among others. His current projects include the development of and numerical methods, new frictional contact models, and high performance, parallel,
direct, and iterative solvers for these.

Hiroshi Matsuike. I am a software engineer working at Sony Computer

Entertainment, Inc. I'm working on developing an in-house
physics engine and on supporting developers who integrate
physics into their games.

Cesar Mendoza. Cesar Mendoza is a senior physics specialist at Eden

Games, an internal game developer studio of the legendary
group Atari. He designs and develops game physics features of EdenGames' proprietary technology. Previously, he
worked for NaturalMotion, Ltd. where he was part of the
core team developing *Euphoria*, a game physics middleware
for full simulation of 3D characters, including body, muscles, and motor nervous systems. He holds a PhD in computer graphics from INRIA, France, and has carried out post-
doctoral stays at CNR, Italy, Trinity College, Dublin, and
Madrid, Spain, in topics related to physical simulation and virtual reality. He has
two MSc in Automatic Control from Imperial College, UK, and from Grenoble
Institute of Technology, France. He has published several international research
papers and usually acts as reviewer in many computer graphics conferences and
journals. His website is found at www.mendozajullia.com/.

Sergiy Migdalskiy. Sergiy earned an MSc in applied mathematics in Ukraine,

and spent most of his time programming. In 2002 he moved to Crytek in Germany, where he specialized in animation, optimization, and porting. Having shipped the PC title *Far Cry*, he moved to Naughty Dog in California in 2004, where he started preproduction work on the PS/3 exclusive *Uncharted: Drake's Fortune*. He worked on animation, camera, main hero control, and other systems, but mostly on physics and collision. Sergiy specialized in high-level PS/3 SPU and math-intensive coding. He wrote the collision and physics simulation systems that shipped in *Uncharted*, which sold over one million copies worldwide. In 2008, Sergiy moved to Valve in Washington and worked on PC and Xbox 360 titles *Left 4 Dead* and *Left 4 Dead 2* that sold multiple million copies to date, and is looking forward to bringing more high quality entertainment to gamers worldwide.

Kiaran Ritchie. Kiaran Ritchie is a Canadian-born technical animator with

professional experience at Factor 5, Lucasfilm Animation, and EA Bioware. His expertise is in creature rigging, deformation systems, and animation pipelines for film, TV, and videogames. Kiaran was the principal author of *The Art of Rigging* textbooks, which have had a major impact on animation and rigging methodologies used in many companies. While at Lucasfilm Animation in California, Kiaran implemented many custom deformation systems still in use on *The Clone Wars* TV show. Since then, he has been concerned with adapting offline deformation systems for use in real-time applications. He currently operates his own independent games studio, Big Fat Alien, out of Westbank, British Columbia. His first game, *BEEP*, relies heavily on physics-based gameplay scenarios powered by the open source Box 2D physics engine. Kiaran is married to Jasmine and they are expecting their first baby to arrive shortly after SIGGRAPH 2010.

Kees van Kooten. Kees van Kooten is working on rendering technologies for interactive medical applications at Virtual Proteins. He graduated cum laude in 2006 at the Eindhoven University of Technology with a degree in Computer Science and Visualization, after which he worked in the games industry for a couple of years. Apart from computer graphics, he has always been especially interested in physics simulation. Both interests were combined in an article for *GPU Gems 3*, containing a physics-based solution to fluid visualization. Lately, Kees has given presentations on rendering and physics at GDC World and GDC Europe. During his spare time, he likes to play drums in his own band.

Jim Van Verth. Jim Van Verth has been working in the game industry for over ten  years, concentrating on 3D graphics and simulation. Currently he is a senior tools and technology engineer at Insomniac Games. Prior to that he was an OpenGL driver engineer at NVIDIA Corporation, and was a founding member of Red Storm Entertainment, where he worked on such titles as Tom Clancy's *Politika, Force 21*, and *Rainbow Six: Lockdown*. He is a regular presenter at game development conferences and expositions, and in particular is the creator of the ever-popular Math for Programmers tutorial at the Game Developers Conference. He is also coauthor of the book *Essential Mathematics for Games and Interactive Applications*, published through Morgan Kaufmann.

Index